Introduction to United States
Public Documents

LIBRARY SCIENCE TEXT SERIES

Joe Morehead

INTRODUCTION TO
United States Public Documents

Second Edition

Libraries Unlimited, Inc.   1978
Littleton, Colorado

LIBRARIES UNLIMITED, INC.
P.O. Box 263
Littleton, Colorado 80160

Library of Congress Cataloging in Publication Data

Morehead, Joe, 1931-
    Introduction to United States public documents.

    (Library science text series)
    Includes bibliographies and indexes.
    1. United States--Government publications.
2. United States. Government Printing Office.
I. Title.
Z1223.Z7M67   1978   015'.73   78-16866

ISBN 0-87287-186-X (cloth)
        0-87287-190-8 (paper)

PREFACE TO THE SECOND EDITION

The purpose of this edition remains the same as that expressed in the preface to the 1975 text: "To set forth an introductory account of public documents, their locus, diffusion, habitation, and use." The audience remains basically the same: institutions of whatever size and type that acquire federal government publications, library school students, professional librarians, and the general user of these ubiquitous materials. The emphasis remains a contemporary one; the reader is urged to consult other historical or specialized studies for information not included in this work. Overall, the salient and conspicuous feature of this edition is the large amount of information that is either new or substantially revised. The considerable changes incorporated reflect the rapid and dramatic response on the part of government to the demands and needs of the community of users.

Chapters 1 through 4 describe the administrative machinery and bibliographic systems by which both government and libraries execute the transfer and sharing of public information. Chapter 5 introduces some of the general checklists, indexes and guides to government materials. Chapters 6 through 11 discuss some of the prominent publications generated by or in support of the activities of the five acknowledged arms of the federal establishment. And Appendix A examines a selected number of special problems in documents librarianship. Appendix B lists abbreviations, acronyms, citations, and personal names used in the text. Following the appendixes are personal author, selected title/series, and subject indexes. Because this is an introduction to the field, I have attempted to do no more than present the contours of information sources and their salient characteristics. The cited materials are exemplary rather than exhaustive or definitive.

The present volume differs significantly from the 1975 edition in several respects. The brief chapter on the record-keeping activities of libraries has been dropped. A full-length treatment of this aspect of internal management is covered in Rebekah M. Harleston and Carla J. Stoffle, *Administration of Government Documents Collections* (Libraries Unlimited, Inc., 1974). The chapters on the publications of the several departments, agencies, and independent establishments now emphasize categories of materials rather than a lengthy recital of individual titles and series. I am aware that by imposing this limitation, everyone's favorite agency or series will be missing. But I am persuaded that the concept "more is less" and its converse justify this change of emphasis.

5

To reflect current interests and trends, a large amount of information treated briefly or not at all in the 1975 edition is explored in this revision. Chapter 4, for example, presents a detailed account of the subventionary activities of certain agencies like the National Technical Information Service, Defense Documentation Center, and Educational Resources Information Center. In addition, five specialized facets of government documentation are treated in Appendix A. This information did not fit appropriately into the conceptual scheme of the chapters, but it is not thereby of lesser importance. Subjects include mapping and charting, census data, computer-based data files, audiovisual materials, and a microform summary.

Generally, the new information in this volume reflects the many prominent changes that have taken place since publication of the earlier work. GPO micropublishing, the current *Monthly Catalog* with its AACR and OCLC connections, the commercial micrographics scene, on-line information retrieval systems in government and legal materials—these developments and others, though they have been around for some time, have only recently made an impact on the control and access of federal publishing. In the last four years there has been an astonishing amount of innovation in a field of librarianship that has been relatively impervious to change.

The technologies of the computer and micropublishing harnassed to the service of information requirements are the agents of rapid change. As these developments permit ever more sophisticated correlations of data, selective dissemination of information will continue to be packaged and repackaged in ways responsive to user needs. Indeed, the rate at which this exposition becomes historical if not obsolescent will provide a conspicuous measure of change and growth in the discipline.

Apart from the basic account of public documents as significant sources of information, this edition, like its predecessor, purports to suggest other themes. The late James Bennett Childs noted that "from one point of view, government publications are a mirror of the functions of a government and of its agencies and its instrumentalities and of its subventions."[1] Accordingly, the text emphasizes the principle of provenance, or issuing agency, in the production and distribution of government information. It is my conviction that knowledge of the structure, organization, and hierarchical relationships among government entities markedly improves the reference capabilities of the documents librarian.

Another theme explicit in Chapter 4 and implicit elsewhere in this account is the difficult quest for an unqualified definition of a government publication. Several definitions were presented in the earlier edition of this text.[2] More recently there was the "Definition of a Public Document" proposed by the Administrative and Organization Task Force of the Government Documents Round Table.[3] Perhaps no wholly satisfactory definition can ever be adduced. Working definitions will always need to be refined and redefined as a consequence of political, social, and technological forces. Nevertheless, the task must be addressed continually. Far from being a harmless theoretical exercise, defining a public document bears substantially on the practical implications of collection development, organization, bibliographical control, and access.

Ultimately, the fundamental theme underlying any account of government publications as crucial sources of information is access. James Madison, in a letter to W. T. Berry in 1822, proclaimed:

A popular government, without popular information, or the means of acquiring it, is but a prologue to a farce or a tragedy; or, perhaps both. Knowledge will forever govern ignorance; and a people who mean to be their own governors, must arm themselves with the power which knowledge gives.[4]

Librarians should not underestimate their shining role in defense of these tenets. Regardless of all the benefits present and future technologies bring to the bibliographic enterprise, the public will continue to rely, perhaps more than ever, upon professional expertise to provide what information is made available. In my 1975 text I made this statement:

Documents librarianship is that most exasperating and rewarding of all tasks, for the peculiar challenge that one faces in this discipline is the need to be a "generalist" in areas that encompass the whole of recorded information. The knowledgeable documents librarian is a necessity, the highly skilled practitioner an exemplar of virtuosity in the profession.[5]

I am convinced that these celebratory remarks remain as fitting and suitable as ever.

Joe Morehead

REFERENCES

1. J. B. Childs, "Government Publications (Documents)," in Allen Kent, et al. (eds.) *Encyclopedia of Library and Information Science*, Vol. 10 (New York: Marcel Dekker, 1973), p. 40.

2. Joe Morehead, *Introduction to United States Public Documents* (Littleton, Colorado: Libraries Unlimited, Inc., 1975), pp. xxiv-xxv.

3. *Documents to the People* 5: 187 (September 1977).

4. In Saul K. Padover (ed.), *The Complete Madison: His Basic Writings* (New York: Harper, 1953), p. 337.

5. Morehead, p. xxiv.

ACKNOWLEDGMENTS

A sense of both pleasure and duty compels me to express my indebtedness to those who have provided a contribution to this endeavor. Too numerous to mention by name in this space are my friends and colleagues in documents librarianship, especially those active in the Government Documents Round Table of the American Library Association. Some of their names appear in the body of the text and in the "Personal Author" index. Others, through informal contact, continue to instruct and inspire. My task in compiling an account of federal government publications and activities bears little significance apart from their words and deeds.

In the preparation of this work several individuals have contributed specialized assistance: Janice A. Sacco, Carol Ann Schlierer, and Donna D. Wanek of the School of Library and Information Science, State University of New York at Albany, for their expert typing skills; Deborah Brewer, Judy Caraghar, and Mary Mitchell, at Libraries Unlimited, for their respective copyediting and typesetting abilities. A special measure of thanks is due Tae Moon Lee, Government Documents Librarian, University Library, SUNY at Albany, who served as my research assistant for this project. His meticulous attention to detail and knowledge of the field were of inestimable help.

Deficiencies in the design, content, and style of the work are my responsibility alone.

TABLE OF CONTENTS

LIST OF ILLUSTRATIONS

1

GOVERNMENT PRINTING OFFICE

If you stand on Capitol Hill, at the top of the high flight of stairs leading into the Senate, and look straight north, you will see the Government Printing Office. It is in dreary contrast to the pure whiteness of the Capitol. A long rectangle of sooty brick, domineered by a scorched cupola, from whose apparent ashes rises the Phoenix of a gilt eagle. . . . Making a straight way from Capitol Hill across Tiber Creek, which you will cross by stepping-stones deposited in its basin, and taking a footpath across lots where geese and pigs browse upon plentiful barrenness, you will reach the printing-house in 10 or 15 minutes, and hear the hum of its machinery.

The near exterior view is no better than the remote one. A huge factory of red brick, about 350 feet long, with the gables and one side facing separate streets, and the other side fenced up to enclose boiler houses, paper storehouses, wagon-sheds, wastepaper barracks, and an accessory wing for stereotyping and for a machine shop—this is all that a passing pedestrian knows of the GPO.

−John B. Ellis, *Sights and Secrets of the National Capital*
(New York: U.S. Publishing Company, 1869)

BACKGROUND

During the eighteenth century, printing was still an infant art; an expert printer, working hard, could hope to accomplish but two or three pages of composition a day. Printing for the early Congresses was handled entirely by private firms. Among these, the firm of Gales and Seaton dominated the printing of congressional proceedings from 1789 to 1818, but the imprint of several other establishments was carried on congressional documents for this period. In 1818 a congressional committee recommended the creation of a government printing office, in order "to produce promptitude, uniformity, accuracy and elegance in the execution of the public printing" for "the work of Congress . . . and that of the various departments." The current system of low bidder, the committee reported, created delays and a product "executed in such an inelegant and incorrect manner, as must bring disgrace and ridicule on the literature, and the press of our country."[1] But nothing came of the proposal, and "half a century would pass before these words would be implemented by action."[2]

Despite a number of acts that Congress passed during the first half of the nineteenth century in an attempt to bring some integrity into the commercial printing of government documents, the system was increasingly beset with corruption and patronage. Profiteering, waste, and egregious inefficiency flourished until Congress passed and President Buchanan signed into law the Printing Act of 1860. The act created a Superintendent of Public Printing to manage the official printing and binding "authorized by the Senate and House of Representatives, the executive and judicial departments, and the Court of Claims." The officers of this new agency were enjoined not to "have any interest, direct or indirect, in the publication of any newspaper or periodical" or other binding, engraving, or procurement activities that would suggest a conflict of interest. If the new Superintendent were to "corruptly collude" with private publishers, a fine and penitentiary sentence awaited him.[3] With these sober warnings, the doors of the GPO were officially opened on March 4, 1861, the same day Abraham Lincoln was inaugurated, on the eve of the Civil War.

In the years following the end of the civil conflict, a number of amendments to the 1860 act attempted to effect firmer control over public printing. Congress in 1876 changed the title of the chief officer to that of Public Printer, the position to be filled by presidential appointment with the advice and consent of the Senate. By 1890, over 1,800 people were employed at the GPO, which was now being bruited in periodical accounts as "the largest printing office in the world." And in 1895 Congress passed a comprehensive act codifying the public printing laws in force and creating the office of Superintendent of Documents.

The Printing Act of 1895 represented the second significant piece of legislation on public printing. In addition to its landmark provisions of the creation of the Public Documents office and the beginnings of a formal depository library system, it consolidated the control and power of the Public Printer as the principal agent for the production of documents. Despite the fact that the 1860 act vested the GPO with the authority to handle "all government printing," a number of agencies were still securing private firms for their publications. Since 1860, however, some units within the federal executive branch had been discovering that the GPO produced a better product at a lower cost, and they began to divert their printing to the young office. The new act placed all federal printing offices under the control of the Public Printer—"those then in operation and any that might be put in operation later." Certain agencies were excepted from this regulation, but the Printer was now empowered to abolish any other printing operations when in his judgment—with the approval of the Joint Committee on Printing—"the economy of the public service would be thereby advanced." With the act of 1895 the primacy of the GPO as printer and publisher for all congressional and much agency printing was clearly intended, and it was thought that the centralization of printing was accomplished.[4]

Over the years, the centralization and control which the Printing Act mandated rapidly deteriorated. Nevertheless, the act of 1895, with the usual amendments refining this and that procedure or introducing a nuance for expediency, served as the basic legal instrument for the activities of the Public Printer until 1962, when major changes in sections of the earlier act were effected. But these changes had more impact upon the depository library program than upon the functions of the Printer. With the passage of time, the GPO has undergone important, even crucial, changes that affect libraries apart from the role of the Assistant Public Printer (Superintendent of Documents) within the GPO's organizational structure. It is to these recent developments that our attention will be directed. In perspective, this brief sketch of GPO history does scant justice to the interesting and often colorful record of "the largest printing office in the world." Two authoritative accounts of the GPO are found in the authorized version, *100 GPO Years, 1861-1961: A History of United States Public Printing* (Washington: Government Printing Office, 1961), and in a work by Robert E. Kling, Jr., *The Government Printing Office* (New York: Praeger, 1970). The former is a chronological report of GPO activities, with numerous citations from the laws enacted over that period, plus accounts from newspapers and other secondary sources that described the unfolding drama. The latter, written by a former Superintendent of Documents, draws heavily upon *100 GPO Years* and carries the story up to 1970.

THE GPO TODAY

Functions

The mission of the GPO is to provide the printing and binding services required by the Congress and the various government departments and agencies in accordance with law and with the *Government Printing and Binding Regulations*. That law has been codified in Title 44 of the *United States Code*, Public Printing and Documents. In order to accomplish this mission, the Public Printer is required to have sufficient equipment and an adequate complement of trained employees to meet the peak-load requirements for the Congress and the urgent needs of the departments. These services, which include the furnishing of blank paper, inks, and similar supplies to all governmental activities on order, cover specifically all congressional work, the bulk of which is produced on very close schedules in order to meet "must" delivery dates.

The GPO is officially an agency of the legislative branch. As early as 1875, Chief Justice Morrison R. Waite, ruling on the GPO's position within the federal establishment, declared:

> In short, the GPO superintendent seems to have a department of his own, in which he is in a sense supreme. Certainly he is not under control of any of the executive departments. Apparently he is more responsible to Congress than to any other authority.[5]

In 1932, a Comptroller General's decision stated that the GPO was indeed a part of the legislative branch not subject to legislation applicable only to the executive departments and independent establishments of the government.[6] The Public Printer "is required by law to be a practical printer versed in the art of bookbinding and is appointed by the President with the advice and consent of the Senate."[7] However, the president does not exercise direct or delegated control of the GPO's management.

The Congressional Joint Committee on Printing (JCP) acts as a functioning arm of Congress but serves the entire government. As the single voice of the Senate and House it is, in effect, an active Board of Directors of the GPO and oversees printing, binding, and document distribution for Congress and other federal entities. The JCP "not only has statutory authority over the establishment of printing capabilities elsewhere in government, but contracts between the GPO and commercial contractors also must be approved by JCP." Moreover, the JCP is charged by law with employing "any measure it considers necessary to remedy neglect, delay, duplication, or waste in the public printing and binding and the distribution of Government publications."[8]

Obeisance to the Congress is an annual ritual when the Public Printer and Assistant Public Printer (Superintendent of Documents) go, hat in hand, to testify before House and Senate subcommittees on legislative branch appropriations and defend their budgetary requests for the forthcoming fiscal year. The published hearings of this testimony provide the best single source of information about the activities and plans of the GPO and are available to depository libraries. Hearings before the House subcommittee carry a SuDocs notation Y4.Ap6/1:L52/year and are sent to depository libraries under Item 1011. The counterpart hearings in the Senate (Y 4.Ap6/2: L51/year; Item 1033) cover much of the same ground, but the House hearings are usually more detailed.

Operations

Fourteen regional printing procurement offices are operational in ten regions throughout the country, with two more in Alaska (Region 11) and Hawaii (Region 12) scheduled but not yet established as of April 1977. They act as brokerage houses; their officials are authorized to advertise for bids or set up an "open-end" contract with commercial printers in the region. Contracts for commercially procured printing have increased, and the trend has been justified as good fiscal policy and good politics. Since the regional procurement system was initiated in 1968, Public Printers have testified that the operation is both efficient and cheap. An estimated 90 percent of commercial printers are categorized as "small businesses," and the GPO works in concert with the Small Business Administration to insure the viability of the arrangement.

If materials are of an unclassified nature, are not required by an agency in a hurry, and are to be printed in an amount that secures the printer a margin of profit, they are let out on a competitive bid basis. In 1961, the percentage of commercially procured printing was 42.5 of the total GPO production. By 1966 "in-house" printing accounted for 50.9 percent of the total, while commercially procured printing accounted for 49.1 percent. In 1974, commercial printing comprised 64 percent of the total.[9]

Field printing constitutes a very small percentage of total GPO printing. A small number of field printing facilities, located on federal property, handle minor requests, primarily of a local nature, that can be carried out more efficiently and with less cost than either commercial procurement or the main Washington plant could do. Most field printing work consists of overnight or daily jobs in small quantities. With some exceptions, these documents are used locally or for internal consumption.

Of value to businessmen is a publication, revised about once a year, titled *How to Do Business with the GPO, a Guide for Contractors* (GP 1.23/4:B96/year; Item 548). An alphabetical list of plants by federal agency authorized to perform printing, and their listing by geographical region, as well as a list of regional printing procurement offices with addresses are found in *Government Printing and Binding Regulations*, which is revised periodically and issued by the JCP (Y 4.P93/1:6/no.; Item 992-A); in these revised issues are found the regulations for printing and binding set forth in updated fashion by the JCP.

Documents produced for the GPO by commercial firms still carry the GPO imprint. They are not to be confused with the large class of "non-GPO" publications produced by the facilities of agencies independent of the GPO. The nature and significance of non-GPO documents in the overall publishing role of the federal establishment will be discussed in Chapter 3.

It should be noted that as a printer, the GPO has no jurisdiction over the content or size of publications. Various factors determine whether an agency will print a publication on its own or send it to the GPO. The agency sends the text copy of its issuance to the GPO's Planning Service department. The planners write up work orders, or "jackets," containing complete printing instructions for the publication. After the jacket is prepared, the decision is reached to either print the publication at the GPO, or to contract it out to a commercial printer. Since the GPO is basically a "black and white print shop," any publication incorporating extensive use of color, or special processes, must be contracted out. One can tell if a particular publication was printed at the GPO or by a contractor by looking at the imprint. A white star in front of the words "Government Printing Office" indicates the publication was printed by a contractor. The absence of the star indicates the job was done at the GPO's own facilities.[10]

Automation and Computer Technology

In 1977 the Public Printer testified before a subcommittee of the House Appropriations Committee that "85 percent of the cost of congressional printing and binding is in the typesetting, not in the paper. . . . Most of the cost is in setting the type."[11] A book page can be set into type in about fifteen minutes by a competent linotype operator, but the composing process, including proofreading, correction, and verification, is lengthy and complex. Accordingly, technological emphasis has concentrated upon shortening and simplifying this process. In 1962 the Public Printer convened a committee to study and recommend a solution to the problems that stem from the reproduction of material produced by high-speed printers on automatic data processing equipment. The committee proposed "a high-speed electronic phototypesetting device operating from magnetic tapes which would produce a fully-formatted page of hard copy," and bids were invited. An award was made to the Mergenthaler Linotype Company, which teamed with CBS Laboratories on the project, and in 1967 the "Linotron" was born.[12]

The Linotron is a custom-made electronic phototypesetting machine that can almost effortlessly link the modern high-speed computer to the old art of printing.

The material to be printed arrives at the machine in the form of encoded magnetic tape from other departmental computers. On instruction from the computer tape, the Linotron finds the character and typeface desired, and at computer speed sets the document a page at a time. Each one thousand characters can be set electronically in any of eight print sizes in a second. What emerges is a film strip that is ready to be developed and turned into hard copy.

A second Linotron system was placed in operation in 1969. By 1970, a former Public Printer was able to state that the systems had saved enough money in two years of operation to be self-sustaining. The acceleration of the printing process by computerized composition has been dramatic. In 1974 the Superintendent of Documents noted that "a page of the Chicago Telephone Directory consisting of approximately 22,000 characters would be completed in about 20 seconds, or at the rate of three pages per minute."[13] Moreover, the system permits reduction of the number of printed pages almost 40 percent; this translates into fewer negatives, fewer plates, less presswork, less paper and, ultimately, lower costs.

In FY 1974 the GPO composed over three-quarters of a million pages on the two Linotron systems. During a 15-month period ending September 30, 1976, an additional million pages were set electronically. The House Information Systems in 1977 was developing a process "whereby much of the material that is presently typeset in hot metal will, in fact, be mostly set as a by-product of a text edit system which they are planning to install. [The GPO is] working closely with them in the development of the system."[14]

Voluminous works such as the *Federal Register*, *Congressional Record*, House and Senate hearings, etc., are being and will be converted to electronic photocomposition. Congressional printing alone, when the total process is automated, will achieve substantial savings on the current cost of printing and binding. And it will reduce the number of employees. Since 1975 the number of GPO employees "has come down 341 ... primarily as the result of better management techniques and utilization of new technology."[15]

Although the Public Printer feels that the GPO is consistently underfunded by Congress, it remains a leader in the application of electronic text processing and photocomposition technology because it has the money to pioneer in printing techniques not available to commercial printing houses. After all, the government is the single largest contributor to the "print explosion"; it is only simple justice that a government agency, with tax dollars, assume the burden and obligation of developing cost-effective automated systems for the printing of documents.

Micropublishing

In 1970 Public Printer A. N. Spence submitted a proposal to the JCP requesting permission to study the feasibility of making GPO publications available in microform "to customers either in addition to or in lieu of printing." JCP gave the Public Printer authority to form an advisory committee, which included representatives from the Library of Congress, American Library Association, and industry. The advisory committee's recommendations included a questionnaire sent to depository libraries, wherein 75 percent of those responding indicated an interest in receiving some documents in microform.

Spence's death and an interregnum in appointment of a new Public Printer delayed implementation of the micropublishing venture. In the summer of 1973 Public Printer Thomas F. McCormick submitted a plan to the JCP to obtain new and additional data on the microform needs of the depository library community. Part II of the 1973 *Biennial Report of Depository Libraries* was another questionnaire designed to determine interest in receiving categories of publications in microform.[16]

The survey was mailed to libraries in late February 1974. When the responses were finally tabulated, the results were basically the same as the earlier survey: an overwhelming number of depository libraries desired that at least some categories of documents be received in microform. In June 1974 McCormick in a formal letter to the JCP requested approval to conduct a pilot microform project in cooperation with selected depository institutions. The purpose of the pilot project was "to examine the adequacy of bibliographic controls, attempt to measure user response, examine the quality of film manufacture, packaging and distribution of the film. The test would provide for system refinement to assure the best possible product in the hands of the Depository Librarians."[17]

On January 9, 1975, the Chairman of the JCP approved the microform pilot project. The project called for the conversion of some 63,000 pages of the *Code of Federal Regulations* (CFR) to a 98-frame nominal 24:1 reduction ratio microfiche for distribution to 22 participating depository libraries for a period of about 4 months.[18] The final report on the pilot project was submitted to the JCP in June of 1976. Titled *Test Results, Government Printing Office Microform Pilot Project* (June 30, 1976), copies were furnished to members of the Depository Library Council to the Public Printer. Later the report was transmitted to all depository libraries with *Daily Depository Shipping List 9301* (November 16, 1976).

Results of the pilot project indicated that, with a few minor exceptions, the program was judged a success. Approval from the Chairman of the JCP was transmitted by letter addressed to the Public Printer on March 25, 1977. The letter stipulated that the microfiche would not be made available for sale by the Superintendent of Documents at this time.[19]

The tortuous progress of this venture aptly illustrates the deliberative nature of government decision making. As former Public Printer McCormick stated:

> While the mills of the Government may appear to grind slowly, there is usually a reason—and that reason often is to avoid anyone being injured financially by the weight of Government action. In early discussions between GPO officials and the Joint Committee on Printing—dating to 1972—several Committee members expressed concern over the possibility of the Government Printing Office competing with private enterprise. It has been GPO's aim not to intrude, where possible, into areas where the private economy would be harmed. The care Congress and we at GPO have exercised has been aimed primarily at assuring that GPO's entry into micropublication is proper, well-planned, and consistent with the needs of the public and the best interests of the industry.[20]

Later in the same remarks, McCormick averred "that the Government Printing Office was never meant to act as a publisher, or a publishing specialist. Neither would we presume to be a micropublisher."[21]

Distribution of documents on microfiche to depository libraries should not be considered a panacea. In the questionnaire distributed in 1974, comments were invited; and a number of documents librarians took the opportunity to respond, some at length. Typical of a thoughtful response was LeRoy C. Schwarzkopf's comments and questions concerning possible problems. Examples include the distribution of numbered publications which are not published in consecutive order; current bills and resolutions with amendments; the numerous loose-leaf issuances, and the like.[22]

It is assumed that the good judgment of documents librarians will prevail. Responses indicated that librarians would prefer current reference materials, including serials and periodicals, to continue being received in hard copy. Suitable for microform are "annual reports, census information, trade reports, agricultural publications, and Defense Department documents . . . ; in short, the materials most in demand in microform are those of a statistical, archival, or research—not topical—nature."[23]

For the reader who wishes to pursue the documentation in more detail, a succinct "bibliographic history," with citations, is offered. The reconstruction of events may be followed in two principal sources: *Documents to the People* (DttP) and *Public Documents Highlights* (PDH). The former is the official publication of the Government Documents Round Table (GODORT) of the American Library Association; the latter is issued by SuDocs (GP 3.27:nos.) and intended primarily for depository librarians. Selected source materials follow.

Documents to the People

DttP, in its January 1975 issue, published a lengthy summary which was presented to the JCP justifying the need for a micropublishing project. The account is given on pages 32-39. It includes a brief history of events beginning in 1970 with Public Printer Spence's proposal, gives a statistical analysis of the 1974 microform preference survey, discusses the choice of the CFR as the pilot project vehicle, the film format, indexing techniques, bibliographic control using the *Monthly Catalog*, microfiche header area presentation, objectives of the pilot project, and cost benefits to the GPO. Following is a list of pilot project depository libraries and selected comments from depository librarians.

The September 1976 issue of DttP (pp. 18-20) contains a thorough analysis of the test project by Frank Edgcombe, microforms librarian at Montclair State College, New Jersey. Topics include distribution of the fiche, quality, bibliographic control, indexing, and usage.

The January 1977 issue of DttP (pp. 9-10) carried a status report on the project by Ray Gulick, GPO Microforms Specialist, which was presented at the Fall 1976 meeting of the Depository Library Council to the Public Printer. Emphasis was placed on the cost benefits to the GPO ($300,000 per year) and the benefits of microform to libraries (faster distribution, reduction in storage space, etc.).

The May 1977 issue of DttP contained news that the JCP had approved the GPO request to convert to microfiche "non-GPO documentation," and to authorize

GPO to convert GPO documents into microfiche "as necessary and as requested by individual depository librarians and when savings in costs are clearly demonstrable." (p. 97).

The June 1977 issue of DttP carried the text of the JCP approval (p. 139), and a report on the program by Jim Livsey,[24] in which he expanded on the categories of documents to be converted. Livsey noted that, concerning documents already in the depository program, "in instances where costs are an overwhelming factor of consideration, depositories will not be given a choice of format." (p. 138).

Public Documents Highlights

The April 1974 issue of PDH (GP 3.27:3) presented a summary of the history and current status of micropublishing at the GPO in conjunction with the microform preference survey, which was received by libraries about that time (p. 1).

The June 1974 issue of PDH (GP 3.27:4) contains a very useful section called "Microform Questions Answered." Responses in the form of questions placed in the survey by librarians were answered on a selected basis and included a number of useful facts (pp. 5-6). A sample question illustrating the process follows:

"Will the fiche go 'out-of-print' or have its 'supply exhausted' as soon as the paper copy?"

A. Retention of the original silver master by the Superintendent of Documents in an archival condition will assure there will never be an "out-of-print" condition. Additional film duplicates or hardcopy can be generated from that master as well as projection printing plates for short-run purposes (p. 5).

The PDH issue of February 1977 (GP 3.27:20) carried a news item about the resolution of the Depository Library Council to the Public Printer officially endorsing the GPO microform program. The Council had reviewed the test results of the pilot project and unanimously resolved that the program proceed. The text of the resolution is given in full (pp. 1, 6). Finally, PDH in its April 1977 issue (GP 3.27:21), printed the text of the letter from the JCP Chairman to the GPO authorizing the program. Here, as elsewhere, PDH and DttP have duplicated information, a satisfactory arrangement because the audience for each publication is not precisely the same.

Other

The April 1974 issue of *Microform Review* carried under the title "Micropublishing and the Government Printing Office/Three Viewpoints" comments by three persons espousing their own view of the microform venture. The first viewpoint was written by James Adler, president of Congressional Information Service, Inc. (CIS). The second viewpoint was conveyed by the GPO. The last viewpoint was carried by Catharine J. Reynolds, government documents librarian and head of the documents division, University of Colorado libraries. The juxtaposition of these points of view presents a clear picture of the often conflicting aims of industry, government, and the user of both products (pp. 85-95).

The March 1976 issue of *Illinois Libraries* (v. 58, no. 3) was devoted to the topic "Documents in Microform." One of the articles, "GPO's Micropublishing Program," was written by Jim Livsey and presented a short history of federal government printing activities, followed by a brief summary of micropublishing plans to that date (pp. 204-205).

Clearly, all this is prologue. Assessment of the GPO micropublishing program is down the road. Whatever the immediate effects, or the modifications and changes that are sure to ensue, it is obvious that the program has momentous and probably irreversible consequences for the issuing of documents and for their use by the public.

Facilities

From the beginning the need for better physical facilities to discharge the responsibilities of the GPO properly was a topic of concern. The author in his 1975 edition of this text has given an account of the tribulations of inadequate physical facilities from 1860 to 1974.[25] Although the answer to GPO's physical plant problems is by no means resolved, some recent developments would seem to indicate guarded optimism.

As of 1977 the Government Printing Office's existing space utilization consisted of the following properties.

GPO Owned Facilities

Buildings 1, 2, 3, and 4 are located on G to H North Capitol Street NW in the District of Columbia. They comprise the "in house" printing and binding plant and administrative offices, and have been considered inadequate since 1939.[26]

GPO Leased Facilities

Documents warehouses are located in Laurel, Maryland, and Alexandria, Virginia; these facilities are used in the operations of the Superintendent of Documents (see Chapter 2). In addition, the GPO leases materials management warehouse space in Franconia and Fairfax, Virginia. Office space for public documents and data systems is located at Union Center Plaza in the District of Columbia, about 1½ blocks from the main GPO on North Capitol Street.

The total amount of square feet for GPO owned and leased facilities is 2,428,000.[27]

The need to improve the present GPO facilities has, as noted, been manifest and generally acknowledged for over three decades. The discussion over the years has centered on where the facility should be located and what type of facility it should be. Efforts were directed toward adding to the present facility. But Public

Printers opposed that suggestion as being cost-ineffective, since the current eight-story plant is inherently inefficient to begin with. Moreover, the decision to find a suitable site that met several criteria became more difficult to resolve than had been expected.

In 1976 the various entities participating in a search for a new location decided upon a site which seemed to satisfy all criteria. To be located at Brentwood Road and T Street NE, between Rhode Island and New York Avenues, the site would presumably meet the following standards:

1.   Increase the efficiency of printing service to Congress and other Federal agencies;
2.   Provide the District of Columbia with a much needed economic base and retain substantial skilled employment to area residents;
3.   Provide a major public building project at a time when the construction industry needs a boost;
4.   Assist in accomplishing the objectives of the National Capital Planning Commission's comprehensive plan for the Nation's Capital;
5.   Provide Government Printing Office employees with a better, healthier working environment;
6.   Provide Federal savings of between $11 and $22 million annually thereby reimbursing construction costs over a relatively short period of time; and
7.   Free up the present Government Printing Office for other Federal purposes.[28]

The site is located about a 10- to 15-minute drive from the Capitol next to a railroad siding. Adequate truck routes are available. And it is next to a Metro station. Proposed is a modern, three-story building which would place the bulk of the production effort on one floor, thus increasing capabilities, productivity and service while improving working conditions and employee safety.

On December 16, 1976, *The Washington Post* carried a lengthy article about the new site.[29] The article, though factual and well-written, left the impression that final approval had been granted. A notice in the March 1977 issue of DttP (p. 80) was necessary to dispel the premature euphoria implicit in the newspaper account.

Indeed, like the snail's progress in formulating and gaining approval for the GPO micropublishing program, the process involved in breaking ground for a new facility is painfully slow and consists of a number of hurdles. The legislative process involves House and Senate committees and subcommittees, floor action, authorization and appropriations measures, liaison with the Congressional Budget Office, and the like. Moreover, the planning stages have involved the active participation of the following groups working with GPO officials:

National Capital Planning Commission
General Services Administration
Metropolitan Washington Board of Trade
Printing Industry of Metropolitan Washington, D.C.
District of Columbia government
Council on Environmental Quality

Joint Industry-Government Advisory Board, GPO
International Printing and Graphic Communications Union
Greater Washington Central Labor Council
Washington Building and Construction Trades Council
Environmental Protection Agency
Department of Transportation[30]

Finally, it is important to note that, if and when final approval is granted, it would take about seven years to build and relocate. At best, the facility would not become a reality until 1983 or 1984.[31]

GPO Publications

According to the March 1977 edition of the *List of Classes of United States Government Publications Available for Selection by Depository Libraries* (GP 3.24:year), only two series from the GPO itself are available to depository institutions: General Publications (GP 1.2; Item 548) and Handbooks, Manuals, Guides (GP 1.23/4; Item 548). Andriot's *Guide to U.S. Government Publications*, however, lists a number of non-depository series: bulletins, pamphlets, circulars, regulations, training series, and the like. Few librarians see these publications, and there is probably little use for them in libraries.

By authority of 44 U.S.C. 309(c) the Public Printer is required to submit an "annual business-type budget program for the operations under the revolving fund" at the beginning of each session of Congress.[32] Pursuant to 44 U.S.C. 508 he is required to submit to the JCP estimates of the quantity of paper of all descriptions needed for the public printing and binding for the ensuing year.

The *Annual Report of the Public Printer* is *not* available to depository libraries. Under authority of 44 U.S.C. 1117, the GPO discontinued *printing* the annual reports in 1947. 44 U.S.C. 1117 permits agencies the option of discontinuing the printing of annual or special reports in order to keep expenditures for printing and binding within appropriations. When this option is exercised, the original copy of the report is kept on file in the office of the heads of the respective departments, independent offices, or establishments for public inspection. Accordingly, typewritten copies of the *Annual Report of the Public Printer* are available for public inspection at the Government Printing Office, and photocopies may be secured for a fee. I trust that the irony of this procedure has not escaped the perceptive reader.

REFERENCES

1. *100 GPO Years, 1861-1961: A History of United States Public Printing* (Washington: Government Printing Office, 1961), p. 15.

2. Robert E. Kling, Jr., *The Government Printing Office* (New York: Praeger, 1970), p. 12.

3. *100 GPO Years*, pp. 31-33.

4. Kling, pp. 33-34.

5. *100 GPO Years*, p. 162.

6. Ibid., p. 163.

7. U.S. Office of the Federal Register. *United States Government Manual, 1976/77* (Washington: Government Printing Office, 1976), p. 51.

8. Kling, p. 136.

9. U.S. Congress, House, Committee on Appropriations, Subcommittee on Legislative Branch Appropriations, *Legislative Branch Appropriations for [FY] 1977*, Hearings, 94th Cong., 2d Sess., February 9, 1976 (Washington: Government Printing Office, 1976), p. 503.

10. PDH 10: 1, 3 (June 1975).

11. *Legislative Branch Appropriations for [FY] 1978* (House), p. 428.

12. Kling, pp. 197-200.

13. W. H. Lewis, "Superintendent of Documents on the GPO and Its Plans," *Illinois Libraries* 56: 262 (April 1974).

14. *Legislative Branch Appropriations for [FY] 1978* (House), p. 428.

15. Ibid., pp. 429-30.

16. DttP 3: 32 (January 1975); PDH 3: 1-2 (April 1974).

17. PDH 4: 1, 4 (June 1974).

18. A list of participating libraries is found in DttP 3: 37 (January 1975).

19. Full text of the letter was published in PDH 21: 1 (April 1977) and DttP 5: 139 (June 1977).

20. PDH 4: 2 (June 1974).

21. Ibid., p. 6. John J. Boyle was appointed United States Public Printer in 1977.

22. Comments and attachments to *Request for Information from Depository Libraries*, Documents Division—McKeldin Library, University of Maryland (1974).

23. PDH 4: 2 (June 1974).

24. Livsey is Director of the Library and Statutory Distribution Service and Microforms Program Manager for the GPO.

25. Joe Morehead, *Introduction to United States Public Documents* (Littleton, Colo.: Libraries Unlimited, 1975), pp. 8-10.

26. Ibid., p. 8.

27. U.S. Congress, House, Committee on Public Works and Transportation, Subcommittee on Public Buildings and Grounds, *Proposed Relocation of the Government Printing Office in Washington, D.C.*, Hearings, 95th Cong., 1st Sess., May 17, 18, 1977 (Washington: Government Printing Office, 1977), p. 79.

28. Ibid., p. 30.

29. Paul Hodge, "New Northeast Site Approved for the Relocation of GPO," *The Washington Post* (December 16, 1976), pp. D.C. 1, D.C. 4.

30. The list is not complete, nor will it be until completion of the project. The land for the new site is owned by four different companies, including Chesapeake & Ohio Railroad System and Trailways Bus.

31. Hodge, p. D.C. 4; DttP 5: 80 (March 1977).

32. *Reports to Be Made to Congress* (95-1: H. doc. 10), p. 52.

2

SUPERINTENDENT OF DOCUMENTS

One studying today the mechanism and administration of the Federal government . . . cannot but be struck with the enormous development of what are called the non-essential functions of government. The power of the government is used in a thousand ways to accomplish ends not in themselves necessary to the maintenance of law and order, but solely to do certain things that are believed to be for the advantage of the people and which cannot be done as well under private auspices.

To the student, the most interesting portion of this work is that undertaken for the purpose of making contributions to human knowledge. Within comparative recent years the government has established numerous scientific and educational bureaus whose sole or chief function is the collection of special information and its publication and distribution among the people. . . .

Unfortunately, the system of issuing and distributing government publications in the past has been such that it would seem that, if deliberate design had been exercised, this task of the student could not have been made a more difficult one. There has been an utter lack of system in the methods employed by the government. Starting from a small beginning, public printing has grown here and there as demands have arisen, until the present enormous output has been reached. Each branch of the government has looked out for its own interests, and the present confused and complicated system has been the outcome. The result of this condition of affairs is that to the majority of persons these publications are closed books. Not only are they in many cases unobtainable, but their very existence is unknown. Most librarians have given up in despair their attempts to obtain complete sets of government documents or to catalog those that they have.

—William Franklin Willoughby, "Government Publications,"
Yale Review (August 1896)

BACKGROUND

The Printing Act of 1895 created the Office of Superintendent of Documents to effect "a more intelligent distribution of Government publications," because the procedures in force at the time were hopelessly chaotic. The first Superintendent, F. A. Crandall, registered dismay at the "bewildering congeries of volumes, numbers, and parts . . . of Congressional documents," and of the overall operation stated:

Of course the present system was not devised by anybody. There was never anybody who could have devised it. Like Topsy, it "jist growed."[1]

Topsy's haphazard growth generated abuse in the dispersal of documents; the Congress was chiefly to blame for the distribution of its quota of publications in a manner "too promiscuous among persons who did not appreciate their true value." Documents had been turning up in secondhand bookstores for sale, "thus abusing the generosity of the Government." Some libraries "were overwhelmed by mountains of government publications, while others received no regular distribution at all." Moreover, "no standard system for titling government documents existed" rendering "practical cataloging . . . virtually impossible."[2] Little wonder that comments like Mr. Willoughby's had been appearing in the press and journals.

While the act of 1860 had endeavored to correct the several problems in the printing of documents, the act of 1895 sought to remedy the defects in distribution. It directed the Superintendent to

receive and care for all surplus documents in the possession of Government offices; assort and catalog them; supervise their distribution and sale; catalog and index monthly and annually all documents published; in fine, to render accessible to librarian and the public generally the vast store of Government publications.[3]

To carry out this mission, a Public Documents Division was established within the GPO; the Superintendent was subordinate to the Public Printer but "was to exercise full authority over the tangled government documents situation."[4] Established in leased quarters on the sixth floor of the Union Building on G Street, NW, near Seventh, accompanied by the usual lamentations of inadequate space, the Division began "the giant task of taking over 134,000 publications accumulated by the departments, hundreds of boxes from the House and Senate document rooms, and over 21,000 publications in the GPO."[5] Distribution to depository libraries was systematized, the enormous job of cataloging was begun, and the sales program was initiated. Thus 106 years after George Washington took the oath of office of President of the United States, a semblance of management was introduced into the dissemination of the publications of the federal establishment.

When the Printing Act of 1895 established the office of Superintendent of Documents (SuDocs), it did not explicitly mandate the creation and maintenance of a library of federal documents. However, a collection developed in the Public Documents Division because of the requirements to "prepare and publish a comprehensive index of public documents" and "a catalog of government publications which shall show the documents printed during the preceding month, where obtainable, and the price." The fledgling "Library" retained at least one copy of every distinct document received for cataloging/indexing purposes. By 1898 the Superintendent had organized the Public Documents Division into six operational units: "Bookkeeping and Correspondence, Sales, Catalog, Library, Mail, and Stock."[6]

Joseph A. King, a former librarian of the Division, was unequivocal in discussing the genesis of the collection. The documents assembled, he noted, constitute "the by-product of one of the functions charged by law to the Superintendent of Documents," namely, the compilation of catalogs and indexes. Writing in 1951, he pointed out that the Library "was established to carry out the will of Congress by publishing this monthly catalog. Though its collection is a by-product, it has become one of the largest collections of United States Government Publications in the world."[7]

The Library was not open to the general public; a small area, however, had been set aside as a reference department for use by the staff for cataloging and by government officials and infrequent visitors doing research in the collection.[8] It is clear that the Library of the Public Documents Division was not a library in any traditional sense. It was, in King's phrase, a "publishing Library" whose physical characteristics were "strictly functional," unable to offer reference or research services because of space limitations, while accumulating materials for cataloging and indexing at a rate that only served to exacerbate the critical lack of space. Over two decades ago King was able to affirm that the Library "is believed to be the most complete collection of its kind in existence."[9]

TRANSFER OF THE COLLECTION TO THE NATIONAL ARCHIVES

Concern for the preservation of the materials appeared to be the major reason for the transfer of the retrospective collection to the National Archives. Exploratory activity began on an informal basis in 1971. In 1972 a *News Release* by the General Services Administration announced that the transfer was taking place. By June of 1975 processing of the collection as an archival unit had been accomplished through the large "Y3" designation (Boards, Commissions, and Committees), reference service was being provided, and researchers could access the materials. Another relocation of the collection was effected, and the collection is now housed in an annex to the National Archives, the former Lansburgh's Department Store, located about a block and a half from the main Archives Building.

Thus the library of the Superintendent of Documents was left with the task of cataloging current material, retaining certain series for internal reference, and sending materials to the Archives on a periodic schedule for interfiling in the retrospective collection.

The arrangement appears to be a satisfactory one. By definition, there is an already existing archival arrangement. Since the SuDocs class notation is based upon provenance, the idea of an archival order is philosophically conformable. Not only is preservation of old materials insured, but access and reference service to the scholarly research community and the larger public are viable.[10]

Over 2 million individual titles comprise the retrospective collection housed in the Archives annex. The collection is accessed by various government and commercial indexes currently available (see Chapter 5).[11] In late 1976 the GPO proposed that the Council on Library Resources undertake a feasibility study and economic analysis "to determine the cost and advisability of cataloging the entire collection, using the Ohio College Library Center [OCLC] and the Anglo-American Cataloging Rules [AACR]." Such a plan, GPO noted, "if economically sound would benefit the nation's library community by providing electronic search and the generation on demand of indexes and bibliographies through computer manipulation. In cooperation with the Library of Congress, magnetic output tapes could be made available to other networking systems throughout the country, thereby facilitating bibliographic control of Government documentation."[12]

REORGANIZATION OF THE PUBLIC DOCUMENTS DEPARTMENT

In December 1970, the Division of Public Documents was renamed the Public Documents Department. On July 1, 1974, the Department was thoroughly reorganized. First, the Superintendent of Documents was upgraded to the position of Assistant Public Printer, reporting directly to the Public Printer. This reassignment was permitted under the provisions of 44 U.S.C. 305, 1702.[13]

The newly designated Assistant Public Printer (Superintent of Documents)[14] is in charge of three major "service" units: Documents Sales, Documents Support, and Library and Statutory Distribution. Documents Sales, as the title suggests, comprises the various aspects of the sales program: management, order processing, warehouse, field operations. Documents Support is concerned with administrative, analysis and review, and receipts and accounts functions. Library and Statutory Distribution, the Service that most affects documents librarians, contains the following "Divisions": Library, Depository Distribution, and Statutory Stock Distribution. Assisting the Superintendent in a staff capacity is a person holding the title "Micropublishing Specialist." A useful chart showing the reorganization was published in the April 1974 issue of *Public Documents Highlights* (GP 3.27:3), p. 3.

Facilities

In late 1974 the Library and Statutory Distribution Service moved to commodious quarters in a building located in Alexandria, Virginia. Two warehouses in Laurel, Maryland, house the sales operation; automated operations have markedly improved the control and shipment of sales stock. Clerical and administrative staff of documents sales has been relocated in office facilities on Union Center Plaza. The reorganization of the Department and the new locations for the units will presumably remain in effect. If and when the GPO gets its new building, these operations wholly or in part may be joined again.

Separating the SuDocs function from the GPO building has been a sanguine development. "The Depository Program, the Library Division, and the *Monthly Catalog* operations have been growing at the old location on North Capitol Street since 1895. Our work has increased. . . . There just wasn't any more room for us to expand. . . . Working conditions were becoming increasingly cramped."[15] Indeed, the need for new facilities was underscored by the rising tide of complaints about inept service to customers of sales publications and to depository librarians in the processing and receipt of subscribed items.

FUNCTIONS

A description of duties is found in every annual volume of hearings held before the House and Senate subcommittees on legislative branch appropriations. The FY 1978 statement of the Superintendent is typical:

The four functions of the Office of Superintendent of Documents are:

(1)   The sale of Government publications produced by or through the Government Printing Office;

(2)   The distribution of Government publications to designated depository libraries;

(3)   The compilation of catalogs and indexes of Government publications, and;

(4)   The mailing of certain Government publications for Members of Congress and other Government agencies in accordance with specific provisions of law or on a reimbursable basis.[16]

The first three functions listed are of central importance to documents librarians. First we shall examine the sales function, emphasizing current tools and methods. Next the compilation of catalogs and indexes will be studied, concentrating on the features of the *Monthly Catalog*. Finally, mailing to members of Congress will be noted. The depository library function, because of its importance and scope, will be analyzed and discussed in Chapter 3.

The Sales Program

In terms of personnel and required resources, the largest program under the Superintendent of Documents is the sale of publications. In 1895 the Superintendent was empowered "to sell at cost any public document in its charge, the distribution of which is not specifically directed by law."[17] His stock for the first years was acquired from extra copies that libraries had been sent or departments had received. Reprint authority for departmental publications was granted in 1904 and for congressional documents in 1922. Far from relying on the leftover largesse of libraries and agencies, the Superintendent today obtains sales publications from the GPO by submitting printing orders for the number of copies he estimates he will need to meet public demand. And demand for public documents is high. In FY 1976 approximately 56 million publications were sold; projections for future years continue upwards. In both fiscal years 1975 and 1976 total program costs exceeded revenue, but each year the amount of the difference grew smaller.[18]

Prices

In 1972 the Public Printer authorized an increase in the sales price of GPO publications of over 70 percent, the first general rise in prices since 1968. In 1973 a new pricing formula resulted in price increases in the same general range as the increases of 1972. Additional price increases of about 20 percent took effect in 1974 and 1975. A chorus of complaints by librarians and other users resulted in many articles in newspapers and journals, and some statements of outrage by members of Congress. Senator Proxmire, for example, was reported as saying that the drastic increases "may serve as effective censors on the publication of vital . . . information" and called the sharp rise in prices "outrageous."[19]

According to GPO policy, "the basic principle which guides the pricing of publications sold by the Superintendent of Documents is that all costs of operating the program should be recovered by the sales revenue."[20] Pricing is governed by 44 U.S.C. 1708, which reads—

> The price at which additional copies of Government publications are offered for sale to the public by the Superintendent of Documents shall be based on the cost as determined by the Public Printer plus 50 percent.

Thus the principle of recovering costs, or as it is frequently called, to conduct a "self-sustaining" operation, tied to the formula, produced inevitably a rise in prices. As a former Superintendent of Documents put it, "The cost of this program [the sale of publications], including labor, material, and overhead incurred in printing, warehousing, and distribution, is to be borne by the users of the publications rather than being subsidized by appropriations from the General Funds of the Treasury."[21]

Defenders of the price increases blamed the rising cost of paper, a postage increase of over 400 percent arising from the Postal Reorganization Act of 1971, labor costs, salary increases, and general inflation. But these words were of cold comfort to customers, who found themselve paying up to 450 percent more for certain subscriptions.[22]

Although there is clearly some justification for increasing prices of government publications from time to time, the dramatic rises since 1972 have greatly exceeded the rise in the Consumer Price Index (CPI) and the rise in prices for commercial publications. Prohibitive prices do become a form of censorship when they adversely affect the ability of libraries to provide public documents for the public to keep informed. The problem is vexing because 44 U.S.C. 1708 is subject to different interpretations.

Because pricing of sales publications will remain of concern to the user of public documents, the reader should consult some useful studies which have been generated as a result of the crisis that began in 1972. Three of the most notable analyses are as follows:

1) *Pricing of Publications Sold to the Public* (GA 1.13:P96/26; Item 546-D) was a report to the JCP by the General Accounting Office (GAO) prepared in 1974 (B-114829). GAO was asked to determine two things: Did the drastic increases embrace the same financial philosophy

which had prevailed in the past, and did the increases change the relationship between the pricing structure and the annual appropriation by the Congress? To both questions the GAO's conclusion was affirmative. Acknowledging that a new pricing formula based upon a different interpretation of "cost" was used to bring GPO sales up to a self-sustaining level again, GAO concluded that no violation of 44 U.S.C. 1708 was made. The Public Printer's interpretation of "cost" also received tacit approval of the House and Senate appropriations committees. GAO further concluded that the relationship between the pricing structure and the annual appropriation had been changed. "In the past GPO requested appropriations for sales program salaries and expenses which were not identified as included when determining selling prices. GPO did not request appropriations for the identified costs but used sales revenue to finance such costs."[23]

2)   LeRoy C. Schwarzkopf, "Pricing Policy of GPO Sales Publications: An Analysis of the GAO Report to the Joint Committee on Printing," was a response to the above report published in DttP (September 1975), pages 25-30. In studying the legislative history of the present pricing formula, the author concludes that legislative intent for "cost as determined by the Public Printer" before addition of the 50 percent surcharge "should be limited to printing and binding costs." Public Printers and Superintendents "had been less than candid in divulging to the Congress the specific pricing formula and the value of its components." Not only was the sales program self-sustaining; "indeed, the profits were so 'excessive' that starting in 1961 and continuing through 1967, and again in 1969, the 'gross profits' from the sales program which were returned to the Treasury exceeded not only the appropriations for the administrative cost of the sales publications program, but also for the administrative costs of the 'non-revenue' producing activities of the Superintendent of Documents (i.e., Depository Library Program, Cataloging and Indexing, and distribution of free publications from Congress and other federal agencies). In 1970 and 1971 the 'earnings' continued to exceed the administrative costs of the sales program. However, with the rise in postal charges in 1972 a large 'deficit' occurred which was covered by appropriations."[24]

Of perhaps even greater importance is the question of the sales program being "self-sustaining." Why should a policy of providing information on the activities of government result in a profit, much less be obliged to recover costs? Schwarzkopf persuasively cites 31 U.S.C. 483a (Section 501 of the Independent Appropriations Act of 1952):

It is the sense of the Congress that any . . . publication . . . issued by any Federal agency . . . shall be self-sustaining to the full extent possible . . . and the head of each Federal agency is authorized by regulation . . . to prescribe such fee, charge, or price . . . to be fair and equitable taking into consideration direct and indirect cost to the

Government, value to the recipient, public policy and interest served, and other interests served. . . .

The phrase "public policy and interest served" have been construed in court decisions to mean that a sales program need be self-sustaining only to the extent that it "serves special beneficiaries." Thus, Schwarzkopf argues, public libraries which benefit the public at large should not, in the light of court opinions, be required to pay anything for public documents.[25]

3) *Pricing of GPO Sales Publications* was also prepared by Schwarzkopf and issued in September 1976. The research for this lengthier analysis was accomplished in the author's capacity as Chairman, subcommittee on pricing, GPO Users Survey, conducted by the Committee on Information Hangups. In his section on "Conclusions and Recommendations," Schwarzkopf finds that the GPO "has since 1936 violated the legislative intent of the law governing the pricing of publications for sale to the public" and recommends urgent revision of the law "to bring it in line with current economic realities, and with general federal policy on user charges." But, as the author notes, "the problem of establishing a fair pricing policy is complicated by the dichotomy of the federal government providing free publications to some individuals or organizations . . . and requiring others to buy them from the Government Printing Office. Many citizens are not aware of this largesse of the federal government."[26]

Schwarzkopf's two studies are superior to the GAO analysis; they are more thorough, scholarly, and keenly analytical. His two major points are well taken: Pricing policy has been disingenuous, and there is no moral or legal basis for an agency like GPO (or for that matter NTIS, etc.) to be fully self-sustaining.

Branch Bookstores

On March 21, 1967, the first retail bookstore for the sale of government publications outside the Washington, D.C., area was opened in the Everett McKinley Dirksen federal building in Chicago. The bookstores are run along the lines of a commercial bookstore; customers may browse and purchase what is available. If a publication is not in stock, forms are conveniently located for mail order service.

Government bookstores are located primarily in federal buildings. However, the General Services Administration began applying a rental charge, forcing the GPO to re-evaluate the location of bookstores in federal buildings. In 1976 a bookstore was opened in a commercial shopping center in Houston. In February 1977 a GPO official reported that the Houston experiment had been a "smashing success."[27]

The Public Printer testified in 1977 that "we are essentially on the break-even basis with the bookstore operations."[28] Continual monitoring of the financial health of the program requires changes from time to time. During 1976 and 1977 the Detroit bookstore was shifted to a better location and the Canton, Ohio, bookstore was relocated in Columbus, Ohio. During FY 1976 the bookstore located in the Forrestal Building on L'Enfant Plaza in Washington, D.C., was closed due to a consistently low volume of business.[29]

Bookstore operations are reported in the Legislative Branch Appropriations hearings, and a current list of GPO bookstores with addresses and phone numbers is found on the inside back cover of the *Monthly Catalog*.

Commercial Sellers

Although a 25 percent discount is allowed to individuals or libraries that purchase 100 or more copies of a single publication mailed to one address, bookdealers, buying for the purpose of resale, may receive the same discount regardless of quantity if the publications are mailed to their place of business. The Superintendent of Documents is empowered to prescribe the terms and conditions under which he authorizes resale by book dealers.[30] But because this is a comparatively low discount percent, booksellers have traditionally been reluctant to become involved in the business of selling documents.

Perhaps this reluctance is changing. In 1976 the GPO arranged to supply college bookstores with government publications; efforts to fill the orders of these retail outlets within 10 working days after receipt proved successful. In addition, an arrangement with "the 200 cooperating associations of the National Park Service where there are stores" to supply publications for sale was hailed by GPO officials as an "innovative" program.[31]

These efforts are not new. In 1972 a retail outlet in a Dayton, Ohio, department store was opened. For this historic occasion, the Superintendent of Documents attended opening ceremonies. The proprietor, who reported initial favorable response, said that his decision to enter this area where no one had dared to venture before was based on the healthy balance sheet of the GPO's San Francisco bookstore.[32]

Dealers and Jobbers

A directory of government documents dealers and jobbers located in the United States was compiled by Linda Siler-Regan, Head, Documents, Microforms and Maps, U.T. at El Paso Library, El Paso, Texas 79968, and was first published in the September 1975 issue of DttP (pp. 40-43). The list was updated in the September 1977 issue of DttP (pp. 209-212), and biennial revisions of the list are planned. The information includes name, address, and phone number; responsible person to contact; and specific information as to type of document handled.

Excluded from this list are those companies dealing wholly or significantly with government publications in microform. A list of micropublishers of federal documents is found in Henry P. Tseng, *Complete Guide to Legal Materials in Microform* and *1976 Supplement* (University Publications of America, Inc.).

Distribution Centers

Sales publications may be ordered by mail from the Central Office (Superintendent of Documents, U.S. Government Printing Office, Washington, D.C. 20402) and from the Public Documents Distribution Center, Pueblo, Colorado 81009. The latter address serves two primary purposes: for ordering titles designated in the *Selected U.S. Government Publications*, and for processing documents issued under the aegis of the Consumer Information Center.

The catalog for consumer information publications is called *Consumer Information*; it is an index brochure, revised periodically, of selected federal publications of consumer interest. Arranged by broad topics (Automobiles, Diet and Nutrition, Older Americans, etc.) with subdivisions, the list includes a number of free publications. The index itself is free and is the provenance of the General Services Administration's Consumer Information Center.[33] There is an edition in Spanish, entitled *Información Para el Consumidor.*

The Pueblo Distribution Center was established in 1972. The year before, a facility for processing documents was created in Philadelphia. The two area distribution centers were established to reduce the workload of the main processing center. On August 27, 1976, the Philadelphia center closed as part of a GPO facilities consolidation, and its functions were absorbed by the Pueblo, Colorado, facility.

Other Agencies

Under the provisions of 44 U.S.C. 1708, the Superintendent "may designate any Government officer his agent for the sale of Government publications under regulations agreed upon by the Superintendent of Documents and the head of the respective department or establishment of the Government." This provision accounts for the numerous publications which can be purchased directly from the "issuing agency." Sometimes the same publication is available from an agency and from SuDocs, an unnecessary and confusing duplication. While the Superintendent remains the chief sales agent for GPO publications, there are "over 125 consigned agents in other Government agencies."[34]

Ordering Sales Publications

Different forms are provided for customers depending upon whether the order is sent to the Pueblo, Colorado, facility or GPO's Central Office. Remittances should be by check or money order payable to the Superintendent of Documents. Operating rules require that SuDocs deposit monies received in the U.S. Treasury within 48 hours of receipt. Because of this requirement, the customer's cancelled check comes back before the order is received.

SuDocs used to supply coupons in units of $0.05, $0.10, $0.25, and $0.50, but effective July 1, 1976, this procedure was discontinued. The most suitable and convenient way to purchase GPO sales publications is by establishing a *Deposit Account.* With a deposit of $50 or more, a prepaid account may be opened, a deposit number is assigned the individual or institution, and deposit order forms may be used to register one's transaction. SuDocs advises that customers maintain a sufficient balance that would cover one's anticipated purchases for a 3-month period.

A multi-digit *stock number* is assigned to a sales publication when it is first printed, and remains with the document until the item is exhausted. If the publication is revised, a new stock number is assigned; if it is reprinted with minor changes, the old number remains. The stock number is a significant piece of information used by SuDocs in its order processing system.

Stock numbers began with a 9-digit number system, but as of 1977 stock numbers consisted of 12 digits arranged as follows:

008-007-12345-1

The first three digits represent the Department, the second three the agency, bureau or service. Thus, 008 refers to the Department of Defense, 007 to Defense Supply Agency. The 5-digit number, called the stem of the stock number, is sequential and does not signify provenance or hierarchy; it is the unique number assigned to the specific publication. The one digit number serves as a numeric check for computer verification of the three preceding numbers. Stock numbers serve as a primary means of identification for the PRF (which will be discussed later) and is the number used by the sales program to process orders.

The Superintendent, like any commercial publisher, tries to anticipate demand for each sales publication, and to print sufficient quantity to meet that demand. From time to time, however, unanticipated publicity creates a greater than expected interest and will occasionally result in a publication being temporarily out-of-print. When this happens, a reprint is ordered, and requests for that publication are "backordered," to be mailed when additional sales stock is received. The reprinting of a publication may take two to four months, but shipment will be made when the new stock becomes available. The Superintendent cannot reprint to accommodate a small market.

Order Processing

The high prices of publications and the inept distribution of materials through the mail have been two of the most vocally criticized areas of the Superintendent's operations. The latter suffered from inadequate bulk warehousing space and facilities at the old location, and the virtual absence of automation.

New warehousing space and computerized systems for bulk sales inventory and order processing have effected a dramatic turnaround in the sales program. A total of 400,000 square feet in two warehouses in Laurel, Maryland, permits access to each pallet without moving others. The entire bulk inventory is now consolidated with a single receiving operation. The second warehouse, known as Laurel II, houses a retail stock distribution function. Material is systematically arranged in stock number sequence in a single area, permitting a much smoother workflow. Retail distribution activities adjacent to bulk stock reduces transportation expenses.[35]

Before the move to Laurel, the operation had to be performed on several floors at the main GPO complex, and the bulk material had to be shipped in from outlying warehouses. The computerized bulk inventory control system significantly reduces delays in replenishing retail stock from bulk storage. The operation now is a one-story arrangement whose benefits have become manifest since the system became fully implemented.

Moreover, an automated data processing system, known as the Sales Order and Information System (SOIS), has resulted in a decided improvement in processing capability. Functional groups under SOIS provide automation management of one-time publication orders; inventory; processing subscription orders and the managing and distribution of subscription stock; refund control; and deposit account maintenance. At the same time, manual systems have been improved; these involve the screening and identifying or orders, and the returning of orders that cannot be fulfilled.[36]

The result of better facilities and automated order processing systems has been salutary indeed. In 1977 the Superintendent was able to state that his office "can now consistently process over 90% of our customer's orders in ten workdays or less compared with 24 workdays in 1973." The volume of complaints has declined, one sturdy index of success.[37]

Publications Reference File

Perhaps the most interesting of the automated systems from the standpoint of documents librarians is the *Publications Reference File* (PRF). Developed principally as an in-house reference tool for filling publications orders, it was evaluated in a library setting by Catharine J. Reynolds in 1974.[38] On December 2, 1976, 100 copies of the PRF were distributed to 100 depository libraries, including regionals, for a two month evaluation period. Receiving libraries were asked to respond concerning the 48:1 reduction ratio 270-frame microfiche format as to its suitability as a continuing depository distribution item on a monthly basis. Moreover, a question was asked as to the PRF's suitability as a sales item for general public use.[39]

The person in charge of the PRF's development and production is Jeanne Isacco, chief of the Information and Storage Section of GPO's sales management division. The distribution pattern of the *Publications Reference File* (GP 3.22/3; Item 552-B) to depository libraries is on a bimonthly schedule: January, March, May, July, September, and November. A *PRF Supplement* will be distributed twelve times a year. For non-depository libraries, the PRF is available bimonthly on subscription. For in-house use at GPO the file is updated weekly. The November 30, 1977, PRF regeneration contained some new features. The full title of the file is now contained in the header area while each sequence begins on a new fiche. Catalog numbers and stock numbers shown in the index frame of each fiche are punctuated.[40]

Basically the PRF is a microfiche catalog analogous to a *Books in Print* for GPO sales publications. The fiche are divided into three sections or sequences, arranged as follows:

1) GPO stock number
2) SuDocs class number

3) Alphabetical dictionary index of interfiled
   a) title
   b) agency series or report numbers
   c) key words or phrases
   d) subjects

Contained in the file are about 20,000 titles in stock and some 2,000 publications that are "New-on-Order" but have not arrived. Moreover, there are some 6,000 publications that are unavailable; these say "exhausted" and are kept in the file for one year. Bibliographic information for each record is complete and includes stock number, SuDocs class number, personal author (if there is one), title, price, issuing agency, descriptive information (i.e., hearing dates, grant number, etc.), series, report number (if one exists), information on superseded publications, and GPO's internal location designation.[41]

The stock number, class number, title, key words or phrases, and authors (there is no listing for corporate authors) are arranged in order on the fiche and can be used for retrieval purposes. The color stripe at the top of the fiche is known as the "header," and the words or numbers printed on the header of each fiche indicate the key phrase of the first record of the first frame on that fiche. By noting the header on two consecutive fiche, one can determine which records are on each fiche.[42]

Once the fiche is determined, one can go to the "index" in the last two frames. A frame contains three to five records, and the "index" lists the first record on each frame. From there it is a matter of locating the entry in the index that precedes the record being sought. Thus the "index frame" on each fiche is not an index per se. Actual indexing is accomplished "by printing the information for each record under each 'index' term. Therefore, there is no separate 'index' resulting in two look-up steps. This is to save time for the reference order clerks."[43]

For example, the publication *Selecting and Growing House Plants* is found in the stock number sequence (001-000-00863), in the class number sequence (A 1.77:82/2), and in the alphabetical sequence under the following "fields of information":

S = for title "Selecting and Growing House Plants"

H = for the series Home and Garden Bulletin 82

P = for keyword "Plants"

H = for subject heading "House Plants"

F = for subject heading "Floriculture"

Each time this record is repeated on the fiche, all the essential bibliographic information is given.[44]

Users are advised not to order any publication listed as "New-on-Order" without a price, since this will result in a buildup of unprocessable orders. There is an error rate on the file of about 5 percent. Although GPO is striving to reduce this rate, it may be unavoidable because of the frequent changes in document status.[45]

The Legislative Indexing Vocabulary of LC's Congressional Research Service is used for subject terms and keywords. But the PRF is not intended to be a standard library tool with all the appropriate LC headings, main entries, and the like. Indeed, the PRF is to be used to identify what is currently for sale, determine the right stock number for ordering purposes, and find the correct price of a publication.[46] As such, it becomes a highly useful tool for librarians and other users. Still in the process of refinement, the PRF represents yet another device using existing technology to make the operations of the sales program more responsive to the general public and to the library community.

Catalogs and Indexes

Under the new organization of the Office of the Superintendent, the Library and Statutory Distribution Service has as one of its three subordinate entities a "Library Division." But the functions of this unit have changed far less since 1895 than the sophisticated technology by which it discharges its duties.

All agencies issue catalogs, or "lists," of their documents at specified or irregular times; these listings are usually free and available to depository libraries [for example, Bureau of the Census Catalog of Publications (C3.163/3; Item 138), Geological Survey Bibliographies and List of Publications (I 19.14/2; Item 619-B), etc.]. But the Library Division of the Assistant Public Printer (Superintendent of Documents), as an issuing agency, is charged with publishing several reference sources that have become basic bibliographic tools for libraries large and small alike. Four of these basic sources will be analyzed in the following pages:

> *Selected U.S. Government Publications* (GP 3.17; Item 556)
> *Price List 36* (GP 3.9; Item 554)
> *Subject Bibliographies* (GP 3.22/2; Item 552-A)
> *Monthly Catalog of United States Government Publications* (GP 3.8; Item 557)

Because these catalogs are central to the bibliographic structure of GPO public documents, librarians must be familiar with them.

Selected U.S. Government Publications

Over 1,500,000 individuals and institutions subscribe to this free listing of documents which purport to be new, relevant, and of general interest. Known popularly as the *Selected List*, the brochure identifies some 150 titles, most of which are annotated, sold by SuDocs. There is a minimum charge of $1.00 for each mail order using the *Selected List*, and stock levels are maintained for one year.[47] A special form is found in each *Selected List*, and, as noted, the Pueblo, Colorado, distribution center is designed to fill orders from this publication using this form. Remittance may be made by check, money order, or charged to one's deposit account.

First issued in 1928, the *Selected List* began as a weekly service, changed to semi-monthly status in 1942, and became a monthly in 1974. The first issue (March 1974) under this schedule was enlarged to include almost 200 publications. Other periodic arrangements have included a January-February 1977 issue (v. 6, no. 1), monthly issues from February through August 1977, and a November-December 1977 issue (v. 6, no. 10).

Arrangement of entries is by broad subject categories such as Business & Industry, Law, Education, Transportation, etc. There are also frivolous headings such as Just for You, Odds 'n Ends, and Thumbs Up (lawn and garden issuances). Features that have appeared over the last few years include a few publications prominently advertised, with more extensive annotations than the other titles; highlights of a prominent government periodical being pushed that month; and "Bulletin Board," a page devoted to items of interest and instructions for subscribers.

Titles listed range from those of obvious general interest (*Camping in the National Park System*) to highly technical (*Stratigraphic Framework and Spatial Distribution of Permeability of the Atlantic Coastal Plain, North Carolina to New York*) to embarrassingly trivial (*Aunt Sammy's Radio Recipes*). The number of esoteric titles has diminished in recent years. Political and economic pressures in the past forced editors of the *Selected List* to include unworthy titles, publications like *Evaluations of Membranes for Hemodialyzers* and *Aerated Lagoon Treatment of Sulfite Pulping*. These publications are known as "dogs," a term used by the staff of the *Selected List* to categorize documents included that are not—by any stretch of the imagination—"popular government titles."[48]

Perennial classics, such as earlier editions of the *Yearbook of Agriculture*, that are kept in print or reprinted, are announced from time to time. Meant to be a current ordering tool, the *Selected List* affords non-depository libraries an opportunity to build a collection tailored to the needs of their clientele.

Price List 36

When in late 1973 the price structure of sales publications underwent precipitous change, a series of subject pamphlets known as *Price Lists* (PLs) became inoperative and were "recalled." For a time it was thought that they would simply be reissued reflecting the new prices. In March 1974, however, the Superintendent announced that, with the exception of *Price List 36* (PL 36), called *Government Periodicals and Subscription Services*, publication of the series would be postponed indefinitely.

Price Lists identified "popular" in-print publications sold by SuDocs and in this respect complemented the *Selected List*. Close to 50 *Price Lists* were issued on an irregular basis. When they were discontinued, only PL 36 remained. As its title suggests, it is an annotated listing of subscription items. Nearly half of the revenue of the sales program is derived from this category, which is divided into two distinct parts: dated periodicals, and publications which consist of a basic volume updated by changes or new material issued for a predetermined or indefinite period.

PL 36 used to be divided into two sections, Section I an alphabetical list of periodicals by title, Section II a similar listing of subscription services. Recent issues have combined both Sections into a single alphabetical arrangement, with a detailed agency index. Order forms are printed in the last pages of PL 36, and remittance is by check, money order, or use of one's deposit account.

A typical periodical listing in the August 1977 edition of PL 36 is structured in the following manner:

```
PROBLEMS OF COMMUNISM.  (Bimonthly.)
  Subscription price: Domestic--$9.35
  a year, $1.60 single copy; Foreign--
  $11.70 a year, $2.00 single copy.
  [PROC] (File Code 2N)

                   Catalog No. IA 1.8:

  Provides analyses and significant
  background information on various
  aspects of world communism today.
```

Indexing services, like the *Monthly Catalog*, are indicated in PL 36 in this fashion:

```
MONTHLY CATALOG OF UNITED STATES
  GOVERNMENT PUBLICATIONS.  Subscrip-
  tion price: Domestic--$45.00 a year,
  $3.25 single copy, $9.00 semi-annual
  index, Jan.-June, $16.00 cumulative
  index, Jan.-Dec., $4.50 serials supple-
  ment; Foreign--$56.00 a year, $4.10
  single copy, $11.25 semi-annual index,
  Jan.-June, $20.00 cumulative index,
  Jan.-Dec., $5.65 serials supplement.
  [MC] (File Code 2A)

                   Catalog No. GP 3.8:

  Lists the publications (printed and
  processed) issued during each month.
  It includes the publications sold by
  the Superintendent of Documents, those
  for official use, and those which are
  sent to Depository Libraries.
```

An example of a typical subscription service is shown in PL 36 as follows:

●CUSTOMS REGULATIONS OF THE UNITED
STATES. Subscription price: Domestic--
$37.00; Foreign--$46.00.
[CRUS] (File Code 1F)

Catalog No. T 17.9:

Subscription service includes the reprint
which incorporates effective material
through 159 and revised pages beginning
with the 160th set for an indefinite period.
In looseleaf form, punched for 3-ring
binder.

Contains regulations made and published
for the purpose of carrying out customs
laws administered by the Bureau of
Customs.

The (●) symbol preceding this title indicates that the basic manual will be followed by additional material or changes as issued.

Subscriptions are accepted for one year only unless otherwise specified. The average processing time for new subscriptions takes 2 to 6 weeks plus mailing time. Discount policy is governed by 44 U.S.C. 1708, and generally follows that noted for publications other than periodicals. PL 36 is revised and issued free on a quarterly basis: February, May, August, and November. Prices are subject to change without advance notice.

Most regulatory publications come under the "subscription service" category. During FY 1977 there were about 420 paid subscription lists, in addition to congressional and agency distribution lists. Maintaining these lists was the first application of automated data processing. Modernizing of the subscription processing system has been an ongoing effort of SuDocs, and a special area has been established in the Laurel facility to improve the distribution of subscription items.[49]

Subject Bibliographies (SB)

With the exception of PL 36, the *Price List* series was replaced by a *Subject Bibliographies* series. This series was made available to depository institutions as announced in *Daily Depository Shipping List 7786* (May 29, 1975) as *Survey 75-7* (May 1975). SB 001, April 7, 1975, *Home Gardening of Fruits and Vegetables*, was the first issued in the series, which has grown rapidly to include almost 300 bibliographies by mid-1977. The titles in the series reflect the scope of government activities, from *Accidents and Accident Prevention* (SB 229) to *Zoology* (SB 124).

Some *Subject Bibliographies* are arranged alphabetically by title or series. Others are assigned broad subject headings and within those headings, titles are listed alphabetically by keyword. Some titles are annotated, others are not. The standard bibliographic information for a listing includes SuDocs class number, the all-important stock number, and the price. A mail order form is included at the back of the particular SB. Like subscriptions in PL 36, orders for publications listed in the SB series are sent to the Assistant Public Printer (Superintendent of Documents), Government Printing Office, Washington, D.C. 20402.

When individual *Subject Bibliographies* are revised, the same base number is continued, with a shilling mark preceding the number of the revision. For example, SB 26/3, *United States Army in World War II*, represents the third revision of that bibliography; SB 25/2 indicates that *Supreme Court Reports* is in its second revised edition.

A *Subject Bibliography Index* has been issued for the SB series. The *Index* (SB-999) contains a multi-purpose order form which can be used to obtain copies of any of the subject bibliographies.

Despite the inconsistent pattern in compiling the various *Subject Bibliographies*, this series represents a major improvement over the earlier *Price Lists* series. In Chapter 5 a discussion of other bibliographic guides to federal publications, both produced by government or commercially, will be assayed.[50] But for SuDocs sales publications, the basic in-print, current awareness publications are the *Selected List*, PL 36, and the *Subject Bibliographies* series.

Monthly Catalog of United States Government Publications

First issued in 1895, the *Monthly Catalog* has endured six name changes. From January 1951 it has been issued under its current title, and librarians know it simply as the *Monthly Catalog* (MoCat). Useful background readings on the MoCat's history and the changes it has undergone include L. F. Schmeckebier and R. B. Eastin, *Government Publications and Their Use* (2d rev. ed.; Washington, Brookings, 1969), pp. 17-20 *et passim*; LeRoy C. Schwarzkopf, "The *Monthly Catalog* and Bibliographic Control of U.S. Government Publications," *Drexel Library Quarterly* 10: 79-105 (January-April 1974), and John A. McGeachy, III, "The *Monthly Catalog*'s First Response to Its 1947 Congressional Charge," LRTS 20: 53-64 (Winter 1976). As Schwarzkopf noted, the MoCat "established its distinctive character early and has witnessed relatively few major changes over the years."[51] All that relative quiescence was rudely shattered with the appearance of the July 1976 issue, which presented to users of this primary bibliographic source the most far reaching change in the publication's eighty-one year history.

Background

In the preface to the July 1976 issue of the *Monthly Catalog of United States Government Publications* there is this succinct, modest statement:

> In response to requests by the library community and the Depository Library Council to the Public Printer, the Assistant Public Printer (Superintendent of Documents) in the summer of 1974 directed the Library Division to join the Ohio College Library Center's on-line cataloging network, convert to the MARC format, and catalog according to the Anglo-American cataloging rules (AACR).

The *Monthly Catalog* utilizes AACR and Library of Congress main entries. Subjects are derived from *Library of Congress Subject Headings* 8th edition and its supplements. The catalog consists of text and four indexes—author, title, subject, and series/report number.

The Government Printing Office considers the *Monthly Catalog* to be an evolving publication. Its scope and timeliness will continue to be of prime importance.

During the 1975 ALA Midwinter Conference (January 21, 1975), the Superintendent of Documents announced "plans to implement the MARC format in the cataloging of publications for the *Monthly Catalog* as of January 1, 1976. . . . The conversion to MARC . . . will make accessible to libraries the *Monthly Catalog* data base in tape form."[52] In October 1975 the GPO "through its Library Division became part of the Ohio College Library Center (OCLC) network" and noted that every "effort is currently being made to speed up issuance of the *Catalog* while making the transition to an AACR/MARC format by July 1976."[53]

The target date of July 1976 was achieved, and was proclaimed in a kind of Bicentennial spasm of joy in the August 1976 issue of *Public Documents Highlights*, under the heading "Monthly Catalog in a Revolutionary Format":

> The July issue of the *Monthly Catalog* is as revolutionary as 1776! New dimensions of 10 1/4" x 7 7/8" frame a MARC style format proceeding from the OCLC data base. Content consists of six parts: a text and five [sic] indexes. Entries in the text are blocked into two columns. Headings separate the larger organizational groupings. Text is arranged by order of SuDocs classification.[54]

The author of that announcement got carried away. The July issue did *not* contain a stock number index, as the piece went on to say. But the compilers of the new, "revolutionary" MoCat could be forgiven their enthusiasm. Clearly, a significant series of developments were taking place, a confluence of technologies where the current household words in the profession—MARC,[55] OCLC, AACR—flowed together to create a *Monthly Catalog* that would have been unrecognizable by F. A. Crandall, the first Superintendent of Documents.

A more measured, detailed account of events leading up to the July 1976 MoCat, with an analysis of its implications, was given in *Documents to the People* 4: 37-42 (May 1976). The author of the report, LeRoy C. Schwarzkopf, noted that at the GPO Library Division in Alexandria, a "single OCLC terminal had been installed during Fall 1975 and the first GPO entry in full MARC format was entered into the OCLC data base on November 20, 1975. Three additional terminals and a line printer are being obtained for use at the GPO Library."[56]

The report identified the salient characteristics of the "landmark" program:

(a)   Cataloging information in a recognized standard format (MARC) entered into a national network data base (OCLC).

(b)   Cooperative cataloging among GPO and other federal libraries.

(c)   Expanded listings in the MoCat to include more non-GPO publications.

(d)   Concern by documents librarians over AACR proposed revisions involving choice and form of entry for corporate bodies.

(e)   Cost and record-keeping implications of producing catalog cards from OCLC data.[57]

Libraries that have OCLC terminals or are connected with computer networks which link up with OCLC can retrieve cataloging information on-line and manipulate it in a variety of ways. Libraries which are not OCLC members may purchase MARC tapes for use in their own computers. Examples of calling up documents on OCLC and learning OCLC terminal use were given in the June and August 1976 issues of *Public Documents Highlights.* Moreover, PDH instituted a section aimed at familiarizing librarians with the policies and procedures employed at the GPO in constructing the MoCat with reference to AACR and their application. How and where GPO differs from AACR in cataloging for the MoCat and the OCLC data base is highlighted.

Cataloging information is inputed to OCLC daily, and OCLC sends GPO bi-weekly tapes of this input. The tapes are sent to computer operations monthly "where they are combined and programmed to provide the listings and indexes for the *Monthly Catalog.* These are edited and returned to the GPO Electronic Photo-Composition Division where they are keyed onto a magnetic tape through a system called ATEX. Corrections are run against the main data base which is updated. The list of corrections is then edited and verified by the Library. The corrected tapes are run on the Linotron Photo-Composition equipment to produce page proofs or film. The proofs are checked by Library personnel before they are released for printing. It is estimated that two weeks elapse between release for printing and start of distribution of the printed catalogs."[58]

Cooperating libraries interact directly with GPO catalogers to reduce duplicate cataloging. Under the auspices of the Federal Library Committee, shared cataloging with other federal libraries is possible. The Federal Library Committee sponsors the FLECC (Federal Libraries' Experiment in Cooperative Cataloging) program in which over 40 federal libraries now participate in the OCLC network. The program is currently designed for monographs only, because GPO is already involved in the CONSER (Conversion of Serials) project for the recataloging of periodicals and serials. The participating libraries consult on decisions regarding name authorities and series treatment. "Following the physical exchange of hard copy, the cooperating agency's cataloging is received at GPO on an OCLC terminal, and is then revised and checked against GPO's authority files for consistency with prior usage in the *Monthly Catalog.*" Early participants were the libraries of the Departments of Health, Education and Welfare, Interior, and Transportation. "Under consideration is a pilot project with the Library of Congress on Congressional hearings. . . . An interesting by-product of these efforts is the eventual establishment of an on-line authority system for U.S. corporate entries."[59] However, as useful as this cooperative venture was proclaimed, it was abandoned owing to the lack of uniform cataloging procedures among the participating agency libraries.

Cooperative cataloging would appear to have the effect of increasing the number of non-GPO publications listed in the MoCat. "By joining OCLC along with more than 40 other federal libraries, GPO may be able to use the input from these other libraries to include more non-GPO publications."[60] It is estimated conservatively that "eight of ten federal publications are non-GPO. . . . Over 300 federal government printing plants are authorized to operate around the country." But it is likely that the micropublishing program more than cooperative cataloging will increase the number of non-GPO materials that can be entered in the MoCat. The GPO is asking a change in the depository law to require non-GPO agencies to supply only two copies of their publications to GPO rather than the full number needed to supply depository libraries. Agencies would be far more likely to send two of their non-GPO publications to be cataloged and filmed for distribution than the hundreds of copies required for the depository system in hard copy.[61]

Traditionally, documents librarians have avoided cataloging government materials by AACR "because of the difficulties in applying the rules in a consistent manner to serve the needs of the user." Instead, they have "come up with their own schemes for cataloging documents, most of these schemes based upon the government body as author." Proposed revisions of the 1967 *Anglo-American Cataloging Rules* must be workable for entering documents into network catalogs and for retrieving the appropriate citations for the user. During 1977 there was deep concern on the part of knowledgable documents librarians that the proposed revisions to AACR'67 "will only generate confusion for users of the bibliographic data created or generated by cataloging librarians. Document materials . . . frequently carry agency names which are highly similar. Without indication of the hierarchical relationship or organizational affiliation, the user cannot safely rely upon the specificity of the bibliographic information which appears on a card or a computer display, nor can one accept place of publication as a reliable discriminating element to resolve the confusion."[62]

Accompanying *Daily Depository Shipping List 9924* (June 30, 1977) was a letter from the Chief of the Cataloging Distribution Service of the Library of Congress to all depository librarians. The letter sought input from depository librarians on how best to structure potential card services to be offered by the Distribution Service. The tape service had just been started, and the letter was simply seeking suggestions at this time. Prospective service ideas which might be derived from GPO *Monthly Catalog* MARC records include printed catalog cards, subscription card services, or a selectively ordered card service.

An earlier plan to provide OCLC cards through the Library and Statutory Distribution Service of the Office of Superintendent of Documents had been abandoned due to lack of interest by depository librarians. After announcing the plan and soliciting comments on a *Shipping List* notice, only 47 positive responses were received.[63]

A preliminary study of printed catalog cards conducted at the University of Illinois at Chicago Circle Library suggested that the "use of OCLC to produce cards for federal documents" would not be cost effective.[64] And, as the letter from the Cataloging Distribution Service correctly observed, "Our contacts with librarians in charge of separately maintained documents collections and librarians cataloging documents for collections which integrate documents with commercially published books indicate that there is a diversity of opinion on how and whether to catalog." It would be pointless to launch an elaborate card service which would not meet the needs of documents librarians.

The Monthly Catalog Today

Features on the pages before the main entries include abbreviations, a useful "Sample Entry," a general information section, "How to Order Publications," new class numbers, corrections for previous MoCats, and an alphabetical list of government authors. Order forms precede the back cover. On the inside back cover is a list of GPO bookstores, and on the back cover a margin index serves to locate the four indexes. Most of these features are found in issues of the MoCat B.C. (Before Computerization).

The significant differences lie in the form of entry and subject access. In 1974 the MoCat developed separate subject, personal author, and title indexes. Current issues are indexed as follows:

Author Index: An alphabetical list of personal authors, editors, co-authors, corporate authors, and conferences.

Title Index: An alphabetical list of titles, series titles, and sub- or alternate titles.

Subject Index: An alphabetical list of subjects based on LC Subject Headings.

Series/report Index: An alphabetical list of report numbers and series statements.

Additional indexes, such as SuDocs class numbers, stock numbers, etc., have been recommended and are being studied by the GPO. The first cumulative index for the "new" MoCat covered the period July-December 1976 in one huge volume. The schedule calls for a semiannual index covering January-June, and an annual cumulation covering the 12 issues plus the *Serials Supplement* for the calendar year.

In each issue, the "Sample Entry" (Figure 1) shows in great detail the bibliographic structure of Library of Congress format. A comparison of two similar publications in the former and the current configuration demonstrates the differences:

Monthly Catalog, April 1975

PRESIDENT OF THE UNITED STATES Washington, DC 20500

```
05759  Economic report of the President, transmitted to Congress
       Feb. 1975, together with annual report of Council of
       Economic Advisers. 1975. iii+359 p.il. [Also issued as
       H. doc. 2, 94th Congress, 1st session.]
       *Paper, $3.25.  ●Item 848

                                                P   38.9:975
```

Monthly Catalog, August 1976

PRESIDENT OF THE UNITED STATES

```
76-3242
                          Pr 38.9:976
United States. President, 1974- (Ford)
     The economic report of the President : transmitted to the
Congress January 1976 / together with The annual report of
the Council of Economic Advisers. -- Washington : U.S. Govt.
Print. Off., 1976.
     282 p.; 24 cm.
     Item 848
     S/N 040-000-00342-8
     pbk.: $2.60
     1. United States -- Economic policy   2. United States --
Economic conditions -- 1945-  I. Ford, Gerald R., 1913-   II.
Title.
OCLC 2158524
```

Figure 1

MONTHLY CATALOG: SAMPLE ENTRY

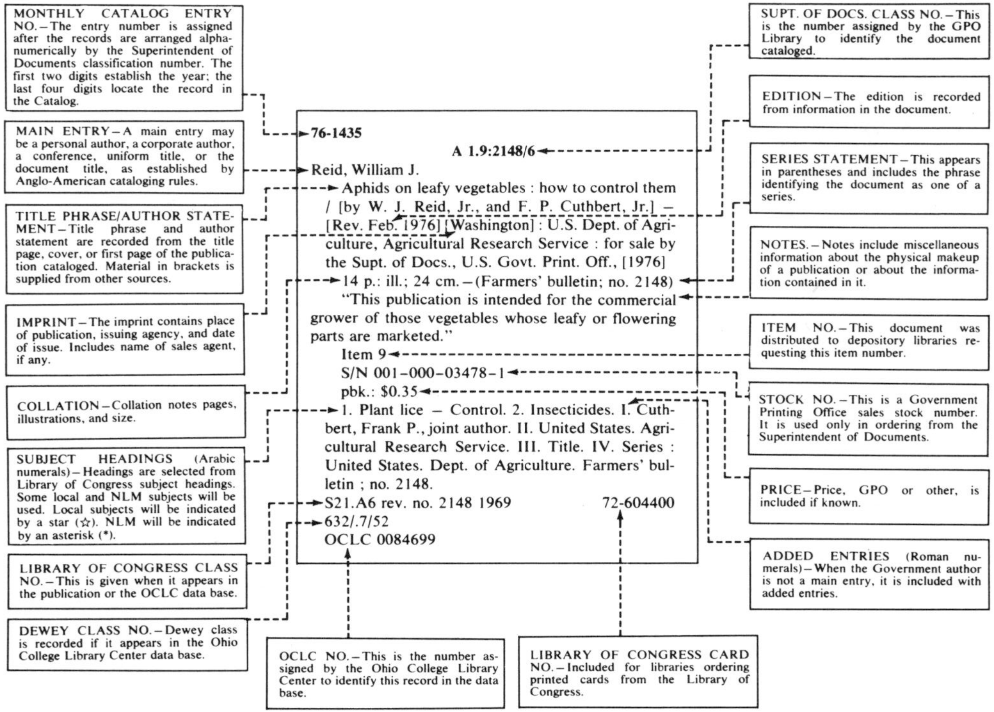

Left-side annotation boxes (bottom):

MONTHLY CATALOG ENTRY NO.—The entry number is assigned after the records are arranged alphanumerically by the Superintendent of Documents classification number. The first two digits establish the year; the last four digits locate the record in the Catalog.

MAIN ENTRY—A main entry may be a personal author, a corporate author, a conference, uniform title, or the document title, as established by Anglo-American cataloging rules.

TITLE PHRASE/AUTHOR STATEMENT—Title phrase and author statement are recorded from the title page, cover, or first page of the publication cataloged. Material in brackets is supplied from other sources.

IMPRINT—The imprint contains place of publication, issuing agency, and date of issue. Includes name of sales agent, if any.

COLLATION—Collation notes pages, illustrations, and size.

SUBJECT HEADINGS (Arabic numerals)—Headings are selected from Library of Congress subject headings. Some local and NLM subjects will be used. Local subjects will be indicated by a star (☆). NLM will be indicated by an asterisk (*).

LIBRARY OF CONGRESS CLASS NO.—This is given when it appears in the publication or the OCLC data base.

DEWEY CLASS NO.—Dewey class is recorded if it appears in the Ohio College Library Center data base.

Right-side annotation boxes (top):

SUPT. OF DOCS. CLASS NO.—This is the number assigned by the GPO Library to identify the document cataloged.

EDITION—The edition is recorded from information in the document.

SERIES STATEMENT—This appears in parentheses and includes the phrase identifying the document as one of a series.

NOTES.—Notes include miscellaneous information about the physical makeup of a publication or about the information contained in it.

ITEM NO.—This document was distributed to depository libraries requesting this item number.

STOCK NO.—This is a Government Printing Office sales stock number. It is used only in ordering from the Superintendent of Documents.

PRICE—Price, GPO or other, is included if known.

ADDED ENTRIES (Roman numerals)—When the Government author is not a main entry, it is included with added entries.

Center entry:

76-1435   A 1.9:2148/6

Reid, William J.
Aphids on leafy vegetables : how to control them / [by W. J. Reid, Jr., and F. P. Cuthbert, Jr.]. — [Rev. Feb. 1976]. Washington : U.S. Dept. of Agriculture, Agricultural Research Service : for sale by the Supt. of Docs., U.S. Govt. Print. Off., [1976]
14 p. : ill. ; 24 cm. — (Farmers' bulletin; no. 2148)
"This publication is intended for the commercial grower of those vegetables whose leafy or flowering parts are marketed."
Item 9
S/N 001-000-03478-1
pbk. : $0.35
1. Plant lice — Control. 2. Insecticides. I. Cuthbert, Frank P., joint author. II. United States. Agricultural Research Service. III. Title. IV. Series : United States. Dept. of Agriculture. Farmers' bulletin ; no. 2148.
S21.A6 rev. no. 2148 1969   72-604400
632/.7/52
OCLC 0084699

Bottom annotation boxes:

LIBRARY OF CONGRESS CARD NO.—Included for libraries ordering printed cards from the Library of Congress.

OCLC NO.—This is the number assigned by the Ohio College Library Center to identify this record in the data base.

Special issues include the September MoCat, which has appended a "List of Depository Libraries as of September 1, [*year*]" and is arranged alphabetically by state and by city within each state. The name of the institution, date it became a depository, and depository number are given. This information is similar to that published in pre-1976 September issues.

A significant change occurred initially in the listing of serials. In earlier MoCats, the February issue contained an appendix that listed periodicals and subscription publications alphabetically by title. In the new format, this appendix was issued in 1977 in a separate volume entitled *Serials Supplement*. Its first appearance came between the April and May 1977 issues, was numbered 988, and covered 1,218 entries. *Serials Supplement* No. 988 (Figure 2, page 66, shows a "Sample Entry") contained the same prefatory material and four indexes as the regular issues.

It may be instructive to compare the bibliographic information provided by *Price List 36*, the "old" February MoCat appendix, and the first *Serials Supplement* for the same periodical:

<u>Price List 36</u> (May 1977)

```
DEPARTMENT OF STATE BULLETIN.  (Weekly.) Subscription
     price: Domestic--$42.50 a year, 85¢ single copy;
     Foreign--$53.15 a year, $1.10 single copy.
     [DSB--File Code 2E]
                                    Catalog No. S 1.3:
     Provides information on the development of
     foreign relations, operations of the State Depart-
     ment, statements by the President and Secretary of
     State, and special articles on international affairs.
```

<u>Monthly Catalog</u> (February 1976)

```
03737 Department of State bulletin, official weekly record of
     United States foreign policy. ([Office of Media Services,
     Bureau of Public Affairs], State Department.)  [Index
     issued separately for each volume.]  *Paper, $42.50 a
     yr., $10.65 additional for foreign mailing; single copy,
     85c.
     ●Item 864
     L.C. card 39-26945            S 1.3:(v.nos.&nos.)
```

Serials Supplement (1977)

STATE DEPARTMENT
Washington, DC 20520

77-6422

S 1.3:(v.nos.&nos.)
United States. Dept. of State.
    The Department of State bulletin. [Washington, U.S. Dept.
of State, Office of Media Services, Bureau of Public Affairs;
for sale by Supt. of Docs., U.S. Govt. Print. Off.]
    tables. 27 cm.
    $42.50 (U.S.) $53.15 (foreign)
    v. 1 - July 1, 1939-
    "Official weekly record of United States foreign policy"
    Indexed by: Public affairs information service
    Indexed by: Reader's guide to periodical literature
    Supersedes the Press releases and the Treaty information
bulletin of the Department of State.
    Item 864
    Weekly
    ISSN 0041-7610
    I. United States. Dept. of State. Bulletin. II. Title.

OCLC 1639364

Inadequate subject access in the subject index of the MoCat is guaranteed if Library of Congress subject headings *only* are used. Enhancement with key words, liberal use of cross references, a thesaurus, or various combinations thereof, are needed to provide better subject access. Under the present usage, a publication entitled *Area Wage Survey: Albany-Schenectady-Troy, New York, Metropolitan Area* (L 2.3:1900-59) cannot be accessed by Albany, Schenectady, or Troy, but can be found using the subject heading "Wages–New York–Albany [Schenectady, Troy] metropolitan area–Statistics–Periodicals."[6][5]

Clearly, refinements will be implemented in future issues of the *Monthly Catalog.* The Depository Library Council to the Public Printer has a Committee on GPO Operations; one of its tasks is to monitor user reactions to the "new" *Monthly Catalog.* Documents librarians were sent a questionnaire in August 1977, and the key questions concerned subject accessibility. The Superintendent of Documents continues to show that GPO is responsive to the community of users of federal documents.

The first year of the "new" MoCat was not without its problems. Because of programming difficulties with the June 1977 issue, catalog entry numbers in the July and August catalogs were duplicated from the June catalog. The computer errors in the June MoCat also resulted in the removal of all the June entries from the 1977 *Semiannual Index.* These errors were rectified by issuing a combined July,

Figure 2

SERIALS SUPPLEMENT: SAMPLE ENTRY

Sample entry (center):

77-6213   HE 1.459: (v.nos. & nos.)

Children today. [Washington] U.S. Dept. of Health, Education, and Welfare, Office of Human Development, Office of Child Development, Children's Bureau; for sale by the Supt. of Docs., U.S. Govt. Print. Off.

20402

v. ill. 27 cm. (DHEW publication; no. (OHD))

$6.10 (U.S.) $7.65 (foreign) $1.00 (single copy) index varies in price

v. 1-   Jan./Feb. 1972-

Indexed by: Education index ISSN 0013-1385

Indexed by: Nursing literature index ISSN 0550-3957

Indexed by: Hospital literature index ISSN 0018-5736

Vols. for (Mar./Apr. 1973-) for sale by the Supt. of Docs. U.S. Govt. Print. Off.

Bimonthly.

Item 449

ISSN 0361-4336 : CODEN: CHTDA

Supersedes: Children

Main series: United States. Dept. of Health, Education, and Welfare. DHEW publication; no. (OHD)

1. Child welfare—United States—Periodicals. 2. Children—Care and hygiene—Periodicals. I. United States. Children's Bureau.

HV741.C5362   72-620933

362.7/05

OCLC 1159272

Left-side callouts:

MONTHLY CATALOG ENTRY NO.—The entry number is assigned after the records are arranged alphanumerically by the Superintendent of Documents classification number. The first two digits establish the year; the last four digits locate the record in the Catalog.

MAIN ENTRY—A main entry may be a corporate author, or the document title, as established by Anglo-American cataloging rules.

SUBSCRIPTION ADDRESS—May include. street address, city, country, and zip code of sales agent.

COLLATION—Collation: notes, illustrations, and size.

PRICE—Price, GPO or other, is included if known.

DATE—Beginning date of publication and/or volume designation.

ITEM NO.—This document was distributed to depository libraries requesting this item number.

ISSN—International standard serial number, assigned or authenticated by the National Serials Data Program. Each number is unique to a title and is part of the international effort for uniform control of serials.

LIBRARY OF CONGRESS CLASS NO.—This is given when it appears in the publication or the OCLC data base.

DEWEY CLASS NO.—Dewey class is recorded if it appears in the Ohio College Library Center data base.

OCLC NO.—This is the number assigned by the Ohio College Library Center to identify this record in the data base.

Right-side callouts:

SUPT. OF DOCS. CLASS NO.—This is the number assigned by the GPO Library to identify the document cataloged.

TITLE PHRASE—Title phrase is recorded from the title page, cover, or first page of the publication cataloged.

IMPRINT—The imprint contains place of publication, issuing agency, and name of sales agent, if any.

SERIES STATEMENT—This appears in parentheses and includes the phrase identifying the document as one of a series.

NOTES—Notes include miscellaneous information about the physical makeup of a publication or about the information contained in it.

PERIODICITY—Current frequency of publication.

LINKING ENTRIES—Provide bibliographic and historical information as well as allowing internal machine linkage between related records in a computer file.

SUBJECT HEADINGS (Arabic numerals)—Headings are selected from Library of Congress subject headings. Some local and NLM subjects will be used. Local subjects will be indicated by a star (✩). NLM will be indicated by an asterisk (*).

ADDED ENTRIES (Roman numerals)—When the Government author is not a main entry, it is included with added entries.

LIBRARY OF CONGRESS CARD NO.—Included for libraries ordering printed cards from the Library of Congress.

August, September 1977 issue (Entries 77-9536 to 77-13039) and by providing correct indexing information for all 1977 catalogs in the 1977 *Cumulative Index.*

While the new *Monthly Catalog* marches on, loose ends still need to be tied. Because the new MoCat's first issue was July 1976 (Entries 76-1 to 76-1433), there needed to be a semiannual cumulative index for the old format covering the period January-June 1976. In addition, the two decennial indexes (1941-1950 and 1951-1960) obviously did not cover sufficient ground. In 1977 libraries received a quinquennial cumulation covering the years 1961-1965 (GP 3.8/3:961-65; Item 557) in two volumes. Future cumulations through June 1976 will presumably close out an era in which the *Monthly Catalog*'s size and format was as familiar to thousands of librarians and users as one's hand.

Classification

The Superintendent of Documents classification system was established in the Library of the Public Documents Department sometime between 1895 and 1903. The first explanation of the system was given in 1903 by William Leander Post, then in charge of the Library, who gave credit for the concept to Adelaide R. Hasse. Ms. Hasse had used the system in assigning classification numbers to a Department of Agriculture List of Publications. The notation expanded as the federal establishment's quantity of publications and issuing units grew, and has changed in some details, but it has retained the principles upon which it was first based. For many years it served as the order or "catalog" number, until that function was replaced by the multi-digit stock number for GPO sales publications.

The SuDocs classification is an alphameric notation based on the principle of *provenance*, whereby the several publications of any government author—a department, bureau, agency, office—are grouped together under like notation. Basically, this sort of arrangement guarantees no inevitable grouping of similar subject matter, and in that sense the purist would argue that the notation is not truly a "classed" system. A book on children's poetry and a guide to the official publications of Swaziland are documents of the same government author (in this case the Library of Congress). In the system, the classification reflects the organizational structure of the United States government, and this is at once the scheme's strength and its weakness.

The concept of provenance avoids the tortuous Procrustean problems of a scheme like the Dewey decimal classification, but it is at the mercy of any government reorganization. Since reorganization happens not infrequently, the publications of some government authors are located in several places in the system. One example will demonstrate the effect of reorganization on classification.

The *Budget of the United States Government* has undergone title changes and agency changes, and its classification has undergone similar changes, as follows:

Class Number	Years
T 51.5:	1923-1940
Pr 32.107:	1941-1946
Pr 33.107:	1947-1954
Pr 34.107:	1955-1961
PrEx 2.8:	1962-

The reclassification that results from reorganization will always cause problems for both the catalogers at GPO and documents librarians and their clientele. When the Department of Health, Education and Welfare was created in 1953 and the functions of the Federal Security Agency, which was thereby abolished, were transferred to the new Cabinet-level entity, publications of the old agency were still designated "FS" for several years. Finally the letters were changed to "HE," reinstating the minor mnemonic advantage but demoralizing documents librarians during a rather lengthy transition.

More recently, an egregious flip-flop took place. For many years, the Census Bureau reported directly to the Secretary of Commerce, and its publications were classed in "C3." In 1972 a reorganization placed the Census Bureau under a newly created entity called the Social and Economic Statistics Administration (SESA). So as not to be accused of delay (as they were in the "FS" to "HE" debacle), the Superintendent with unaccustomed alacrity changed the class to "C56." In 1975 SESA was abolished, Census resumed its former place in the Commerce hierarchy, and now the current publications are back in the familiar "C3." At this writing it is too early to observe the full effect of the establishment of a Department of Energy (PL 95-91; 91 Stat. 565, August 4, 1977) on reclassification, but Title III, Sections 301-310 of PL 95-91 suggests wholesale changes in provenance.

When changes in reorganization require changes in the classification of documents, librarians have three basic options. They may continue the old notations; they may assign new notations as issued and change all the notations on the older publications to conform to the new notation; or they may assign new notations as issued and leave the old letters and numbers on the earlier materials. The last strategy appears to accommodate the fewest disadvantages, but librarians responsible for segregated documents collections have not formed a consensus as to which option is better. Indeed, the problem of reclassification is a vexing one, and the literature of librarianship is liberally sprinkled with debate on the issue.[66] Despite the fact that browsing is discouraged by the very nature of a provenance system of classification, users and librarians alike find it annoying to have the publications of the *Index-Catalog of the Library of the Surgeon-General's Office* shelved in four places. Whatever options librarians choose, the larger factor of the role of government publications in the overall collection will dictate the decision; in any case, rigidity in the decision-making process should be eschewed.

A Brief Explanation of the System

The explanation that follows is based primarily on *An Explanation of the Superintendent of Documents Classification System* (Washington: Government Printing Office, 1973) and John L. Andriot, *Working with U.S. Government Publications, Preprint No. 1: The Superintendent of Documents Classification Scheme, an Explanation and Current Agency Outline* (McLean, Va.: Documents Index, 1973).

The basic arrangement is the grouping of subordinate units with the parent organization, so that each full notation reveals the responsible *issuing agency* (provenance) and its place in the organizational structure of the federal establishment. But the classification scheme does not necessarily show "authorship" in the sense of an individual or, more commonly, a corporate body responsible for the *intellectual content* of the publication. Hence, issuing agency is not to be confused with "corporate author," even though in many instances the two may be the same.

One example of many may suffice to show this distinction. *Analysis of Federal and State Campaign Finance Law* was prepared *by* the Congressional Research Service of the Library of Congress *for* the Federal Election Commission. It was *issued* by the Commission, hence its SuDocs class notation reflected that provenance (Y 3.E 2/3:2 1 44/2; Item 1091-A). But the main entry in the September 1976 *Monthly Catalog* reads "United States. Library of Congress. Congressional Research Service. American Law Division." In the *Author Index* to the issue of the MoCat where this entry was listed there is no listing for Federal Election Commission.[67]

The full class number can be divided into three major elements: author symbol, series designation, and book number. The combination of author and series designations is called the "class stem." The book number is that which gives the publication its unique identification and rounds out the notation. An example follows:

	Symbol	Designation	Hierarchy
	L	Parent Agency	Department of Labor
class stem	2	Sub Agency	Bureau of Labor Statistics
	.3	Series or generic type	Bulletin (series)
book number	:1902	Individual publication	Bulletin 1902

As is so common in federal publications, this series is a "monographic series" in which Bulletin 1902 is *Analysis of Work Stoppages, 1974*. Remember that the phrase "author symbol," which has been used for years, is a misnomer in the sense illustrated by the above example of the Federal Election Commission. Andriot uses the phrase "agency section," which is more accurate.

Letters are ascribed to the parent agency, as "A" for Agriculture Department, "Ju" for Judiciary, "FT" for Federal Trade Commission. To set off the subordinate bureaus and offices, numbers are added to the letters, the digit "1" assigned to the secretary's or administrator's office of the parent organization. Succeeding numbers are applied, in order, to the lesser agencies. This alphameric notation represents the bureau or office, for example:

Agriculture Department (Secretary's Office and Department Series)	A 1.
Forest Service	A 13.
National Agricultural Library	A 17.
Communication Office	A 21.

The next segment in the scheme is a number following the period. It designates a specific series, periodical, continuation, or generic type. Numbers .1 through .8 are reserved for the following types of publications:

.1   Annual (CY or FY) Reports
.2   General Publications
.3   Bulletins
.4   Circulars
.5   Laws (administered by the agency)
.6   Regulations, rules, and instructions
.7   Press Releases
.8   Handbooks, Manuals, Guides

Other generic types which recur but which are not assigned a specific number include Addresses (speeches), Bibliographies and lists of publications, maps and charts, and posters.

New series closely related to already existing series are designated by use of the shilling mark after the number assigned to the existing series, followed by a digit for each related series starting with "2." For example:

A 89.4   Farmer Cooperative Service Circulars
A89.4/2   Farmer Cooperative Service Educational Circulars

This device is also used for superseded periodicals, to wit:

C 1.58/2   *Commerce America*; supersedes
C 1.58   *Commerce Today*

Notations assigned to subunits of a large Department like Health, Education and Welfare (HEW) in multiples of 10 still retain the eight "form" designations, for example:

National Institutes of Health

HE 20.3001   Annual Report
HE 20.3002   General Publications
HE 20.3006   Regulations, rules, and instructions
HE 20.3008   Handbooks, Manuals, and Guides

By combining the "author" symbol and series designation, the class stems are obtained for the several series issued, for example:

A 1.1:   Annual Report, U.S. Department of Agriculture
D 205.6:   Regulations, rules, instructions, Judge Advocate
           General, Navy Department
HH 6.5:   Laws, Federal National Mortgage Association

Now we can turn our attention to the notation that follows the colon. For numbered series, these "book numbers" reflect a simple numerical sequence. For example, Department of Agriculture Leaflet 381 would be A 1.35:381. For revisions of numbered publications, the shilling mark and number corresponding to the revision are added. Thus when Leaflet 381 first appeared in revised form, the notation read A 1.35:381/2.

General Publications (.2) are usually monographs, and these unnumbered publications are given a book number based upon the keyword in the title, using the 2-figure Cutter table. Revisions of unnumbered publications are identified by addition of the shilling mark and, if applicable, the last three digits of the year of revision. If necessary, shilling marks following the original Cutter number further distinguish the individuality of the work. The dash (-) is also employed to extend the numbers within the SuDocs class system; it is often used to designate a reprint of an individual edition.

The system described above governs the classification of most government publications. There are special forms employed by certain entities; these consist of classes assigned to

a)   some series issued by the Interstate Commerce Commission,
b)   boards, commissions, and committees established by act of Congress or under authority of an act of Congress, not specifically designated in the executive branch nor as completely independent agencies,
c)   the several publications of the Congress and its committees,
d)   multilateral international organizations in which the United States participates, and
e)   publications of the President and the Executive Office of the President including committees and commissions established by executive order and reporting directly to the President.

The classification and designation of the special forms will be noted in succeeding chapters as the publications themselves are discussed. A number of other minor wrinkles to the system will not be described here, and the reader is referred to the two publications cited above that include greater detail. Since one of them is an official government document, let us apply what has been discussed to an analysis of its unique classification number:

```
              An Explanation of the Superintendent of Documents
                          Classification System
                        GP 3.2:C 58/6/rev. 973
```

	Symbol	Provenance and Hierarchy
	GP	Government Printing Office (Parent Agency)
class stem	GP 3	Assistant Public Printer, Superintendent of Documents (Sub Agency)
	GP 3.2:	General Publications series
	C58	Cutter table based on keyword (Classification) in title
book number	C58/6	Sixth edition
	C58/6/rev. 973	Sixth edition slightly revised in 1973

Although the SuDocs class system, like other notation schemes, conveys an initial appearance of difficulty, it becomes easily comprehensible with frequent use. Since major bibliographic tools such as the *Monthly Catalog* are organized in SuDocs class order, early familiarity with the system will enable the librarian to relate organizational structure to issuance, resulting in faster and more accurate service to the user.

By-Law Distribution of Documents

The Statutory Stock Distribution Division of the Library and Statutory Distribution Service is responsible for providing centralized mailing services to Congress and federal agencies. During the 15-month period ending September 30, 1976, the "by-law" distribution program funded the distribution of over 74 million publications.[68] Some of these mailings are performed at no charge to the agency in accordance with specific provisions of law. However, agency-initiated mailings are performed only on a reimbursable basis.

In hearings over the years, members of the Legislative Branch Appropriations subcommittee have expressed mild concern over the magnitude of this function of the Superintendent of Documents' program. In recent hearings in the House, lists of the publications authorized by law, by resolution, and specifically by many sections of 44 U.S.C., which are mailed to members and to agencies, have been printed for the public record.[69] The anomaly is that the Superintendent offers a number of these publications for sale to the public, while members and certain agency heads receive many copies of a particular document free. Most of these extra copies are sent to designated constituents free. The knowledgeable documents librarian will learn how to take advantage of this unfair situation.

Distribution to Depository Libraries

In 1977 there were over 1,200 designated depository libraries in the United States and its territories. The distribution of documents to these libraries, the last of the four major functions of the Superintendent to be noted in this chapter, is of paramount importance. Accordingly, the depository library program and its various provisions and activities will be fully discussed in the next chapter.

REFERENCES

1. *100 GPO Years*, pp. 75-76.

2. Kling, p. 112.

3. *100 GPO Years*, p. 75.

4. Kling, p. 112.

5. *100 GPO Years*, p. 75.

6. Ibid., p. 79. See also Kling, pp. 35, 112-14.

7. Joseph A. King, "The United States Government Printing Office Library," *D.C. Libraries* 22: 2 (January 1951).

8. Ibid., p. 4.

9. Ibid., pp. 3, 4. Cf. L. F. Schmeckebier and R. B. Eastin, *Government Publications and Their Use* (2d rev. ed.; Washington: Brookings, 1969), p. 132: "There is probably no complete collection of government publications in existence, but the one in the Public Documents Library is probably the most nearly complete."

10. A detailed analysis of this historic transfer is found in Joe Morehead, "Transfer of the Public Documents Library to the National Archives," *Government Publications Review* 3: 1-14 (1976).

11. Ibid., pp. 6-7.

12. PDH 19: 1 (December 1976).

13. U.S. House. *Legislative Branch Appropriations for [FY] 1975* [Hearings], p. 363.

14. Following Carper W. Buckley's long tenure as Superintendent (1953-1970) there have been several persons who have not held the job long: Robert E. Kling, Jr., Rowland E. Darling (Acting), Wellington H. (Wimpy) Lewis, and, effective July 20, 1975, Carl A. LaBarre.

15. PDH 6: 2 (October 1974).

16. U.S. House. *Legislative Branch Appropriations for [FY] 1978* [Hearings], p. 484.

17. *100 GPO Years*, p. 76.

18. U.S. House. *Legislative Branch Appropriations for [FY] 1978* [Hearings], p. 484.

19. *The New York Times*, 14 November 1973, p. 22.

20. U.S. House. *Legislative Branch Appropriations for [FY] 1978* [Hearings], p. 484.

21. W. H. Lewis, "Superintendent of Documents on the GPO and Its Plans," *Illinois Libraries* 56: 264 (April 1974).

22. One result of rising prices appeared as a notice in the January-February 1977 issue of *Selected U.S. Government Publications:* "Due to continued increases in our operating costs and to avoid increasing the prices of all the publications in our sales inventory, we have instituted a minimum mail order charge of $1.00 per order." (p. 13).

23. *Pricing of Publications Sold to the Public* (1974), pp. ii-iii.

24. Schwarzkopf, "Pricing Policy...," pp. 27, 28-29, 30.

25. Ibid., pp. 29-30. Cases cited were 415 U.S. 336, 415 U.S. 345, 335 F2d 304, and 379 U.S. 966.

26. LeRoy C. Schwarzkopf, *Pricing of GPO Sales Publications* (Washington: Committee on Information Hangups, September 1976); [available on microfiche or hard copy through ERIC Document Reproduction Service; ED 126 956], pp.

28-29. A thorough summary of the pricing issue is found in Arthur D. Larson, "The Pricing of Documents by the Government Printing Office: Survival Response by an Agency in Crisis," *Government Publications Review* 4: 277-313 (1977).

27. DttP 5: 80 (March 1977).

28. U.S. House. *Legislative Branch Appropriations for [FY] 1978* [Hearings], p. 494.

29. U.S. House. *Legislative Branch Appropriations for [FY] 1977* [Hearings], p. 535.

30. 44 U.S.C. 1708.

31. DttP 5: 79-80 (March 1977).

32. *Publishers' Weekly* (March 20, 1972), p. 42.

33. The present publication replaces the discontinued *Price List 86*, also titled *Consumer Information.*

34. U.S. House. *Legislative Branch Appropriations for [FY] 1978* [Hearings], p. 484.

35. U.S. House. *Legislative Branch Appropriations for [FY] 1977* [Hearings], p. 535.

36. U.S. House. *Legislative Branch Appropriations for [FY] 1978* [Hearings], pp. 433-34, 485-86.

37. Ibid., p. 486.

38. Catharine J. Reynolds, "The Public Documents Department Microfiche Information Retrieval System," *Microform Review* 3: 269-72 (October 1974).

39. *Daily Depository Shipping List 9343*, 3d Shipment (December 3, 1976), contains a list of libraries by state and library depository number that received the PRF.

40. *Daily Depository Shipping List 10*, 446 (December 21, 1977), p. 3.

41. DttP 5: 79-80 (March 1977).

42. U.S. Superintendent of Documents. *PRF User's Manual: How to Use the Microfiche File* (1976; mimeographed), p. 1.

43. DttP 5: 79 (March 1977).

44. *PRF User's Manual*, p. 5.

45. DttP 5: 133 (June 1977).

46. DttP 5: 79 (March 1977).

47. U.S. House. *Legislative Branch Appropriations for [FY] 1977* [Hearings], p. 535.

48. Lyle Chastaine, "An Analysis of the Selected List of U.S. Government Publications," May 1975 (unpublished paper, School of Library and Information Science, State University of New York at Albany).

49. U.S. House. *Legislative Branch Appropriations for [FY] 1977* [Hearings], p. 536; *[FY] 1978* [Hearings], pp. 485-86.

50. An example of a useful non-government bibliographic series is that prepared by the Missouri State Library, coordinated by Maggie Johnson and Lucy Rauch. See DttP 3: 45-46 (September 1975).

51. Schwarzkopf, "The *Monthly Catalog* and Bibliographic Control of U.S. Government Publications," p. 83.

52. PDH 9: 1 (April 1975).

53. PDH 14: 1 (February 1976).

54. PDH 17: 1 (August 1976).

55. MARC is the acronym for "machine-readable cataloging." See *Information on the MARC System*, 3d ed. (Library of Congress, MARC Development Office, 1973).

56. "MARC, AACR, OCLC and the New Monthly Catalog," DttP 4: 38 (May 1976).

57. Ibid., pp. 38-39.

58. DttP 5: 6 (January 1977). Users of the ATEX system include *Newsweek*, *U.S. News & World Report*, *Reader's Digest*, the *Chicago Sun Times*, the *Louisville Courier-Journal*, *National Geographic*, *Forbes*, the *Economist*, and the Central Intelligence Agency.

59. PDH 21: 1-2 (April 1977).

60. DttP 4: 39 (May 1976).

61. DttP 5: 97 (May 1977).

62. Ibid., pp. 98-99.

63. *Daily Depository Shipping List 9293* (November 11, 1976).

64. DttP 4: 26 (November 1976).

65. *Monthly Catalog* (May 1977), entry 77-7251.

66. For comprehensive summaries of arguments concerning this enduring problem, see Forrest C. Palmer, "Simmons vs. Schwarzkopf: The Great Class(ification) Debate," *Southeastern Librarian* (Fall 1977), pp. 163-66; and Michael Waldo, "An Historical Look at the Debate Over How to Organize Federal Government Documents in Depository Libraries," *Government Publications Review* 4: 319-29 (1977).

67. *Monthly Catalog*, September 1976 (entry 76-5654).

68. U.S. House. *Legislative Branch Appropriations for [FY] 1978* [Hearings], p. 435.

69. *[FY] 1976* [Hearings], pp. 734-36; *[FY] 1977* [Hearings], pp. 505-507; *[FY] 1978* [Hearings], pp. 441-50.

3

DEPOSITORY LIBRARY SYSTEM

With the subsequent growth and shifting of population and the various changes in the boundaries of Congressional districts, many depository libraries are not now located so as to serve the districts for which they were originally designated. But other depository libraries cannot be selected under the present law for the new and large centers of population. . . . On the other hand, many districts apparently do not desire or cannot assume the burden of having a depository for government publications. . . . The . . . vacant designations cannot, however, be assigned to libraries in other districts. Consequently many important libraries are compelled to obtain government publications by haphazard importuning of Congressmen and the departments.

The selective privilege granted depository libraries a few years ago has also disclosed the fact that many of the present designations are either unwilling or lack the facilities to provide sufficient space for adequate deposits of government publications, thereby making their designation as depositories of little service to the public.

—Annual Report of the Public Printer, 1926

BACKGROUND

Before designated depositories were established, and before the Printing Act of 1895 set up a systematic approach, special legislation was passed at various times, which provided for the printing of copies of the House and Senate *Journals*. These were issued in sufficient number to be distributed to the executives of the several states and to each of the state and territorial legislatures. Provision was also made at times to supply the acts, documents, and reports, as well as the *Journals*, to incorporated universities, colleges, and historical societies. During the 13th Congress, 2d session, a resolution was adopted embodying earlier ad hoc legislation that directed "for every future Congress" a limit of two hundred in addition to the usual number, "and this, of course, was more than sufficient for the needs at that early day."[1] Joint resolutions of 1840 increased that number to three hundred. By contrast, during fiscal year 1978, the number of publications distributed to depository institutions was over 18 million.

In the mid-nineteenth century, the Secretary of the Interior was charged with the distribution of publications to institutions, which now included public and school libraries, atheneums, literary and scientific societies, and boards of trade. During that time Congress and the departments had authority to continue their own distribution policies. These had become so indiscriminate that the first Superintendent of Documents asserted that publications were disbursed "with such liberal prodigality as to cheapen them in the estimation of the people at large." Unsolicited documents "were not only not appreciated but were regarded with contempt." Urging a more rational policy, he noted that "on the one hand, horse or cattle books were sent to districts in which automobiles and electric cars held sway and where cattle were represented only in butcher shops and dairies. On the other hand, rural districts were flooded with *Flags of Maritime Nations* . . . instead of books published specially for their use."[2]

Librarians unhappy with the unsolicited receipt of documents "of every nature" for their designated institutions had to wait until 1922 for relief from what the first Superintendent called "chronic document indigestion." The appropriation for that fiscal year provided that libraries could select those categories of publications most suitable for their clientele, and the selective deposit system was born.

The plan that had evolved with its several amendments by 1962 included 594 depository libraries, located in all of the states and most of the territories. The mechanics of distribution allowed "at least one mailing a day" to every depository. But changes in the demographic pattern, owing to redistricting and to economic shifts, created the need for new depositories in areas where no vacancies for an additional designation existed. Moreover, depository libraries could not dispose of documents no longer needed nor able to be housed properly, and some librarians complained that they lacked important "non-GPO" publications, which were excluded from depository distribution. On the other hand, they faulted the existing system for its inadequacies in supplying important GPO documents. In response to these and other complaints the GPO and the Superintendent applied their efforts to effect new legislation. The result, the Depository Library Act of 1962, represented the most significant major changes in depository legislation in over six decades.[3]

The Depository Library Act of 1962 (76 Stat. 352), as amended, is codified as Chapter 19 of Title 44, *United States Code*, "Public Printing and Documents." Pursuant to the statutory language, the Superintendent of Documents issued a manual, *Instructions to Depository Libraries* (revised July 1974). The manual superseded the edition of September 1967 and, according to the prefatory note, was "designed to provide guidance regarding the duties and privileges of libraries designated as depositories for U.S. Government publications."

All documents librarians working in the over 1,200 designated depository institutions must be familiar with the provisions of 44 U.S.C. 1901 *et seq.* the *Instructions* as they appear in revised editions, and current information on depository developments. These may be usefully perused in issues of *Documents to the People, Public Documents Highlights*, the annual Legislative Branch Appropriations hearings, and notices found in the *Daily Depository Shipping List*. In addition, articles that appear in the professional literature on depository problems and prospects become obligatory reading. Because developments in the depository system appear to change with a degree of rapidity not found in earlier years, it is the professional task to keep abreast of current trends.

INSTRUCTIONS

The manual entitled *Instructions to Depository Libraries* (GP 3.26:D44/year) was revised in 1974 and again in November 1977; and the 1977 revision was issued to depository libraries in February of 1978. The current *Instructions* consists of 12 sections and Exhibits A through E. Exhibit A features a sample Item card, Exhibits B(1) and B(2) are examples of a *Daily Depository Shipping List*, Exhibit C is a claim form, Exhibit D is a sample form for amending selections of Items, and Exhibit E is a form used to confirm a classification number. Moreover, the 1977 *Instructions* have two Appendixes. Appendix A is an alphabetical list, by state and by library, of designated regional depository libraries as of November 1977. Appendix B is a list of those periodicals mailed automatically and not listed on the *Shipping List*.

Section 1 consists of general information and is largely hortatory. The documents librarian is reminded that one should select only those categories best suited to patrons' needs, that documents on deposit remain the property of the federal government, that use of the SuDocs class scheme is not mandatory, and that government materials may circulate and be treated with the same care as "privately published material, such as books and periodicals."

Section 2 concerns the responsibilities of regional depositories. Unlike other depository libraries, regional depositories "*must receive and retain* at least one copy of *all* Government publications made available to depositories . . . either in printed or microform copy (except those authorized to be discarded by the Superintendent of Documents)." Regionals must "provide interlibrary loan and reference service to designated depository and non-depository libraries" and must also assist selective non-Federal libraries "in the disposal of unwanted Government publications as provided by law."[4] An important feature of the role of regionals is that by virtue of their mandatory retention of all depository categories, selective depository libraries may dispose of unwanted materials after a period of five years. The *Instructions* state that the regional "may refuse to grant permission for disposal of any publication that it feels should be kept by one of its depositories for a longer period of time," but this interpretation of the statutes governing disposal is dubious.

A system of disposition then follows in Section 2, followed by suggestions that the regional depository librarian should make periodic visits to selective depositories within his or her jurisdiction to maintain familiarity with "the operations and needs" of these libraries.[5]

Section 3 contains simple instructions when writing SuDocs, instructions which, sadly, are not followed in many instances.

Section 4 deals with the biennial report required of all designated depository libraries, consisting of a questionnaire that must be answered fully and promptly. This section also makes note of Depository Library Inspectors, a resource permitting the effective implementation of 44 U.S.C. 1909.

Section 5 discusses the right of a library to relinquish its depository status, and conversely, the right of SuDocs to terminate its status if the library fails to maintain the standards required by law.

Section 6 treats of selection tools, among them the *List of Classes of United States Government Publications Available for Selection by Depository Libraries* (GP 3.24:year). Arrangement is by SuDocs class number, title of series or Item, and depository Item number. Figure 3 (p. 80) is an example of a page from the revised June 30, 1977, *List of Classes*. The *List* is revised periodically and is furnished to depository libraries as issued.

After the 1974 *Instructions* were published, the Superintendent of Documents decided to issue, as a complement to the *List of Classes*, a document entitled *Inactive or Discontinued Items from the 1950 Revision of the Classified List, Revised (date)* with the class number GP 3.24:year/app. Figure 4 (p. 81) shows a typical page of this publication.

Section 7 is concerned with the notification of new series for depository institutions by means of a periodic *Survey* sent to libraries. Instructions for selecting new Items listed on the *Survey* are given.

Section 8 continues the discussion of selection procedures. The *Instructions* emphasize that in the selection of Items (categories or series), publications cannot be furnished retroactively. New selections take effect "only when new issues in the series selected are ordered printed." Moreover, depository institutions should review all current selections "to determine whether the library is receiving material which is not being used and to eliminate wasteful use of taxpayers' money and unnecessary costs to the Federal Government in supplying material which is not needed."

Section 9 deals with the *Daily Depository Shipping List*, which will be discussed below.

Section 10 discusses the mechanics of claiming for copies of publications selected but not received, and duplicate shipments.

Section 11 consists of a list of 14 types of material that may be discarded by all depository libraries, including regionals. Note well that these categories of documents *have nothing to do* with the five-year disposal policy of selective depository libraries. Categories, which are not inclusive, that the SuDocs permits all depository libraries to discard include superseded editions of a publication, earlier issues of a document that has been cumulated, old looseleaf pages upon receipt of replacement pages, and the like. Note too that this is *not a mandatory disposal list*. For purposes of scholarship or archival control, a library may wish to hold earlier editions of an important work, or earlier bills and resolutions.

Section 12 permits all designated depositories, including regionals, to substitute microform for any holdings of hard copy, "provided the microcopies are properly referenced, can be readily located, and are easily accessible to users." This Section does not apply only to the GPO micropublishing program, but involves all microcopies purchased commercially or otherwise acquired.

Figure 3

LIST OF CLASSES OF UNITED STATES GOVERNMENT PUBLICATIONS AVAILABLE FOR SELECTION BY DEPOSITORY LIBRARIES

C 3.134/4: Congressional District Data (CDD series) 140–B–1

C 3.138/3: Current Business Reports: Monthly Retail Trade Sales and Accounts Receivable (BR–series) 147–B

C 3.138/3–2: Current Business Reports: Annual Retail Trade 147–B

C 3.140/2: Government Employment (GE series) 148–A

C 3.145: State & Local Government Special Studies 148–A

C 3.145/6: Quarterly Summary of State and Local Tax Revenue (GT series) 146–E

C 3.150: U.S. Foreign Trade: Schedules 148

C 3.158: Current Industrial Reports (non-GPO) 142–A

C 3.163/2: Bureau of Census Catalog: Monthly Supplements 138

C 3.163/3: Bureau of Census Catalog of Publications 138

C 3.163/4: Bibliographies and Lists of Publications 138

C 3.164: Foreign Trade Reports 144

C 3.186: Current Population Reports 142–C

C 3.191/2: Government Finances (GF series) 146–E

C 3.191/3: Government Finances and Employment at a Glance 146–L

C 3.202/18: Census of Business: Special Reports 133

C 3.204: County Business Patterns (CBP series) 133–A–1 to 133–A–53

C 3.205/3: International Statistical Programs Office ISPO (series) 146–F

C 3.205/4: ISP Supplemental Course (series) 146–F

C 3.205/6: International Research Documents (ISP–RD-series) 146–F

C 3.211/5: Special Current Business Reports: Monthly Department Store Sales in Selected Areas (BD series) 148–B

C 3.212: Technical Papers 151–A

C 3.212/2: Technical Notes (numbered) 151–C

C 3.214: Working Papers (numbered) 151–B

C 3.215: Current Housing Reports 141–A

Construction Reports:

C 3.215/2: —Housing Starts, C20-(series) 140–A–1

C 3.215/3: —Value of New Construction Put in Place, C30-(series) 140–A–2

C 3.215/4: —Housing Authorized by Building Permits and Public Contracts, C40-(series) 140–A–3

C 3.215/5: —Authorized Construction, Washington, D.C. Area, C41-(series) 140–A–4

C 3.215/8: —Residential Alterations and Repairs, Expenditures on Residential Additions, Alterations, Maintenance and Repairs, and Replacements, C50-(series) 140–A–5

C 3.215/9: —New One-Family Homes Sold and for Sale, C25-(series) 140–A–6

C 3.215/9–2: —Price Index of New One-Family Houses Sold, C27-(series) 140–A–7

C 3.215/13: —Housing Completions, C22-(series) 140–A–8

C 3.215/15: —New Residential Construction in Selected Standard Metropolitan Statistical Areas, C21-(series) 140–A–9

Census of Population:

C 3.223: —General Publications 154
—State and Area Series 159–A–1 to 159–A–54

C 3.223/2: —Preliminary Reports 159–A–1 to 159–A–54

C 3.223/4: —Advance Reports 159–A–1 to 159–A–54

C 3.223/5: —Number of Inhabitants 159–A–1 to 159–A–54

C 3.223/6: —General Population Characteristics 159–A–1 to 159–A–54

C 3.223/7: —General Social and Economic Characteristics 159–A–1 to 159–A–54

C 3.223/8: —Detailed Characteristics 159–A–1 to 159–A–54

C 3.223/9: —Characteristics of the Population (bound volumes) 159–A–1 to 159–A–54

C 3.223/10: —Final Volumes (Other than by States and Areas) 159

C 3.223/11: —Census Tract Reports 159

C 3.223/12: —Supplementary Reports 154

C 3.223/13: —General Demographic Trends for Metropolitan Areas 159–A–1 to 159–A–54

C 3.223/13–2: —Geographic Identification Code Scheme 154

C 3.223/16: —Evaluation & Research Reports (ER series) 154

C 3.223/17: —Employment Profiles of Selected Low-income Areas (PHC (3) series) 159–A–1 to 159–A–54

Census of Housing:

C 3.224/3: —States and Small Areas 156–A–1 to 156–A–54

C 3.224/4: —Metropolitan Housing 156–A–1 to 156–A–54

C 3.224/5: —City Blocks 156–A–1 to 156–A–54

C 3.224/6: —Components of Inventory Change 155

C 3.224/7: —Residential Finance 155

C 3.224/8: —Special Reports for Local Housing Authorities, Series HC (S1) 155

C 3.224/9: —Final Volumes (other than by States and areas) 155

C 3.224/10: —Subject Reports, HC (7) Series 155

C 3.227: Census Tract Memo 131–C

Figure 4

INACTIVE OR DISCONTINUED ITEMS
FROM THE 1950 REVISION OF THE CLASSIFIED LIST

474 Annual Report FS 13.101: (Food and Drug Administration).

475–C Leaflets FS 13.117: (Food and Drug Administration, Health, Education, and Welfare Department)

475–S Banned Toy List HE 20.4024: (Food and Drug Administration, Health, Education, and Welfare Department)

476 Notices of Judgment under Caustic Poison Act FS 13.112: (Food and Drug Administration, Health, Education, and Welfare Department)

477 Notices of Judgment under Federal Food, Drug and Cosmetic Act FS 13.108: (Food and Drug Administration, Health, Education, and Welfare Department)

478–A Report on Enforcement and Compliance FS 13.118: (Food and Drug Administration, Health, Education, and Welfare Department)

479 Service and Regulatory Announcements Caustic Poison FS 13.110: (Food and Drug Administration, Health, Education, and Welfare Department)

480 F.D.C. Regulations (by part numbers) FS 13.106/2: (Food & Drug Admin. HEW Dept.).

480–A Student Reference Sheet SR (series) FS 13.122: (Food & Drug Admin., HEW Dept.).

481 Annual Report FS 2.1: (Public Health Service). years.

482 Cancer Series FS 2.57: (Public Health Service).

483 Community Health Series FS 2.35: (Public Health Service).

483–A Current Literature on Venereal Disease FS 2.11/2: (Public Health Service, Health, Education, and Welfare Department)

483–B Directory of State, Territorial, and Regional Health Authorities (annual) HE 20.2015/2: (Health Service and Mental Health Administration)

483–C Directory of Local Health and Mental Health Units HE 20.2015: (Health Service and Mental Health Administration).

483–D Dictionaries, Glossaries, etc. FS 2.88: (Public Health Service, H.E.W. Dept.).

483–E–4 Addresses EP 4.12: (Programs Office EPA).

483–E–5 Community Affairs Bulletin (irregular) HE 20.1311: (National Air Pollution Control Administration).

483–F Environmental Health Series HE 20.1011: (Environmental Health Service, HEW Dept.).

483–G Flouridation Census (annual) HE 20.3112; (Health Professions Education and Manpower Training Bureau, HEW).

483–H Rheumatic Fever Memo FS 2.312: (Public Health Service HEW Dept.).

483–H–1 General Publications (Unnumbered publications of a miscellaneous nature.) HE 20.2052: (Health Maintenance Organization Service HEW Dept.).

483–H–2 Handbooks, Manuals, Guides HE 20.2058: (Health Maintenance Organization Service, HEW Dept.).

483–J Guidelines for (various health professionals & sub-professional) in Home Health Services FS 2.6/8: (Public Health Service HEW Dept.).

483–K Federal Research & Development Planning & Programming: Sulfur Oxides Pollution Control (annual) FS 2.93/4: (Public Health Service, HEW Dept.).

483–M ORP/SID (series) EP 6.10/2: (Radiation Office, EPA).

483–O Injury Control Research Laboratory: Research Report ICRL/RR (series) HE 20.2859: (Community Environmental Management Bureau, HEW Dept.).

483–P Grants-in-Aid and Other Financial Assistance Programs, HE 20.2016: (Health Services and Mental Health Administration HEW Dept.).

483–Q Workshop Series of Pharmacology Section N.I.M.H. (numbered) FS 2.310: (Public Health Service, HEW Dept.).

483–R Emergency Health Services Digest (numbered) HE 20.2013/2: (Health Service and Mental Health Admin. HEW Dept.).

483–S APTIC Bulletins HE 20.1303/2: (National Air Pollution Control Administration HEW Dept.).

483–T–1 General Publications HE 20.2002: (Health Services and Mental Health Administration HEW Dept.).

483–T–2 Handbooks, Manuals, Guides HE 20.2008: (Health Service and Mental Health Administration HEW Dept.)

483–T–3 Indian Health Program (annual) HE 20.2014: (Health Services and Mental Health Administration HEW Dept.).

483–T–4 Bibliographies and Lists of Publications HE 20.2012/2: (Health Services and Mental Health Administration HEW Dept.).

483–T–5 Laws HE 20.2005: (Health Services and Mental Health Administration HEW Dept.).

483–U Computer Research & Technology Division: Technical Reports HE 20.3011: (National Institute of Health HEW Dept.).

483–V–1 General Publications HE 20.2752: (Maternal and Child Health Service HEW Dept.).

483–V–2 Bibliographies and Lists of Publications HE

SELECTION TOOLS

Item cards, the *Daily Depository Shipping List*, and forms for claiming publications selected but not received constitute three important procedures in the administration of a depository collection. A summary of their purpose and use follows.

Item Cards

Section 6 of the *Instructions* sets forth the procedure whereby a "Classified List" of series or categories, in the form of 3-by-5-inch cards, is made available to depository libraries. Two sets of cards, arranged numerically by Item number sequence, are furnished to depository libraries at the time of their designation. One set is retained by the library for its records, the other is used to make selections. Selections are made by returning to the Library Division, Superintendent of Documents, one Item card for the series desired, properly identified with the library's assigned depository library number. Newly designated depository libraries should make their selection of Items within 30 days from the time the deck is received.

The assigned Item number remains the controlling designation for that category regardless of a change of title or reorganization of the issuing agency. Items may be considered generic categories, but they do not reflect the number or ratio of publications to Items. Libraries selecting Item 577 will receive one copy of the annual *United States Government Manual.* On the other hand, selecting Item 557 will insure receipt of all issues of the *Monthly Catalog* for the year. Other Items cover series with an indeterminate number of individual publications. Slip laws, treaty series, Supreme Court reports, and General Publications series are examples of this indeterminate category. Moreover, an Item number assigned to a series may also govern the distribution of a closely related series of like nature. Thus the Economic Development Administration's Maps and Charts series (C 46.17) and Directory of Approval Projects series (C 46.19/2) are both received under Item 130-J even though the class notation for the two series differs.

For depository libraries an ongoing selection process is accomplished by means of a periodic *Survey.* Distributed as a special section of a numbered *Daily Depository Shipping List*, the duplicate Item cards are reproduced on the *Survey* sheet itself. If selection is desired, one card is clipped for the library's file, the other is returned to Library Division (SLL), Assistant Public Printer (Superintendent of Documents), Washington, D.C. 20401. If a sample copy of the new Item is not received, the library cannot make a claim, since often not enough sample copies of the publication representing the series are produced for distribution.

Until 1978 the policy of the Library Division had been to annotate Item cards only when the Item category was not self-explanatory. This was in violation of 44 U.S.C. 1904. As a result of a Study Committee on Federal Documents Depository Survey Items (Federal Documents Task Force, GODORT) chaired by Tae Moon Lee, the Superintendent began complying with the provisions of 44 U.S.C. 1904 properly. Figure 5 shows an annotated Item card on *Shipping List 10,654* (March 10, 1978), *Survey* 78-37.

Figure 5

ITEM CARD

```
Item 315-F-2

    DEFENSE INTELLIGENCE AGENCY

Review of Soviet Ground Forces       D 5.209:
            (monthly)

Provides up-to-date information on wide variety
of topics of general interest throughout the Dept.
of Defense. Consists of translations of selected
recent articles from Soviet press and background
articles written by DIA analysts on Soviet tactics,
training, and equipment, organization, etc. Each
expected to be 75 pp.

Survey 78-37          Depository Library No.____
```

Daily Depository Shipping List

The *Daily Depository Shipping List* is perhaps the single most important internal working document for the administration of depository collections. For obvious reasons, no depository Item number has been assigned to this publication, but it is available for sale from SuDocs and carries a class notation (GP 3.16/3). Every depository library receives a copy of each *Shipping List*, even though none of the Items listed were selected by an individual library. That is, the *Shipping List* serves as an invoice for the shipment. Upon receipt of a package, the indicated Item numbers should be checked against the library's selections (the active Item card file) to determine whether any Items have been omitted from the shipment.

As noted, the *Shipping List* includes the periodic *Survey* of new Items. Moreover, it is a quick means of informing depository libraries of corrections of previous lists, changes in class number, and notices and special announcements. Figure 6 (p. 84) shows a typical *Shipping List*.

Claims

Shipping Lists should be retained for at least 45 days in order to make claims for Items previously selected but not received in the depository shipment. Claims for non-receipt must be postmarked within 15 days from the date of receipt of the *Shipping List*. No claims will be honored for material which is over 45 days old. It

Figure 6
DAILY DEPOSITORY SHIPPING LIST

GPO Form 3452
(3–75)

DAILY DEPOSITORY
SHIPPING LIST 9925

Assistant Public Printer
Superintendent of Documents
Library Division (SLL)
Washington, D.C. 20402

4th   Shipment of June 30, 1977

Page __1__ of __1__ Pages

Claims for nonreceipt of publications on this list under item numbers previously selected by a library **must be postmarked** within fifteen days of receipt of this shipment. *(Instructions to Depository Libraries, Revised July 1974, Page 12.)*

ITEM NUMBER	TITLE	CLASSIFICATION
42–C	AER No. 374, Residential and Regional Distribution of Benefits Under the Allowance for Basic Living Expenses (ABLE) Welfare Reform Proposal, June 1977	A 1.107:374
84	Forestry Research, What's New in the West? July 1977	A 13.2:F 76/84
126–D–3	OT Rpt. 77–122, Extended Area Test System in the 136–148 MHz Band...An EMC Assessment, May 1977	C 1.60/3:77–122
142–A	CIR: Consumption on the Woolen and Worsted Systems, March 1977, M22D(77)–3	C 3.158:M22D(77)–3
208–B–7	NESS–88, National Environmental Satellite Service Catalog of Products, June 1977	C 55.13/2:NESS 88
247	NBS SP 500–12, Computer Science & Technology: Data Compression—A Comparison of Methods, June 1977, S/N 003–003–01797–3, *$1.50	C 13.10:500–12
259	Manual of Patent Examining Procedure Third Edition, Rev. No. 52, April 1977	C 21.15:961/rev.52
455–C	Vocational Education and Career Education-A Symbiotic Relationship, 1977	HE 19.110:B 98
552–A	SB–023, Hearing and Hearing Disability, May 4, 1977	GP 3.22/2:023/2
563	Federal Specification: BB–H–1168B, May 9, 1977	GS 2.8:BB–H–1168B
610–A	CFS No. 7287, Frozen Fishery Products, April 1977 (Preliminary)	C 55.309/2:7287
629–C	Final Environmental Impact Statement Proposed Development of Oil Shale Resources, Vol. 1,	I 53.19/2:Oi 5/5v.2
637–A	IC 8744, Underground Mine Communications (In Four Parts) 3, Haulage Systems, 1977	I 28.27:8744
664–F	REC–ERC–76–13, Chemical and Vegetative Stabilization of Soils, January 1977	I 27.60:76–13
740–A	Supreme Court Decision No. 75–1805, Decided June 16, 1977, *45¢	Ju 6.8/b:976/75–1805
834–C	Transportation: The Diverse Aged, Policy Report One, May 1976, S/N 038–000–00318–6, *	NS 1.2:T 68/2/no.1
838–E	Postal Contracting Manual, Pub. 41, Trans. Let. 25, June 27, 1977, *on sub	P 1.12/6:971/trans.25
982–D–1	Program Evaluation Support for the Motor Vehicle Diagnostic Inspection Demonstration Projects, Volume 2: Costs and Benefits, Final Report, May 1977	TD 8.2:D 54/3/v.2
1035	Hearings: Community Credit Needs S/N 052–070–04101–3	Y 4.B 22/3: C 73/13
1070–M	Perspectives on Federal Retail Food Grading, June 1977, S/N 052–003–00384–8, *	Y 3.T 22/2:2 F73/3

*For Sale by the Superintendent of Documents.

is not necessary to retain the *Lists* past this point if a library maintains other adequate records of what has been mailed.[6]

The Superintendent of Documents provides claim forms for depository publications selected but not received (Figure 7). Instructions for claiming an entire shipment or just one or more Items in a shipment are given, but to be sure that depository librarians understood the procedure, it was spelled out in *Public Documents Highlights* issues of June 1975 (p. 3) and December 1975 (p. 4). Moreover, in the April 1976 issue of PDH (p. 2), announcement was made of a formal "claims" unit at the Library and Statutory Distribution Service in Alexandria, which addition "will make claims handling much faster than previously."

Figure 7

CLAIM FORM

UNITED STATES GOVERNMENT PRINTING OFFICE

CLAIM FOR DEPOSITORY PUBLICATIONS SELECTED BUT NOT RECEIVED

All claims for nonreceipt of depository publications must be postmarked within 15 days from the date of receipt of the Daily Depository Shipping List on which they appear. Only one item may be requested on each claim form. When filing a claim for an entire shipment, circle the items on the Daily Depository Shipping List to which you are entitled, and attach it to your completed claim form.

A false statement on this application is punishable by law (U.S. Code, Title 18, Section 287).

Mail claims to: Assistant Public Printer
(Superintendent of Documents)
Library Division (SLL)
Washington, DC 20401

I certify that this depository library did not receive the following item listed on Daily Depository Shipping List No._____, dated_____. This item number was previously selected by the depository. The Daily Depository Shipping List on which this publication was listed was received on_____ .

Item Number...

Title ....

....

Classification ....

Signature of librarian authorized to make claim ....

Depository Library No. .... Date ....
☐ *Check here if Regional Library.*

PLEASE **PRINT OR TYPE** ADDRESS ON LABEL BELOW INCLUDING **YOUR ZIP CODE**

GPO Form 3481
....

| U.S. GOVERNMENT PRINTING OFFICE
ASSISTANT PUBLIC PRINTER
(SUPERINTENDENT OF DOCUMENTS)
WASHINGTON, D.C. 20401

OFFICIAL BUSINESS
—
Penalty For Private Use
$300 | **Depository Library No.** ....

Name ....

Street address ....

City and State....................................... ZIP Code .... | POSTAGE AND FEES PAID
U.S. GOVERNMENT PRINTING OFFICE
377
SPECIAL FOURTH-CLASS RATE
BOOK |

Another problem arises when libraries receive Items they did not request. If an unselected Item happens to be an expensive publication, such as a bound serial set volume, it should be returned to the Library Division. However, "unbound, inexpensive items, can be treated in the same manner as unselected survey items. That is: kept as samples, given away, or disposed of through paper recycling, etc."[7] If by inadvertence, a depository library receives a duplicate shipment, it should notify the Library Division immediately by phone or mail. Duplicate shipments "often mean that there is a discrepancy with the mailing labels and we would like to correct it as soon as possible. If another factor is the cause of the duplication early handling of the problem is also important."[8]

CURRENT DEVELOPMENTS AND PRACTICES

Availability of government publications to depository libraries is authorized by appropriate sections in Title 44 of the *United States Code.* Crucial are 44 U.S.C. 1902, 1903, which read in part:

Government publications, except those determined by their issuing component to be required for official use only or for strictly administrative or operational purposes which have no public interest or educational value and publications classified for reasons of national security, shall be made available to depository libraries through the facilities of the Superintendent of Documents for public information. Each component of the Government shall furnish the Superintendent of Documents a list of such publications it issued during the previous month, that were obtained from sources other than the Government Printing office. (44 U.S.C. 1902)

The Superintendent of Documents shall currently inform the components of the Government ordering printing of publications as to the number of copies of their publications required for distribution to depository libraries. The cost of printing and binding those publications distributed to depository libraries obtained elsewhere than from the Government Printing Office, shall be borne by components of the Government responsible for their issuance; those requisitioned from the Government Printing Office shall be charged to appropriations provided the Superintendent of Documents for that purpose. (44 U.S.C. 1903).[9]

When publications are printed by the Government Printing Office (or by contract), the Library Division is furnished with information on the publication— issuing agency, title, series, etc.—and a jacket number (work order control number) is also assigned. The Division then decides how many copies are needed for depository distribution. For new Items, the response from the *Surveys* determines the number of copies needed for distribution of future issues. Thus control of GPO printed publications for deposit is reasonably secure.[10]

Non-GPO Publications

Non-GPO publications are those printed or processed by the agencies' own printing or mimeographing equipment. It has been estimated that "eight of ten federal publications are non-GPO" and "over 300 federal government printing plants are authorized to operate around the country."[11] To insure that publications printed by the agencies become part of the depository program as required by Title 44, "Circular Letter 100 was sent to all Federal agencies in July 1974 reminding them of their legal responsibilities. ... The extent to which the agencies comply with this law determines what publications a library will receive in a certain class."[12] But note that 44 U.S.C. 1903 requires that the agency foot the printing and binding bill for the extra copies necessary to meet depository demands. And since 44 U.S.C. 1902 gives the issuing agency the right to determine whether the publication is suitable for depository distribution, the agencies have not only little incentive to cooperate but also a handy loophole for not cooperating. As Livsey has suggested, if the agencies were required to send only two copies of their publications to the Library Division, they could be converted to microfiche and distributed in that format. "At present, field agencies publishing in small quantities are frightened away by the hundreds of copies required by the depository system."[13]

Despite these obstacles, more non-GPO publications are being included in depository shipments as time goes by. "When the GPO Library learns about a non-GPO publication which was not distributed, it contacts the issuing agency to obtain (if possible) enough copies for distribution to all depositories selecting the appropriate item, as a minimum enough for distribution to regional depositories. A request then is made for future issues of the publication; retroactive distribution of earlier issues is not provided by depository law."[14]

Every current edition of the *List of Classes* indicates those non-GPO publications which are available to depository libraries. A sample of non-GPO depository series taken from the March 1977 revised *List of Classes* is shown in Table 1 (p. 88).

Table 1

CATEGORIES OF NON-GPO SERIES
AVAILABLE ON DEPOSIT

Issuing Agency	Category	Depository Item Number
Agriculture Department	Annual Report	6
Census Bureau	Report of Cotton Ginnings	141
	Current Industrial Reports	142-A
Bureau of Mines	Mineral Trade Notes	638-B
	International Coal Trade	637-C
	International Petroleum Annual	642-A
Bureau of Labor Statistics	Estimated Retail Food Prices by City	768-I
Unemployment Insurance Service	Significant Provisions of State Unemployment Insurance Laws	761-A
Women's Bureau	Family and Property Law	781-A
Employment and Training Admin.	Unemployment Insurance Statistics	758
	Unemployment Insurance Claims	761-B

[It should be noted that the above series, available in hard copy, may in the future become available on microfiche pursuant to phase one of the GPO micropublishing program.]

Microform Distribution

The GPO micropublishing program has been discussed at length in Chapter 1. As previously noted, in a letter dated March 25, 1977, Senator Howard W. Cannon, chairperson of the Joint Committee on Printing, gave the Public Printer official authorization to provide depository institutions with publications in a microformat. Specifically the letter authorized the GPO "to convert to microfiche, as necessary and as requested by individual depository libraries, that category of publications identified as 'non-GPO documentation'" and "to convert to microfiche, as necessary and as requested by individual depository libraries and when savings in costs are clearly demonstrable, that category of publications identified as 'GPO documentation'."[15] GPO officials and, indeed, the library community are hopeful that this authorization will encourage the agencies to distribute more non-GPO publications to depository libraries. As if in anticipation of this, "many agencies . . . are switching to fiche with great speed. In the future, agencies will make the decision on the format of individual publications, and GPO will distribute either paper copies or fiche."[16]

Following the JCP approval, the GPO promulgated *Government Printing Office Instruction 565.1* (September 30, 1977), which established responsibilities and procedures for the conversion and distribution of publications in a microfiche format of selected GPO and non-GPO publications. The first phase of the micropublishing program involves what *Instruction 565.1* calls "Non-GPO Depository" titles, those procured or produced by agencies in either their own printing plants or purchased through sources other than GPO. Two copies of these publications will be forwarded to the Library Division for entry into the *Monthly Catalog*, "if appropriate," and "some of the material will be converted to the microfiche format for distribution to Depository Libraries."

Two types of film will be placed in distribution. Regional depository libraries will receive archival silver film as well as a second set on non-silver microfiche. The silver film will be held by the Regionals as the archival copy, while the second set will be used by patrons. Selective depositories will receive third generation non-silver film. None of the distribution microfiche will contain color striping in the header area; this will permit depository libraries to make additional duplicate microfiche while retaining the information contained in the header area.

The objectives of this phase of the project are several: to improve bibliographic control, provide the public with information that in the past has not been readily available, and relieve agency printing plants of the financial burden of producing sufficient hard copy titles for distribution to depository institutions. Moreover, these regulations will result in a more faithful implementation of the appropriate provisions of Title 44 of the *United States Code.*

It is important to note that these instructions do not pertain to the filming of scientific and technical information now being handled by "such organizations as the National Technical Information Service, Defense Documentation Center or other authorized offices" (see Chapter 4). In an attachment to *Instruction 565.1*, there is a list of the types of material considered unsuitable for depository distribution in microfiche:

1. Flyers announcing meetings and conferences to be held.
2. Publications reading "For official use only," "For administrative use," "For use by Government agencies only," and similar restricting phrases.
3. Any security classified material.
4. Addresses multilithed for release to newspapers.
5. Preprints from publications sent to depositories later in bound form.
6. Ephemeral material.
7. Posters.
8. Maps.
9. Charts.
10. Individual publication announcements.

In addition to increasing the availability of non-GPO publications, the *Instruction* permits "GPO Depository" titles to be offered to depository libraries "that will provide clear cost reductions." In addition, the Superintendent of Documents is authorized to undertake the microfiche conversion of publications without securing the permission of the issuing agencies.

Fortunately, *Instruction 565.1* provides a definition of GPO and non-GPO documentation for purposes of the depository library program. Non-GPO documentation is defined as "materials printed in authorized agency printing plants or contractor printing plants that are available only in limited quantities and not currently offered to the Depository Libraries." GPO documentation is defined as "that material printed in or through Government Printing Office facilities that is made available to Depository Libraries on a continuing basis."

Automatic Distribution of Selected Periodicals

The August 1975 issue of *Public Documents Highlights* carried a list of 52 publications, primarily periodicals, which were to be mailed directly from the contractor or printer to designated depository libraries. Later, this number was dramatically reduced. In the June 1977 issue of PDH, the list was reduced to sixteen. William J. Barrett, Deputy Assistant Public Printer, was quoted in DttP as saying "It is not expected that there will be any further change in the direct mail program."[17]

The list includes publications like the *Federal Register*, daily *Congressional Record*, House and Senate *Calendars*, *Weekly Compilation of Presidential Documents*, and *Commerce Business Daily*. Direct mailing of these publications assures more timely receipt by depository libraries. Since these publications are not mailed on a shipping list, there is no specific deadline for filing a claim for non-receipt. Librarians can make a claim when one of the following conditions has been met:

1) You have not received a particular issue of a periodical but have received subsequent issues,
2) you have heard that other libraries have received the particular issue that you are missing, or
3) the time of the month when you usually receive issues of a specific periodical has passed.[18]

Inspection Program

According to 44 U.S.C. 1909, "The Superintendent of Documents shall make firsthand investigation of conditions for which need is indicated and include the results of investigations in his annual report." But without adequate staffing, the Superintendent himself could not carry out even the spirit, much less the letter, of the law. A promising solution to that problem was effected by the creation of two positions in the office of the Superintendent of Documents of Depository Library Inspectors. The Inspectors assumed their duties in November 1974.[19]

During FY 1975, 224 depository libraries in 17 states were inspected. The current *Instructions to Depository Libraries* is employed as a checklist tool. "The availability of all depository documents to the general public and how this access is provided is one of the most important aspects of the inspection."[20] In general, the duties of the Inspectors encompass the extent to which the depository fulfills the obligations of the program as set forth in Chapter 19 of Title 44 and in the *Instructions*. Suggestions are made "in a spirit of helpfulness, rather than fault-finding." Moreover, the inspection program may help documents librarians petition administrators for an upgrading of services.[21]

In the March 1977 issue of DttP, the Deputy Assistant Public Printer was able to state that "more than two-thirds of all the libraries have had a visit to date and we hope that the balance will be visited by the end of 1977." No immediate plans are being made to increase the number of Inspectors, and the projection is that the two will be able to inspect each depository library once every three years.[22]

Depository Library Council

The Depository Library Council to the Public Printer was formally established in 1972 to provide advice on matters dealing with the depository library program and the sales service program of the Superintendent of Documents. Originally, the body was called the Depository Library Advisory Council, but the name was changed to avoid the suggestion that the Council was subject to the provisions of the Federal Advisory Committee Act (PL 92-463; 86 Stat. 770). The Council is presently composed of 15 members nominated by various library associations of the United States and appointed by the Public Printer to serve for a period of three years. Each year five new members are appointed to replace five outgoing members. Council members encourage librarians who work with documents, whether in a depository or non-depository institution, to write or telephone any member of the Council regarding an idea, complaint or suggestion.[23]

The Council usually meets twice a year to advise the Public Printer. Working committees of the Council include micrographics, GPO operations, depository libraries, and the national depository system. Travel and other expenses for Council members to attend meetings are borne by SuDocs appropriations.[24]

Proposed Standards and Guidelines

The Standards Committee of the Depository Library Council worked during 1974 "on a report that would provide an inspection tool for the Superintendent of Documents, a guide for the education of documents librarians, and a tool for communication with library administrators." At the October 1974 meeting of the Council two reports were presented by the Standards Committee to the Council: one report covered minimum standards for the depository system; the other, a longer draft, set forth guidelines for the depository system. "The Council agreed to recommend to the Public Printer that both [standards and guidelines] be adopted provisionally for a period of twelve months beginning January 1, 1975, and that these be used by the Superintendent of Documents and cooperating libraries as appropriate in the inspection of depository libraries during the year."[25]

Published as a *Special Supplement* to the December 1975 issue of *Public Documents Highlights*, the two separate reports were brought together under the rubric *Proposed Standards & Guidelines*. Minimum Standards would be mandatory and enforceable under present law; Guidelines would be voluntary but would provide an incentive to upgrade the performance of depository libraries. An analysis of the problems in formulating standards and guidelines was published in the March 1976 issue of DttP.[26] And when the standards and guidelines were printed in the *Special Supplement* to PDH (December 1975), comments were requested from all depository librarians.

A number of individual librarians as well as professional groups responded to the first draft.[27] Comments on the 1975 version were considered at the October 1976 meeting of the Depository Library Council, and changes were made. Minor amendments were made at the April 1977 meeting of the Council on the advice of the General Counsel of the GPO.

The revised *Proposed Standards & Guidelines* was published as a *Special Supplement* to the August 1977 issue of *Public Documents Highlights*. Missing from this revision is a section in the December 1975 *Special Supplement* which set forth proposed changes in depository procedures that would require either administrative or statutory action. The revised standards and guidelines are divided into twelve sections, with subparts for each section. Major topics include objectives of the system, the duties of the SuDocs, new depository designations, regional depository obligations, service to users, etc. *Appendix A* is a list of 23 titles of official government publications that *all* depository libraries should have "available for immediate use." In early 1978 depository libraries received a copy of the guidelines in the form of a 15-page brochure entitled *Guidelines for the Depository Library System*. It consists of the guidelines as adopted by the Depository Library Council October 18, 1977, the list of those 23 indispensable titles, and the by-laws of the Council as amended October 18, 1977.

Regional Depository Libraries

One of the significant achievements of the Depository Library Act of 1962 was the establishment of the regional depository library concept. 44 U.S.C. 1912 and Section 2 of the *Instructions to Depository Libraries* (1977 revision) set forth eligibility requirements and duties and functions. 44 U.S.C. 1912 permits each state (and Puerto Rico) to have two regional depositories. Most states have found that one regional serves the needs of the selective depository libraries well. However, as of December 1977 the following states, in addition to Puerto Rico, either did not have regionals or were not served by a regional: Alaska, Arkansas, Delaware, Missouri, Rhode Island, South Carolina, South Dakota, Tennessee. The states of New Hampshire and Vermont are served by the University of Maine library in Orono.

Some states have two regional depository libraries: Alabama, Arizona, Colorado, Louisiana, Michigan, Nebraska, New Mexico, North Dakota, Texas, and Wisconsin. In Arizona and New Mexico, for example, two of the ten depository libraries in the entire state are regionals! Conversely, states like California, New York, and Ohio, with many selective depository libraries, are served by one regional.[28]

This uneven pattern causes alarm, given the crucial role of regionals in assuring the deposit of at least one copy in microform or hard copy of every available depository Item. States without regionals cannot participate in the machinery provided for disposal of unneeded documents, nor can they avail themselves of the depository network through workshops, training sessions, and consultive services. PDH has shown its concern in an article, more in the spirit of an editorial, appearing in its October 1975 issue.[29]

SUMMARY

The Depository Library Act of 1962 wrought important changes in the system of distributing publications for public use and information. Clearly, access to public information has improved over the last decade and a half; there is little doubt that the Superintendent of Documents strives to be responsive to the depository library community.

Nevertheless, there is always room for improvement. The first working draft of the Standards Committee of the Depository Library Council to the Public Printer included the following suggestions for further enhancing the depository program:

1. That regional depositories be entitled to a second copy of the publications in all categories, if desired, either in microform or hard copy;

2. That 44 U.S.C. 1903 be amended so that the SuDocs, through his own appropriations, is able to obtain more non-GPO publications for the depository system;

3. That there be further improvement of the *Monthly Catalog*, specifically in its indexing, its periodic cumulations, and the timeliness of its publishing;

4. That provision be made for a National Depository Library at the head of the system which now comprises a network of selective and regional depositories;

5. That federal financial support be given to defray direct costs incurred by a regional depository in discharging its responsibilities to its selective members;

6. That selective depositories be required to accept a minimum percent of the Items available; and

7. That 44 U.S.C. 1909 be amended to require a minimum of 25,000 titles other than government publications as an eligibility requirement.[30]

Some of these suggestions may come about without the need for administrative or legislative action. For example, it is hoped that the availability of Items in microform will encourage selective depositories to subscribe to more categories, inasmuch as the hoary and venerable "lack of space" argument would no longer be valid. The crucial element in the continuing relationship between the GPO and the library community is that of flexibility and common sense. GPO's response to initiatives by individual documents librarians and to the promptings of GODORT in the last few years does indeed warrant a cautious optimism for the future. That optimism may be justified in terms of past performances. As Schwarzkopf stated, "Despite its faults, the Depository Library Program has been, and continues to be, an effective and economical program to provide public access to official publications of the United States Government. During 1976 there were 1,196 depository libraries to whom were sent over 15 million free publications. The cost of the entire program to the United States Government in 1976 was six and one half million dollars, which included the cost of the publications, shipping charges and administrative costs. Most American taxpayers would consider this money well spent."[31]

REFERENCES

1. U.S. Congress. Joint Committee on Printing. *Government Depository Libraries: The Present Law Governing Designated Depository Libraries*, Committee Print, 95th Cong., 1st Sess., rev. April 1977, p. 4.

2. *100 GPO Years*, pp. 79, 90.

3. Carper W. Buckley, "Implementation of the Federal Depository Library Act of 1962," *Library Trends* 15: 27-28 (July 1966).

4. Regionals have no jurisdiction over federal depository libraries, which are designated by a special provision of the 1962 act. 44 U.S.C. 1907 notes: "Depository libraries within executive departments and independent agencies may dispose of unwanted Government publications after first offering them to the Library of Congress and the Archivist of the United States."

5. See the excellent article by LeRoy C. Schwarzkopf, "Regional Depository Libraries for U.S. Government Publications," *Government Publications Review* 2: 91-102 (1975).

6. PDH 9: 3-4 (April 1975).

7. PDH 17: 3 (August 1976).

8. PDH 10: 3 (June 1975).

9. As of April 1977. See note 1, *supra*, p. 41.

10. PDH 8: 3 (December 1974).

11. DttP 5: 97 (May 1977).

12. PDH 8: 3 (December 1974).

13. DttP 5: 97 (May 1977).

14. DttP 5: 8 (January 1977).

15. PDH 21: 1 (April 1977).

16. DttP 5: 97 (May 1977).

17. DttP 5: 77 (March 1977).

18. PDH 11: 2 (August 1975).

19. PDH 8: 1 (December 1974).

20. PDH 11: 2 (August 1975).

21. Dan MacGilvray, "Depository Library Inspection Program," DttP 4: 18-19 (June 1976).

22. DttP 5: 77 (March 1977).

23. U.S. House. *Legislative Branch Appropriations for [FY] 1976* [Hearings], p. 759; *Daily Depository Shipping List* 9775 (May 9, 1977).

24. U.S. House. *Legislative Branch Appropriations for [FY] 1975* [Hearings], pp. 400-402.

25. DttP 3: 21 (January 1975). The working draft of the proposed guidelines and minimum standards is found on pp. 23-30.

26. Catharine J. Reynolds, "Standards for Depository Libraries, Goals and Roadblocks," DttP 4: 45-46 (March 1976).

27. See Rebekah Harleston and L. C. Schwarzkopf, *Reactions to Proposed Standards & Guidelines for the Depository Library System* (1976). Available from ERIC Document Reproduction Service [ED 126 957].

28. Schwarzkopf, note 5, *supra*, pp. 93-94. PL 95-261 (April 17, 1978) provides for the designation of accredited law schools as depository libraries.

29. "Regional Libraries Needed," PDH 12: 1, 2 (October 1975).

30. *Special Supplement* to *Public Documents Highlights* (December 1975), pp. 5-6.

31. LeRoy C. Schwarzkopf, "The Depository Library Program and Access to Official Publications of the United States Government," a paper delivered at the meeting of the I.F.L.A. Section on Official Publications, 1977 World Congress of Librarians, Brussels, Belgium, September 7, 1977, p. 8.

4

NON-DEPOSITORY PUBLICATIONS

Since World War II the federal government has greatly increased its scientific and technical activities and directly or indirectly is supporting much of the scientific research and development being carried on in the United States. This has been a matter of growing concern to some private publishers, with some fears voiced that the federal government might dominate the scientific publishing field. However, most government agencies have encouraged federal scientists to publish reports in nongovernment scientific and technical journals. . . .

The publications in this field include many noteworthy and valuable contributions in almost every branch of the physical and social sciences. . . . If the field is approached by way of the subject matter, a listing would include almost every field of scientific inquiry and human interest. It would comprise subjects of interest to the specialist in every branch of science, to the workers in diverse fields of industry, to the traveler, to the teacher, to the engineer, to the manufacturer, to the merchant, to the housewife, and to the general seeker after knowledge for its own sake. . . .

It may appear inconsistent that so little space is devoted to a group that includes so large a number of publications of importance, but the only alternative is a voluminous cataloging of publications in many diverse fields.

−Laurence F. Schmeckebier and Roy B. Eastin,
Government Publications and Their Use (2d rev. ed.;
Washington: Brookings, 1969)

INTRODUCTION

Schmeckebier and Eastin correctly recognized the difficulty if not the futility of trying to discuss the often confusing domain of "non-depository" publications. For when we begin this journey, we leave the mere maze of government documentation and enter a dark forest, where few Tigers burning bright illumine the way. As we noted in Chapter 3, documents produced by agencies other than the GPO will increasingly find their way into the depository system by virtue of *Instruction 565.1*. But the vast majority of technical report literature, federally sponsored, remains exempted from depository distribution.

To understand why this should be the case, we must examine the several provisions of legislation and recognize that the crucial matter of "legislative intent" is unclear, thus giving rise to interpretations where the interest of one group is pitted against the interest of another body. The result is confusion and, often, acrimony.

First, let us note 44 U.S.C. 1902. It states that publications of the federal government "shall be made available to depository libraries" with the following exceptions: "those determined by their issuing component to be required for official use only or for strictly administrative or operational purposes which have no public interest or educational value and publications classified for reasons of national security."

Then, 44 U.S.C. 1903 adds another category to be exempted from the depository system: "so-called cooperative publications which must necessarily be sold in order to be self-sustaining."

Finally, let us review the brief and inadequate "definition" of a government publication that stands at the beginning of Chapter 19 (Depository Library Program) of Title 44 of the *United States Code*: "Government publication, as used in this chapter, means informational matter which is published as an individual document at Government expense, or as required by law." (44 U.S.C. 1901).

What does this mean? For one thing, the "definition" includes the phrase "at Government expense" and that would seem *not to exclude* federally funded documentation from potential entry into the depository distribution system. On the other hand, 44 U.S.C. 1902 and 1903 appear to *exclude* the following categories of publications, no matter what their source may be:

1. Official use only;
2. Having no public interest or educational value;
3. Classified for national security; and
4. "Cooperative" publications that need to be sold to be self-sustaining.

Fortunately, many types of publications are added to the depository distribution system through the machinery of the *Survey*. Examples of publications which were removed from "non-depository" status include the *Library of Congress Information Bulletin* (Item 785-C), the Senate Executive Documents and Reports series (Item 1008-A-1), and the committee prints of several Congressional committees (various Items). Is it to be presumed that these publications now possess an educational value or a public interest that for years they did not have? Publications classified for security reasons do become declassified and made available to depository institutions. Internal administrative documents clearly having no public interest are not desired by depository libraries. The issue of cooperative publications that must be sold to be self-sustaining is painful and unresolved, and will be explored at length later in this chapter.

We are continually reminded of the problem of non-depository documents because we are made aware of their existence bibliographically. LeRoy C. Schwarzkopf made an analysis of 16,770 titles entered in the January to November

1973 issues of the *Monthly Catalog*. Of the total number of titles, 34 percent were non-depository. Of these, 15 percent were distributed by the issuing agency, 2 percent were sold by the issuing agency, 8 percent were sold by NTIS, 3 percent were sold by the GPO, and 6 percent were not available for sale or distribution.[1] Note here the illogic suggested by the percentages. Five percent of this group were sold either by the issuing agency or by GPO; surely a publication worthy of sale is worthy as a depository document. Fifteen percent were deemed of sufficient interest by someone to be distributed to a person or persons interested in their contents. The eight percent sold by NTIS represent a bibliographic duplication of information since, as we shall see, NTIS has its own comprehensive catalogs. It would be soothing if we could assume that the six percent not available for sale or distribution were truly publications either classified, for official use only, "cooperative," or having no educational value and public interest.

It is easy to determine via the *Monthly Catalog* those publications not available to depository libraries. Every publication not identified by a "black dot" or "bullet" symbol (●) must be obtained by other than depository means.[2] Select any *Monthly Catalog* and scan the entries; you will find numerous titles which are non-depository publications. Remember, too, that these represent only those publications that have made their way to the Library Division to become bibliographically born. In addition, "there has been a trend during the last few years for more and more publications to be published through NTIS, ERIC, private contractors, and so on. This means that they are no longer automatically made depository items."[3] The number of government publications, including contract reports funded by a federal agency, is immense. Accordingly, even regional depository libraries cannot rely upon the depository apparatus for building a collection of "government publications" (in the broadest sense of 44 U.S.C. 1901) that will be wholly responsive to the needs of a heterogeneous clientele.

SOURCES OF NON-DEPOSITORY PUBLICATIONS

The sources discussed below comprise some of the major services for acquiring and controlling non-depository publications. They include in their bibliographic apparatus large numbers of publications that are not, by even the most liberal definition, properly speaking, a "government document." Nevertheless, they are in some fashion associated so closely with government that the community of professional documents librarians includes them among its accepted responsibilities.

National Technical Information Service

The National Technical Information Service is a federal agency located within the Department of Commerce. According to the *United States Government Manual*, it was established on September 2, 1970, "to simplify and improve public access to Department of Commerce publications and to data files and scientific and technical reports produced by Federal agencies and their contractors. The agency is obligated by Title 15 of the *United States Code* to recover its cost from sales to users."[4] Its immediate predecessors were the Clearinghouse for Federal Scientific and Technical Information (1964-1970) and the Office of Technical Services (1946-1964).

The Service, known by the acronym NTIS, is described in its promotional literature as the "central source for the public sale of Government sponsored research, development and engineering reports and other analyses prepared by Federal agencies, their contractors or grantees" and a central source "for Federally generated machine processable data files." NTIS ships over 19,000 information products daily, supplies the public with about 4 million documents and microforms yearly, and has over 100,000 titles in current shelf stock.[5]

The NTIS Charter

NTIS is governed by the provisions of 15 U.S.C. 1151-1157. As an agency of the federal government dealing with so-called "cooperative publications" (44 U.S.C. 1903), NTIS consistently maintains that it is exempt from participation in the depository library system. The crucial provision is found in 15 U.S.C. 1153. It is worth quoting the applicable words, because the greatest and most vociferous attack on NTIS policies arises from a failure to determine the legislative intent of the mandate that NTIS officials assume. 15 U.S.C. 1153 says in part:

> The Secretary [of Commerce] is authorized ... to establish ... a schedule or schedules of reasonable fees or charges for services performed or for documents or other publications furnished under this chapter.

> It is the policy of this chapter, to the fullest extent feasible and consistent with the objectives of this chapter, that each of the services and functions provided herein shall be self-sustaining or self-liquidating and that the general public shall not bear the cost of publications and other services which are for the special use and benefit of private groups and individuals; but nothing herein shall be construed to require the levying of fees or charges for services performed or publications furnished to any agency or instrumentality of the Federal Government, or for publications which are distributed pursuant to reciprocal arrangements for the exchange of information or which are otherwise issued primarily for the general benefit of the public.

The convoluted wording of this provision is a paradigm of legislation badly written. Indeed, to resolve the problem, the Public Printer in 1974 requested the Comptroller General of the United States to decide whether the Depository Library Act of 1962 is applicable to publications issued by NTIS. His ruling (Decision Number B-114829, June 27, 1975) was lengthy, but the last paragraph, which summarized his decision, was published in DttP:

> To summarize, we agree with NTIS that its publications may generally be regarded as "cooperative publications." We also agree that those NTIS publications of a specialized and limited interest nature are to be self-sustaining under 15 U.S.C. 1153 and are therefore exempt from the

Depository Library Act under 44 U.S.C. 1903. At the same time, we conclude that both statutes, as well as the legislative history discussed herein, indicate a different treatment for NTIS publications that are "issued primarily for the general benefit of the public." Thus we agree with GPO that the latter are subject to the Library Act. It is recognized that it may be difficult to apply precisely the foregoing distinction; and this task must be left to resolution between NTIS and GPO. However, we are inclined to favor the general framework indicated in GPO's letter to us, which suggests coverage for " . . . certain serial publications (by NTIS); e.g., *Government Reports Announcements and Index* and the *GRA Annual Index*, which are of widespread public interest, most especially to the library community."[6]

Thus the Comptroller General's decision gave the controversy back to GPO and NTIS to resolve, while appearing to side with GPO that NTIS materials issued for the "general benefit of the public" should not be excluded from the depository system. That this problem must be resolved, by new legislation if necessary, was underscored by a recommendation contained in the final report of the National Study Commission on Records and Documents of Federal Officials, dated March 31, 1977:

> 3.   Most documents containing technical information either produced by private agencies under Government contract, or prepared by Federal agencies, remain outside the depository system, although the National Technical Information Service (NTIS) indexes, catalogs, and sells them in paper copies, microforms, punched cards, or on magnetic tape. NTIS does not participate in the Depository Library Program, holding that the act creating the Service provides that the public cannot bear the cost of its publications. Librarians, however, assert that NTIS can and should participate in the Depository Library Program because the same act states that NTIS can freely distribute information "for the general benefit of the public" (15 U.S.C. 1153). The question of whether technical material handled by NTIS should be offered to the Depository Library System should be resolved. The current interpretation of the mandate of NTIS has greatly extended the definition of technical material while at the same time it has increased the cost of copies so that such material is now available only to wealthier libraries. Means should be found to assess the need by depositories for the kind of material processed by NTIS and a solution found to bring that material into the Depository Library System by, if necessary, clarifying the law.[7]

The Commission in its final report noted that NTIS "has greatly extended the definition of technical material." The question was pointedly brought up in a panel discussion at the 1975 annual program of GODORT on the bibliographic control of federal government publications. Among the panelists was Marvin Wilson, Assistant Director (Production) at NTIS. The question addressed to him and his answer follow:

Q: Why is *Commerce Today* [now called *Commerce America*] and similar non-scientific and technical materials included in *GRA*? Why is coverage not limited to scientific, technical, and engineering titles?

A: There are two reasons for this. The first is clear and straight-forward. When NTIS was reconstituted from the Federal Clearinghouse in 1970 the Secretary of Commerce directed that NTIS would maintain centralized bibliographic control of Department of Commerce publications.

The second is an attempt by NTIS to make all possible useful information known to the users of all our products. We view many reports that may not be termed scientific or technical in the strictest sense as still being useful to our users. Research emphasis changes constantly and today research in Social or Behavioral Sciences is just as important in the scientific and technical community as research in Physics or Chemistry was a few years ago. Also the use of technical reports has changed from being primarily a help in further research to being used both as a research aid and a tool for implementing technology. . . . For this reason we do acquire and announce some non-technical reports as available from NTIS but in other cases we announce alternate sources for the material.

A related reason is the NTIS machine-readable data base. Our data base is maintained by more than 30 large information centers. Thousands of profiles and on-line requests are processed by these centers daily. If NTIS did not include the non-technical reports in the data base this user community which does not rely on printed catalogs would be deprived of these reports.[8]

Here we have, in these discussions, the phenomenon of an agency (NTIS) aggressively seeking not only to consolidate but to expand its bureaucratic position, and a less aggressive agency (GPO) unwilling or unable to counteract or blunt the enlarging, encroaching domain and sphere of influence of NTIS. Losers in the battle thus far have been the depository library community and, through it, the general public.

NTIS Products and Services

It is somewhat difficult to keep abreast of NTIS products and services because the agency is continually changing the scope and indeed the name of its various information products and the bibliographic tools by which they can be accessed. As of late 1977 here were some of the basic products and services offered by NTIS.

NTISearch

NTISearch (pronounced en-tee-search) provides access to over 400,000 reports on completed federal government research and other analyses. The

NTISearch information collection covers federally sponsored research projects from 1964. The collection is updated by the daily addition of about 200 new research reports.

The NTISearch program consists of two types of services: *Published Searches* and *On-Line Searches.*

Published Searches are bibliographies developed by information specialists at NTIS from an on-line interactive bibliographic retrieval system. Most of the *Published Searches* are prepared from the NTIS data base, but some are prepared from the Engineering Index, Inc. (Ei) and the American Petroleum Institute (API) data bases. These are updated at regular intervals and are available in paper copy or microfiche.

On-Line Searches may be subscribed to if the *Published Search* does not fully satisfy the information needs of the user. These are customized to the user's specific needs. One may simply call an on-line search telephone number to initiate a search. Moreover, at the user's request, NTIS will include, with each search, specially priced microfiche of the entire texts of the summarized reports. NTIS research reports cited in NTISearches are available in one or more of the following forms: paper copy, microform (microfiche or microfilm), magnetic tape, and punched cards.

SRIM

SRIM is an acronym for *Selected Research in Microfiche.* It used to be called SCIM (Selected Categories in Microfiche) and before that was known as SDM (Selective Dissemination of Microfiche). The current version is an automatic biweekly service available from NTIS to help the user expand coverage of federal government research and development (R&D) in selected categories. The selected research report is available in microfiche. This full text service is further refined by *SRIM Profile*, based on the user's own specifications. As with NTISearch customized service, a SRIM information specialist will work directly with the user to develop a selection strategy based upon index keywords assigned to all NTIS reports.

NTIS developed a *SRIM Index* in 1977 and made it available to subscribers in 1978 as an optional service. The *Index* is produced in microfiche and paper copy and is sorted into six sequences: subject, contract number, corporate source, personal author, report/accession number, and title. *SRIM Index* is distributed quarterly and cumulates for the calendar year, the last quarter being an annual index.

An NTIS Deposit Account is necessary for SRIM service, which can be established with a minimum deposit of $25 for SRIM and $125 for *SRIM Profile*. SRIM categories range from administration to urban technology and include education, law and humanities as well as biomedical technology and engineering. NTIS promotional materials on SRIM emphasize features like its complete text delivery, fast service two weeks after publication, savings of space, easy retrieval, savings of money, simplified research procedures, and convenience.

WGA

Weekly Government Abstracts (WGA) consist of weekly newsletters in some 26 categories, each carrying summaries (abstracts) of most unclassified federally funded research as it is completed and made available. The report summaries are usually prepared by the author. The last issue of the year of each WGA is a subject index containing up to 10 cross references. Annual subscription rates, as of 1977, ranged from $45 to $165 (for *Government Inventions for Licensing*). Categories include business and economics, energy, health planning, library and information sciences, and physics.[9]

Other

In addition to the above basic services, the various NTIS catalogs and brochures continue to list the kinds of materials and subjects it makes available. A 1976-77 sample would include Internal Revenue Service (IRS) summary ZIP Code data; docketed civil tax cases pending in the appellate, claims, district and tax courts; National Library of Medicine's on-line data bases (MEDLINE/TOXLINE); censuses of population and housing; energy SOS (Standing Order Service) for full text of all printed reports on energy published by NTIS; petroleum statistics reports; Nuclear Regulatory Commission reports; U.S. Patent Classification on microfilm; translations of news reports from the People's Republic of China; and Parkinson's disease citations.

The vastness of scope of NTIS operations results from its diversity of clients. Not only are federal agencies registered with NTIS: the Service is the national marketing coordinator for a number of so-called "Special Technology Groups." These groups recover their costs by making their products and services publicly available through NTIS. Included are such entities as the Engineering Sciences Data Unit in London, and the Chemical Propulsion Information Agency located at Johns Hopkins University in Maryland. Thus are the lines between publications of the public and private sector blurred in the workings of an information agency like NTIS.

Bibliographic Control

While the several NTIS announcements proclaim special services and provide an overview of products, *Government Reports Announcements & Index* (GRA&I) is a semimonthly indexing and abstracting service for comprehensive bibliographic coverage. Although sold through NTIS, it is available to depository libraries (C 51.9/3; Item 270).

Report entries are arranged by subjects. The "subject field and group structure" categories were endorsed by the Committee on Scientific & Technical Information (COSATI) of the Federal Council for Science & Technology in 1964, hence are called COSATI subject fields. As of 1977 there were 22 subject fields, from Aeronautics to Space Technology. Field 5, "Behavioral and Social Sciences," includes subdivisions such as history, law, humanities, personnel selection, and psychology. The rest are primarily scientific and technical.

Main entries contain the standard bibliographic information, including an abstract of the report. Figure 8 shows a sample main entry with the identifying features of the publication.

Figure 8
GOVERNMENT REPORTS ANNOUNCEMENTS AND INDEX: SAMPLE MAIN ENTRY

SAMPLE ENTRIES

MAIN ENTRY

Report entries are arranged by subject group and field. Within fields they are arranged alphanumerically by NTIS order number (accession number); alphabetic data precedes numeric.

Field 10 ENERGY CONVERSION
(NON-PROPULSIVE)

Group 10A Conversion Techniques

Order number —— PB-254 315/5GA   PC A16/MF A01 ——— Price codes

Corporate author — Smithsonian Science Information Exchange, Inc., Washington, D.C.

Personal author — Information on International Research and Development Activities in the Field of Energy, David F. Hersey. May 76, 370p* NSF/RA-760057, Grant NSF-AER74-20678 ——— Report title

Keywords — descriptors & identifiers — Descriptors: *Directories, *Indexes (Documentation), *Energy, Research projects, Foreign countries, Bibliographies, Abstracts. Identifiers: Announcement bulletins.

This directory is the product of a data collection effort undertaken by the Smithsonian Science Information Exchange (SSIE) on behalf of an interagency committee formed under the U.S. State Department to provide international cooperation in energy research and development. Included is information covering 1766 ongoing and recently completed energy research projects conducted in Canada, Italy, the Federal Republic of Germany, France, the Netherlands, the United Kingdom, and 25 other countries. In addition to the title and text of project summaries, the directory contains the following indexes: Subject Index, Investigator Index, Performing Organization Index, and Supporting Organization Index. — Abstract of report

Index entries are by subject, personal author, corporate author, contact grant number, and accession/report number. Figure 9 (p. 105) shows sample index entries related to the main entry.

Figure 9

GOVERNMENT REPORTS ANNOUNCEMENTS AND INDEX:
SAMPLE INDEX ENTRIES

INDEX ENTRIES

Index entries are arranged alphanumerically. Titles are included in all indexes except the Contract Number index.

SUBJECT

ENERGY
Information on International Research and Development Activities in the Field of Energy.
PB-254 315/5GI   10A

Entries are sequenced by major subject term (the keywords with an asterisk) and by NTIS order number.

PERSONAL AUTHOR

HERSEY, DAVID F.
Information in International Research and Development Activities in the Field of Energy.
PB-254 315/5GI   10A

Entries are sequenced by personal author, report title, and NTIS order number.

CORPORATE AUTHOR

SMITHSONIAN SCIENCE INFORMATION EXCHANGE, INC., WASHINGTON, D.C.
Information on International Research and Development Activities in the Field of Energy.
(NSF/RA-760057)
PB-254 315/5GI   10A

Entries are sequenced by corporate author name, original report number, and NTIS order number. The monitor agency number is given following the report title.

CONTRACT GRANT NUMBER

NSF-AER74-20678
Smithsonian Science Information Exchange, Inc., Washington, D.C.
PB-254 315/5GI   10A

Entries are sequenced by contract or grant number, corporate author, and NTIS order number.

ACCESSION/REPORT NUMBER

PB-254 315/5GI
Information on International Research and Development Activities in the Field of Energy.
PB-254 315/5GI   10A   PC A16/MF A0I

Entries are sequenced by NTIS order, original report, or monitor agency number. Price codes are given in this index.

Preceding the entries in each fortnightly issue of GRA&I is information about NTIS, how to order, NTIS products, product formats, a list of the COSATI subject fields, and key NTIS telephone numbers for subscriptions, NTISearches, etc.

Government Reports Annual Index (C 51.9/4:year; Item 270) is published in six sections. Section 1 is usually a subject index (A-L) and section 2 concludes the listing (M-Z). Section 3 is the personal author index. Section 4 is the corporate author index. Sections 5 and 6 comprise the contract number index and accession/report number index.

GRA&I and MoCat

GRA&I is the basic bibliographic tool for summaries of government research. Unlike the *Monthly Catalog*, it is hampered by the lack of a title index. However, it has an abstracting capability that the MoCat does not possess. The relationship between the MoCat and GRA&I bears a few comments.

　　　Librarians have for some time desired closer cooperation between the MoCat and GRA&I. But "without some enforced bibliographic control it would be very difficult to coordinate [GRA&I] and the *Monthly Catalog*, primarily due to the different missions and operating procedures by GPO and NTIS." Put another way, "NTIS is obligated to furnish the [Library Division of the SuDocs] copies of only publications they initiate, which they do." The problem relates to the Depository Library Act and to NTIS's enabling legislation. "Most users of GPO and NTIS documents are aware that few NTIS documents are printed by GPO. Since GPO does not have copies available as a result of override printing, the documents are not distributed to the Depository Libraries. Also, because the documents are not sent to GPO for printing or distribution, they are not cataloged for inclusion in the *Monthly Catalog.*"[10] And this brings us right back to the need for clarification of the appropriate provisions of Titles 44 (Chapter 19) and 15 (Chapter 23) of the *United States Code.*

　　　Meanwhile, the bibliographic overlapping in GRA&I and MoCat often causes confusion among users of both indexes. A good deal of the same material finds its way into both tools, especially concerning COSATI Subject Field 5, "Behavioral and Social Sciences." Note, for example, how the periodical *Commerce America* is covered bibliographically in GRA&I and in the *Monthly Catalog*'s *Serials Supplement* (1977):

<u>GRA&I (March 5, 1976)</u>

```
PB-248 151-01/GA        PC-GPO/MF$2.25-NTIS
Department of Commerce, Washington, D.C.
Commerce America. Volume 1, Number 1,
January 5, 1976.
5 Jan 76, 44p
Paper copy available from GPO.

Descriptors: *Commerce, *Periodicals, Interna-
tional trade, Negotiation, Manufacturing,
Technology innovation, Product development,
Quality of life, Environmental impacts, Design,
Energy conservation, Research.

Contents:
   Stage is set to begin earnest bargaining at
     multilateral trade negotiations in Geneva;
   Computer can help U.S. producers retain
     technical leadership;
   Designers can make life more livable,
     explain the unexplainable;
   Economic highlights;
   Energy management digest;
   Domestic business report;
   International commerce report.
```

Serials Supplement (1977)

77-5569

C1.58/2:(v. nos. & nos.)
Commerce America. Washington U.S. Dept. of Commerce;
for sale by the Supt. of Docs., U.S. Govt. Print. Off.
20402
ill. 28 cm.
$29.80 (U.S.) $37.25 (foreign) $1.15 (single)
v. 1-Jan. 5, 1976.
Item 127-A
Biweekly.
ISSN 0361-0438
Supersedes: Commerce today
1. United States--Commerce--Periodicals. I. United
States. Dept. of Commerce.
HF1.C38
330.9/73/092
OCLC 2246954

Similarly, the *Survey of Current Business* is listed in both the MoCat and GRA&I. One can purchase both periodicals from SuDocs in paper copy and from NTIS on microfiche. Both are depository Items. Other publications listed in both catalogs include a number of Census Bureau documents. Often a publication, such as the *Bureau of the Census Catalog*, is listed in GRA&I with the notation that the publication is available *only* in paper copy from GPO. The same publication, listed in the *Serials Supplement*, makes no reference to NTIS.

One expects Commerce Department publications, however unscientific or non-technical they may be, to be listed in GRA&I. But in August 1977 a Bureau of Labor Statistics (Department of Labor) news release announced a number of Comprehensive Employment and Training Act (CETA) studies of employment and unemployment as being "available *only* from the National Technical Information Service." And this type of series, which documents librarians expect to find listed in the MoCat, creates bibliographic confusion. Indeed, Census Bureau publications are available from at least three different sources: SuDocs, NTIS, and the Bureau's Data User Services Division. And they are probably available from the several regional offices of the Bureau as well as from one's Representative. Moreover, they are available for sale by commercial publishers in either microform or paper copy.

When NTIS is the issuing agency itself, it is supposed to provide copies of its publications for depository distribution. Thus we find that GRA&I is a depository Item. But the various WGA titles are not available on deposit. Both are listed in the *Serials Supplement* (1977) to the MoCat and are assigned SuDocs class numbers. The March 1977 *List of Classes* shows seven series available from NTIS to depository institutions.

As noted, the vast bulk of materials available through NTIS are "government publications" only in the sense that they are sponsored or funded by a government agency. Usually in these cases the contractor or grantee publishes the report. Many of these reports make their way into the MoCat. A typical MoCat entry for this type of contract technical report is shown below:

Monthly Catalog, September 1976

76-5515
                 NAS 1.26:2641
Fahmy, Abdel A.
    Investigation of thermal fatigue in fiber composite materi-
als/ Abdel A. Fahmy and Thomas C. Cunningham;
prepared by North Caroline State University, Raleigh, N.C.,
for Langley Research Center.--Washington: U.S. National
Aeronautics and Space Administration; Springfield, Va: for
sale by the National Technical Information Service, 1976.
    v, 56 p.: ill.; 27 cm.--(NASA contractor report; NASA
CR-2641)
    Cover title.
    Bibliography: p. 56.
    pbk.: $4.25
    1. Composite materials. 2. Fibers. I. Cunningham,
Thomas G., jt. auth. II. United States. Langley Research
Center, Hampton, Va. III. United States. National Aeronau-
tics and Space Administration. IV. Title. V. Series: United
States. National Aeronautics and Space Administration.
NASA contractor report; NASA CR-2641.

OCLC 2363032

Since GRA&I is a comprehensive semimonthly indexing and abstracting serial for federally sponsored technical reports in the NTIS data base, one wonders why it is necessary to include a relatively small number of these publications in the MoCat at all.

Limitations of NTIS

J. C. Meredith, in his excellent article "NTIS Update: A Critical Review of Services" (*Government Publications Review* 1: 343-61, 1974), sets forth with clarity the major limitations of NTIS:

1. It is a passive acquisitions system;
2. Coverage of materials in subject fields is uneven;
3. "Soft" discipline categories diminish the "scientific and technical" nature of the services.

As a "secondary depository apparatus" of the federal government, NTIS "exercises virtually no control over input." Passive acquisition results in lack of quality control. Input does not fall "neatly within conceptual boundaries"; even categories like Education crawl in under the benevolent but undisciplined subcategory in Field 5 called "Personnel selection, training, and evaluation." As Meredith points out, the criticism of GRA&I reflects faults of the system rather than defects intrinsic to the index itself.[11]

Meredith correctly points out that NTIS "has always had a problem of domain ... conferred on it by the looseness of the enabling legislation ..." It "accepts almost anything and everything that is submitted by a Federal agency, contractor, or grantee, as long as it is accompanied by the usual fee." The agency's promotional materials "contain misstatements and halftruths." The fuzzy language of the law permits the Director of NTIS to "disregard the needs and expectations of anyone not identified with 'industry and business,' including many of the people who generated the information in the first place." Indeed, the several dubious characteristics of practice, which NTIS officials call their "mandate," lead Meredith to summarize his analysis with these harsh but just words: "It is impossible to describe NTIS without a degree of asperity bordering—at times—on censure."[12]

Background Readings

Considering the controversy surrounding NTIS, one would conclude that the issue has received attention in the professional literature. In addition to Meredith's analysis, which should be required reading for anyone involved with these materials, other useful information has been published. Catherine Ettlinger, "NTIS: The Nation's Biggest Publisher," *Government Executive* (February 1974), pp. 42-48, describes the products and services of NTIS and gives its Director a chance to voice his philosophy of how NTIS should be administered. Bo W. Thott, "The National Technical Information Service," *Drexel Library Quarterly* 10: 39-52 (January-April 1974) presents an account of NTIS functions written by an employee of the agency. In the same issue of *Drexel Library Quarterly* (pp. 123-46), Evelyn M. Fass, "Government Information Services: Or, of Needles and Haystacks," gives a useful analysis of the bibliographic control furnished by GRA&I, the *Monthly Catalog*, *Scientific and Technical Aerospace Reports*, and *Nuclear Science Abstracts*. Joseph G. Coyne, "The National Technical Information Service," *Illinois Libraries* 56: 269-71 (April 1974) provides a brief account of the agency and future developments; Coyne, like Thott, is an employee of NTIS. Frederic J. O'Hara, "Views and Over-Views On/Of U.S. Government Documents," *Government Publications Review* 4: 51-57 (1977) gives the genesis and history of NTIS, describes GRA&I, NTISearch, WGA, and SRIM, and lists the COSATI subject fields and the groups within them. Of great interest is a sequence of challenge and response involving Irving M. Klempner, professor, School of Library and Information Science, SUNY at Albany, and William T. Knox, former NTIS Director, published in various issues of *Special Libraries*.[13] This exchange is well worth reading, for it provides a splendid example of two viewpoints, unalterably opposed, that define the crucial problem of NTIS and its lack of responsiveness to the general public. Finally, the issues of DttP cited in this analysis prove useful for current awareness.

Concluding Comments

In 1974 the Director of NTIS, the late William T. Knox, was quoted as expressing a desire that the agency become a quasi-government corporation. "I don't think NTIS can be a private firm like McGraw Hill. It's still got to have Government involvement in one way or another because it serves Government agencies. My point is that I don't think NTIS operates as effectively as it could while entirely in a Government department."[14] In another interview, Knox conceded that making NTIS a corporation would increase the cost of the information it would sell. In that same interview Knox complained that SuDocs "has interpreted the depository libraries statute in such a way that GPO is distributing free to 700 libraries the annual *Government Reports Index*. . . . " That represents a loss of income to NTIS; "the result is that those who buy our publications are paying the cost" of free distribution by GPO.[15]

It is clear from statements like these that NTIS and the depository library program are doing battle over a philosophy of public service, and the issue is exacerbated by fuzzy legislation. The National Study Commission on Records and Documents of Federal Officials was absolutely right in its recommendation, which bears repeating: *"Means should be found to assess the need by depositories for the kind of material processed by NTIS and a solution found to bring those materials into the Depository Library System by, if necessary, clarifying the law"* [emphasis added by author].

Defense Documentation Center

The Defense Documentation Center (DDC) is one of five service centers under the Defense Logistics Agency of the Department of Defense (DoD). The Defense Logistics Agency was formerly known as the Defense Supply Agency; its name was changed by DoD Directive 5105.22 (January 22, 1977). DDC facilities are housed in Alexandria, Virginia.

According to the *United States Government Manual* DDC "is responsible for the development, maintenance, and operation of the management information system in the field of scientific and technical information; acquisition, storage, announcement, retrieval, and provision of secondary distribution of scientific and technical reports; and primary distribution of foreign technical reports."[16]

Defense and associated contractor researchers are required to deposit information both classified and unclassified into various data banks in the DDC depository. "There are four major data collections . . . of which the oldest and largest is the Technical Report collection, established after World War II, which now has over one million separate report titles on completed research."[17] R&D activities within the U.S. government and their associated contractors, subcontractors, and grantees, with current government contracts, are eligible to receive most of the information from the data banks. There are collections, however, which contain proprietary data or information compiled for the specific purpose of DoD management decisions which are made available to Defense components only.

Several publications exist for the DDC user community on a periodic basis to announce the existence and availability of DDC programs, products and services: *Technical Abstract Bulletin* (TAB), *Technical Abstract Bulletin Indexes* (TAB-I), *Annual Indexes, TAB Quarterly Indexes, Bibliography of Bibliographies*, and the *DDC Digest*. With the exception of the *DDC Digest*, and some reports included in the *Bibliography of Bibliographies*, the above publications are classified. In 1967 TAB was given a "confidential" security classification, and in 1971 that security label was placed on the *TAB Indexes*, thus removing them from public access.

However, as Robert H. Rea points out, "more than half of the reports received at DDC are made available to NTIS."[18] DDC serves the general public through the following programs:

Unidentified Requests: DDC performs searches in response to letters from individuals or institutions (private and governmental) concerning the availability of technical reports. The requestor is advised if the report is available, and how and from what source copies may be obtained. When a DoD-sponsored report is not available in the public domain, DDC will ask for a review of the report by the military controlling office to determine if the existing distribution limitation can be waived. If release is approved, DDC will furnish a copy, subject to the conditions placed on its release.

Service to Legal Profession: Attorneys often contact DDC in a search for substantiating evidence regarding proposed or anticipated litigation; these requests usually concern announcements of specific reports to the general public, and disposition of patent ownerships resulting from particular research projects sponsored or co-sponsored by DoD. DDC representatives initiate these searches, but this service is subject to a charge based on personnel costs.

Unclassified/Unlimited DoD Reports: By contractual agreement with NTIS, DDC provides copies of R&D reports that are not classified and are sponsored, or generated, by DoD. Moreover, reports which were formerly classified or limited are furnished as soon as they are declassified and delimited, and made available through NTIS.

NTIS then announces the reports in GRA&I. The order number (or "accession/report number") assigned to documents sponsored by DoD is prefixed by the letters "AD." This symbol is a holdover from the old Astia (Armed Services Technical Information Agency) Document designation.[19] Documents are not supplied by DDC but are ordered directly from NTIS; in addition, the service charges for the publications are determined by NTIS.

National Aeronautics and Space Administration

Along with the Department of Defense and the Department of Energy, the National Aeronautics and Space Administration (NASA) is a major agency for the generating of technical report literature. Its chief bibliographic tool is *Scientific and Technical Aerospace Reports* (STAR), a semimonthly indexing/abstracting service.

STAR is available for sale by SuDocs and to depository libraries (NAS 1.9/4; Item 830-K). Cumulative index volumes are published semiannually and annually (NAS1.9/5; Item 830-K).

STAR announces current publications in the following areas: 1) NASA, NASA contractor, and NASA grantee reports; 2) reports issued by other federal government agencies, domestic and foreign institutions, universities, and private firms); 3) translations in report form; 4) NASA-owned patents and patent applications; and 5) dissertations and theses.

An arrangement between NASA and the Smithsonian Science Information Exchange (SSIE) permits the insertion of a separate section of information on aerospace-related activities entitled *On-Going Research Projects.* The insert gives titles of active NASA grants and university contracts, summary portions of recently updated *NASA Research and Technology Operating Plans* (RTOPs), and notices of non-NASA research projects that were funded in the most recent or current fiscal year; the latter are selected by SSIE. The subject scope of STAR includes all aspects of aeronautics and space research and development, supporting basic and applied research, and applications. Aerospace aspects of earth resources, energy development, conservation, oceanography, environmental protection, urban transportation, and other topics of national priority and public policy are also covered.

STAR uses ten major subject divisions, further divided into over 70 specific subject categories and one general category/division. The major subject divisions are listed in the table of contents, together with a note for each that defines its scope and provides cross-references. Abstracts in STAR are grouped by specific category, the categories appearing in sequential order.

Documents announced in STAR are available either in paper copy or in microform from the following sources: NTIS, SuDocs, NASA Public Document Rooms (Washington, D.C.), University Microfilms (dissertations), and the U.S. Patent Office. NASA patent application specifications are sold in paper copy or microfiche by NTIS, while printed copies of patents which are not microfiched are available for purchase from the Commissioner of Patents.

STAR, GRA&I and MoCat

Documents reported in STAR, GRA&I and the *Monthly Catalog* in the subjects that relate to NASA's mission present a splendid example of bibliographic duplication. Let us tread gingerly through this thicket.

Because NASA is one of the federal agencies that registers reports with NTIS, its documentation finds its way into GRA&I. Indeed, Meredith notes that NASA-related documents account for 12 percent of reports summarized in GRA&I.[20] A report announced in STAR but available through NTIS looks like this:

STAR (September 8, 1977)

N77-26337#   Oxford Univ. (England). Dept. of Engineering
Science.
ANALYSIS OF NITROGEN AND AIR LIQUEFACTION SYSTEMS
K.G. Narayankhedhar 1976 74p. refs
(QUEL-1163/76) Avail: NTIS HC A04/MF A01
   The existing liquefaction systems were analyzed
over a wide range of operating conditions to arrive
at the optimum operating conditions for each of the
systems. Results are presented in the nondimensional
parameters, namely, figure of merit and fraction
of the total flow of gas which is liquefied. A low
pressure turbine cycle (turbine operating between
atmospheric and sub-atmosphere pressures) is suggested
which obviates the necessity of an oil-free compressor.
A detailed analysis of this cycle leading to the optimum
operating conditions is also presented.
                                          Author (ESA)

Note that "N-numbers" are assigned by NASA, as "AD numbers" are attached to
DDC documentation. In GRA&I a NASA-sponsored technical report available from
NTIS refers the user to STAR for the abstract:

GRA&I (September 2, 1977)

N77-23123/1GA   PC A03/MF A01
Boeing Commercial Airplane Co., Seattle,
Wash.
FLEXSTAB: A Summary of the Functions and
Capabilities of the NASA Flexible Airplane
Analysis Computer System.
E.N. Tinoco, and J. E. Mercer, Feb 75, 43p
NASA-CR-2564, D6-41098
Contract NAS2-5006

Descriptors: *Aerodynamic   stability.
*Aeroelasticity, Computer programs, *Nasa pro-
grams, Aerodynamic loads, Hardware, Subsonic
speed, Supersonic speeds.
Identifiers: FLEXSTAB computer program.

For abstract, see STAR 1514.

Not to be excluded from this bibliographic feast, the *Monthly Catalog* lists both NASA agency publications and sponsored contract reports. The rationale for announcing the former cannot be challenged; here is an example of a NASA publication issued by the agency itself in its well-known NASA SP-series. Note that it is both sold by SuDocs and available to depository institutions:

Monthly Catalog (May 1977)

77-7310

NAS 1.21:345

Alfven, Hannes, 1908-
  Evolution of the solar system/Hannes Alfven and Gustaf
  Arrhenius.--Washington: National Aeronautics and Space
  Administration, Scientific and Technical Information Office:
  for sale by the Supt. of Docs., U.S. Govt. Print. Off., 1976.
    xii, 599 p.: ill., graphs; 26 cm.- (NASA SP ; 345)
    Includes bibliographical references and index.
  •Item 830-1
  S/N 033-000-06613-6
  cloth: $11.00
    1. Solar system. 2. Mechanics, Celestial. I. Arrhenius,
  Gustaf. II. United States. National Aeronautics and Space
  Administration. Scientific and Technical Information Office.
  III. Title. IV. Series: United States. National Aeronautics
  and Space Administration. NASA SP; 345.
  QB501.A528
  521/.54
  OCLC 2318404

But we also find in the MoCat listings such as the one below. This report was prepared by a private organization under a NASA contract, and is available *only* through NTIS:

Monthly Catalog (September 1976)

76-5519

NAS 1.26:2665

Wezernak, C.T.
  Spectral reflectance and radiance characteristics of water
pollutants/C.T. Wezernak, R.E. Turner, and D.R. Lyzenga:
prepared by Environmental Research Institute of Michigan,
Ann Arbor, Mich. for Langley Research Center--Washington
U.S. National Aeronautics and Space Administration;
Springfield Va.: for sale by the National Technical
Information Service, 1976.
    xiii, 218 p: ill.; 27 cm.--(NASA contractor report;
NASA CR-2665
    Cover title.
    Bibliography: p. 214-218.
    pbk: $7.75
    1. Water--Pollution. 2. Specular reflectance. 3. Or-
ganic water pollutants. I. Turner, R.E., jt. auth. II. Lyzen-
ga, D.R., jt. auth. III. Environmental Research Institute of
Michigan. IV. United States. Langley Research Center,
Hampton, Va. V. United States. National Aeronautics and
Space Administration. VI. Title. VII. Series: United States
National Aeronautics and Space Administration. NASA con-
tractor report; NASA CR-2665.

OCLC 2325731

The most charitable view one can summon concerning this sales, indexing, and distribution pattern is that it partakes of a Kafkaesque unreality.

Department of Energy

One of the large producers of information whose contract report literature found its way into the NTIS apparatus was the Atomic Energy Commission (AEC). It was abolished by the Energy Reorganization Act of 1974 (88 Stat. 1237; 42 U.S.C. 5814) and its functions transferred to the Energy Research and Development Administration and the Nuclear Regulatory Commission. While the Nuclear Regulatory Commission (NRC), an independent agency, awards contracts for research, its primary purpose is focused on the use of nuclear energy to generate electrical power, and it fulfills its responsibilities through a system of licencing and regulating nuclear reactors and other nuclear facilities. The Energy Research and Development Administration (ERDA), however, became the primary research entity for all other energy technologies. And during its brief life, ERDA registered reports with NTIS.

On August 4, 1977, the president signed PL 95-91 (91 Stat. 565; 42 U.S.C. 7101) establishing a Department of Energy (DOE) and bringing the number of Departments of the federal government up to twelve. On September 13, 1977, Executive Order 12009 was signed, prescribing October 1, 1977, the effective date of the Department of Energy Organization Act, and directing that the transfer of functions commence.

And quite a transfer it was! The new Department, pursuant to Title III of the Act, consolidated all functions of the Federal Energy Administration (FEA), Federal Power Commission (FPC), and ERDA, and these entities ceased to exist. Moreover, energy-related functions were transferred from the Departments of Interior, Housing and Urban Development (HUD), Transportation, Defense, and Commerce; and from two independent regulatory agencies, the Interstate Commerce Commission (ICC) and the Securities and Exchange Commission (SEC). And the Department of Energy will participate in the energy activities of other federal agencies such as the Rural Electrification Administration.

ERDA, FEA, and the FPC, as well as components of the Departments noted above, have been participating in the NTIS system, and energy-related research will continue to provide a large number of contract technical literature available through NTIS. And while GRA&I will provide the bibliographic apparatus for these reports, the *Monthly Catalog* will provide bibliographic control for publications produced by the DOE and its components. Indeed, *Daily Depository Shipping List 10,175* (September 23, 1977) in *Survey 77-257* offered to depository libraries the first DOE title in its General Publications series (E 1.2; Item 429-A). And *Shipping List 10,213* (October 4, 1977) carried the following announcement:

NEW CLASSES

The following Superintendent of Documents classification numbers will be used for publications of the Department of Energy and its subordinate administrations:

E 1.   Secretary of Energy
E 1.100   Office of Inspector General
E 2.   Federal Energy Regulatory Commission
E 3.   Energy Information Administration
E 4.   Economic Regulatory Administration

Individual classes will be assigned as the publications are received.

Energy Documentation

The major bibliographic tool now issued by the Department of Energy is *Energy Research Abstracts* (ERA), a semimonthly service that provides abstracting and indexing coverage of all scientific and technical reports, journal articles, conference papers, books, patents and theses originated by DOE, its laboratories, energy centers, and contractors. ERA is available on deposit (E 1.17; Item 474-A-6) and for sale from SuDocs. The subject matter includes all of DOE's research and development programs for energy systems and related technologies. Moreover, ERA covers other federally sponsored energy information and the international literature on reactor technology, waste processing and storage, fusion technology, and non-nuclear information obtained from foreign governments under agreements for cooperation.

ERA consists of a main entry section and indexes by personal author, corporate author, subject, and report number. The technical reports abstracted in ERA are largely available from NTIS, but some are available from SuDocs, the Technical Information Center in Oak Ridge, Tennessee, and elsewhere. Sources for ordering reports are listed in the report number index.

INIS Atomindex

For many years librarians and their public enjoyed the free use of *Nuclear Science Abstracts* (Y 3.At 7:16; Item 1051-A) through the depository library system. Issued by AEC, *Nuclear Science Abstracts* (NSA) was a semimonthly indexing/abstracting service for the literature of nuclear science and engineering. Quinquennial cumulative indexes were published by GPO and made available to depository libraries from 1948 to 1973.

The *Nuclear Science Abstracts* final issue was that of June 30, 1976 (Volume 33, Number 12). It was replaced by *INIS Atomindex*, which is published by the International Atomic Energy Agency (IAEA), one of the so-called specialized agencies within the United Nations family. *Atomindex* is a product of the International Nuclear Information System (INIS), which maintains a data base for IAEA and its member states identifying publications relating to nuclear science and its peaceful applications. *INIS Atomindex* is available for sale in the United States through UNIPUB, P.O. Box 433, Murray Hill Station, New York, N.Y. 10016.

A semimonthly abstracting journal, *INIS Atomindex* provides essentially the same literature coverage as did *Nuclear Science Abstracts.* When ERA was being issued under the provenance of the defunct ERDA, it was claimed that the literature coverage in *INIS Atomindex* did not duplicate the material indexed in ERA. However, the large amount of nuclear research reports listed in current issues of ERA suggests that there may be overlapping between the two indexes.

Each issue of *INIS Atomindex* consists of a main entry section and is indexed by subject, personal author, corporate author, report, standard and patent number. Entries are assigned a sequential reference number (RN) and arranged alphabetically by author within subject categories. Each entry consists of a bibliographic description, followed by an abstract or a set of descriptors. The subject headings under which the entry is indexed in the subject index are given at the end of each entry.

The big three—Defense, NASA, Energy—account for most of the technical reports in the NTIS bibliographic system and, as we have observed, most of them are not available in the depository library program. But other agencies that register reports with NTIS include the Environmental Protection Agency; National Science Foundation; independent entities like the Federal Trade Commission and the Federal Communications Commission; and components of the Departments of Agriculture; Commerce; Health, Education and Welfare; Housing and Urban Development; Interior; Labor; State; Treasury; and Transportation. Indeed, so vast is the bibliographic net cast by NTIS that overload is, if not a reality, then certainly an imminent danger. The Committee on Information Hang-Ups (CIH) in 1971 criticized NTIS's indexing in language that, if anything, is more applicable today: "We do not know what is in it [GRA&I] or what is not in it. Contents are not limited by subject or source ... and there is duplication of material indexed elsewhere.... The use of computer tapes from other information centers, as NTIS now uses them, makes an index that is too big and too inconsistent in bibliographic form.... The sheer bulk of the indices not only creates, but magnifies the importance of small errors, inconsistencies, and omissions."[21]

Joint Publications Research Service

Located in Springfield, Virginia, the Joint Publications Research Service (JPRS) selects, translates, and abstracts foreign language political and technical media for federal agencies. Most JPRS reports are concerned with publications in communist countries, though materials from all nations may be translated. About half of the reports are in the scientific and technical fields. A standing order service provides for the automatic mailing of reports on a continuing basis, as translations are completed. Subscribers must open an NTIS Deposit Account with a minimum deposit of $25, which may also be used to order any other NTIS products or services. Single copies of back issues are available. An index to JPRS translations is available from the Micro Photo Division of Bell & Howell. Called the Bell & Howell *TRANSDEX Index*, it comprises a keyword section, a names section, and a bibliographic listing section. In addition, the *Index* includes a brief section which correlates series titles with the specific document numbers.

In the past, JPRS publications were not a depository Item. But *Daily Depository Shipping List 10,368* (November 23, 1977), *Survey 77-333* offered JPRS series on microfiche (Y 3.J66:13/nos.) with Items 1067-L-(nos.). Initial series on this *Survey* included translations on Eastern Europe, Japan, Latin America, Western Europe, and Sub-Saharan Africa. Clearly, this represents a competition of sorts with NTIS. Curiously, JPRS serials are not available from NTIS in microfiche.

Foreign Broadcast Information Service

The March 1977 edition of the *List of Classes* indicates that only the four-part reference work *Broadcasting Stations of the World* is available to depository institutions from the Foreign Broadcast Information Service (FBIS). Its contents are described in Chapter 7. But NTIS offers a subscription to *FBIS Daily Reports*, which consists of translations and analyses of information collected daily from foreign broadcasts, news accounts, commentaries, newspapers, periodicals, and government statements published in the previous 48 to 72 hours.

NTIS subscription permits selective regional coverage or worldwide coverage; the geographical areas are similar to those covered in JPRS translations: China, the Soviet Union, Latin America, etc. Here the emphasis is on coverage of current political and social events. Subscription is either in paper copy or microfiche.

However, GPO invaded NTIS's territory in the distribution (but not the sale) of *FBIS Daily Report* series. *Daily Depository Shipping List 10,477* (*Survey 78-8*) of January 5, 1978, announced the availability to depository libraries of the *Daily Reports* on microfiche (PrEx 7.10; Items 856-B-nos.) covering Western Europe, Sub-Saharan Africa, the Soviet Union, People's Republic of China, Middle East and North Africa, Latin America, Eastern Europe, and Asia and the Pacific.

Library of Congress Photoduplication Service

The LC Photoduplication Service operates under a revolving fund to provide photoreproduction of material in the Library's collection for a fee. These services include "electrostatic positive prints, facsimile prints, 35mm microfilm negatives, 35mm microfilm positives, photoprints from 35mm microfilm, photographic negatives, photographic prints, view photographs, and blue line or black line prints. The Photoduplication Service also assists other units of the Library in preservation of their collections."[22]

Subject to copyright and other restrictions, the Service supplies photo-reproduction of materials to government agencies, institutions, and individuals. The time required for processing orders varies from a few days to several months depending on the size of the job, type of reproduction required, completeness of reference, and availability of material. Certain newspapers, periodicals, and government gazettes (primarily foreign titles) are microfilmed on a continuing basis.

Retrospective files of similar publications (including domestic titles), manuscript collections, etc., are filmed as special or cooperative projects. Research libraries can request that their name be placed on the mailing list to receive announcements of such filming projects.

Documents available from LC Photoduplication Service include microfilm of presidential papers (see Chapter 6) and early State records of the United States. Moreover, the Service is the custodian of "over 160,000 scientific and technical reports released through the Publication Board of the Department of Commerce as well as more than 46,000 [reports of the now-defunct Atomic Energy Commission] and 30,000 technical translations published prior to June 1, 1961."[23]

Educational Resources Information Center

The Educational Resources Information Center (ERIC) is operated by the National Institute of Education (NIE), an entity of the Department of Health, Education, and Welfare. ERIC was established by the U.S. Office of Education in the mid-1960s when the literature of education was relatively uncontrolled. At that time, research reports submitted to the Office of Education by contractors and grantees usually received scattered distribution and soon vanished. ERIC was designed to correct this situation by providing a more solid base for acceptance and use of worthwhile educational developments.

ERIC's data bank consists largely of "fugitive" educational materials which are not readily or easily located through the primary journals and their indexing tools. These include "noncopyrighted, unpublished educational materials such as project reports, speech texts, research findings, locally-produced materials, and conference proceedings."[24]

Because of the decentralized nature of U.S. education, ERIC consists of a network of clearinghouses integrated through a computerized facility known as ERIC Central in Washington, D.C. As of 1977 there were 16 clearinghouses, based primarily with universities and professional associations, each specializing in a particular subject area of education and responsible for collecting all relevant unpublished, noncopyrightable material of value in that area. "Virtually all observers of ERIC have concluded over time that the network of clearinghouses does a better job of ferreting out the current literature of education than one single information center in Washington could ever do."[25]

ERIC Services

ERIC units, in addition to the clearinghouses, include the ERIC Document Reproduction Service (EDRS), ERIC Processing and Reference Facility, and Macmillan Information.

EDRS

EDRS is located in Arlington, Virginia, and contracts to operate microfiche reproduction service for the ERIC system. All documents for which reproduction permission has been obtained and announced in *Resources in Education* are forwarded to EDRS where they are microfilmed and converted to microfiche. ERIC users can purchase documents available for sale from EDRS in either microfiche or paper copy. Because a number of libraries subscribe to the ERIC microfiche collection, EDRS issues annually a *Directory of ERIC Microfiche Collections*. It is organized by state and within state alphabetically by name of institution. The *Directory* includes all current subscribers, along with past subscribers whose collections cover a 2-year period or more.

ERIC Processing and Reference Facility

Under the policy direction of ERIC Central, the Processing and Reference Facility, located in Bethesda, Maryland, receives, edits and prepares abstracts from the clearinghouses to go into *Resources in Education*. In addition, the Facility monitors changes and additions to the ERIC *Thesaurus* and publishes the *ERIC Data Base Users' Interchange*, which contains information, ideas, papers and commentaries to regular users of ERIC; *Interchange* is free and is issued irregularly.

Macmillan Information

Macmillan Information, a division of the Macmillan Publishing Company (New York City), publishes a number of ERIC-related items, including the *Thesaurus of ERIC Descriptors, Current Index to Journals in Education, ERIC Educational Documents Abstracts*, and *ERIC Educational Documents Index*. In addition, Macmillan Information issues *ERIC Bibliographies*, which provide access to all documents processed by ERIC on a given subject.

Bibliographic Tools

The amalgam of information aids provided by both public and private sectors is evident in ERIC, for the federal government, Macmillan, and Prentice-Hall are or have been involved in the ERIC enterprise.

Resources in Education (HE 19.210; Item 466-A) is a monthly indexing/ abstracting service which is both available for sale through SuDocs and to depository institutions. Formerly known as *Research in Education*, it indexes and abstracts the documents in the ERIC system. There are semi-annual indexes.

Resources in Education (RIE) is indexed by subject, author, institution, and clearinghouse number/ED-number cross referenced. About 80 percent of material cited in each issue is available from EDRS in either microfiche or photocopy format. The remaining 20 percent is available from the publisher or issuing source of the document. Also included in the monthly issues are new thesaurus terms, other ERIC products, and sections on how to order ERIC publications and documents. Figure 10 shows a sample entry with an explanation of the several bibliographic units. The ERIC accession number, an "ED-number," is sequentially assigned to documents as they are processed.

Figure 10

RESOURCES IN EDUCATION: SAMPLE ENTRY

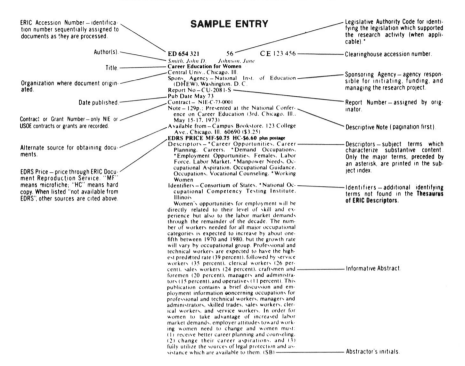

*The key to these codes is as follows:

Code	Description	Code	Description
08	Adult and Vocational Education, Public Law 88–210	52	Library Research and Development, Public Law 89–320, Title II, Part B
16	Captioned Films for the Deaf, Public Law 85–905	56	New Educational Media, Public Law 85–864, Title VII, Part A
24	Cooperative Research, Public Law 89–10, Title IV	64	New Education Media, Public Law 85–864, Title VII, Part B
32	Disadvantaged Students Program, Public Law 89–10, Title I	72	Research in Foreign Countries, Public Law 83–480
40	Handicapped Children and Youth, Public Law 88–164	80	State Educational Agencies Experimental Activities, Public Law 89–10, Title V. Section 505
48	Language Development, Public Law 85–864, Title VI	88	Supplementary Centers and Services, Public Law 88–10, Title III
		95	Other Office of Education Programs

Current Index to Journals in Education (CIJE) is a monthly indexing/ abstracting service published by Macmillan Information, with semi-annual cumulations. Because RIE was unable to incorporate the vast amount of literature on education published in journals, CIJE was created for that purpose. It is devoted exclusively to the periodical literature, and it covers over 700 publications.

All articles listed in CIJE are indexed by one of the 16 ERIC clearinghouses or by Macmillan Information. Citations to journals in a particular issue of CIJE represent the titles received by the various processing centers during the month previous to publication. CIJE is compiled by means of computer manipulation of the data received from the ERIC clearinghouse.

CIJE's main entry section is arranged alphabetically and numerically by clearinghouse accession number, an identification of the specific clearinghouse that was responsible for preparing the bibliographic citation and assigning the indexing terms. A list of ERIC clearinghouses and their identifying letter codes can be found on the inside of the front cover of the CIJE issues. Descriptive terms preceded by an asterisk (*) represent *descriptors* (sometimes called subject headings) which are listed in the subject index. Bracketed items are additional identifying terms not found in the *Thesaurus of ERIC Descriptors.* Following the descriptors are annotations or résumés which briefly describe the article; these are compiled at the various processing centers in the ERIC network.

In addition to its main entry section, CIJE is indexed by subject, author, and "journal contents." A journal article may be listed under as many as five descriptors in the subject index. Authors' names are given in full when available. If co-authors are responsible for the article, both names are indexed. If more than two authors are given with the article, only the first author is indexed. The journal contents index is arranged alphabetically by journal title and date; each article listed is in EJ (*ERIC Journal*) accession number sequence. In addition to the indexes, there is a list of new thesaurus terms in each issue of CIJE.

University Microfilms International (UMI) provides a reprint service for many of the journals indexed in CIJE. There is a standard price for each article and it must be prepaid; deposit accounts are available.

In addition to the two major indexes, RIE and CIJE, a principal ERIC reference tool is the *Thesaurus of ERIC Descriptors.* Published by Macmillan Information,[26] it is the source of subject headings used in RIE and CIJE and provides the system for retrieving document and journal citations in ERIC collections. Since the most common search method of ERIC is a "subject" approach, the use of the controlled vocabulary, by means of "terms" which appear in the *Thesaurus,* is a valid way of quickly doing a manual search.

Moreover, computer searches in the ERIC system must be translated into ERIC descriptors using the *Thesaurus* and set up using Boolean connectors. Computer searches are available from many university libraries, state departments of education, educational information centers, research centers, commercial organizations, and from some of the ERIC clearinghouses. A list of the ERIC data base search services is available from User Service Coordinator, ERIC Processing and Reference Facility, Bethesda, Maryland.

Other guides to ERIC include *ERIC Educational Documents Abstracts,* which is a multi-volume series that brings together all the summaries of the report literature selected by the clearinghouses for indexing and listing in RIE; *ERIC Educational Documents Index* are multi-volume subject-author indexes providing titles and identification/accession numbers to the documents and report literature announced in the monthly issues of RIE. Both are available from Macmillan Information in hard copy volumes.

Complete Guide and Index to ERIC Reports Thru December 1969 (Englewood Cliffs, N.J.: Prentice-Hall, 1970), a one-volume work, serves primarily as a cumulative index to ERIC literature on curricula, educational media, and teaching methods. The work is indexed by subject (ED number), author, clearinghouse number (referencing the ED number) and numerical title (by ED number).

RIE, MoCat, and GRA&I

Because the vast bulk of documentation that finds its way into the ERIC system is not issued by RIE, very little would be expected to appear in the *Monthly Catalog.* As noted, however, RIE itself is sold through SuDocs and made available to depository institutions. The March 1977 edition of the *List of Classes* showed that the ERIC Clearinghouse for Social Studies issues a Social Sciences Educational Interpretive Series (HE 18.13; Item 461-D-4), which was not abolished according to the March 1977 *Inactive or Discontinued Items* . . . list. But it is clear that for ERIC materials one would consult RIE or CIJE.

Peculiarly, some material on education finds its way into GRA&I. Documents indexed under "education" in the subject index portion of *Government Reports Annual Index* fall "discreetly" into COSATI Field 5, group structure "Personnel Selection, Training, and Evaluation." As Meredith notes, "During one period, NTIS took in 103 such documents, while ERIC processed 12,339, so the incursion is numerically insignificant."[27] Two examples of materials appropriate to RIE but found in GRA&I follow:

```
Will the Real Community College Stand Up.
PB 234 955/3GI   74-22 5I PC$8.75/MF$2.25

Early Childhood Education in Yugoslavia:
A Special Issue of Selected Bibliography
of Yugoslav Educational Materials.
TT-73-56029   74-24   5I   PC$3.25/MF$2.25
```

The latter, being a technical translation, can be justified somewhat more rationally than the former.

Of importance to students of library science and to professional librarians is the ERIC Clearinghouse on Information Resources (IR). On January 1, 1977, this clearinghouse moved from Stanford University's School of Education to the School of Education at Syracuse University. Applicable areas include "management, standards, operation, and use of libraries and information centers, the technology to improve their operations, and the education, training, and professional activities of librarians and information specialists."[28]

Background Readings

Useful information in the professional literature on ERIC and related activities includes the following:

Joshua I. Smith, "Documents Processing at ERIC/CLIS," *Illinois Libraries* 56: 266-68 (April 1974) is a discussion of the basic structure of ERIC by a former director of the ERIC Clearinghouse on Library and Information Science. Bernard M. Fry and Eva L. Kiewitt, "The Educational Resources Information Center: Its Legal Basis, Organization, Distribution System, Bibliographic Controls," *Drexel Library Quarterly* 10: 63-78 (January-April 1974), as the title suggests, discusses the genesis of ERIC and its several functions. Robert Roth, "Educational Resources Information Center," *Government Publications Review* 1: 183-85 (Winter 1973) concentrates on the functions of EDRS and the ERIC Processing and Reference Facility. "Understanding ERIC," *American Libraries* 7: 532-33 (September 1976) is a brief account of ERIC services.

Documents Expediting Project

Located within the Exchange and Gift Division, Processing Department, Library of Congress, the Documents Expediting Project (DocEx) provides member libraries a centralized service for acquiring non-depository publications not available for purchase either through GPO or from the issuing agency. DocEx tries to avoid duplicating the distribution policies of other agencies. For example, it does not distribute what NTIS sells, while NTIS does not sell what the Expediter distributes. If an issuing agency offers a publication for sale, DocEx does not include it in its acquisitions policy. And Items made available to depository libraries usually do not get included in what DocEx supplies.

Each library chooses its own subscription rate which, in 1976, ranged from $225 to $750 annually in increments of $25. A subscription entitles member libraries to all publications distributed by DocEx. But when the Project is unable to obtain enough copies of a publication for the entire membership, those libraries paying the higher rates receive the available copies.

DocEx advertises its services by claiming to secure elusive publications of agencies, thus saving librarians time and effort in writing the issuing entities and searching lists and specialized bibliographies. In 1973 the Library Division of the Superintendent of Documents reported that "all government publications received from the Documents Expediter are entered in the *Monthly Catalog* unless the publication is considered for administrative use or internal use only. Contract reports issued by non-Government agencies, for the most part, are not entered in the *Catalog* unless the publication clearly indicates the Government office is the publisher, and claims the document as its own publication."[29] Nevertheless, the Work Group on Bibliographic Control, Federal Documents Task Force (GODORT), continued to show concern about the failure of the MoCat to list many publications distributed by DocEx. In reply to inquiries, the chief of the Exchange and Gift Division, in a letter dated August 18, 1975, stated that "we have been sending copies of all these publications to the SuDocs Library after holding them to first make sure that they are not duplicated by the receipts of our Federal Documents Section and to remove the excepted categories which have not been listed by the *Monthly Catalog*."[30] The excepted categories remain the two noted above.

Examples of publications that have been issued by DocEx to subscribers include many monographs and speeches from different agencies, the annual reports of the Bonneville Power Administration and Federal Reserve System, Smithsonian

Institution research reports, and the CIA's *Reference Aid* series (discussed in Chapter 7). Moreover, DocEx will endeavor to fill special requests for non-current federal publications, those that may be out of print or the elusive "last copy" of a scarce item.

There is an irony to the DocEx operation. Whether consciously or not, the GPO conspires to erode the Project's capability. At the prompting of GODORT, the Depository Library Council, and other interested groups, GPO continues to expand its offerings to depository institutions; and every new Item offered potentially reduces what DocEx can supply. For example, a list of DocEx titles and groups of publications issued in April 1974 showed that among the publications offered through DocEx were Congressional committee prints, Senate executive documents, and Senate executive reports.[31] But the Senate executive documents and reports were made a depository Item in 1977, and the number of committee prints available to depository institutions has risen.

Indeed, if all committee prints were released for depository distribution, DocEx would be deprived of its most marketable commodity. Note this interesting statement from the 1976 *Annual Report of the Librarian of Congress*:

> The Documents Expediting Project suffered a net loss of seven member libraries, despite the fact that Stanford University, Yale University, the Air University, and one law firm joined the project. Most of the defections appear to have been prompted by the change in GPO policy under which many congressional committee prints were made depository items for the first time. Before that, membership in the project was virtually the only means of ensuring some measure of coverage for these publications.[32]

In fact, fewer than 50 percent of the total number of unclassified prints were available to depository libraries by the end of 1977. And the statement is incorrect in its claim that "membership in [DocEx] was virtually the only means of ensuring some measure of coverage for [prints]": *CIS Microfiche Library* supplies the most comprehensive coverage of committee prints.

But it is true that GPO "competes" with DocEx. Perhaps the *Annual Report* of the National Fertilizer Development Center, Tennessee Valley Authority, will never become a depository Item, but even that probability is suspect. The first phase of the GPO micropublishing program involves "non-GPO Depository" titles, that is, publications "that are procured or produced by agencies in either their own printing plants or purchased through sources other than GPO. . . . It is expected that about 6,000 such titles will be converted [to a microfiche format for distribution to depository libraries] during the first year of the program."[33] This strikes at the heart of the DocEx program, and bids fair to reduce greatly the quantity it distributes.

Readex Microprint Corporation

Unlike the other sources discussed in this chapter, Readex Microprint Corporation has no direct connection with the federal government. Although it is one of many commercial firms engaged in the business of reproducing federal documents for sale, it enjoys a history of supplying libraries with non-depository publications virtually unique in its field.

Since 1953 Readex has been making all non-depository publications listed in the *Monthly Catalog* available in its microprint edition. According to Readex's 1977 catalog, a subscription to the 1976 non-depository collection sold for $3,300, but because of an increase in the number of publications listed in the "new" MoCat, Readex set the 1976 subscription at a per-card price of $0.30. The project is a cooperative venture involving the Library Division of the Superintendent, the Documents Expediting Project, and the LC Photoduplication Service. The materials are arranged by the Library Division in the order in which they appear in the *Monthly Catalog*; then they are forwarded to the LC Photoduplication Service where they are filmed at Readex's expense. Thus the *Monthly Catalog* entry number serves as the basic unit of bibliographic control, and the *Monthly Catalog* serves as a book catalog for accessing the microprint collection.

Microprint comes to libraries in plastic boxes in the shape and size of a royal octavo volume (6½x10-inches), and is shelved in the same manner as books; no special equipment is needed for storage. Specifications for paper and printing to insure archival permanence are set forth by the U.S. National Bureau of Standards. The Readex Universal Micro-Viewer provides magnification, while the Dennison-Readex Unitform Enlarger-Printer produces enlarged electrostatic copies from the microform.

Since 1956 Readex has been offering all depository publications listed in the *Monthly Catalog* in their microprint edition. Moreover, Readex has filmed the following federal series, which can be purchased as separates or in various groupings:

U.S. Serial Set, 1789– [34]

U.S. Surgeon-General's Office Index-Catalogue

House and Senate Bills, 1957-1965
Congressional Hearings and Committee Prints, 1956–

JPRS Reports 1958– (Those entered in MoCat only)

In addition, Readex offers in separate units the publications of over 70 agencies, including serials like the *Federal Register* and the Patent Office *Official Gazette*. Separate units combine all depository and non-depository publications of the issuing agency entered in the *Monthly Catalog*, as well as the periodicals and other serials (subscription services) listed in the *Serials Supplement* (1977) or the February issue of the MoCat. An *Index to U.S. Government Serials (1950-1960) as Published by Readex Microprint Corporation* was compiled under the direction of Margaret Rich and was made available to Readex subscribers by the company.[35]

SUMMARY

The provisions of Title 44 of the *United States Code*, however vague or indirect their language, suggest that publications produced by an agency or instrumentality of government or at government expense, and having public interest or educational value, are to be made available to depository libraries. However, as we noted in Chapter 3, the majority of documents produced by agencies in their own printing plants or by contract have not yet found their way into the depository system. Moreover, the enormous amount of technical report literature, funded by government, is excluded from the depository system by virtue of its so-called "cooperative" status. And there is no doubt, in the judgment of the library community, that some of the latter do possess public interest and do have educational value. When we couple the precluding legislation of Title 44 with the enabling legislation of Title 15 of the *United States Code*, the result is a hodgepodge of multiple distribution, sales, and bibliographic confusion.

What, then, can be done? Pursuant to the approval of the Depository Library Microform Project by Senator Cannon, *Government Printing Office Instruction 565.1* (September 30, 1977) set forth regulations by which "non-GPO" titles can be brought into the depository system by conversion to microfiche format. This will help to solve one part of the problem.

In order to bring appropriate cooperative publications into the system, existing legislation must be amended. During the meeting of the Depository Library Council to the Public Printer in October 1977, a draft of proposed amendments to Title 44 of the *United States Code* was circulated. Prepared by the ALA Ad Hoc Committee on Federal Depository Legislation, the proposed amendments included a change in 44 U.S.C. 1903. The Committee recommended deleting the language that exempts cooperative publications from the system, to wit, *"but not so-called cooperative publications which must necessarily be sold in order to be self-sustaining."* The Committee's explanation follows:

> It is suggested that the underlined part of the above sentence be deleted. Many so-called cooperative publications, such as those sold by service agencies like ERIC and NTIS, contain extremely important information which should not, by law, be kept from depository libraries. Such publications are generally tax-supported in part (usually the research or writing of the document), which should justify their being supplied to GPO by the issuing agency for distribution to depository libraries and free access for the public.

44 U.S.C. 1911 states in part that depository libraries "shall make Government publications available for the free use of the general public." Unfortunately, the current situation does not reflect that grand design.

REFERENCES

1. LeRoy C. Schwarzkopf, "The *Monthly Catalog* and Bibliographic Control of U.S. Government Publications," *Drexel Library Quarterly* 10: 87-88 (January-April 1974).

2. When the *Monthly Catalog*'s July 1976 issue first appeared in its new LC format, the black dot was missing in the entry. At the insistence of depository librarians, it was restored with the April 1977 issue.

3. Bernadine E. Hoduski, "The Federal Depository Library System: What Is Its Basic Job?" *Drexel Library Quarterly* 10: 111 (January-April 1974).

4. *United States Government Manual, 1976/77*, p. 149.

5. *NTISearch* (NTIS-PR-186, June 1977), p. c.

6. DttP 3: 41 (November 1975).

7. DttP 5: 200 (September 1977).

8. DttP 3: 41-42 (November 1975).

9. The bimonthly *NTIS Search* is a depository Item (188-A-1), but WGA, while carrying a SuDocs class number (C 51.9/nos.), is not available to depository libraries.

10. DttP 3: 37, 40-41 (November 1975).

11. Meredith, pp. 344-46 *et passim.*

12. Ibid., pp. 357-58.

13. William T. Knox, "Special Libraries and NTIS," *Special Libraries* 67: 45-48 (January 1976); letter, Irving M. Klempner, *Special Libraries* 67: 397-400 (August 1976); defense by Knox, *Special Libraries* 68: 6A-7A (April 1977); rebuttal by Klempner, *Special Libraries* 68: 6A (May/June 1977).

14. Catherine Ettlinger, "NTIS: The Nation's Biggest Publisher," *Government Executive* (February 1974), p. 48.

15. "New Plan for NTIS?" *American Libraries* 5: 285-86 (June 1974).

16. *United States Government Manual, 1977/78*, pp. 229-30.

17. Herman W. Miles and Joan L. Sweeney, "Dialog with Defense Documentation Center," *Special Libraries* 67: 499 (November 1976).

18. Robert H. Rea, "The Defense Documentation Center," *Drexel Library Quarterly* 10: 23 (January-April 1974).

19. Meredith, p. 346.

20. Ibid. Meredith found that 32 percent of the total documentation in a typical issue of GRA&I consists of reports channeled through the Defense Documentation Center.

21. Quoted in Fass, p. 136.

22. U.S. Congress. Joint Committee on Congressional Operations. *Inventory of Information Resources for the U.S. House of Representatives*, Committee Print, 94th Cong., 2d Sess., 1976, p. 49.

23. U.S. Library of Congress. *A Directory of Information Resources in the United States Federal Government* (LC 1.31:D62/4/974; Item 787-A), p. 225.

24. James W. Brown, et al., *ERIC: What It Can Do for You/How to Use It* (Stanford Center for Research and Development in Teaching, School of Education, Stanford University: Stanford, California, January 1977), p. 1.

25. Robert Roth, "Educational Resources Information Center," *Government Publications Review* 1: 183 (Winter 1973).

26. *Daily Depository Shipping List 9194* (October 4, 1976) noted that the "sixth edition of *Thesaurus of ERIC Descriptors* is now being published by Macmillan Information. It is not being financed by accountable public funds and cannot be made a depository distribution item."

27. Meredith, pp. 345-46.

28. *ERIC: What It Can Do for You/How to Use It*, p. 5.

29. DttP 1: 9 (September 1973).

30. DttP 4: 35 (May 1976).

31. *Proceedings of the Senate Executive Journal*, which are printed in very limited quantity, are available through DocEx.

32. *Report of the Librarian of Congress* (LC 1.1:976; Item 785), p. 6.

33. *Government Printing Office Instruction 565.1* (September 30, 1977), pp. 1-2.

34. As of 1977 the Serial Set groups covered the period 1789-1935; Readex announces succeeding groups as issued.

35. Margaret Rich, "Indexing of Serial Publications in the Readex Microprint Collection of U.S. Government Documents," *Government Publications Review* 3: 109-111 (1976).

5

SELECTED GENERAL GUIDES TO FEDERAL PUBLICATIONS

When the members of the Joint Committee on Printing of the 47th Congress commenced the direction of the work thus entrusted to them, they were in the position of Christopher Columbus when he steered westward on his voyage of discovery, confident that a new world existed, but having no knowledge of its distance or the direction in which it lay. . . . On the first of March, 1883, the work was placed under the superintendence of the subscriber, with directions to follow the plan approved by the committee, and to employ fourteen gentlemen, who were designated. . . . Unfortunately, not one of the clerks employed possessed any experience in the performance of such work, and some proved to be so entirely incompetent that no use could be made of what they did; but by the patient and diligent application of the others, 63,063 books, pamphlets, and documents were found and catalogued.

> —Preface to Ben Perley Poore's *Descriptive Catalogue of the Government Publications of the United States, September 5, 1774-March 4, 1881* (48th Cong., S. misc. doc. 67)

INTRODUCTION

The bibliographic apparatus of United States public documents is as complex and variegated as the unwieldy corpus of materials it attempts to encompass. Indexes, lists, guides, bibliographies, whatever the name assigned to them, exhibit—like the complex materials they enumerate—a pattern that is irregular and often confusing. This should come as no surprise to the user of federal public documents. The bibliographic enterprise always falls short of its ideal.

A note of optimism, however, must be sounded when one compares recent bibliographic enterprises with early nineteenth century endeavors. In part the history of current federal indexing and bibliographic publishing, especially in the private sector, has been an attempt—largely successful—to correct the errors and omissions of former bibliography while enhancing the whole.

We have come a long way since Ben Perley Poore compared his task, in the above quote, to that of "Christopher Columbus when he steered westward on his voyage of discovery." Developments in micropublishing and computer-generated information have created a revolution in bibliographic control and retrieval. Fortunately, government publications have come within the purview of our present technological expertise. And not a moment too soon. For the publishing activities of the federal establishment are worldwide in scope, and the subject matter is universal. No theme, however fey, antic, arcane or ostensibly inapposite, remains far from the omniverous curiosity of government. By definition, the bibliographic "ideal" is unattainable, but attempts to achieve it are not the less noble.

This chapter will survey some of the more important retrospective and current guides that purport to organize this vast and bewildering mass of information.

Background Sources

Even a list of guides to the guides cannot claim to be complete. Outstanding earlier resources include Anne M. Boyd, *United States Government Publications* (3d ed. rev. by Rae E. Rips; New York: Wilson, 1949), and Laurence F. Schmeckebier and Roy B. Eastin, *Government Publications and Their Use* (2d rev. ed.; Washington: Brookings, 1969). A comprehensive, annotated guide is John Brown Mason, *Research Resources: Annotated Guide to the Social Sciences, Volume 2* (Santa Barbara, Calif.: ABC-Clio, 1971). James Bennett Childs, "Government Publications (Documents)," in Allen Kent, et al., (eds.) *Encyclopedia of Library and Information Science, Vol. 10* (New York: Marcel Dekker, 1973) presents an excellent summary of United States government publications in his survey of the bibliographic structure of worldwide government publishing.

The literature of librarianship contains numerous articles about federal government publications. Important collected issues include the July 1966 *Library Trends*; the June 1971 issue of *Illinois Libraries*; the January-April 1974 issue of *Drexel Library Quarterly*; and the April 1974 issue of *Illinois Libraries. Documents to the People* and *Government Publications Review* are periodicals devoted entirely to the publications and activities of governments at all levels. Indeed, the decade of the 1970s has witnessed a dramatic increase in the attention toward and interest in the publications of federal and other governmental entities.[1]

Of recent interest and importance are two guides which supply invaluable bibliographic information for anyone working with government publications. Both sources go beyond federal publications to include state, local, and international documents.

Draft Syllabus of Resources for
Teaching Government Publications

The Education Task Force of GODORT, under the direction of Coordinator M. Dean Trivette, assembled a highly useful guide to government documents. The section on federal publications (pp. 21-67) includes citations to abstracting and indexing services, background readings, cataloging and classification, depository library system, Congress, laws, maps, microforms, and many more topics. Issued to GODORT members in 1976 in hard copy, it is available from ERIC in both bound copy and microfiche (ED 125 668; IR 003 784).

Government Publications: A Guide to Bibliographic Tools

The fourth edition of this guide was published by the Library of Congress in 1975 and made available for sale by the Superintendent of Documents. Prepared by Vladimir M. Palic, it is the latest edition of what was begun by James Bennett Childs in 1927 under the title *An Account of Government Document Bibliography in the United States and Elsewhere.* It is noted in the "Foreword" to this edition that "Childs' was a 78-page pamphlet containing approximately 400 entries whereas this book of over 400 pages cites more than 3,000 titles."

Part I covers federal government publications (pp. 11-80) and includes guides and general bibliographies, Congress, the departments and agencies, and the Supreme Court. The index includes selected personal and corporate authors, titles of works, names of geographical areas, and names of international governmental organizations.

Some of the sources that follow will be brought up again in later chapters as their significance impels more detailed analysis. Other important instruments of bibliographic control not included in this section will be given coverage in the chapters that ensue, for the bibliographic mosaic must be assembled piece by piece.

CATALOGS, INDEXES, AND CHECKLISTS

Government Documents

Poore

Pursuant to a law enacted in 1882, which authorized the preparation of a "Descriptive Catalogue of all publications made by the authority of the government of the United States and the preceding government of the Colonies, and all departments, bureaus and offices thereof, from July 4, 1776 to March 4, 1881,"[2] Ben Perley Poore and a ragtag group of helpers assembled "the first and only attempt to make a complete list of all government publications—executive, legislative, and judicial";[3] the result was a *Descriptive Catalogue of the Government Publications of the United States, September 5, 1774-March 4, 1881.* The volume was 1,392 pages, consisting of 1,241 pages of catalog and 151 pages of index. The index was euphemistically deemed "far from complete or satisfactory. It is sufficient to condemn it to state that there are no cross references."[4] Moreover, Poore's *Catalogue* omitted many departmental publications.

Poore's is arranged according to the publication's date of issue. Each entry is annotated, but the chronological format mandates a superior index. Because of the lack of differentiation and specificity in the index, the *Catalogue* is a time-consuming drudgery to use. First issued as Senate Miscellaneous Document 67, 48th Congress, Poore's *Catalogue* has since been reissued in a 1962 Johnson reprint.

Greely

Adolphus Washington Greely was a soldier, scientist, and arctic explorer who published works on meteorological, electrical, and geographical subjects, and who found time to supervise a compilation of congressional publications for the early Congresses. Entitled *Public Documents of the First Fourteen Congresses, 1789-1817—Papers Relating to Early Congressional Documents*, it was issued in one volume as Senate Document 428, 56th Congress, 1st session. A supplement was published in Volume 1 of the *Annual Report* of the American Historical Association for 1903; the two studies were reprinted in one volume by Johnson in 1963.

Although there is some overlapping with Poore, Greely's list pertains to publications of Congress and not necessarily to those ordered compiled or printed by Congress. Arrangement is chronological by Congress, followed by a 45-page index of names (but not subjects). The compiler endeavored to give a complete listing for the period 1789-1817, but there are many omissions; no attempt was made to include departmental publications as such.

Checklist

After Ames (see below) had directed and supervised the publication of two earlier editions of a checklist for both departmental and congressional publications, the Superintendent of Documents in 1911 issued the *Checklist of United States Public Documents, 1789-1909* (Kraus reprint, 1962). The *Checklist* reproduced the shelflist of the Public Document Department Library. It is arranged in three sections: congressional edition by serial number; departmental edition by SuDocs class number; and miscellaneous publications of Congress. Planned in two volumes, the index volume was never issued. Librarians and those conversant with government structure are best equipped to handle this source. The failure of earlier compilers to include departmental documents is significantly remedied by the *Checklist*.

Tables and Index

Picking up where Greely stopped, the *Tables of and Annotated Index to the Congressional Series of United States Public Documents* was published in 1902 (Mark Press reprint, 1963) and lists publications of the 15th to the 52d Congresses,

1817-1893. The first section of the book, the "Tables," gives series information, with notes on contents and on omission or duplication in the Serial Set. The second section, the "Index," is a useful reference by subject and name, with the accompanying serial number of the bound congressional set.[5]

The index is deliberately selective, covering little more than 50 percent of the numbered *documents* and *reports* issued from 1817 to 1893. The compilers expressed their disdain for many congressional materials. In the preface it is noted that an effort was made "to extricate the more important documents from the scattered mass of worthless matter which composes nearly one half the congressional set."[6] Like Greely's compilation, the *Tables and Index* includes only congressional publications. However, because many executive publications were issued in their "Congressional edition," the guide has limited usefulness in this area. The peculiarities of issuing publications in more than one edition will be discussed in the next chapter.

Ames

Poore's comprehensive general catalog included publications up to 1881, and John Griffith Ames carried the listing from that year to 1893, the first edition covering the years 1889-1893. Ames, who was the Superintendent of Documents in the Interior Department, called his second edition *Comprehensive Index to the Publications of the United States Government.* It was brought out in 1905 in two volumes (issued as House Document 754, 58th Congress, 2d session; Edwards reprint, 1953, 2 volumes in 1). But, like Poore, Ames omitted a number of departmental publications. Arrangement is alphabetical by subject with a personal name index at the end of volume 2. The usefulness of the index, as opposed to Poore's, is manifest: subordinate sections of a book are indexed separately, and serial numbers are given in tables under the subject "Congressional Documents" in volume 1.

Document Catalog

Covering the years 1893-1940, this biennial work, whose title was *Catalogue of the Public Documents of the ... Congress and of All Departments of the Government of the United States for the Period from March 4, 1893 to December 31, 1940,* is an analytic dictionary catalog. It represents the first truly systematic effort to record public documents issued by the federal establishment.

The *Document Catalog* is a joy to use. Entries are under both personal and governmental authors, subject, and frequently title. It includes a complete list of executive orders issued during the period covered. Proclamations are listed, as are periodicals that were issued regularly. Processed as well as printed documents made available to the Superintendent are included, but no claim to completeness is made for the processed materials. A list of government offices appears at the end of each catalog to serve as a guide to government organization. Beginning with the 56th Congress, the serial number was included in brackets to permit easy access to the bound volumes of the Serial Set.

For all its accuracy, however, the *Document Catalog* was doomed by a fatal dose of overenthusiasm in the 1895 legislation, which mandated the publishing of the *Monthly Catalog* during the very years when the *Document Catalog* was being compiled. From the beginning it was three years late in appearing; World War I retarded publication of its biennial editions to the extent that they appeared nine years after the close of the Congress covered. It was finally discontinued with Volume 25, issued in 1947 but covering the 76th Congress (1939-1940).

Document Index

An alphabetical subject (or inverted title) listing for the congressional documents and reports only, the full title was *Index to the Reports and Documents of the . . . Congress, with Numerical Lists and Schedule of Volumes, 1897-1933*. Libraries that have the *Document Catalog* rarely need to use this sessional tool, unless the client has only the number of the document or report. This publication was superseded by the *Numerical Lists and Schedules of Volumes*.

Numerical Lists

The *Numerical Lists and Schedule of Volumes* is simply that section of the *Document Index* consisting of the reports and documents in numbered sequence (the "Lists"), and a grouping of numbered reports and documents by volumes (the "Schedule") of the congressional set. Since 1933 the *Numerical Lists* has been the main *sessional* key to the bound volumes known as the Serial Set. Lists and schedules for an entire Congress were included in the biennial *Document Catalog*, but owing to its increasingly tardy appearance, libraries that subscribed to the Serial Set needed a more prompt key. With the discontinuance of the *Document Catalog*, the *Numerical Lists* and the *Monthly Catalog* now furnish the information necessary to pursue the congressional *reports* and *documents*. Because of its essential value in this respect, the *Numerical Lists* will be considered in more detail in the next chapter.

Monthly Catalog

Current use of this basic source was discussed in Chapter 2. Historically, the *Monthly Catalog* was created by the Printing Act of 1895, wherein the Superintendent of Documents was directed "to prepare and publish a Monthly Catalog of Government publications, which shall show the publications printed during a month, where obtainable, and the price thereof." However, the same Act instructed the Superintendent "to prepare and print at the close of each Congress a Comprehensive Index [*Document Catalog*] of public documents [and] to prepare and print at the close of each regular session of Congress a Consolidated Index [*Document Index*] of congressional documents."[7] Thus the *Monthly Catalog* was to remedy the haphazard system of distribution and sales and provide "a reasonably early notice of all works printed by the government and how they could be obtained."[8] The *Document Catalog*, a "retrospective" tool virtually from its inception, was to be the exemplary bibliographic achievement. But as the cost of compiling and printing the biennial work grew ever more burdensome, and as the *Monthly Catalog* improved its coverage,[9] however slowly, the Superintendent was compelled to re-examine both programs. Upon his recommendation to the Joint Committee on Printing, the latter index became the single official source of publications as mandated by Section 62 of the 1895 Printing Act.

A privately published work in ten volumes known as *Hickcox's Monthly Catalogue* was the precursor of the monthly publication.[10] Between 1941 and 1947 three supplements to the *Monthly Catalog* were issued "to cover publications which had been omitted from the *Monthly Catalog* and which would have appeared in the biennial *Document Catalog.*"[11] The internal improvements beginning with the September 1947 issue, the re-emergence of personal authors in 1963, the decennial indexes and, of course, the great evolution of the MoCat beginning with the July 1976 issue—all have been measures designed to make the *Monthly Catalog* a guide fully justifying the discontinuance of the *Document Catalog*. But those who mourn the demise of the magnificent *Document Catalog* are not wholly irrational in their grief.

The foregoing attempts to place the general catalogs, indexes and checklists in chronological sequence by period covered, an arrangement that is graphically presented in Table 2; the works are referred to by popular (short) title. Another perspective on the sequence is shown below.[12]

Executive *and* Congressional Publications	Congressional Publications only
Poore	Greely
Ames	Tables and Index
Checklist	Document Index
Document Catalog	Numerical Lists
Monthly Catalog	

Because of the limitations inherent in each of these resources, the librarian will often have to direct the client to more than one source, especially if the client is seeking citations prior to 1893. Moreover, the only way to become familiar with the construction of the early indexes and lists is through much practice in the working situation.

Table 2

CHRONOLOGY OF OFFICIAL GENERAL CATALOGS, INDEXES AND CHECKLISTS

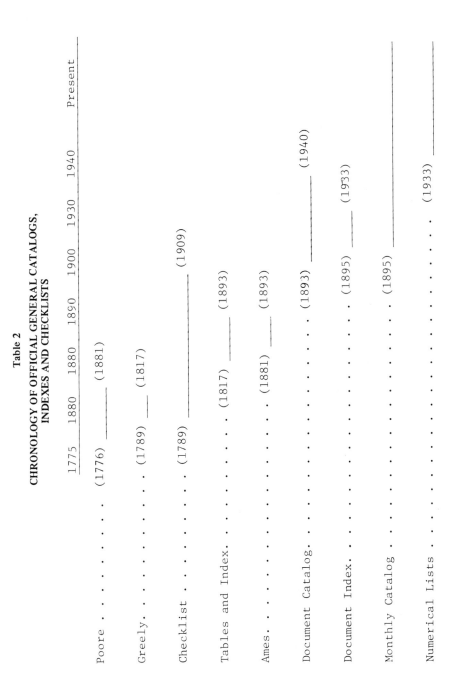

	1775	1880	1880	1890	1900	1930	1940	Present
Poore	(1776) ——— (1881)							
Greely	(1789) ——— (1817)							
Checklist	(1789) ——————— (1909)							
Tables and Index	(1817) ——— (1893)							
Ames	(1881) ——— (1893)							
Document Catalog	(1893) ——————— (1940)							
Document Index	(1895) ——— (1933)							
Monthly Catalog	(1895) ————————————							
Numerical Lists	(1933) ————————————							

Commercial Publications

Never has the rectification of shortcomings in the several guides noted above been more diligently pursued than in the last few years. The following commercial firms and their publications demonstrate significantly and, indeed in some cases, spectacularly, the bibliographic endeavors toward that end.

Carrollton Press, Inc., and United States Historical Documents Institute, Inc.

Both Carrollton Press (CP) and the United States Historical Documents Institute (USHDI) are owned by the same person, William W. Buchanan. CP was incorporated in 1967, and USHDI was founded in 1970. Both firms share the staffs and facilities of offices in Arlington, Virginia, with an indexing and microfilming installation in Inverness, Scotland.

Checklist of United States Public Documents
1789-1975 (USHDI)

A "dual media" edition (indexes in hard copy and text in microform), *Checklist '75* contains some 1,300,000 shelflist cards arranged on microfilm according to the SuDocs class system. Because it is the shelflist of the library of the Superintendent, it includes in one place all the bibliographic information contained in the *1909 Checklist*, the *Document Catalog* (1893-1940) and the *Monthly Catalog* (1895-1975). Moreover, there are entries for thousands of publications never listed in the above guides.

Accompanying the microfilm are twenty-one hardcover volumes of indexes, broken down in the following manner:

a)   *Cumulative Title Index to U.S. Government Publications, 1789-1975* in sixteen hardcover volumes, compiled by Daniel Lester and Sandra Faull. This is a single-alphabet listing of all titles contained in the shelflist of the SuDocs Library. Bibliographic data provided include, in addition to the title, the SuDocs class number, the date of the information in the document, and the microfilm reel number on which the full description can be found in *Checklist '75*.

b)   Index I, *Superintendent of Documents Classification Number Index of U.S. Government Author-Organizations, 1789-1975*, a single volume list of names of more than 8,300 government "author-organizations" in SuDocs class number indicating microfilm reel numbers.

c)   Index II, *U.S. Government Author-Organization Index, 1789-1975*, a single volume index arranged alphabetically by the official names of the agencies in b) above. This index may be most profitably used if one knows the first significant word in the name of the government entity.

d)   Index III, *Departmental Keyword Indexes to U.S. Government Author-Organizations, 1789-1975*, a single volume index for which an entry has been made for each significant word in the name. Thus for the 8,300 agencies over 32,000 output entries are listed.

e)   Index IV, *U.S. Government Serial Titles, 1789-1975*, a single volume index which lists more than 18,000 current and discontinued serial titles. Because of the complicated histories of many of these publications, this volume is more than simply an alphabetical list. Bibliographic histories and other information are given, which means that Index IV may be profitably used by itself.

f)   Index V, *Master Keyword Index to the Publication-Issuing Offices of the U.S. Government, 1789-1975*, a single volume index that provides a form of subject access to the collection. The issuing entities are covered under 33,000 subject-oriented keyword entries. SuDocs class numbers and microfilm reel numbers are given for each entry.

Many libraries subscribed to *Checklist '70*, the predecessor of *Checklist '75*, which covered the same material in the dual-media format from 1789-1970, and included *Indexes I-V*. The addition of the *Cumulative Title Index* in sixteen volumes and the five-year supplementation mark the features of *Checklist '75*. The five hardbound indexes for the earlier *Checklist '70* were compiled by Daniel and Marilyn Lester and were computer-generated.

The United States Monthly Catalog Reference System (CP)

A trio of publications comprise the *Monthly Catalog Reference System*, as follows:

Cumulative Subject Index to the Monthly Catalog of U.S. Government Publications, 1900-1971—Issued in fifteen hardcover volumes, the *Cumulative Subject Index* provides subject access to the *Monthly Catalog* in one file. It represents "a massive merging of entries in all previously published official cumulative indexes to the *Monthly Catalog*: 49 annual indexes . . . ; the two decennial indexes; and one six-month index."[13] It is an excellent and instructive example of a rather successful attempt to overcome the inadequacies of the official *Monthly Catalog*, specifically the failure of the Superintendent of Documents to provide timely cumulations over the years.

To accompany the *Cumulative Subject Index*, a microfilm edition of the complete backfile of the *Monthly Catalog* (1895-1971) was prepared by the Photoduplication Service of the Library of Congress and was sold by CP. The 53-reel set contains the text of the *Monthly Catalog*, its three World War II supplements (1941-1946), its two *Decennial Indexes* (1941-1950; 1951-1960), and some 60 pre-1900 issues which were not indexed.

The Monthly Catalog of U.S. Government Publications, 1895-1924 with Superintendent of Documents Classification Numbers Added—For the years 1895-1924 the official *Monthly Catalog* did not include the SuDocs class number with its entries. The task of adding some 100,000 class notations was completed by Mary Elizabeth Poole and her staff at the D. H. Hill Library of North Carolina State University, Raleigh. The pre-1925 numbers, fortunately, were being used by the Public Documents Library during that time; and Ms. Poole was able to assemble all but a few class numbers for the 360 issues published before 1925. The popular title for this reprint is *Classes Added MoCat 1895-1924*.

Monthly Catalog of U.S. Government Publications, 1925-1962—Rounding out the trio of publications that comprise the *Monthly Catalog Reference System* is a facsimile reprint edition of the MoCat in 76 hardcover volumes. For those libraries wishing to fill gaps in their holdings, individual volumes are offered separately.

Documents Office Classification (USHDI)—The indefatigable Ms. Poole compiled the fifth edition (1977) of *Documents Office Classification* (DOC) in three hardcover volumes. This is a revised version of the fourth edition (1974) and is correlated to *Checklist '75*. DOC contains thousands of entries arranged by SuDocs number with title and reference to earlier and later class numbers. An alphabetical index appears at the end of each volume listing the names of over 2,000 author-organizations along with their current, earlier, and later SuDocs class numbers. *Index I* of *Checklist '75* can be used as an index to DOC to provide more complete author indexing. Ms. Poole was able to accomplish her DOC primarily because of USHDI's microfilm edition of the SuDocs' shelflist card file.

Cumulative Subject Index to the Monthly Catalog of U.S. Government Publications, 1895-1899 (CP)—This publication fills the last indexing gap in the official run of the GPO MoCat. Issued in two hardcover volumes, it was compiled by producing original entries for the 35 catalogs which had no indexing.

Cumulative Index to Hickcox's Monthly Catalog of U.S. Government Publications, 1885-1894 (CP)—As noted, the precursor of the official MoCat was published by John J. Hickcox in ten annual catalogs. This edition provides cumulative subject and author access. Both *Hickcox's* and the *Cumulative Subject Index, 1895-1899* were prepared by Edna Agatha Kanely for Carrollton Press. *Hickcox's* cumulation in this edition is published in two hardcover volumes.

Hickcox's Monthly Catalog of U.S. Government Publications, 1885-1894, Classed Added (CP)—Mary Elizabeth Poole prepared a reprint edition of *Hickcox's* work and has added SuDocs class numbers for the years 1885-1894. The SuDocs numbers may be useful when requesting copies of older publications now housed in the National Archives and shelved by SuDocs class number. The reprint edition is issued in six clothbound volumes.

Cumulative Subject Guide to U.S. Government Bibliographies, 1924-1973 (CP)—A useful spin-off from the *Cumulative Subject Index to the Monthly Catalog*, this seven-volume hardcover compilation describes all bibliographic references in the *Monthly Catalog* for those years. Entries include not only separate bibliographies but thousands of entries of proceedings, journal articles, and the like, with references appended. The latter information was not indexed in the MoCat from 1948 on. The result is a total of more than 40,000 entries covering "bibliographies" in the broadest sense of the word for 50 years of MoCats.

A "dual media" package, the *Guide* is an index to *U.S. Government Bibliography Masterfile, 1924-1973*, which contains the full text of the references on microfiche. An annual updating service is available to subscribers in the dual-media format.

Other CP and USHDI Guides

The above publications represent a systematic effort to enhance access to the information originally listed in the *Monthly Catalog* and its predecessor, and to the extent that that material overlaps, the venerable *Document Catalog*. Other useful and interesting products and services that have been distributed by CP/USHDI include:

The Declassified Documents Reference System (CP)—In a dual media self-contained format, the *System* consists of top secret, secret, and confidential federal documents which have been declassified under the provisions of EO 11652 and the Freedom of Information Act. Access to this collection provides the student and scholar the means for critical re-evaluation of historical events of great magnitude. Documents have been secured from a number of departments and agencies, including State, Defense, CIA, and White House.

Abstract Catalogs are published quarterly, accompanied by a separate cumulative *Subject Index*. The complete 1975 collection consisted of 1,618 documents contained on 186 microfiche. A *Retrospective Collection* has been issued. It consists of three hardcover volumes. Part one is a two-volume *Catalog of Abstracts* and the second part is a one-volume *Cumulative Subject Index*. The latter combines entries from the *Retrospective Collection* and the *1975 Annual Collection*.

The microfiche contains the full text of all documents indexed in the hardbound volumes and the quarterly issues. It is arranged in the same sequence as are the entries in the *Catalogs*. Thus the *System* consists of quarterly abstracts which cumulate annually, cumulative subject indexes, and the text on microfiche.

The National Union Catalog of U.S. Government Publications Received by Depository Libraries, 1974 (CP)—This is a four-volume set showing the depository libraries in the United States and the categories of Items they subscribed to as of November 1973. It may have some value as an interlibrary loan tool, or as a directory to students who need to know if a library nearby has a run of publications within a certain Item. However, its value as a source of information useful to clients can be maintained only if it is issued at least biennially.

Annual Reports Series (CP)—Carrollton Press has compiled a set of *Papers and Annual Reports of the American Historical Association, 1884-1914* (issued in the House *documents* series), and the *Annual Reports and General Appendices of the Smithsonian Institution, 1846-1912* (also issued in the House *documents* series). Both series include cumulative author-subject index volumes.

Congressional Information Service, Inc.

Another commercial publisher that has attempted, with singular success, to rectify the bibliographic shortcomings of retrospective and current guides to federal publications is Congressional Information Service, Inc. (CIS). CIS began auspiciously in 1970 with the publication of *CIS/Index* and has been issuing a series of products and services ever since. These bibliographic sources have been distinguished by their quality and accuracy.

CIS/Index

CIS/Index appears monthly with an annual cumulation (*CIS/Annual*). Moreover, there is a *CIS/Five-Year Cumulative Index* (1970-1974) to the *Abstract* volumes covering that period. The monthly issues both index and provide abstracts for Congressional publications: hearings, committee prints, reports and documents, Senate executive reports and documents. Annotated listings in the multiple-access *Index* section are correlated to document descriptions in the *Abstracts* section. Moreover, *CIS/Annual* provides a guide to multi-volume hearings and legislative histories. Figure 11 shows a sample abstract in *CIS/Index*.

Like some of the products of CP/USHDI, the *CIS/Index* is a dual-media, self-contained reference system. Through the *CIS/Microfiche Library*, the full text of congressional materials (except interim legislative calendars) is available. The manifold uses of this excellent source are explored in more detail in Chapter 6.

CIS/Congressional Bills, Resolutions, and Laws

CIS offers microfiche files of bills and laws that are probably the most complete in existence. The materials are filed sequentially by bill number within bill category. The different versions of legislation are arranged chronologically behind the introduced version. Beginning with the 93rd Congress collection, all enacted public and private laws are included. As of 1977, *CIS/Bills on Microfiche* collections were available from the 90th Congress (1967-68). Supplementation is produced every two years after the completion of a Congress.

CIS/U.S. Serial Set Index, 1789-1969

This prodigious undertaking makes available a systematic search of the Serial Set in one location. Consisting of twelve separate cumulative parts totaling 36 volumes, access is by subject and keywords, private relief and related actions, and numerical lists and schedules of serial volumes. Accompanying the *Index* is the full text on microfiche.

American Statistics Index (ASI)

In some respects ASI is an even more awesome accomplishment than *CIS/Index*. ASI identifies, indexes, and provides abstract information for the publications of more than 400 sources in the executive branch, Congress, and other entities. It is by far the single most comprehensive finding aid to federal government statistics in existence.

Like *CIS/Index*, ASI is issued monthly with an *ASI Annual Supplement*. Access is through an index with multiple entry approaches to the abstracts. The *Index* issues cumulate quarterly, and are organized by subjects and names, categories, titles, and agency report numbers. The abstracting is so thorough that even citations to magazine articles of statistical content are set forth. Special features of the *ASI Annual* include Census Regions and Divisions, Standard

Figure 11
CIS/INDEX: SAMPLE ABSTRACT

SAMPLE ABSTRACT

The following sample entry shows the information contained in a typical abstract

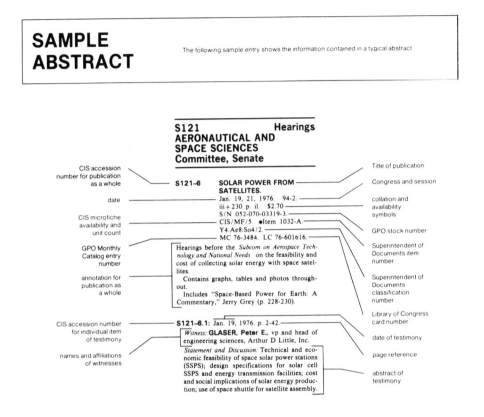

NOTE 1 — AVAILABILITY: Publications that carry a price are sold by the Superintendent of Documents, Washington, D.C. 20402.

Publications that carry no price may be requested in writing from the issuing committee; such requests are honored when possible. It is suggested that requests be accompanied by a return address label for each document requested. Write to Senate committees at Washington, D.C. 20510; and to House committees at Washington, D.C. 20515.

The following symbols are used to give additional information about the availability of publications:

Publications marked with a bullet (●) and an Item Number are sent to Depository Libraries. (Not all Depository Libraries collect all Item Numbers, however).

Publications marked with a single dagger (†) are distributed by the issuing committee, but usually are available only in limited quantities; reports and documents are distributed by the House or Senate Documents Room.

Publications marked with a double dagger (‡) are printed for official use, and often are not available for distribution to the public.

Publications marked with a diamond (♦) are specifically designated by the issuing committee as not available for distribution.

Microfiche copies of all publications abstracted in the CIS/Index are sold by Congressional Information Service in either complete collections, or individually. For details, see your librarian or write the publisher.

NOTE 2 — IDENTIFICATION NUMBERS: Wherever possible, a Superintendent of Documents classification number, a Library of Congress number, and a GPO monthly catalog entry number have been given for each publication. However, not all Congressional publications have been assigned these identification numbers. Publications (particularly committee prints) which do not appear in the GPO Monthly Catalog do not receive entry numbers or Superintendent of Documents classification numbers. Wherever such identification numbers have been assigned and made available to us at press time, they have been included in the CIS/Annual.

Metropolitan Statistical Areas (SMSA), Standard Industrial Classifications (SIC), and other official classifications.

Through the *ASI Microfiche Library*, the full text of documents indexed and abstracted in ASI may be purchased. Figure 12 shows a sample abstract in ASI.

Figure 12

ASI: SAMPLE ABSTRACT

AcCIS—The *CIS/Index* and *American Statistics Index* data bases are searchable on-line through the computer facilities of System Development Corporation (SDC). The user can order needed source materials from the computer via the service described below.

CIS and ASI Documents on Demand—The SDC search is a bibliographic, not a full-text, service. However, individual copies of documents can be ordered on demand while one is still connected to the computer, or by the more conventional means of using the *CIS/Index* and ASI as catalogs. Each document is assuredly always "in stock"; from the master file diazo duplicates are made and shipped by first class mail within 24 hours.

In sum, Congressional Information Service has accomplished for the publications of the Congress and federal statistics what CP/USHDI has done for the departmental publications of government and general bibliography. CIS has not only improved upon the earlier bibliographic sources for retrospective ease of searching, but also has given libraries current indexing and abstracting capabilities of greater sophistication than are found in official publications like the *Monthly Catalog* and its satellites. Despite the improvements in the MoCat, the user will gravitate toward *CIS/Index* and ASI to pinpoint congressional and statistical information.

Andriot

John L. Andriot has published several guides to federal documents. Before CIS and CP/USHDI began producing comprehensive tools that provided access to government materials, Andriot's guides were widely used and their value justly acknowledged.

Guide to U.S. Government Publications

The 1977 edition of Andriot's *Guide to U.S. Government Publications* is arranged by SuDocs class number, with an "Agency Index" and a "Title Index." Both indexes are arranged alphabetically by keyword of agency or title. It is a guide to the important series, including periodicals, currently being issued by the federal government. Many entries are annotated. Important monographs of reference value within the series are individually noted.

This edition is being issued in hardcover volumes. Volume numbers and the SuDocs classes they comprise are shown as follows:

Volume	Classes
1	A
2	C-H
3	I-S
4	T-Z
5	Index to Vols. 1-4

Upon completion of the five-volume set, each volume will be revised, updated, and reissued at six-month intervals. In an appendix section of each volume, there is a list of new SuDocs class numbers which appeared in the "New Classification Numbers" section of the MoCat and the *Daily Depository Shipping Lists*; this list will cumulate so that users need only refer to the most recent volume.

Andriot's *Guide* has undergone transformations during its history. It was published as the *Guide to U.S. Government Serials and Periodicals* in various editions from 1959 until 1973, when its contents were enlarged and the name changed to its current title. From June 1973 until June 1976, it was issued as a looseleaf service in two volumes. Volume 1 covered the publications of those entities currently in existence in 1973. Volume 2 consisted of a list of agencies no longer in existence and discontinued SuDocs class numbers. The looseleaf service permitted supplementation on a quarterly basis.

With a return to bound volume format, a significant degree of recency is lost, especially if reorganization mandates large changes in provenance and a consequent magnitude of change in SuDocs classification owing to reorganization. Moreover, in the present format, the discontinued series are interfiled with current publications, thus making it more difficult and more confusing to pinpoint with ease the two. Having discontinued series in a separate volume was an arrangement superior to the present one.

Guide to U.S. Government Statistics

The fourth edition of this work was published in 1973. In the foreword to his third edition (1961), Andriot declared his intention to issue the *Guide* biennially, a wish that went palpably unrealized. The fourth edition is an annotated guide to over 1,700 recurring U.S. government publications "from one-page releases to huge compilations of historical data." Over 3,000 titles in major statistical numbered series are listed. For each agency Andriot lists basic statistical series in SuDocs class order with information as to the kinds of statistical data given. There is a subject index, but it is not as detailed or analytical as one would like.

Unfortunately, this effort bears comparison with ASI, and was published before ASI came to the attention of reviewers. It is hardly possible for Andriot to compete successfully with a current indexing/abstracting source like ASI. Nor is there any need to. Andriot can thus expend his talents in improving his *Guide to U.S. Government Publications* and leave federal statistics to ASI.[14]

Checklist of Major U.S. Government Series

Volume 1 of the *Checklist*, entitled *Department of Agriculture*, was issued in 1973 and covered 23 prominent numerical series being issued at that time by the Department of Agriculture. There is a title index but no subject index. Arrangement of Volume 1 was in typical SuDocs class order. Andriot stated that this volume was the first of a projected twenty to thirty volume set of checklists covering the major series, both numbered and unnumbered, published by departments and independent agencies. Priority was to be given to those agencies that do not publish cumulative lists of their series on a periodic basis. However, Volume 1 of this *Checklist* was incorporated into Volume 1 (Class A) of the 1977 *Guide to U.S. Government Publications.* Thus at this writing it is unclear whether Andriot plans to continue this series independent of material that will appear in the hardcover volumes of the *Guide.*

Pierian Press

Cumulative Personal Author Indexes to the Monthly Catalog

Just as Carrollton Press enhanced the use of the official MoCat by providing a cumulative subject approach, so Pierian Press has provided access to personal authors of federal documents. Decennial and quinquennial personal author indexes to the MoCat have been issued in four volumes covering the years 1941-1970. *The Cumulative Personal Author Indexes* consist of alphabetical lists of all personal names that have appeared in the entries of the *Monthly Catalog* for those years. Authors in these lists include virtually every relationship of personal author to cited publication—editor, compiler, translator, researcher, lecturer, joint author, illustrator—including a systematic author approach to Joint Publications Research Service (JPRS) translations.

These author indexes are significant because from September 1947 to December 1962 personal authors were omitted from the MoCat indexes, including the two decennial cumulative indexes (1941-1950 and 1951-1960). The *Document Catalog* (1893-1940) did include personal authors. Pierian Press's contribution is an invaluable aid to searching the MoCat.

Bibliography of United States Government
Bibliographies, 1968-1973

Compiled by Roberta A. Scull, *Bibliography* contains over 1,200 annotated entries with a title and subject index. Emphasis is on general, scientific, and social science bibliographies issued serially or as monographs by the federal government. A number of detailed appendixes offer information on ordering, availability, and price. Periodic supplements updating this basic volume will be published in issues of *Reference Services Review* (RSR).[15]

Government Documents in the Library Literature,
1909-1974

Compiled by Alan Edward Schorr, this guide is a comprehensive bibliographic coverage of literature on United States, state, municipal, United Nations, and League of Nations documents. There are over 1,200 references covering the years 1909-1974, divided into four sections with subdivisions by topics. The guide is accessed by two indexes: a geographical index by state and a personal name index. The author is Government Publications and Map Librarian, and Assistant Professor of Library Science at the University of Alaska, Fairbanks.

G. K. Hall & Co.

Bibliographic Guide to Government Publications—U.S.

This is an annual subject bibliography which brings together publications cataloged by the Research Libraries of the New York Public Library with additional entries from Library of Congress MARC tapes. Access is by main entry, added entries, titles, series titles, and subject headings.[16]

Body

Annotated Bibliography of Bibliographies on
Selected Government Publications and Supplementary Guides
to the Superintendent of Documents Classification System

The first issue of this series was published in 1967 by Alexander C. Body (925 Westfall, Kalamazoo, Michigan) and was followed by numbered *Supplements.* A typical issue consists of extensive annotations of selected government bibliographies issued by federal agencies. Arrangement is by SuDocs class number with useful appendixes including a classified list of government authors, departments and agencies, and an index.

Columbia University Press

A Popular Guide to Government Publications

The fourth edition of W. Philip Leidy's *Popular Guide* (1976) consists of several thousand titles selected from materials issued by the various agencies between 1967 and 1975. Arrangement is under 119 topics. There is a detailed, analytic index. Standard bibliographic information includes author if known, issuing office, year of publication, pagination, and stock number for ordering purposes.

Libraries Unlimited, Inc.

Several useful guides to federal materials have appeared from Libraries Unlimited. *Government Reference Books: A Biennial Guide to U.S. Government Publications* has been issued in the following periodicity:

Years Covered	Compiler
1968/69	Sally Wynkoop
1970/71	Sally Wynkoop
1972/73	Sally Wynkoop
1974/75	Alan Edward Schorr

The 1974/75 volume contains over 1,300 entries, an increase of 25 percent over the third edition. Containing descriptive annotations, the work is a guide to bibliographies, directories, handbooks, statistical compendia, dictionaries, gazetteers, etc. Bibliographic information for each entry is complete. Entries are grouped under four broad subject sections (social sciences, science and technology, humanities, general reference) with alphabetically arranged subject subdivisions. Access is through personal author, title, and subject indexes.

Other guides published by Libraries Unlimited include Linda C. Pohle, *A Guide to Popular Government Publications: For Libraries and Home Reference* (1972) and Sally Wynkoop, *Subject Guide to Government Reference Books* (1972). The former emphasizes popular publications, while the latter emphasizes comprehensive works and serial publications, omitting pamphlets and ephemera.

Other

Omnibus guides to reference sources inevitably list many government publications and works about them. Standard classics like Winchell's *Guide to Reference Books* and its *Supplements*, and Wynar's *American Reference Books Annual*, should not be overlooked. Official government issuances such as the *National Union Catalog* and *New Serial Titles* include, of course, government publications. Commercial sources range in scope from comprehensive to highly selective and in price from expensive to reasonable. As one can see from this small but exemplary sample, smaller libraries unable to afford the publications of CP/USHDI or CIS (or whose clientele make it unnecessary to purchase these tools) will find no dearth of guides to the mazeway of government publications.

Miscellaneous Non-Bibliographic Sources

Directory of Government Document Collections
& Librarians

In 1974 the Government Documents Round Table of ALA published a *Directory* with the assistance of Congressional Information Service. The *1978 Directory of Government Document Collections & Librarians* represents an improvement over the 1974 edition. Arranged in seven sections, the *Directory*'s entries give detailed information on the holdings of federal, state, local, foreign, and international publications for almost 2,300 libraries in the United States. The entries are arranged in geo-alphabetical order. Other sections of the *Directory* include information on library school instructors in government documents, a special collections index, and the names and addresses of key people and organizations in government documents activities.

Citation Manual for United States Government Publications

Compiled by George D. Brightbill and Wayne C. Maxson and published by the Center for the Study of Federalism, Temple University, Philadelphia (1974), the *Citation Manual* provides a useful guide to conventions of footnoting or otherwise referencing the numerous forms documents take. Because it is specifically concerned with federal government documents, its value as a specialized style manual is patent.

CONCLUSION

Thanks to the twin technologies, computer-assisted publishing and micrographics, bibliographic control has traveled great distances since the heroic but inadequate efforts of individuals like Poole and Ames. Yet expanding the scope and quality control of government information seems only to reveal the need for more and better systems. Indeed, the sheer amount of information continues to expand more rapidly than the apparatus that seeks to contain it and render it manageable. The task often resembles the one designed to punish Sisyphus.

REFERENCES

1. For example, the entire March 1976 issue of *Illinois Libraries* is devoted to documents in microform.

2. W. F. Willoughby, "Government Publications," *Yale Review* (August 1869), p. 159.

3. Schmeckebier, p. 6.

4. Willoughby, p. 160.

5. The Serial Set will be analyzed in Chapter 6.

6. Schmeckebier, p. 33.

7. *100 GPO Years*, p. 76.

8. Willoughby, pp. 163-64.

9. For instance, after 1936 there was a pronounced increase in the number of "processed" publications cited in the *Monthly Catalog*.

10. John H. Hickcox, *United States Government Publications: A Monthly Catalogue* (Washington: W. H. Lowdermilk, 1885-1894). Irregularly issued over this period, it contains many entries not listed elsewhere.

11. Schmeckebier, p. 26.

12. Bearing in mind, of course, the omission of many departmental publications and the overlapping periods covered.

13. From a review by LeRoy C. Schwarzkopf in *American Reference Books Annual* (1975), entry 102, pp. 47-48.

14. See the excellent review, written before ASI was available in sufficient numbers to analyze adequately, of Andriot's *Statistics* by Arne Richards in *Government Publications Review* 1: 91-96 (Fall 1973).

15. The first annual supplement to *Bibliography of United States Government Bibliographies, 1968-1973* was published in the July/December 1975 issue of RSR.

16. For a critical and largely negative review of this publication, see RQ 14: 54-55 (Fall 1974).

6

LEGISLATIVE BRANCH MATERIALS

What is the spirit that has in general characterized the proceedings of Congress? A perusal of their journals, as well as the candid acknowledgments of such as have had a seat in that assembly, will inform us, that the members have but too frequently displayed the character, rather of partisans of their respective States, than of impartial guardians of a common interest. . . .

—The Federalist, XLVI (Madison)

The necessity of a Senate is not less indicated by the propensity of all single and numerous assemblies to yield to the impulse of sudden and violent passions, and to be seduced by factious leaders into intemperate and pernicious resolutions.

—The Federalist, LXII (Madison)

INTRODUCTION

The framers of the Constitution had no major doubts about Congress as *primus inter pares*. In historical fact Congress antedates both the presidency and the judicial branch. The first federal Congress made the arrangements for counting the ballots of the first electoral college and for inaugurating George Washington and John Adams as the first executive officers. The office of Attorney General and the Departments of War, State, and Treasury were established by acts of the first Congress. Congressional legislation was needed to erect the system of federal courts and to establish the Supreme Court. It is no accident of organization or style that the framers began the noble document with that unequivocal statement, "All legislative powers herein granted shall be vested in a Congress of the United States which shall consist of a Senate and House of Representatives."

Although slow to change, the Congress does attempt on a continuing basis to restructure its committees and supporting agencies.[1] According to the 1976/77 edition of the *United States Government Manual,* there were eight agencies serving the Congress. We discussed the duties of the Government Printing Office and the Assistant Public Printer (Superintendent of Documents) in Chapters 1 and 2. The other units are the Architect of the Capitol, United States Botanic Garden, General Accounting Office, Library of Congress, Cost Accounting Standards Board, Office of Technology Assessment, and Congressional Budget Office. Brief descriptions of the activities of these agencies are contained in the *Manual,* and detailed accountability is set forth in the annual *Legislative Branch Appropriations* hearings. This chapter will first consider some publications of selected agencies. Following that will be a discussion of the important kinds of materials that issue from the House of Representatives and the Senate. Finally, the legislative process will be assayed, with reference to the significant indexes and guides published by both government and by private companies in aid of tracing legislation.

GENERAL ACCOUNTING OFFICE

The General Accounting Office (GAO) was created by the Budget and Accounting Act of 1921 (31 U.S.C. 41), and its activities have been extended by subsequent legislation. The GAO assists the Congress, its committees and individual members, in carrying out their legislative and review responsibilities. Furthermore, it carries out legal, accounting, auditing, and claims settlement functions with respect to programs and operations as assigned by the Congress; and it makes recommendations designed to provide for more efficient and effective government operations. Technically, this agency has a certain degree of independence within the legislative branch. It is under the control and direction of the Comptroller General of the United States and his Deputy, appointed by the President with the advice and consent of the Senate for terms of 15 years.

Reports to Congress by the Comptroller General

The investigatory scope of the GAO being large, the series of Reports to Congress (GA 1.13; Item 546-D) contain a number of useful studies. Unfortunately, some of these reports were non-depository while others were received under the appropriate Item. Examples: *Pricing of Publications Sold to the Public* (GA 1.13:P96/26; Item 546-D) and *Agency Printing and Duplicating Operations Need Management Improvements, Multiagency* (GA 1.13:P93/11; Non-Depository), both issued in November 1974.

The problem of the availability of GAO reports on deposit was rectified by the GPO micropublishing program. *Daily Depository Shipping List 10,301* (November 3, 1977) announced a shipment of 355 *Reports* in a microfiche format. The *Reports* were produced within GAO. Regional Depository Libraries received both second generation archival silver film as well as a set of third generation non-silver film. Selective depositories received third generation non-silver film if they subscribed to Item 546-D.

Congressional Sourcebook Series

The GAO in 1976 began issuing Congressional Sourcebooks (GA 1.22; Item 545-E), a series of directories reflecting an inventory of program-related information. The purpose of the Sourcebooks is to help identify relevant and reliable information which may be needed by the Congress to carry out its legislative oversight and budget control responsibilities. Volumes in this series include *Requirements for Recurring Reports to the Congress* (GA 1.22:R29), *Federal Program Evaluations* (GA 1.22:P94), and *Federal Information Sources and Systems* (GA 1.22:In3). Available to depository libraries in hard copy, they may be requested on microfiche by writing to the GAO Distribution Section, Room 4522, 441 G Street NW, Washington, D.C. 20548. Each of these directories has a citation section arranged by executive agency and indexes by subject, budget function/ subfunction, and issuing agencies. Moreover, *Requirements for Recurring Reports to the Congress* has a law index and a congressional recipient index.

LIBRARY OF CONGRESS

In 1800 Congress passed a law appropriating $5,000 "for the purchase of such books as may be necessary for the use of Congress" (2 Stat. 56). Subsequent legislation (2 U.S.C. 131-168d) expanded the scope of the Library of Congress (LC). For FY 1978, the Librarian of Congress requested an overall appropriation of $173,600,000.[2] Although under the law, the Library's first responsibility is service to Congress, its range of acvities has come to include the entire governmental establishment and the public at large, so that in fact it is this country's national library.

In the *List of Classes*, March 1977 revision, some twenty offices, departments, and divisions within LC made available almost fifty series to depository libraries. Some representative publications, by issuing unit, will be indicated here.

Office of the Librarian

The *Annual Report of the Librarian of Congress* (LC 1.1; Item 785) for the fiscal year includes the activities of LC's various departments and offices. Published as a supplement to the Annual Report, the *Quarterly Journal of the Library of Congress* (LC 1.17; Item 788) is a handsomely designed and illustrated periodical covering the various activities of the Library. The *Library of Congress Information Bulletin* (LC 1.18; Item 785-C), a weekly newsletter, is available free to educational or publicly supported libraries and research institutions.

Neither *New Serial Titles* (LC 1.23/3) nor *New Serial Titles, Classed Subject Arrangement* (LC 1.23/5) are available on deposit to institutions. The former, subtitled "A Union List of Serials Commencing Publication After December 31, 1949," is prepared under the sponsorship of the Joint Committee on the Union List of Serials. It appears in eight monthly issues, four quarterly issues, and in annual cumulations which are self-cumulative through periods of five or ten years. Its companion, the *Classed Subject Arrangement*, is a monthly.

LC's National Referral Center for Science and Technology Publications has issued several directories since it was established in 1962. These compilations, covering engineering, water, general toxicology, and the biological sciences, are based on a register of information resources available to the Center. A useful title in this series is *A Directory of Information Resources in the United States Federal Government, with a Supplement of Government Sponsored Information Analysis Centers.* It is a 416-page listing of federal departments and agencies, indicating the unit's areas of interest, publications, and information services.

General Reference and Bibliography Division

The General Publications Series (LC 2.2; Item 806-C) contains a number of useful monographs, while the Handbooks, Manuals, and Guides Series (LC 2.8; Item 806-B) features guides to published official records of various countries. *Children's Books* (LC 2.11; Item 806-I) is an annual list of books published during the year in the United States for children from preschool through junior high school. A brief synopsis of the books is given in addition to the standard bibliographic data. Of outstanding reference value is the *Guide to the Study of the United States of America* (LC 2.2: Un3/4; Item 806-C), a comprehensive listing of bibliographical studies on the United States. In it are described approximately 10,000 books reflecting the development of life and thought in this country.

Copyright Office

On October 19, 1976, President Ford signed the bill for the general revision of the United States copyright law, a landmark piece of legislation (PL 94-553; 90 Stat. 2541). The new law supersedes the copyright act of 1909, and, with some exceptions, became effective on January 1, 1978. Under its provisions, there will now be a single system of statutory protection for all copyrightable works, published or unpublished.

The new copyright legislation is complex and represents a fundamental legal and philosophical change over the act of 1909, which was a direct descendant of the original British Copyright Act of 1710, the statute of Queen Anne. It is difficult to foresee what problems may arise in the new copyright act, but the provisions of PL 94-553 will have a profound effect upon the library community.

Useful publications that issue from the Copyright Office include the Circular series (LC 3.4/2; Item 802-A) and the famous *Catalog of Copyright Entries* (LC 3.6/5). The former consists of a number of helpful pamphlets, such as *Publications of the Copyright Office* (Circular 2), *General Information on Copyright* (Circular 1), *Copyright Law of the United States of America* (Circular 91), and *Highlights of the New Copyright Law* (Circular R99). Subjects in the Circular series are revised from time to time and cover, in addition to the titles above, such topics as copyright fees, books and pamphlets, audiovisual materials, and poems and song lyrics.

Catalog of Copyright Entries, 3d Series

This massive work is divided into several sections:

Part	Description	Item Number
1	Books and Pamphlets; including serials and contributions to periodicals	791
2	Periodicals; including domestic and foreign periodicals and newspapers	793
3,4	Dramas and works prepared for oral delivery	794
5	Music; published and unpublished music materials	795
6	Maps and Atlases; domestic and foreign maps, atlases and other cartographic works	797
7-11A	Works of art, reproductions of works of art, scientific and technical drawings, photographic works, prints and pictorial illustrations	798
11B	Commercial Prints and Labels	799
12, 13	Motion Pictures and filmstrips	800
14	Sound recordings	795

These parts were available to depository libraries as of the March 1977 revision of the *List of Classes.* However, the testimony of the Register of Copyrights, Barbara Ringer, in FY 1978 legislative branch appropriations hearings, suggests that the Copyright Office is going to have to change "all of our procedures, all of our forms, all of our correspondence, all of our manuals of practice, and all of our regulations" to meet the requirements of the new law.[3] Therefore, the *Catalog of Copyright Entries*, as shown above, may change and the reader is advised to consult current documents if applicable.

Manuscript Division

Presidents' Papers Index Series

Pursuant to PL 85-147 (1957), the Librarian of Congress was authorized to arrange, index, and microfilm the papers of the Presidents of the United States housed in LC's collections. Now completed, the index series covers Presidents Washington to Coolidge. The indexes themselves are available to depository libraries (LC 4.7; Item 811-B), essentially names of correspondents with descriptive information about each document and a key to its location on the microfilm. The complete 3,073-reel set of presidential papers sells for $31,705 from LC's Photoduplication Service (Washington, D.C. 20540)[4] and for non-depository libraries, the various *Indexes* may be purchased from the Superintendent of Documents.

Congressional Research Service

The Congressional Research Service (CRS), formerly known as the Legislative Reference Service, provides a number of information services to members of Congress and their staffs, congressional committees, subject specialists who perform research for the Congress, and a limited number of researchers at the General Accounting Office. Among these services are a mechanized selective dissemination of information (SDI) operation, and a "hot line" telephone reference capability.[5] The Legislative Reorganization Act of 1970 directed the CRS, upon request, to advise and assist congressional committees in analyzing and evaluating legislative proposals, and to provide whatever other research and analytical services the committees consider appropriate. Any member can direct the Service to provide him or her with a concise memorandum of the purpose, effect, and relevant legislative history of any measure scheduled for hearings.

Digest of Public General Bills and Resolutions

The principal purpose of the *Digest* is to furnish, in summary form, the essential features of public bills and resolutions with their changes during the legislative process. The *Digest* is normally issued during each session of a Congress in two cumulative issues with monthly supplements and a final edition at the conclusion of the session.

The *Digest*, which used to be published in eight parts, is, as of 1977, issued in four parts:

Part 1: Action Taken during the Congress. This part reflects action taken throughout the Congress, including first session action in second session publication. It is divided into two sections, "Public Laws" and "Other Measures Receiving Action." The first section contains digests of public laws in numerical order of enactment, their legislative histories, and a cross-index of public laws and originating legislation. "Other Measures Receiving Action" numerically lists the latest revised digests with their legislative histories, including, if appropriate: date reported from committee, report numbers, dates considered on floor, date passed, conference action, and date of presidential action.

Part 2: Digests of Public General Bills and Resolutions. This part includes digests of all public bills and resolutions in numerical order as introduced. If a measure is identical to one introduced in the same session, reference is made from higher numbered measures to the earlier measure. For a typical page in this part, see Figure 13, page 158.

Part 3: Indexes to Digested Bills and Resolutions. This part provides indexes by sponsor and co-sponsor, identical bills, short titles, and subjects.

Part 4: Factual Descriptions. This part is required by clause 5(d) of House Rule X; factual descriptions consist of 100 words or less of the subject matter of bills and resolutions. In Part 2, private measures are identified by bill number only. But in Part 4, private as well as public bills are described.

Each supplement contains the digests or bill titles when appropriate, and factual descriptions of bills introduced since the previous cumulative issue or

Figure 13

DIGEST OF PUBLIC GENERAL BILLS AND RESOLUTIONS

H.R. 1236 Mr. Roberts; 1/4/77. Post Office and Civil Service

Repeals the Postal Reorganization Act. Reenacts provisions relating to the postal service which were in effect immediately prior to the enactment of such Act.

H.R. 1237 Mr. Roe; 1/4/77. Post Office and Civil Service

See digest of H.R. 519

H.R. 1238 Mr. Roe; 1/4/77. Post Office and Civil Service

Extends to 25 years the period during which preferential mail rates shall apply to publications mailed by any veterans' organizations.

H.R. 1239 Mr. Roe; 1/4/77. Post Office and Civil Service

Prohibits interference with the right of any officer or employee of the Postal Service to have direct oral or written communication with a Member of Congress or with any committee of Congress on an unofficial and informal basis in connection with the employment of such officer or employee or pertaining to the Postal Service in any way.

Forbids the Postal Service from taking any disciplinary action or from discriminating against any officer or employee due to such communication.

H.R. 1240 Mr. Roe; 1/4/77. Public Works and Transportation

See digest of H.R. 1174

H.R. 1241 Mr. Roe; 1/4/77. Public Works and Transportation

Directs the Secretary of the Treasury to determine for each fiscal year the amount of taxes attributable to each State which are paid into the Highway Trust Fund. Directs the Secretary of Transportation to insure that each State will be apportioned an aggregate amount of at least 80 percent of the amount of such taxes in Federal-aid highway program funds.

H.R. 1242 Mr. Roe; 1/4/77. Public Works and Transportation

See digest of H.R. 1054

H.R. 1243 Mr. Roe; 1/4/77. Public Works and Transportation

Authorizes the Secretary of Transportation, with the approval of the Secretary of the Treasury, to guarantee any person against loss of principal and interest on securities, obligations, or loans issued to enable certain motor carriers engaged in express service to refinance existing obligations and for other corporate and related purposes consistent with their responsibilities as common carriers.

Requires the Secretary to make specified findings in writing before making any guarantee pursuant to this Act including the unavailability of other practicable means of obtaining financial assistance. Specifies additional conditions which must be met regarding any stocks guaranteed under this Act.

Stipulates that the aggregate unpaid principal amount of securities, obligations, and loans outstanding at any one time which are guaranteed under this Act may not exceed $25,000,000.

Requires the Interstate Commerce Commission to advise the Secretary quarterly regarding the performance of each common carrier applying for assistance under this Act. Authorizes the Secretary to take appropriate action, including the termination of the United States obligation in the event that the common carrier fails to provide reasonably adequate service.

Directs the Secretary to report to the President and the Congress within one year after the enactment of this Act regarding the Department's activities pursuant to this Act. Specifies information which must be included in such report.

H.R. 1244 Mr. Roe; 1/4/77. Public Works and Transportation

Elderly and Handicapped Americans Transportation Services Act - Amends the Federal Aviation Act of 1958 to allow airlines to offer free or reduced rate transportation to persons 65 years of age or older, and for handicapped persons and their necessary attendants.

Amends the Interstate Commerce Act to allow common carriers subject to the provisions of such Act to provide free or reduced rate transportation to persons 65 years of age or older and to handicapped persons and their attendants.

Amends the Urban Mass Transportation Act of 1964 to direct the Secretary of Transportation, in providing assistance under such Act, to give preferential treatment to State and local public bodies which agree to adopt and maintain specially reduced rates, not exceeding 50 percent of the regular rates, for handicapped persons and persons over 65. Authorizes the Secretary to make grants and loans to States and local public bodies in order to assist them in providing mass transportation services which will meet the needs of handicapped persons and persons over 65.

Authorizes the Secretary to prescribe standards for the design of buildings, structures, and facilities which are provided with financial assistance under the Urban Mass Transportation Act to insure that persons 65 or over and the physically or mentally handicapped will have ready access to, and use of, those buildings, structures, and facilities.

Amends the Older Americans Act of 1965 to authorize the Secretary of Health, Education, and Welfare to make grants for special transportation research and demonstration projects for the handicapped and the elderly. Authorizes appropriations of $15,-000,000 for fiscal year 1974 and $25,000,000 for fiscal year 1975 to carry out such grant program.

H.R. 1245 Mr. Roe; 1/4/77. Public Works and Transportation

Directs the Secretary of Transportation to require that all projects receiving Federal financial assistance for mass transportation purposes be designed and operated so that such transportation facilities, equipment and services can be utilized by elderly and handicapped persons.

H.R. 1246 Mr. Roe; 1/4/77. Public Works and Transportation

Sludge Management Act - Directs the Administrator of the Environmental Protection Agency to study the environmental, health, and economic effects of subsurface landfilling sludge on soils and ground water, and alternate methods of sludge disposal. Directs the Administrator to develop guidelines for sludge disposal and land-spreading in order to protect the public health and welfare.

Authorizes the Administrator to make grants to States and localities of up to 40 percent of the cost of removal of sludge from navigable waters of the United States or any adjacent shoreline. Directs the Administrator to establish an Environmental Protection Agency Task Force on sludge removal. Authorizes the establishment of programs of training, demonstration, and surveys relating to the restoration of water quality where degraded by sludge.

Directs the Administrator to establish criteria for regulating and controlling the transportation, storage, and disposal of hazardous sludge. Establishes a permit program for activities relating to hazardous sludge two years after the enactment of this Act.

Establishes procedures for adoption and approval of State hazardous sludge permit programs in accordance with criteria prescribed by the Administrator.

Amends the Federal Water Pollution Control Act to prohibit grants for treatment works, after September 30, 1976, unless the applicant demonstrates that adequate confined disposal methods will be provided.

H.R. 1247 Mr. Roe; 1/4/77. Public Works and Transportation

Authorizes the Administrator of the Environmental Protection Agency to provide financial and technical assistance to States and localities for the construction or acquisition of sewage sludge disposal facilities. Stipulates that such grants shall equal 75 per-

supplement, as well as a subject index of those bills. When a cumulative issue is published in a session, all prior issues for that session (both cumulative and supplements) should be discarded. The final issue for a session should be retained permanently.

Prepared by the Bill Digest Unit, American Law Division, Congressional Research Service of the Library of Congress, the *Digest* is one of the more widely used guides to the legislative process. Moreover, it is the only source that offers summaries, or digests, of the text of the legislation.

Subject Cataloging Division

Subject Headings Used in the Dictionary Catalogs of the Library of Congress

In 1975 the *Eighth Edition, Library of Congress Subject Headings* (LC 26.7; Item 823) was made available to depository institutions in both hardcopy and in a *Microfiche Edition* (Item 823-A-1). The microfiche format (98-frame 24:1) was the result of a joint undertaking between the Depository Distribution Service and the Library of Congress, and was made available to depository subscribers before the hardcopy was distributed.[6] Moreover, under the same Item (823-A-1) depository institutions may receive *Library of Congress Subject Headings in Microform, Quarterly Cumulation* (LC 26.7/2).

Library of Congress Classification Schedules

Classification Schedules (LC 26.9; Item 819) are issued irregularly in volumes, parts, and subclasses. They constitute the complete LC classification scheme from A (General Works: Polygraphy) to Z (Bibliography and Library Science). In 1974 the U.S. Historical Documents Institute, Inc., made available a 15-volume clothbound set of *Combined Indexes to the Library of Congress Classification Schedules.* Divided into five sets, the *Combined Indexes* are organized in the following manner.

Set I is an author/number index to the *Schedules.* Set II is a biographical subject arrangement. Set III consists of a classified index to persons in the *Schedules.* Set IV is a geographical name index. Set V is a subject keyword index.

Processing Department

This department, which includes the Card Division, is responsible for issuing massive bibliographic sources like the *National Union Catalog* (LC 30.8) and the *Subject Catalog* (LC 30.8/3). These sources are not depository Items; they are available for sale by the Cataloging Distribution Service Division, Building 159, Navy Yard Annex, 20541.

However, the venerable *Monthly Checklist of State Publications* (LC 30.9; Item 816), which began in 1910, is available to depository institutions. It is a bibliographical record of documents and publications issued by the several states and received in LC. Because the Library of Congress receives from the states only a fraction of the total publications produced at that level of government, the *Checklist* is of limited value. There is an annual index, and the June and December issues contain periodical listings.

Congressional Budget Office

The Congressional Budget Office (CBO) was established by the Congressional Budget Act of 1974 (88 Stat. 302; 2 U.S.C. 601). The CBO provides Congress with basic budget data and with analyses of alternative fiscal, budgetary, and programmatic policy issues. Moreover, CBO provides periodic forecasts and analyses of economic trends. The agency "keeps score" for Congress by monitoring the results of Congressional action on individual authorization, appropriation, and revenue bills against the targets or ceilings specified in concurrent resolutions. To achieve this end, CBO has developed a sophisticated automated scorekeeping data base.[7]

The March 1977 edition of *List of Classes* showed five series available to depository libraries from the CBO: General Publications (Y 10.2; Item 1005-C); Handbooks, Manuals, Guides (Y 10.8; Item 1005-B); Background Papers (Y 10.9; Item 1005-A); Technical Analysis Papers, a numbered series (Y 10.11; Item 1005-D); and Budget Issue Papers (Y 10.12; Item 1005-E).

GENERAL PUBLICATIONS OF THE CONGRESS

As a rule, materials initiated by or required by the Congress fall into two categories: 1) publications of the Congress as a whole, or by one chamber; and 2) publications of the committees or subcommittees of Congress. Because the President, for example, is required by Article II, Section 3, of the Constitution to communicate with Congress, presidential messages are published by the Congress (in the *documents* series), whereas, of course, they initiate in the executive. Moreover, the Superintendent's notation scheme for publications of the Congress employs a *classified* and a *designated* symbol system, or a combination of both.

The Congressional Record (CR)

Oceans of ink have been spilled detailing the peculiarities of this publication, the glory and ultimate folly of the Congress.[8] The daily *Congressional Record* (CR), issued when Congress is in session, carries an X/a class notation (Item 994), and includes a fortnightly index. The permanent, bound edition of the CR (X; Item 993) is designated by Congress and session, with individual book numbers made up of volume and part. Due to revision and rearrangement, the pagination of the bound *Record* differs from that of the daily edition.

Members of Congress used to be permitted to insert "speeches" not actually delivered on the floor in such a way that the reader had no way of knowing that the member was absent. However, on March 1, 1978, JCP regulations were amended to identify statements or insertions in the *Record* where no part of them was spoken.

Unspoken material must now be preceded by a "bullet" symbol (●). But this attempt at major reform appears more cosmetic than substantive. A member of either chamber need only deliver the first sentence of his or her remarks verbally, and the entire statement will then appear without the "bullet" symbol. The new rule and the exceptions that significantly diminish the integrity of the provision were published in the *Congressional Record* (daily edition), February 20, 1978, p. H1193.

The *Record* consists of four sections: the proceedings of the House and of the Senate; the Extensions of Remarks; and the Daily Digest. Each section is paged continuously and separately during each session, and each page in each section is preceded by a letter prefix as follows: "S" for Senate, "H" for House, "E" for Extensions of Remarks, and "D" for Daily Digest.

It costs over $300 to print each page of the *Record* in its various editions, including the indexes. For FY 1978, the Public Printer's justification for the cost of the CR included the following information:

> The proceedings of the Senate and House of Representatives are printed daily in the Congressional Record. Approximately 40,600 copies are printed daily and distributed as provided by law (44 U.S.C. 906), and are charged to the appropriation for printing and binding for Congress. There are also printed daily about 8,800 additional copies which are delivered and charged to Government departments on requisition and to the Superintendent of Documents for sale to subscribers. After the close of each session, the daily proceedings are consolidated, indexed, and about 2,500 copies printed as the bound edition of the Record. About 1,500 of these sets are distributed to departments, depository libraries, and public sales. An estimated 57,000 pages will be required in fiscal year 1978 and the cost will be approximately $16,309,000.[9]

In the proceedings sections and the Extensions of Remarks are found numerous items that were published in the *Washington Post* and the *New York Times*.[10] The Extensions of Remarks section contains traditionally extraneous material, although "germane" material does appear in this section if printing requirements and deadlines necessitate its appearance. All the news that fits may show up in the Extensions of Remarks: a potpourri of trivia intermingled with some important information. In 1972 the Joint Committee on Printing had to remind members not to include extraneous matter in the proceedings sections. Exceptions included "(a) excerpts from letters, telegrams, or articles presented in connection with a speech delivered in the course of debate; (b) communications from State Legislatures; and (c) addresses or articles by the President and the members of his cabinet, the Vice President, or a Member of Congress."[11]

Until the 90th Congress, 2d session, the Extensions of Remarks was called the Appendix. Separately paged, it formed a part of both the daily and the permanent editions from the 75th Congress, 1st session, through the 83d Congress, 2d session. Beginning with the 77th Congress, 1st session, each page number was preceded by the designation "A." With the 84th Congress, 1st session, the Appendix pages were *omitted* from the permanent edition. Thus from 1955 to 1968 material in the

Appendix could be consulted only in the daily edition. The *index* to the permanent edition, however, cited references to Appendix material appearing in the daily edition. Libraries were forced to retain the Appendix pages from the daily edition and shelve them in proper sequence with the permanent edition. After the Appendix was omitted from the permanent edition, materials considered germane to legislation were inserted in that edition at the point when the legislation was under discussion. With the 90th Congress, 2d session, the "Appendix," now the Extensions of Remarks, was restored to the permanent edition of the *Record.* Moreover, beginning with that Congress and session, the last page of each daily edition has carried an alphabetical listing of members whose extended remarks appear in that issue, with page numbers.

The Daily Digest section includes "Highlights" of the legislative day, chamber action which summarizes bills introduced and reported, resolutions agreed to, quorum calls, bills signed by the President, committee meetings, and a schedule of House and Senate meetings for the following day.

The bi-weekly Index and the master index for the bound edition of the *Record* are composed of two parts: an index to the proceedings, including material in the Extensions of Remarks; and a History of Bills and Resolutions. The index has a subject and name approach. The History is arranged by bill number. Bill number references are cumulative, however, so that with the latest index one can trace the history of a bill in page references to its introduction, committee report, debate, amendment(s), and enactment or defeat of the measure.

Amendments proposed in the House are noted in the Proceedings section. Although most of the work on bills is done in committee, only a summary of committee activity appears in the Daily Digest. The Digest, however, does include names of witnesses testifying before committee.

The *Record* contains recurring features of some reference value, such as a list of members with state and party affiliation; standing committees with names of members; U.S. judicial circuits with justices assigned and their territories; the various appellate courts and judges; names and home addresses of official reporters; Supreme Court justices and their home addresses; and the several laws and rules in effect for publication of the *Record.*

When Congress is in session, the visitor in the gallery of either chamber of the Congress sees the proceedings and debates being taken down by official reporters. By law the *Record* is supposed to be substantially a verbatim report of proceedings. But the privileges of "leave to print," revision (including the expunging of material), and alteration of members' remarks serve to define and qualify the word "substantially." In 1974 stenotype machine operators appeared on the floor of the Senate as part of the regular debate-recording operation. Prior to that the Senate's official reporters of debate recorded debate by shorthand. As of this writing the House has not succumbed to the advanced technology.

Commercial Sources

The *Federal Index* (Cleveland, Ohio: Predicasts, 1976) includes as one of its sources the *Congressional Record*, and provides citations to that source for proceedings, bills, and resolutions. The *Federal Index Annual* covers all information contained in the monthly issues. The first *Federal Index Annual* included information contained in Volume 1 of the *Federal Index* (October 1976 to September 1977) in one hardcopy volume. A subscription to the *Annual* and the monthly issues entitles the user to access the *Federal Index* file on the Lockheed (LIS) Dialog System (see Appendix A-III).

Capitol Services, Inc., a Washington, D.C.-based commercial publisher, issues a sequence of information services and products for clients involving the *Congressional Record* and the *Federal Register. CSI Congressional Report* contains a daily summary of House and Senate proceedings, organized by subject and referencing *Congressional Record* pages. Special editions of *Congressional Record Abstracts* are published each day following a meeting of the Congress and include topics such as energy, national defense, and foreign affairs. The abstract summaries cover new legislation introduced, co-sponsorships, floor actions and debate, committee actions and schedules, and communications from the executive. The *Master Edition* of *Congressional Record Abstracts* contains a comprehensive summary of the substantive content of each issue of the *Congressional Record.* Organized by subject, the scope of coverage is similar to the *special editions.*

Finally, a data base called *CRECORD* prepared by Capitol Services, Inc., is available on-line through System Development Corporation (SDC) Search Service Data Bases. Entry date into the SDC system for *CRECORD* was January 1976. Updating frequency is weekly, with about 1,750 items added to the data file weekly. Computer-connect time, as of 1977, was $80 an hour. The supplier does handle off-line prints. *CRECORD* covers the activities on the floor of Congress; proceedings are indexed and cross-referenced in about 275 legislative areas. It must be noted that *CRECORD* is a bibliographic search tool, not a full-text on-line service.

The United States Historical Documents Institute, Inc., issued a dual media reference collection entitled *Proceedings of the U.S. Congress 1789-1964.* This compilation includes the CR and its predecessors: *Annals of Congress* (1789-1824), *Register of Debates* (1824-1837), and *Congressional Globe* (1833-1873). On 35mm microfilm is the full text of the material, while 101 hardcopy volumes provide indexing access to the texts.

Information Handling Services (Englewood, Colorado) offers on microfiche the *Congressional Record, 1949-1974.* Included with the full text are the indexes. One may also subscribe to a current, updating service on standing order.

Readex Microprint Corporation offers the *Congressional Record*, daily edition, from 1957 to date as a separate.

Journals of the House and Senate

Like the *Congressional Record*, the House *Journal* (XJH; Item 1030) and Senate *Journal* (XJS; Item 1047) are assigned a classed notation but also have a series designation. The journals of Congress are the only publications required by the Constitution. Article I, Section 5 states: "Each House shall keep a Journal of its Proceedings, and from time to time publish the same. . . . " Consequently, the *Journals*, not the *Record*, are the official documents for the proceedings of Congress.

Both journals are published at the end of a session. The House *Journal* has appendixes that include proceedings subsequent to *sine die* adjournment, Rules of the House, questions of order decided in the House for that session, and a History of Bills and Resolutions. The Senate *Journal* has a History of Bills and Resolutions, arranged similarly to the House *Journal*: bills, joint resolutions, concurrent resolutions, and resolutions are organized by number, title, and action. The *Journals* have a name/subject/title index.

The House *Manual*, which contains the annotated rules of the House of Representatives, notes that members may decide what proceedings will be included in the *Journal*, "even to the extent of omitting things actually done or recording things not done." Nevertheless, the rules suggest that the *Journal* "ought to be a correct transcript of the proceedings of the House."[12] Rule IV of the Senate simply states that "the proceedings of the Senate shall be briefly and accurately stated in the *Journal*. Messages of the President in full; titles of bills and joint resolutions, and such parts as shall be affected by proposed amendments; every vote, and a brief statement of the contents of each petition, memorial, or paper presented to the Senate, shall be entered." Because the *Journals* are putatively a faithful record of activities, excluding debates, they provide easier access to retrospective procedural information than does the *Congressional Record.*

House General Publications

This category is classified but not designated. The notation Y 1.2 is followed by a Cutter number; Item 998 covers documents issued in this series. Many of the publications carried in this category are available for sale through the Superintendent, and most of the individual issues are compilations of laws grouped in related subjects: agriculture, bankruptcy, interstate commerce, social security, veterans, etc. A prominent exception is the quadrennial *Platforms of the Democratic Party and the Republican Party* (Y 1.2:P 69/year), prepared by the Clerk of the House of Representatives. It contains the text of the platforms adopted by the two parties at their respective national conventions held to nominate the presidential candidates.

The several compilations of laws are updated irregularly. Typical examples include *Laws Relating to Social Security and Unemployment Compensation* (Y 1.2:So 1) and *Atomic Energy Act of 1946 and Amendments* (Y 1.2:At 7). The series is compiled under the supervision of the Superintendent of the House Document Room.

A useful series covering House members is available to depository libraries. Titled *Annual Reports of Political Committees Supporting Candidates for House of Representatives* (Y 1.2/4; Item 998-C), it is compiled under the direction of the Clerk of the House and issued pursuant to the provisions of the 1971 Federal Election Campaign Act (PL 92-225, February 7, 1972). The Superintendent of Documents has been offering these reports for sale as separates.

House Calendars

Rule XIII of the House *Manual* delineates the handling of business reported from committees. The official document conveying this aspect of the legislative process is the *Calendars of the United States House of Representatives and History of Legislation* (Y 1.2/2; Item 998-A), which is published daily when the House is in session. Each issue is cumulative, and in every Monday issue there is a subject index of all legislation, both House and Senate, which has been reported by the committees and acted upon by either or both of the chambers, with the exception of Senate resolutions not of interest to the House and special House reports. Because of its ease of use and its cumulative features, many documents librarians find the *Calendars* to be the single most useful tool for the tracing of a bill's history.

Sections include "Bills in Conference" and "Bills through Conference," both arranged by *date*, with bill number, title of bill, House and Senate conferees, conference report number, and action taken. For "Bills through Conference" additional information includes public or private law numbers and date of approval. Following those tables, the various calendars are represented. The documents librarian will find the *Union Calendar* and *House Calendar* to be of the greatest value for legislative matters.[13] They are arranged by date with bill or report number, member and committee, title, and calendar number. Tables are also provided for the *Private Calendar, Consent Calendar,* and *Calendar of Motions to Discharge Committees.*

Tables on public and private laws are included, arranged by Congress and law number, referencing the bill number. Of perhaps most significance is a section entitled "Numerical Order of Bills and Resolutions Which Have Passed Either or Both Houses, and Bills Now Pending on the Calendars." Arranged numerically (and easily accessible through the subject index) by House bills, joint resolutions, concurrent resolutions, and resolutions, followed by similar tables for the Senate, it gives each bill's history to date. Similar or identical bills, and bills having reference to each other, are indicated by numbers in parentheses. Reference features include Special Legislative Days and Status of Major Bills, a table giving the legislative history of the bill, divided into Legislative Bills and Appropriation Bills.

The final edition of the *House Calendar* includes a list of bills that failed to become law as well as a summary of actions on all House and Senate bills and resolutions for the complete Congress. Issued biennially, it provides a Status of Major Bills table for each session of the Congress and notes vetoes as well. For bills that become law, the final edition of the *House Calendar* has a numerical listing of Public Law numbers, referencing bill numbers.

Senate General Publications

Classified in Y 1.3 (Item 998), publications in this series are new or recurring monographs compiled in the Senate Library under the direction of the Secretary of the Senate.

Presidential Vetoes: Record of Bills Vetoed and Action Taken Thereon by the Senate and House of Representatives, First Congress through the Ninetieth Congress, 1789-1968 (Y 1.3:V64/2) provides the reader with a comprehensive list of vetoes in one volume.

Nomination and Election of the President and Vice President of the United States, Including the Manner of Selecting Delegates to National Political Conventions (Y 1.3:P92/4/976) is a publication issued quadrennially with supplements as needed in the interval between presidential elections. It includes an analysis of election laws.

Factual Campaign Information (Y 1.3:C15/2/year) is revised biennially or as needed to serve Senators in their campaigns: every two years one-third of the Senate faces re-election.

Federal Election Campaign Laws (Y 1.3:C15/4) gathers in codified form the most pertinent and current federal election campaign laws, with citations to the *United States Code.*

Cumulative Index of Congressional Committee Hearings

The basic volume of this useful *Index* (Y 1.3:H35/2/yr./supp. no.; Item 998) with its *Supplements* provides an index to all the printed House and Senate hearings not confidential in character in the collection of the Senate Library. The series began with *Index of Congressional Committee Hearings Prior to January 3, 1935 in the United States Senate Library*, which is available in a 1968 Kraus reprint. The *Cumulative Index of Congressional Committee Hearings* for the 74th through the 85th Congress (1935-1959) was issued in 1959. Thereafter quadrennial supplements have been published.

Quadrennial Supplement to Cumulative Index of Congressional Committee Hearings for the 86th and 87th Congresses was followed by a *Second Quadrennial Supplement* (88th and 89th Congresses), a *Third Quadrennial Supplement* (90th and 91st Congresses), and a *Fourth Quadrennial Supplement* covering hearings during the 92d and 93d Congresses (1971-1974). The *Fourth* follows the same basic arrangement as the initial *Cumulative Index* and succeeding *Supplements*. Hearings are listed by subject matter, by committee, and by bill number, where applicable. However, the index to committee prints, one of the Appendixes in earlier editions, is omitted from this volume and a separate publication is planned.

In the *Fourth Quadrennial Supplement*, Appendix materials include executive hearings held by the Senate Foreign Relations Committee (1947-1950) published in the 93d Congress, and corrections for all the previous editions and supplements. This *Supplement*, like its immediate predecessor, was produced by the electronic photocomposition system of the GPO which permits computer storage of entries and utilization of the Linotron 1010 phototypesetting device.

Volume and tab numbers are those assigned by the Senate Library for reference to its own collection. The index's value as a bibliographic checklist for published hearings is limited by the absence of SuDocs class numbers for each entry. A study was conducted in 1975 to determine the feasibility of including the SuDocs number as part of each entry of the index, but it was decided that the undertaking was impracticable.

For the full text of hearings indexed in these volumes from the first issued in 1839 through 1969, Greenwood Press (Westport, Connecticut), an affiliate of Congressional Information Service, Inc., offers a microfiche edition. Moreover, Greenwood has assembled on microfiche a card-file *Witness Index to the US Congressional Hearings, 1839-1966*. From 1970 to date the CIS/Microfiche Library carries the full text of all published hearings.

Senate Calendar of Business

Less important than the House *Calendars* in tracing legislation, the *Senate Calendar of Business* (Y 1.3/3; Item 998-B) should be a selection of large depository libraries. Designated by Congress and Calendar Number following the Y 1.3/3 classification, the *Calendar of Business* is not cumulative and does not have an index; it is issued daily when the Senate is in session.

Pursuant to Rule VIII in the Senate *Manual*, there is a section in the Senate *Calendar* called "General Orders," which organizes legislation by order number, bill number and sponsor, title, and report number. "Bills in Conference" is a section arranged by date sent to conference, with bill number, brief title, Senate and House conferees, Senate report number, and current status. A separate table gives "Status of Appropriation Bills" and is arranged by bill number with brief title and legislative history to date. Ready reference information in the *Calendar of Business* includes the members and office locations of the Senate standing, special, and select committees.

Public Bills and Resolutions

The classification Y 2 was originally assigned for congressional bills and resolutions, followed by the Congress, session, and bill or resolution number. The category of public bills and resolutions is made available to depository libraries under Item 1006.

Defining accurately the borderline differences between *public* and *private* bills has been a vexing problem for lawmakers and scholars. The principal criterion of division seems to be legislative intent with an effort toward historical consistency and precedent. A bill that becomes law does not carry an indication of whether it is public or private, yet the Office of the Federal Register, in issuing the *Statutes at Large*, makes precisely that distinction. Save for the scholar-specialist's needs, libraries have little call for private bills or laws, although peculiarly House and Senate *reports* on private bills are available on deposit in unbound form (Item 1008-B) and in the bound volumes of the Serial Set (Item 1007-B).[14]

Bills (H.R.; S.)

The term *bill* is used in enacting new legislation or in amending previous legislation, and appears in the form shown in Figure 14, p. 168. It is by far the most common form of legislation. Bills may originate in either the House or the Senate, except for bills raising revenue which, according to Article I, Section 7, of the Constitution, shall originate in the House. It is also customary, but not necessary, that general appropriation measures originate in the House.

Joint Resolutions (H.J. Res.; S.J. Res.)

At one time the joint resolution was used for purposes of general legislation; but the two houses finally concluded that a bill was the proper instrumentality for

Figure 14
BILL: INTRODUCED PRINT

95TH CONGRESS
1ST SESSION

H. R. 9130

IN THE HOUSE OF REPRESENTATIVES

SEPTEMBER 15, 1977

Mr. PREYER introduced the following bill; which was referred jointly to the Committees on House Administration and Government Operations

A BILL

To amend the Freedom of Information Act to insure public access to the official papers of the President, and for other purposes.

1   *Be it enacted by the Senate and House of Representa-*

2   *tives of the United States of America in Congress assembled,*

3   TITLE I

4   SEC. 101. This Act shall be entitled the "Presidential

5   Papers Act of 1977".

6   SEC. 102. Section 2107 of title 44, United States Code,

7   is hereby amended by striking the short title and all of the

8   language which follows, substituting in lieu thereof the

9   following:

10   "SEC. 2107. OFFICIAL PAPERS OF THE PRESIDENT.—

    I

this purpose. However, the legal effect of joint resolutions is the same as that of bills. They may be used for "incidental or inferior" legislation, such as establishing the date for the convening of Congress, or "unusual" legislation, such as the Tonkin Gulf Resolution (H.J. Res. 1145, adopted August 7, 1964). The prescribed form of joint resolutions uses the word "resolved" rather than the phrase "be it enacted."

Amendments to the Constitution are proposed in the form of joint resolutions (Figure 15). Their passage through the legislative process is similar to that of ordinary joint resolutions, except for the two-thirds vote of both houses required by Article V of the Constitution. While all other joint resolutions, like bills, must be signed by the President to become law, constitutional amendments do not require his signature. After ratification by the legislatures of three-fourths of the states, the amendment is filed with the Administrator of General Services, who is responsible for its certification and publication.

Figure 15

HOUSE JOINT RESOLUTION

95TH CONGRESS
1ST SESSION
H. J. RES. 159

IN THE HOUSE OF REPRESENTATIVES

JANUARY 19, 1977

Mr. GAYDOS introduced the following joint resolution; which was referred to the Committee on the Judiciary

---

JOINT RESOLUTION

Proposing an amendment to the Constitution of the United States
guaranteeing the right to life to the unborn, the ill, the aged,
or the incapacitated.

1   *Resolved by the Senate and House of Representatives*

2   *of the United States of America in Congress assembled*

3   *(two-thirds of each House concurring therein),* That the

4   following article is proposed as an amendment to the Consti-

5   tution of the United States, which shall be valid to all intents

6   and purposes as a part of the Constitution only if ratified

7   by the legislatures of three-fourths of the several States

8   within seven years from the date of its submission by the

9   Congress:

I

Concurrent Resolutions (H. Con. Res.; S. Con. Res.)

This form does not have the force of law. Concurrent resolutions are used for matters in which the two chambers have a mutual interest. They are used to express an opinion, a "sense of" the House and Senate. They are identified and/or published in the *Congressional Record*, and later appear in the journals of the two chambers. Although they do not require the signature of the President, they are published in the *Statutes at Large* (Figure 16).

Figure 16

HOUSE CONCURRENT RESOLUTION

95TH CONGRESS
1ST SESSION

H. CON. RES. 60

IN THE SENATE OF THE UNITED STATES

SEPTEMBER 28 (legislative day, SEPTEMBER 22), 1977
Referred to the Committee on Rules and Administration

CONCURRENT RESOLUTION

1   *Resolved by the House of Representatives (the Senate*

2   *concurring),* That the Joint Committee on the Library is

3   authorized and directed to procure a bust or statue of Martin

4   Luther King, Junior, and to cause such sculpture to be

5   placed in a suitable location in the Capitol as determined by

6   the Joint Committee on the Library.

7   SEC. 2. Expenses incurred by the Joint Committee on

8   the Library in carrying out this concurrent resolution, which

9   shall not exceed $25,000, shall be paid out of the contingent

10 fund of the House on vouchers approved by the chairman of

11 the joint committee.

   Passed the House of Representatives September 26, 1977.

   Attest: EDMUND L. HENSHAW, JR.,

                                              Clerk.

V

Resolutions (H. Res.; S. Res.)

Known as "simple" resolutions, they govern the action of only one house and are used for the concern only of the chamber passing them. They affect procedural matters of the body to which they relate, need no presidential signature, and may be found in the *Congressional Record*, and later appear in the House and Senate *Journals* (Figure 17).

Figure 17

HOUSE RESOLUTION

95TH CONGRESS
1ST SESSION

H. RES. 837

IN THE HOUSE OF REPRESENTATIVES

OCTOBER 17, 1977

Mr. BINGHAM submitted the following resolution; which was referred to the
Committee on House Administration

RESOLUTION

1   *Resolved,* That there shall be printed for the use of the

2   Committee on International Relations one thousand copies of

3   the committee print entitled "The Coordination of United

4   States International Economic Policy".

V

The majority of bills are printed only once. About 12 percent are reprinted at various steps in the legislative process. The first printing is known as the "introduced print," but when reported from committee there is a "reported print" with calendar number and House or Senate report number indicated. When passed by one body and sent to the other house, the bill is called "an act" and is known as a "referred (act) print." When reported from committee in that body there can be another printing. There are other variations and some problems associated with the total distribution of bills including all amendments, but organizing bills by number and session is a routine task in libraries.[15]

When the retrospective holdings of the Public Documents Library were transferred to the National Archives, there were only a relatively small number of bills and resolutions saved. In remarks preceding the section "Y 2. Bills and Resolutions of Senate and House" of the *Checklist, 1789-1909* one finds the following:

> Bills and resolutions of the 2 Houses of Congress are not sent to libraries. The only provision of law requiring their preservation is sec. 82 of the general printing act of Jan. 12, 1895, which provides that 4 sets shall be found, of which 2 are deposited in the Senate document room and 2 in the House document room at the Capitol. . . . The files of Senate and House bills and resolutions in the Public Documents Library are very incomplete and no attempt is made here to list them. The few that it does have are arranged by the number of the Congress and session.[16]

The effect of section 82 of the 1895 Act seems to have influenced SuDocs depository policy to the present. All depository libraries, including regionals, are permitted to dispose of House and Senate bills and resolutions "one year after the adjournment of the Congress."[17] As a consequence there are few depository institutions in this country that boast of a substantial retrospective collection of these valuable publications. Fortunately, the Library of Congress houses a complete collection of the printed versions of public and private bills and resolutions in each parliamentary stage.

Access to LC's collection is now possible through *CIS/Bills on Microfiche* series, covering the 90th through the 94th Congress. For each Congress, the bills on microfiche are filed sequentially by bill number within bill category. The different versions of a bill are arranged chronologically behind the introduced print. In addition, beginning with the 93d Congress, the text of the public or private slip law is available for the enacted bills. Readex Microprint offers the text of bills and resolutions covering the years 1957-1965 during which time they were listed by bill number in the *Monthly Catalog*. Another source of bills in microform is the *Legislative Histories* issued by Information Handling Services (Englewood, Colorado). Typically, the *Histories* include the House or Senate bill with its various versions, including amendments.

Finally, the most current search strategy for determining the status of a bill or resolution when the Congress is in session is to telephone the *Bill Status Office* (202/225-1772) located in the Rayburn House Office Building. Inquiries may be accommodated by means of bill number, sponsor or co-sponsor, referral Committee, date introduced, or subject matter.

CONGRESSIONAL COMMITTEE PUBLICATIONS

The several standing, joint, and select or special committees of the House and Senate issue a large body of materials. They are both classed and designated. Numbered series are easily controlled. Other categories are somewhat elusive. The lack of uniformity in printing and distribution of publications of Congress causes problems in access and bibliographic control. Although virtually every congressional committee has been assigned an Item number for deposit, not all publications issued by committees are available on deposit.

Like other aspects of government reorganization, the committees of Congress suffer changes from time to time. In 1975, the House Committee on Foreign Affairs changed its name to the Committee on International Relations, and the SuDocs class notation also changed from Y 4.F76/1 to Y 4.In 8/16. In 1977 the Senate engaged in a flurry of committee reorganization. During that year the Committee on Public Works became the Committee on Environment and Public Works. The Committee on Labor and Public Welfare is now the Committee on Human Resources. The Interior and Insular Affairs Committee, reflecting the new energy concern, became the Committee on Energy and Natural Resources. And several other committees of the Senate underwent change of name. Joint committees did not escape reorganization. For example, the Joint Committee on Internal Revenue Taxation became in 1977 simply the Joint Committee on Taxation, forcing a change in SuDocs classification from Y 4.In 8/11 to Y 4.T 19/4.

Legislative Calendars

Individual committees issue calendars on an irregular schedule. Often overlooked in reference work because they are not depository Items, the committee calendars represent yet another index to legislation. Since they cumulate, the final issue covers an entire Congress. They are classed in Y 4. followed by a Cutter symbol for the specific committee. Following the Cutter symbol, the calendars are designated by Congress and calendar numbers.

A typical legislative calendar includes information on presidential messages referred to committee; status of bills referred to committee on which action has been taken; notice of miscellaneous publications by the committee; nominations before the committee and committee action; hearings held, arranged by bill number; House and Senate bills and resolutions referred to committee, arranged by date; and separate author and subject indexes.

Legislative calendars were indexed in the 1977 *Serials Supplement* to the *Monthly Catalog* in the "Title Index" as this example shows:

Legislative calendar—United States House of

Representatives. Committee on Armed

Services, 77-6603

Codes

Previous editions of the *United States Code* have been published in 1926, 1934, 1940, 1946, 1952, 1958, 1964, 1970, and 1976. Cumulative annual *Supplements* appear between editions. Many of the general and permanent laws which are required to be incorporated in current editions of the U.S.C. are inconsistent, redundant, and obsolete. Accordingly, the Office of the Law Revision

Counsel is engaged in a comprehensive project to revise and enact the *Code* into law, title by title. As of 1977, bills have been passed to revise, codify and enact into law some nineteen titles. In addition, bills relating to other titles are continually being prepared for introduction. When the task is finally completed, all the titles of the *United States Code* will be legal evidence of the general and permanent laws. Recourse to the *Statutes at Large* for this purpose will then be unnecessary.

Formerly the *Code* was classed in Y 4.J89/1: Un3/3. However, *Daily Depository Shipping List No. 10,378* (November 28, 1977) announced that the 1976 edition of the *Code* (Volume One, Titles 1-7) would be classed in Y 1.2/5:(yr./vols.). The depository Item number (991) remains the same. The 1976 edition, containing the general and permanent laws of the United States in force as of January 3, 1977, was prepared and published under the authority of Title 2, *United States Code*, Section 285b, by the Office of the Law Revision Counsel of the House of Representatives with the assistance of the West Publishing Company, the commercial firm that issues the *United States Code Annotated.* The official version includes tables covering presidential documents (see Chapter 7), conversion tables from the *Statutes at Large* to the *Code, District of Columbia Code* sections classified to the *U.S. Code*, an "Index of Acts Cited by Popular Name," and a general subject index.

The House Judiciary Committee continues to issue the *District of Columbia Code* and *Supplements* (Y 4.J89/1:D63/24; Item 990).

Code Finding Aid

A useful finding aid for accurate citations to the *United States Code* is issued by the Office of the Federal Register. *How to Find U.S. Statutes and U.S. Code Citations* (3d rev. ed.; 1977) is an eight-page guide designed to enable the user who has a reference to the *Revised Statutes, Statutes at Large*, name or number of public law to find the appropriate citation to the U.S.C. or to its *Supplements.* Moreover, references make note of commercial publications like U.S.C.C.A.N., *United States Code Annotated, United States Code Service*, and *Shepard's Acts and Cases by Popular Name.*

Directories

The *Congressional Directory* (Y 4.P93/1:1; Item 992) is a basic reference source issued once every Congress, with a supplement for the second session. Issued by the Joint Committee on Printing, its contents vary from time to time. Standard information usually includes, in addition to the biographical section of members, committee and sub-committee listings; foreign representatives and consular offices in the United States; maps of congressional districts; State delegations; press representatives and services; and a host of other useful ready reference materials. The *Directory* is available on microfiche from 1909 to date from Information Handling Services.

A commercial directory is edited by Charles R. Brownson. It is entitled *Congressional Staff Directory*, and includes House and Senate assignments to committees and sub-committees, biographies of the staff, and a list of almost

10,000 cities and towns with their congressional districts and members. A companion volume to this directory is called *Advance Locator for Capitol Hill*. Issued as a "pre-publication supplement" to the *Congressional Staff Directory*, it contains biographical briefs, suite numbers, extensions, district offices, and updated information for the executive branch.

The Washington Monitor, Inc. (Washington, D.C.) publishes the *Congressional Yellow Book*, a looseleaf directory issued quarterly. It contains directory-type information of members of Congress, their committees and key staff aides. Also included are key personnel of the Library of Congress, Government Printing Office, and General Accounting Office.

Biographical Directory of the American Congress

Earlier editions of this compilation have been issued under different names since 1859. Cumulative issues covering the years 1774-1949 and 1774-1961 were issued as House *documents*. The *Biographical Directory 1774-1971* (Item 995-G) was issued as 92-1: S. doc. 8 [Serial 12938]. It includes almost 11,000 short biographies of members of the House and Senate for those years. A feature of this edition is biographies of Presidents who were not members of Congress. The *Biographical Directory* is updated by the annual *Congressional Directory*. A microfilm edition of the *Biographical Directory 1774-1971* is available commercially from Dataflow Systems Incorporated, Bethesda, Maryland.

Hearings

The type of information contained in committee hearing transcripts can generally be categorized in one of the following ways:

1. Exploratory hearings provide testimony and data about general topical areas;

2. Legislative hearings provide testimony and data about one or more specific pieces of legislation;

3. Evaluative and oversight hearings provide testimony and data about the economy and efficiency of program operations; and

4. Appropriation hearings provide interconnected testimony and data about department or agency operations, oversight activities, and comparative fiscal information.[18]

Hearings do not constitute a real series, although some committees have serialized their publications for their own convenience. Some hearings are designated alphabetically, some numerically. Some series run through a session, some through a Congress. Hearings are classed in Y 4 and are often issued in "Parts" when multi-volumed. Hearings are also designated by other devices. The Watergate hearings, for example, were conducted in phases, and the issuing notation read: Y 4.P92/4: P92/phase 1/bk. 4, etc.

An example of accessing hearings through the *Monthly Catalog*'s subject index is as follows:

        Consumer Protection--Law and legislation--

    United States

        Consumer fuel discloser act of 1975:

        hearing before the Subcommittee for

        Consumers of the Committee on Commerce,

        United States Senate, Ninety-fourth

        Congress, first session, on S. 1508. . .

        October 29, 1975. . ., 76-3606

But by far the most useful current source for hearings is *CIS/Index*, which indexes by witness as well as by subject or committee/subcommittee. Moreover, the *CIS/Annual* provides a guide to multi-volume hearings, information which was not available at the time monthly coverage was provided.

Information Handling Services (IHS) includes hearings in its *Legislative Histories on Microfiche*. Berman Associates' *Checklist of Congressional Hearings* is a service which lists hearings promptly after they are printed and provides a concise explanation of the topic covered and the name of the particular committee from which a copy may be requested free of charge.

Virtually all committees of Congress make their hearings available to depository libraries unless they are classified or otherwise limited in distribution. When a hearing held in executive session is declassified, it will be offered on deposit and on the cover will indicate its declassification, often with phrases such as "Secret Hearing Held on (date); Sanitized and Made Public on (date)."[19]

Committee Prints

Committee prints are publications prepared for the use and reference of a given committee, either as staff or consultant research studies, activity reports, or compilations of materials of general interest. Many committee prints are working studies prepared in the course of formulating legislation, and as such are useful to legislators and the general public.

Committee prints continue to be issued in an inconsistent manner. Many do not have numbering or series designation. Some are offered to depository libraries, others are not. Some are placed on sale by SuDocs, others may be requested from the committee, secured through one's Representative, ordered by subscription through the Documents Expediting Project, or purchased in microform editions such as *Readex* or *CIS*.

Sometimes a committee print, in revised form, is reissued as a *document* or *report* in the numbered Serial Set. Other peculiar variations in distribution and form occur. For example, 94-2: S. doc. 247 was sent to depository libraries as Serial 13140-5 but was made available for sale in the "committee print edition" *only* under S/N 052-070-03373.

Like hearings, executive reports and documents, and other congressional materials, committee prints are most easily accessed through *CIS/Index* and its cumulations. Since so many committee prints contain valuable information, the lack of a systematic distribution policy for these publications remains a concern for the documents librarian.[20] Often the useful print will be made available on deposit: *Citizen's Guide to Individual Rights under the Constitution of the United States of America*, October 1976 (Y 4.J89/2:R44/976; Item 1042); *Transportation of Radioactive Material by Passenger Aircraft*, September 1974 (Y 4.At 7/2:R11/18; Item 999); *Mobil Oil Corporation: Failure to Deliver Natural Gas to the Interstate Market*, February 1976 (Y 4.In 8/4:Oi 5/7; Item 1019). More often, however, valuable committee prints will not be assigned depository status: *Annual Report of the Congressional Research Service of the Library of Congress for Fiscal Year 1975* (April 1976); *Background Information for Alaska Lands Designations* (April 1977); *Hospital Cost Containments* (May 1977); *Electric Utility Sector: Concepts, Practices, and Problems* (May 1977); *International Narcotics Control Community* (February 1977).

Committee prints promptly announced in *CIS/Index* without Item number designation may subsequently receive depository distribution, but the process is patently inadequate.

A retrospective collection of committee prints on microfiche is published by Greenwood Press (Westport, Connecticut) covering the years 1911-1969. The collection is available in two parts: Group 1: *US Congressional Committee Prints, 61st-91st Congress, 1st Session, in the US Senate Library* and Group 2: *US Congressional Committee Prints, 65th-91st Congress, 1st Session, Not in the US Senate Library*. The latter group consists of prints that were filmed at the Library of Congress and the National Archives.

Reports and Documents

The next section of this chapter will provide an analysis of the *reports* and *documents* that comprise the famous Serial Set. However, some recurring publications of general reference value are issued in this Congressional series. Many librarians choose to separate these publications from their Serial number order in the bound set and have them classed in the general reference collection.

Reports and *documents* are designated by Congress, session, and number, although they are numbered consecutively through a Congress. Some are issued in Serial Set binding only; others appear first in unbound form and later are incorporated into the bound Serial volumes. The following publications represent a selected number of *documents* in this series which are of more than routine interest.

House Manual

The full title of this publication is *Constitution, Jefferson's Manual, and Rules of the House of Representatives* (94-2: H. doc. 663; Item 1029) and it is issued biennially in Serial binding [13152]. The reason for the lengthy title is that the parliamentary practice of the House derives from four sources: the Constitution, *Jefferson's Manual*, the rules adopted by the House itself from the beginning of its existence, and decisions of the Chairman of the Committee of the Whole. In the years from 1797 to 1801 Thomas Jefferson, then Vice President of the United States, prepared the notable work that has come to be known as *Jefferson's Manual*. This *oeuvre* contributed significantly to House procedures, and many provisions of *Jefferson's Manual* still govern the body.

Deschler's Precedents

Deschler's Precedents of the United States House of Representatives (94-2: H. doc. 661) is the latest in a distinguished series of volumes analyzing the precedents of the House. Issued as Serial 13151-1, the author, Lewis Deschler, was Parliamentarian of the House from 1928 to 1974. The early precedents of the House, dating from the First Congress, are found in Asher Hinds' monumental work published in 1907. This was supplemented by Clarence Cannon in a comprehensive study of House precedents from 1908 to 1936.[21]

PL 93-554 (88 Stat. 1777) requires that the precedents be updated every two years. It will be the function of the present volumes to review the precedents from 1936 through the first session of the 93d Congress, and subsequent precedents will be issued in supplements to Deschler's edition to be prepared for each Congress.

Senate Manual

At the commencement of each new Congress, the Senate Committee on Rules and Administration prepares and issues a revised edition of that body's rules, regulations, statutes, and other materials relating to the operation and organization of the Senate. The full title of the document is *Senate Manual, Containing the Standing Rules, Orders, Laws, and Resolutions Affecting the Business of the United States Senate; Jefferson's Manual; Declaration of Independence; Articles of Confederation; Constitution of the United States, etc.* (94-1: S. doc. 1; Item 1048). Like the *House Manual*, the value of the *Senate Manual* lies in its gloss on the rules governing this body. The *Manual* for the 94th Congress was issued as Serial volume 13103.

Senate Procedure

The revised edition of *Senate Procedure: Precedents and Practices* (93-1: S. doc. 21; Item 995-G) was written by Floyd M. Riddick, Senate Parliamentarian, and issued as Serial volume 13028. Copyrighted by the author under the provisions of PL 92-386 (86 Stat. 559), *Senate Procedure* is over 1,000 pages and is a compilation of Senate rules, arranged alphabetically by subject or procedure.

Reports to Be Made to Congress

Rule III, clause 2, of the Rules of the House of Representatives require the Clerk of that body to compile a list of reports "which it is the duty of any officer or department to make to Congress." Usually revised annually, the current edition (95-1: H. doc. 10; Item 996) gives detailed information on reports which must be submitted by the President, by heads of independent agencies, by Cabinet-level departments and specific agencies within those departments, by the judicial and legislative branches, and by federally chartered private corporations. For each report listed, the document gives the title of the report, its statutory authority, and the date by which the report is to be transmitted to the Congress. There is an index of reporting departments and agencies.

United States Contributions to International Organizations

Issued as an annual report on United States contributions to all the international bodies in which the U.S. participates as a member for the fiscal year, *Contributions* (94-2: H. doc. 333; Item 996) is arranged by international body, with a useful summary of the purpose, structure, origin and development of the body. Tabular data include U.S. contributions to international organizations from 1946 to the present.

Constitution of the United States of America—
Analysis and Interpretation

PL 91-589 (December 24, 1970) mandates that the Congressional Research Service of the Library of Congress issue a new edition of the *Constitution Annotated* (its popular title) every ten years and to supplement the basic volume with cumulative pocket parts every two years. The basic volume (92-2: S. doc. 82 [12980-7]; Item 995-G) consists of an analysis of the Constitution and its amendments together with historic and leading Supreme Court decisions construing each provision. It also includes federal, state and local laws determined to be unconstitutional and Supreme Court decisions overruling previous decisions.

The *1974 Supplement* (93-2: S. doc. 134) was issued as Serial volume 13067-12 and covers the October 1972 and 1973 terms of the high court to July 25, 1974. It continues in the same format as the basic volume and is to be inserted in the pocket on the inside back cover of that volume. The *1976 Supplement* (94-2: S. doc. 200 [13140-2]) cumulated the material covered in the *1974 Supplement* and covers the period from the end of the main edition through July 6, 1976. Although, as noted, the basic volume was prepared with a place for pocket parts, the 1976 cumulation, 224 pages in length, is too large to be conveniently inserted there.

Executive Documents and Reports

Senate Executive Documents and Reports finally became a depository Item. On *Daily Depository Shipping List 10,027* (*Survey 77-206*, August 5, 1977) the Documents and Reports were offered to depository institutions under Item 1008-A-1. They are classed in Y 1 and designated by Congress and session.

Senate executive documents are a *lettered* series by which the President and Secretary of State transmit to the Senate Foreign Relations Committee the text of treaties requesting advice and consent. For example: *Treaty with the Swiss Confederation on Mutual Assistance in Criminal Matters*, February 18, 1976 (Y 1.94/2:F).

Senate executive reports are a *numbered* series which appear to serve two purposes: 1) When issued by the Senate Foreign Relations Committee, they recommend to the full Senate that a treaty proposed by the President (in a Senate executive document) be approved by virtue of the Senate's "advice and consent" duty under the Constitution. For example: recommending ratification of the Patent Cooperation Treaty (Y 1.93/1: rp. 20). 2) When issued by any Senate committee with the appropriate oversight function (including Foreign Relations), they recommend confirmation of presidential nominations of high officials in the executive and judiciary. An example of this kind of executive report is *Consideration of Harold Brown to Be Secretary of Defense*, a report issued by the Senate Armed Services Committee, January 18, 1977 (Y 1.95/1: rp. 2).

Because the *Monthly Catalog* indexes executive reports and documents, they are carried in Readex's depository publications series. For best access, however, the indexing and abstracting capabilities of *CIS/Index* should be exploited (see Chapter 7).

Memorial Addresses

Eulogies delivered in the House or Senate upon the death of a member of Congress or former member are classed Y 7.1, the last active symbol in the SuDocs classification system.[22] Libraries subscribing to Item 1005 receive these addresses in handsome, bound volumes with the Y 7.1 notation. Following the colon, individual book numbers are assigned by using the 3-figure Cutter table based on the name of the deceased member.

When Presidents or presidential appointees who have held high office in the executive or judiciary are memorialized, the compilations of tributes are issued in the Congressional series. The distinction is not always observed, however. Memorial issuances in the case of persons who have enjoyed distinguished careers both in the Congress and in other government positions are not always consistent.

Some examples will illustrate the pattern. Memorial services in Congress for General Eisenhower were issued as 91-1: H. doc. 195 [12852-9]. Eisenhower, of course, never served in the Congress. Tributes in eulogy of John F. Kennedy, who served in the House and Senate before becoming President, appeared as 88-2: S. doc. 59 [12624]. Tributes to James F. Byrnes, who served in both houses and on the Supreme Court and held office in the federal executive, showed up as 92-2: S. doc. 77 [12980-6]. Memorial tributes for Harry S. Truman, senator and President, was issued as 93-1: H. doc. 131 [13034-3]. And addresses in the

Congress in memory of Kenneth B. Keating, a senator who also served as ambassador to India and Israel, appeared as 94-1: S. doc. 74 [13105-3] .

Normally, compilations in the Congressional series by-pass the unbound House or Senate *documents* series (Item 996) and are sent to libraries in "Serial Set binding" (Item 995-G).[23] Because of this pattern, depository libraries that wish to ensure receipt of all memorial addresses should subscribe to Items 1005 and 995-G.

THE SERIAL SET

The peculiar pattern of distribution of memorial addresses noted above is but one instance of the difficulty of fully comprehending the legendary series known variously as the serial number set, sheep set, congressional set, or congressional series. The Serial Set looms Sphinx-like over the federal documents landscape. Throughout its enigmatic history it has included the House and Senate *Journals*, executive and miscellaneous publications of both bodies, reports on private and public legislation, the annual reports of the executive and independent agencies, reports on audits of federally charted private corporations, investigative and background studies, proceedings of certain societies and associations, and much more. Schmeckebier and Eastin present a thorough account of the historical Serial Set.[24] This discussion will be concerned with the present use and control of the publications that comprise the series. The basic composition of the Serial Set is deceptively simple: it consists of two categories of congressional publications— House and Senate *reports*, and House and Senate *documents*.

Reports

For both the House and the Senate, this series consists of 1) miscellaneous reports on public bills; 2) miscellaneous reports on private bills; and 3) special reports. The first two categories constitute the vast majority of *reports*. All *reports* are designated by Congress, session, and individual number, and the numerical designation extends throughout a Congress.

Committee reports which accompany public and private bills voted out of committee describe the purpose and scope of the bill and the reasons for its recommended approval. Reports on public bills, particularly appropriation bills, are required to contain various fiscal and budget information, including an estimate of the costs to be incurred (or revenue to be raised or lost) in the fiscal year the bill is reported and the five succeeding fiscal years. Conference reports, which are required by House Rules to be printed in full in the *Congressional Record*, must be accompanied by an explanatory statement prepared jointly by the House and Senate conferees, sufficiently detailed and explicit to inform members of the effect that the amendments or propositions contained in the report will have upon the original measure.[25] Reports on public bills are of great significance in the legislative process because they establish legislative intent and are used by the executive departments and the courts as the primary source of information regarding the purpose and meaning of the legislation.[26]

Special reports include investigative activities of committees, pro forma orders for a recurring publication to be printed, summaries of legislative and oversight activities of committees, studies of matters relating to public policy, and the like. Some examples indicate the scope and variety of reports in this category:

Legislative History of Committee on Foreign Relations (94-1: S. rp. 37)

Legislative Review during 93d Congress, Senate Committee on Rules and Administration (94-1: S. rp. 90)

Disapprove Construction Projects on Island of Diego Garcia (94-1: S.rp. 202)

Congregate Housing for Older Adults (94-1: S. rp. 478)

Oversight Report on Assistance to Indochina Evacuation (94-1: H. rp. 205)

Minority Enterprise and Allied Problems of Small Business (94-1: H. rp. 468)

Effects of New York City's Fiscal Crisis on Small Business (94-1: H. rp. 659)

Proceedings Against Henry A. Kissinger (94-1: H. rp. 693)

Documents

House and Senate *documents*, like *reports*, are designated by Congress, session, and individual number. Throughout this text, the word "documents" has been used in a generic sense, synonymous with "publications" or "materials." For Serial Set publications in this series, the word assumes a specificity not encountered elsewhere.

The kinds of materials ordered to be published as House or Senate *documents* are many and varied. In the "Miscellaneous" series bound in Serial volumes bearing the same base serial number with the issues in the group differentiated (e.g., 13109-1, 13109-2, 13109-3, etc.) one finds presidential messages, including vetoes; reports on rescissions and deferrals of budget authority; budget amendments; the President's State of the Union address; a few annual reports of agencies and federally chartered private corporations; reference works such as *How Our Laws Are Made*, *Biographical Directory of the American Congress*, *Inaugural Addresses of the Presidents of the United States*, House and Senate *Manuals*, and other issuances often difficult to categorize.

Reports on audits of government corporations are usually grouped into a Serial volume. The reports are required to set forth the scope of financial audit, documentation of the body's assets and liabilities, income and expenses, and activities for the fiscal year. Listed with statutory authority in *Reports to Be Made to Congress* (itself issued as a House *document*), the corporations include Federal Crop Insurance Corporation, U.S. Railway Association, Tennessee Valley Authority, National Flood Insurance Program, etc.

Inconsistencies have always characterized the *documents* series. The *Annual Report to Congress, Boy Scouts of America*, is frequently offered as a sales item and is advertised in *Selected U.S. Government Publications*. But when it is issued in the *documents* series, it is bound in one volume with the *Annual Report of the Girl Scouts* and sent to libraries that subscribe to depository Item 995-P. The *Annual Report of the National Academy of Sciences FY 1972* was sent to depository institutions in its "departmental edition" (NA 1.1; Item 830) whereas the *Annual*

Reports of that entity for FY 1973 and 1974 were issued together as a Senate *document* in Serial volume 13105-4.

Availability

According to the "General Information" section of the *Monthly Catalog*, "subscription service has been implemented" for House and Senate *reports* and *documents*. But "in most cases, single copies of publications in these groups . . . are not sold. Sales copies of a few of the more important ones are printed, and you will find the sales prices listed in the individual entries." For non-depository libraries, the *CIS/Microfiche Library* offers all *reports* and *documents*. In addition, individual copies may be obtained from the House and Senate Document Room, from the issuing committee, or from one's Representative.

Indexing

Reports are indexed in many places. As soon as a bill has been reported out of committee, it is assigned a report number. Thus it is easy to access the report through the index to the *Congressional Record*, the *House Calendar*, *Digest of Public General Bills*, House and Senate *Journals, Monthly Catalog*, CCH *Congressional Index*, and other sources. *CIS/Index*, of course, both abstracts and indexes *reports* and *documents*.

For *documents* the *Monthly Catalog* and *CIS/Index* are useful sources.

Numerical Lists and Schedule of Volumes

The *Numerical Lists* (GP 3.7/2; Item 553) is classed and designated by Congress and session. It bridges the gap between the numerical assignments of individual *reports* and *documents* and their appearance in Serial Set binding. The *Lists* are compiled under the direction of the Assistant Public Printer (Superintendent of Documents) and issued sessionally from that provenance. *Lists* are not only a depository Item but are sold by SuDocs.

Unbound copies of *reports* and *documents* are received in depository libraries under the following Items:

Reports on Public Bills (including "Special Reports")	1008-A
Reports on Private Bills	1008-B
Documents	996

When issued they receive an individual number as noted in the examples on the preceding pages. During each session most of the *reports* and *documents* are accumulated into bound volumes and the volume is assigned a serial number. Some *reports* and *documents* are never issued in unbound form but are sent to depository libraries "in Serial Set binding." Nevertheless, these publications are assigned an individual number as well as a serial number.

If you know the individual *report* or *document* number, the *Numerical Lists* is the finding aid by which you convert that number into the serial number. But the *Numerical Lists* have no subject approach. However, having determined the *report* or *document* number from other indexing sources, it is an easy matter to convert using the *Lists*.

The title of this publication literally identifies its two-part arrangement, as follows:

Part 1, the "Numerical Lists" (Figure 18), gives all House and Senate *reports* and *documents* by individual number, title, and a volume/serial designation. The serial number is followed by subdivisions numbered -1, -2, -3, etc., so that grouping of like categories all have the same base serial number.

Figure 18

NUMERICAL LISTS

NUMERICAL LISTS

Of the Reports and Documents of the 94th Congress, 1st Session

SENATE REPORTS

No.		Vol.; serial
1.	24th annual report of activities of Joint Committee on Defense Production, with material on mobilization from departments and agencies. 2 pts	3-2; **13098-2**
2.	Supplemental expenditures by Special Committee on Aging	1-1; **13096-1**
3.	Increase limitation on expenditures by Committee on Rules and Administration	1-1; **13096-1**
4.	Additional expenditures by Committee on Rules and Administration	1-1; **13096-1**
5.	Regional rail reorganization act amendments of 1975	1-1; **13096-1**
6.	Attorney General's salary	1-1; **13096-1**
7.	Maritime Administration authorization, fiscal 1975	1-1; **13096-1**
8.	Increase amount of uranium distributed to International Atomic Energy Agency	1-1; **13096-1**
9.	Increase amount of uranium distributed to European Atomic Energy Community	1-1; **13096-1**
10.	Extend research agreement for cooperation between U.S. and Israel concerning uses of atomic energy	1-1; **13096-1**
11.	Suspend Presidential authority to impose fees on or adjust petroleum imports	1-1; **13096-1**
12.	Increase temporary limit on public debt	1-1; **13096-1**
13.	25th annual report of Select Committee on Small Business, U.S. Senate, 93d Cong. 2d sess	3-3; **13098-3**
14.	Designate March 13, 1975, Music in Our Schools Day	1-1; **13096-1**
15.	Authorize the President to issue proclamation designating March 1975 Youth Art Month	1-1; **13096-1**
16.	Forest pest control	1-1; **13096-1**
17.	Funds for study of U.S. foreign policy	1-1; **13096-1**
18.	Establish Naval and Marine Museum in Charleston, S.C.	1-1; **13096-1**
19.	Senate delegations responding to invitations from foreign governments	1-1; **13096-1**
20.	Amend act of June 30, 1954, continue civil government Trust Territory of Pacific Islands	1-1; **13096-1**
21.	Further urgent supplemental appropriations, 1975	1-1; **13096-1**
22.	Interparliamentary activities and reception of foreign officials	1-1; **13096-1**
23.	Resolution disapproving deferral of budget authority	1-1; **13096-1**
24.	Budget rescission bill	1-1; **13096-1**
25.	Further continuing appropriations, 1975	1-1; **13906-1**
26.	Standby energy authorities act	1-1; **13096-1**
27.	Implement new congressional budget procedures, fiscal 1976	3-1; **13098-1**
28.	Surface mining control and reclamation act of 1975	1-1; **13096-1**
29.	Nurse training and health revenue sharing and health services act of 1975	3-4; **13098-4**

Part 2, the "Schedule of Volumes," (Figure 19), shows the individual *reports* and *documents* included in each bound volume. The "Date of Receipt" column is a handy place for librarians to note the bound issues that have been received and to discard all issues received in slip form. Grouping bound volumes into Miscellaneous Reports on Public Bills and Miscellaneous Reports on Private Bills was begun with the 84th Congress; grouping of Special Reports commenced with the 88th Congress.

Figure 19
SCHEDULE OF VOLUMES

SCHEDULE OF VOLUMES

Of the Reports and Documents of the 94th Congress, 1st Session

Note.—For explanation regarding the distribution, etc., of the bound set of Congressional documents and reports listed below see the Preface.

SENATE REPORTS

			Serial no.	Date of receipt
Vol.	1–1.	Nos. 2–12, 14–26, 28, 30, 32–36, 38–48, 50–51, 53–57, 59, 62–63, 65: **Miscellaneous reports on public bills. I**	13096–1	
Vol.	1–2.	Nos. 66–78, 81–86, 88–89, 91, 93–94, 96–114, 118–132: **Miscellaneous reports on public bills. II**	13096–2	
Vol.	1–3.	Nos. 133–190: **Miscellaneous reports on public bills. III**	13096–3	
Vol.	1–4.	Nos. 191–201, 203–220, 251–255, 257–260, 262–282: **Miscellaneous reports on public bills. IV**	13096–4	
Vol.	1–5.	Nos. 283–296, 298–312, 314, 316–328: **Miscellaneous reports on public bills. V**	13096–5	
Vol.	1–6.	Nos. 329–345, 347–383, 385–389, 399–408, 410, 412: **Miscellaneous reports on public bills. VI**	13096–6	
Vol.	1–7.	Nos. 414–418, 420–421, 423–424, 426–432, 434–436, 438–445, 447, 449, 451–455, 457–464, 466–470, 472–476, 479–486: **Misscellaneous reports on public bills. VII**	13096–7	
Vol.	1–8.	Nos. 487–498, 500–502, 504–532: **Miscellaneous reports on public bills. VIII**	13096–8	
Vol.	1–9.	Nos. 533, 535–545, 547–558, 560–565, 567–578, 580–588: **Miscellaneous reports on public bills. IX**	13096–9	
Vol.	2.	Nos. 79–80, 115–117, 221–249, 261, 297, 346, 384, 390–398, 437, 448, 450, 471, 477, 546, 566, 579: **Miscellaneous reports on private bills**	13097	
Vol.	3–1.	Nos. 27, 31, 37, 49, 52, 58, 60–61, 64, 87, 90, 92, 95, 202, 256, 313, 315, 411, 413, 419, 422, 425, 456, 478, 503, 534, 559: **Special reports**	13098–1	

House and Senate *documents* are grouped in a "Miscellaneous" category and the base serial number is also subdivided. Other *documents*, issued in Serial Set binding only, are listed by title in the "Schedule of Volumes." Some of these are not labelled "Miscellaneous" but are available under that Item (995-G). Still others are available under other Items. The peculiar nature of these categories becomes academic if the user knows the *report* or *document* number; the *Numerical Lists* will get one to the Serial Set.

Occasionally addenda to a volume of *Numerical Lists* are issued providing important information about series. For example for the 93-1 *Lists* Addendum II (GP 3.7/2: 93/1/add. 2) notified librarians that Volume 2 of the *Annual Report of the American Historical Association*, entitled *Writings on American History*, is no longer issued as a government publication. Following that announcement a list of House *document* numbers and serial volume numbers assigned already will remain blank. Addendum I for that same session informed librarians that the *Decisions of the Commissioner of Patents and United States Courts in Patent and Trademark Cases* would no longer be issued. The 1968 edition of this House *document* was the last published serial volume.

Serial Set "Editions"

For the House and Senate *documents* series, there are publications which are sent to depository libraries in their "departmental edition." Notification of this procedure is given in every issue of the "Schedule of Volumes" section of the *Numerical Lists.* Preceding the titles of these "departmental" *documents*, there is this explanatory note:

The documents listed below originated in executive departments and agencies. They were or will be furnished to depository libraries and international exchanges at the time of printing in the format used by the departments and agencies. They will not be furnished as Congressional documents nor in the volumes as indicated hereby.

These publications typically consist of annual reports of the departments and agencies, including the independent and regulatory entities, and recurring reference sources such as the *Yearbook of Agriculture, Budget, Statistical Abstract of the United States*, and *Economic Report of the President.* Under the appropriate statutory authority, these kinds of publications are transmitted by the executive to the Congress. When ordered to be printed as a House or Senate *document*, they are assigned an individual number and eventually a serial number for binding. A publication thus designated becomes part of the "congressional edition" and is distributed in that form to the libraries of the House and Senate, the Library of Congress, the National Archives, and the office of Assistant Public Printer (Superintendent of Documents). Depository libraries that wish to have these publications in their "departmental edition" must have subscribed to them in advance under the appropriate Item number.

One illustration will shed light on this seemingly confusing distribution policy. In a recent *Numerical Lists* one finds a typical issuance of this kind following the "Schedule of Volumes" explanatory note:

House Documents	Serial No.

Vol. 21   No. 267: Statistical abstract of United
States, 1975, with supplement 13129

This entry indicates that in its "congressional edition" the 1975 *Statistical Abstract* was issued as 94-1: H. doc. 267, Serial 13129. By inference one knows that for a depository library subscribing to Item 150, the publication would have been received in its "departmental edition" and classified in its C 3.134 SuDocs notation.

Publications of that size normally by-pass the unbound (slip) form of the *document* and are received by the Library of Congress, House and Senate libraries, etc., in Serial Set binding only. This procedure is common for *documents* received by depository libraries in the "congressional edition" also. If you were accessing such a *document* using the *Monthly Catalog*, here is the way an entry would read:

77-7532

94-2: S. doc. 264

Elson, Edward Lee Roy, 1906-

Prayers offered by the Chaplain of the Senate of the

United States / Rev. Edward L. R. Elson, at the opening

of the daily sessions of the United States Senate, during

the Ninety-fourth Congress, 1975-1976. -- Washington: U.S.

Govt. Print. Off., 1976.

vii, 152 p. : port. ; 20 cm. -- (Senate document - 94th

Congress, 2d session; no. 94-264)

To be sent to depository libraries as Serial 13140-6.

pbk.

1. Legislative bodies -- Chaplains' prayers.   Prayers.

I. Title.   I. Series: United States. 94th Congress, 2d session,

1976.   Senate.   Document; no. 94-264.

OCLC 2829959

Note that although libraries will receive Serial 13140-6 if they subscribe to Item 995-G (the *Monthly Catalog* was remiss in failing to give the depository Item number in this example), they will not receive in slip form House *document* 94-264 under Item 996. Individual numbers are always assigned to the publications of the Serial Set regardless of the manner of distribution.

It is useful for librarians to make a periodic examination of the House and Senate documents segregated in the "Schedule of Volumes" section of the *Numerical Lists* so that accountability for the missing serial numbers in the bound volumes of their Serial Set can be maintained. Regional depository libraries, of course, will receive the entire series in its various forms. Selective depositories that wish the full run of the Serial Set will have to be aware of the following pattern and Item distribution:[27]

Table 3

TYPES OF MATERIALS IN THE SERIAL SET

Description	Item No.
Unbound H & S Reports	
On public bills and special reports	1008-A
On private bills	1008-B
Bound H & S Reports	
On public bills and special reports	1007-A
On private bills	1007-B
Unbound H & S Documents	
"Miscellaneous" documents	996
Bound H & S Documents	
"Miscellaneous" documents	995-G
and	
American Legion, Proceedings of National Convention	995-I
Appropriations, Budget Estimates	995-E
Boy Scouts of America and Girl Scouts of U.S.A., Annual Reports	995-P
Daughters of American Revolution, Annual Report of National Society	995-B
Disabled American Veterans, National Report	995-J
House Manual	1029
Secretary of Senate, Report	995-M
Senate Manual	1048
United Spanish War Veterans, Proceedings of National Encampment	995-K
Veterans of Foreign Wars of U.S., Proceedings of National Convention	995-L
Veterans of World War I of U.S., Proceedings of National Convention	995-Q

Serial Set Commercial Sources

Readex Microprint

When Readex entered the field of government publications, the Serial Set was the first publication recommended by librarians for issuance in a Microprint edition. As of 1977 Readex's publishing schedule of Serial Set volumes included the *American State Papers* (serial numbers 01-038) through the 71st Congress (1929-1931). Users of the Readex series must rely upon the various nineteenth century bibliographic sources and current indexes such as the *Monthly Catalog* and *Numerical Lists.*[28]

CIS US Serial Set

Congressional Information Service provides retrospective access to the Serial Set in a dual-media format. *CIS US Serial Set Index, 1789-1969*, is produced in twelve parts. Each part, in three clothbound volumes, includes a subject/keyword index; an index of names of individuals and organizations that were recipients of private relief and related congressional actions; and a complete numerical listing and schedule of serial volumes. Through this single-source, comprehensive index, the user can access the *CIS US Serial Set on Microfiche, 1789-1969* for the full text of the series. With its quality microfiche and comprehensive, sophisticated index, the CIS product, though expensive, is of immense value to the scholar, student, and layman for its genealogical utility.[29]

THE LEGISLATIVE PROCESS

Many are the ways in which legislation originates. In modern times the "executive communication" has become a prolific source of legislative proposals. Article II, section 3, of the Constitution obliges the President to report to the Congress from time to time on the state of the Union and to recommend for consideration such measures as he deems necessary and expedient. This takes the form of a letter from a member of the President's Cabinet or the head of an independent agency—or even from the President himself—transmitting a draft of a proposed bill to the Speaker of the House and the President of the Senate. The communication is then referred to the standing committee having jurisdiction over the subject matter embraced in the proposal.

Legislation may be conceived and drafted by interest groups—bar associations, labor unions, chambers of commerce, professional societies—or indeed by individuals. If a member is favorably disposed toward the drafted legislation, he may introduce such measures. Of course, legislative ideas come also from members themselves, initially arising from campaign pledges made or, after taking office, experience learned in the need for amendments to existing statutory law or the repeal of laws.

Whatever the origin, *introduction* of legislation can be made only by a member of Congress. Bills and resolutions are the forms of legislation, and they may be introduced in either chamber. Of the thousands of pieces of legislation introduced every Congress, relatively few are ever reported out of committee, and fewer still become law.

The booklet *How Our Laws Are Made* was first issued by the House Judiciary Committee in 1953 and since that time it has undergone many revisions and editions.[30] It is the single most useful discussion of the legislative process ever published in the form of a government document and contains, in addition to a lucid explanation of the process, a number of illustrations. While attempting to compress the legislative process somewhat in the following pages, the author draws freely upon the booklet.

In addition to *How Our Laws Are Made*, two other sources provide useful information for students of the legislative process. *Enactment of a Law: Procedural Steps in the Legislative Process* (94-2: S. doc. 152) traces a bill originating in the Senate through both chambers to enactment, with illustrations of the bill in its parliamentary stages, committee reports, and public law. Eugene Nabors, "Legislative History and Government Documents—Another Step in Legal Research," *Government Publications Review* 3: 15-41 (1976), is an excellent technical analysis of the legislative process, replete with specimens of the documents generated in the procedure.

Stages of a Bill

The voyage of a bill through Congress begins when it is introduced by a member. In the House, legislation may be sponsored by up to 25 members; the Senate permits unlimited multiple sponsorship. In the House it is no longer the custom to read bills, even by title, at the time of introduction. The bill is introduced simply by placing it in the "hopper" provided for the purpose at the side of the Clerk's desk in the House Chamber. The Senate's procedure is more formal; a Senator who wishes to introduce a measure rises and states that a bill is offered for introduction, and the bill is read by title for the first and second reading.

In the House the title is entered in the *Journal* and printed in the *Congressional Record*. Frequently, Senators obtain consent to have the bill printed in the body of the *Record* following their formal introductory statement. The bill is assigned a number by the Clerk and referred to the appropriate committee. The first printing is known as the "introduced print"; an example of this printing is reproduced in the section of this chapter that discussed bills and resolutions (see Figure 14, page 168).

The chairman of the committee to which a bill has been referred may send the bill to a subcommittee for consideration. Bills of sufficient importance get public hearings. After hearings are completed, the committee or subcommittee will consider the bill in a session that is popularly known as the "marking-up" session. Here a vote is taken to determine the action of the committee. It may decide to report the bill favorably or unfavorably, or to suggest that it be "tabled." If the committee votes to report the bill favorably to the full House or Senate, one of the members is designated to write the committee report. A new version of the bill, called a "reported print," is ordered to be printed. In the example, note that H.R. 8629 in its "reported print" stage has the calendar number and the committee report number on the bill. The date of the "introduced print" is given, along with the name of the bill's sponsor and the date of report out of committee (Figure 20).

Figure 20
BILL: REPORTED PRINT

Union Calendar No.182

90TH CONGRESS
1ST SESSION

H. R. 8629

[Report No. 509]

IN THE HOUSE OF REPRESENTATIVES

APRIL 17, 1967

Mr. CELLER introduced the following bill; which was referred to the Committee on the Judiciary

JULY 25, 1967

Reported with an amendment, committed to the Committee of the Whole House on the State of the Union, and ordered to be printed

[Omit the part struck through and insert the part printed in italic]

A BILL

To amend the Act of July 4, 1966 (Public Law 89–491).

1   *Be it enacted by the Senate and House of Representa-*

2   *tives of the United States of America in Congress assembled,*

3   *That* the Act of July 4, 1966 (80 Stat. 259), *is hereby*

4   *amended as follows:*

5   1. By adding in section 2 (b) (3) the words *"the*

6   *Secretary of Commerce,"* after the words, "the Secretary

7   of Defense,".

8   2. By deleting in section 3 (d) the words *"two years*

9   *after the date of the enactment of this Act,"* and *inserting*

10   in lieu thereof *"July 4, 1969."*.

The *report* of a committee on a measure that has been approved must include 1) the committee's oversight findings and recommendations, 2) the statement required by the Congressional Budget Act of 1974, if the measure provides new budget authority or new or increased expenditures, 3) the estimate and comparison prepared by the Director of the Congressional Budget Office, and 4) a summary of the oversight findings and recommendations made by the Committee on Government Operations whenever they have been submitted to the legislative committee in a timely fashion to allow an opportunity to consider them during the committee's deliberations on the measure.

Moreover, a committee *report* on a bill or joint resolution of a public character must contain a detailed analytical statement as to whether the enactment of the measure into law may have an inflationary impact on prices and costs in the operation of the national economy. Each such *report* must also contain an estimate by the committee of the costs which would be incurred in carrying out the measure in the fiscal year reported and in each of the five succeeding fiscal years.

In the example, note that an amendment is set forth at the beginning, with its explanation. Following are the purpose and scope of the bill, with detailed reasons for recommendation of approval. The name of the member of the committee who wrote the report is given, as are the bill number and name of committee (Figure 21, p. 193).

Like most measures, the bill we are using as an example originated in the House and passed that chamber as amended. Debate on the floor might have produced hundreds of amendments, as happens when the measure is extremely complex, controversial, or lengthy. There is an "enrolling Clerk" in each chamber who prepares an "engrossed copy" of the bill as passed, with all amendments. At this point the measure ceases technically to be called a bill and is termed "an act," signifying that it is the act of one body of the Congress, although it is still popularly referred to as a bill. The engrossed bill is printed on blue paper and delivered to the Senate. There it is referred to the appropriate Senate committee. At this point the bill is again reprinted and is known as an "Act print" or "Senate referred print."[31]

The process now repeats itself. The Senate committee issues a *report* (Figure 22, p. 194) and, as often happens, the Senate version differs from that of the House. The vehicle for resolving differences between the two chambers is known as the *conference.* Managers, or *conferees*, are appointed from each body, and they attempt to effect a compromise that both chambers can agree to. How legislation is managed in a conference committee is most lucidly explained in *U.S. News & World*

Figure 21
HOUSE COMMITTEE REPORT

| 90TH CONGRESS
1st Session | HOUSE OF REPRESENTATIVES | REPORT
No. 509 |

AMERICAN REVOLUTION BICENTENNIAL COMMISSION

JULY 25, 1967.—Committed to the Committee of the Whole House on the State
of the Union and ordered to be printed

Mr. ROGERS of Colorado, from the Committee on the Judiciary,
submitted the following

REPORT

[To accompany H.R. 8629]

The Committee on the Judiciary, to whom was referred the bill
(H.R. 8629) to amend the act of July 4, 1966 (Public Law 89–491),
having considered the same, report favorably thereon with an amendment and recommend that the bill do pass.

The amendment is as follows:

On page 2, strike lines 3 through 5 and insert in lieu thereof the
following:

"SEC. 7. (a) There is authorized to be appropriated not
to exceed $450,000 for the period through fiscal year 1969."

EXPLANATION OF AMENDMENT

The purpose of the amendment is to limit the authorization for
appropriations to $450,000 during the period through fiscal year 1969.

PURPOSE OF THE BILL

The purpose of H.R. 8629 is threefold: First, it would add the
Secretary of Commerce as an ex officio member of the Commission;
second, it would extend the date on which the Commission shall report to the President by 1 year—from July 4, 1968, to July 4, 1969;
third, it would authorize the appropriation of public funds to finance
the work of the Commission.

STATEMENT

Public Law 89–491, approved July 4, 1966, established the American
Revolution Bicentennial Commission to commemorate the American

[Rule XIII of the Rules of the House now require the report to contain an estimate of the costs involved in the reported bill except as to certain committees.
Rule XI also requires that when a record vote is taken, on a bill being reported by a committee, the report shall include the result of that vote]

Figure 22

SENATE COMMITTEE REPORT

Calendar No. 592

90TH CONGRESS *1st Session*	SENATE	REPORT No. 609

EXTENDING THE AMERICAN REVOLUTION BICENTENNIAL COMMISSION

OCTOBER 11 (legislative day, OCTOBER 10), 1967.—Ordered to be printed

Mr. DIRKSEN, from the Committee on the Judiciary,
submitted the following

REPORT

[To accompany H.R. 8629]

The Committee on the Judiciary, to which was referred the bill (H.R. 8629) to amend the act of July 4, 1966 (Public Law 89–491), having considered the same, reports favorably thereon with an amendment and recommends that the bill as amended do pass.

AMENDMENT

On page 2, after line 4, insert the following:

4. By deleting in section 2(b)(1) the word "Four" and inserting in lieu thereof the word "Six"; and by deleting in section 2(b)(2) the word "Four" and inserting in lieu thereof the word "Six".

PURPOSE OF AMENDMENT

The purpose of the amendment is to increase the Senate membership on the Commission from four members to six members, and to increase the House of Representatives membership on the Commission from four members to six members.

PURPOSE

The purpose of the proposed legislation, as amended, is fourfold: First, it would add the Secretary of Commerce as an exofficio member of the Commission; second, it would extend the date on which the

[With certain exceptions, the Legislative Reorganization Act of 1970, requires the report to contain an estimate of the costs involved in the bill]

Report LXXXIII: 80 (November 21, 1977), including its formation, membership restrictions, bargaining strategies, voting procedures, and possible rejection by either or both of the chambers. A *conference report* is written and bears the provenance of the chamber where the legislation originated (Figure 23). Only when the bill has been agreed to in identical form by both bodies can it be "enrolled" for presentation to the President, who vetoes it or signs it into law.

Copies of the enrolled bill are usually transmitted by the White House to the various departments interested in the subject matter so that they may advise the President. The bill may become law without the President's signature by virtue of the Constitutional provision that if he does not return a bill with his objections

Figure 23

CONFERENCE COMMITTEE REPORT

90TH CONGRESS	HOUSE OF REPRESENTATIVES	REPORT
1st Session		No. 987

AMERICAN REVOLUTION BICENTENNIAL COMMISSION

NOVEMBER 28, 1967.—Ordered to be printed

Mr. ROGERS of Colorado, from the committee of conference, submitted the following

CONFERENCE REPORT

[To accompany H.R. 8629]

The committee of conference on the disagreeing votes of the two Houses on the amendment of the Senate to the bill (H.R. 8629) to amend the act of July 4, 1966 (Public Law 89–491), having met, after full and free conference, have agreed to recommend and do recommend to their respective Houses as follows:

That the Senate recede from its amendment.

> BYRON G. ROGERS,
> BASIL WHITENER,
> ANDREW JACOBS, Jr.,
> RICHARD H. POFF,
> CHARLES E. WIGGINS,
> *Managers on the Part of the House.*
> EVERETT M. DIRKSEN,
> JOHN L. MCCLELLAN,
> *Managers on the Part of the Senate.*

within ten days (Sundays excepted) after it has been presented to him, it shall be a law just as if he had signed it. However, if the Congress adjourns within that period of time, it is known as a "pocket veto" and does not become law. In a regular "veto," the President returns the bill to the originating chamber with his objections. As we noted, veto messages are published in the *documents* series of the Serial Set. To override a veto requires a two-thirds vote in both chambers.

Stages of a Law

Provenance for the first official publication of the law shifts from Congress to the Office of the Federal Register, General Services Administration. Known as the "slip law," it takes the form of an unbound pamphlet, printed by photoelectric offset process from the enrolled bill signed by the President. At the Office of the Federal Register it is assigned a Public Law number; these numbers run in sequence, starting anew at the beginning of each Congress.

Public slip laws are classed in GS 4.110 (Item 575) and designated by Congress and number. Private laws are not depository Items. Both public and private laws, however, are available for sale by SuDocs. The Office of the Federal Register, which prepares the slip laws, provides marginal editorial notes giving citations to laws or treaties mentioned in the text. Citations are also given to the *United States Code*, thus enabling the user to determine immediately where provisions of the statute will appear in the *Code*. Note in our example the "legislative history" which appears at the end of a typical slip law (Figure 24).

A chronological arrangement of the slip laws in bound volumes is published as the *Statutes at Large*. Compilation and indexing are the responsibility of the General Services Administration; the Office of the Federal Register issues the *Statutes at Large* (GS 4.111; Item 576) by volumes, in sessional arrangement. When the appropriate volume arrives in one's library, the slip laws covered in that compilation may be discarded.

Like the slip law, the version that appears in the *Statutes at Large* includes the bill number and the date of enactment into law. The "legislative history" found on the slip law is now published in tabular form in the *Statutes*, providing the user with a handy reference to the bill, reports, and dates of consideration and passage. This "Guide to Legislative History of Bills Enacted into Public Law" first appeared in the *Statutes at Large* in 1963 (Figure 25, p. 198).

Statutes of a permanent and general character in force are consolidated and codified in the *United States Code*. Because the official edition of the *Code* is not annotated, it is not as useful as two annotated, privately published editions. *United States Code Annotated* (U.S.C.A.) and *United States Code Service* (U.S.C.S.) are annotated to judicial decisions construing the *United States Code* sections, and make reference to other legal sources outside official statutes.

Figure 24

SLIP LAW WITH LEGISLATIVE HISTORY

Public Law 94-400
94th Congress, S. 3542
September 7, 1976

An Act

To authorize the Secretary of the Interior to make compensation for damages arising out of the failure of the Teton Dam a feature of the Teton Basin Federal reclamation project in Idaho, and for other purposes.

Be it enacted by the Senate and House of Representatives of the United States of America in Congress assembled, That the Congress finds that without regard to the proximate cause of the failure of the Teton Dam, it is the purpose of the United States to fully compensate any and all persons, for the losses sustained by reason of the failure of said dam. The purposes of this Act are (1) to provide just compensation for the deaths, personal injuries and losses of property, including the destruction and damage to irrigation works, resulting from the failure on June 5, 1976, of the Teton Dam in the State of Idaho, and (2) to provide for the expeditious consideration and settlement of claims for such deaths, personal injuries, and property losses.

Teton Dam, Idaho. Damages, compensation.

SEC. 2. All persons who suffered death, personal injury, or loss of property directly resulting from the failure on June 5, 1976, of the Teton Dam of the Lower Teton Division of the Teton Basin Federal reclamation project which was authorized to be constructed by the Act of September 7, 1964 (78 Stat. 925) shall be entitled to receive from the United States full compensation for such death, personal injury, or loss of property. Claimants shall submit their claims in writing to the Secretary, under such regulations as he prescribes, within two years after the date on which the regulations required by section 5 are published in the Federal Register. Claims based on death shall be submitted only by duly authorized legal representatives.

Casualty or property losses, claims.

43 USC 616nn.

SEC. 3. (a) The Secretary of the Interior, or his designee for the purpose, acting on behalf of the United States, is hereby authorized to and shall investigate, consider, ascertain, adjust, determine, and settle any claim for money damages asserted under section 2. Except as otherwise provided herein, the laws of the State of Idaho shall apply: *Provided,* That determinations, awards, and settlements under this Act shall be limited to actual or compensatory damages measured by the pecuniary injuries or loss involved and shall not include interest prior to settlement or punitive damages.

Investigation.

(b) In determining the amount to be awarded under this Act the Secretary shall reduce any such amount by an amount equal to the total of insurance benefits (except life insurance benefits) or other payments or settlements of any nature previously paid with respect to such death claims, personal injury, or property loss.

(c) Payments approved by the Secretary under this Act on death, personal injury, and property loss claims, shall not be subject to insurance subrogation claims in any respect under this Act but without prejudice under other laws as provided in subsection (f).

(d) The Secretary shall not include in an award any amount for reimbursement to any insurance fund for loss payments made by such company or fund.

(e) Except as to the United States, no claim cognizable under this Act shall be assigned or transferred.

LEGISLATIVE HISTORY:

HOUSE REPORT No. 94-1423 (Comm. on the Judiciary).
SENATE REPORT No. 94-963 (Comm. on Interior and Insular Affairs).
CONGRESSIONAL RECORD, Vol 122 (1976):
    June 17, considered and passed Senate.
    Aug. 24, considered and passed House, amended.
    Aug. 25, Senate concurred in House amendments.
WEEKLY COMPILATION OF PRESIDENTIAL DOCUMENTS, Vol. 12, No. 37:
    Sept. 7, Presidential statement.

Figure 25

GUIDE TO LEGISLATIVE HISTORY IN STATUTES AT LARGE

GUIDE TO LEGISLATIVE HISTORY OF BILLS ENACTED INTO PUBLIC LAW—Continued

NOTE: Companion bills are in parentheses

Public Law No.	Date approved 1967	81 Stat.	Bill No.	Report No. and Committee reporting — House	Report No. and Committee reporting — Senate	Dates of consideration and passage (Congressional Record, Vol. 113 (1967)) — House	Dates of consideration and passage — Senate
90-160	Nov. 28	517	S. J. Res. 26	646 Judiciary	241 Judiciary	May 25	May 18; Nov. 17
90-161	Nov. 28	518	H. R. 8632		752 Judiciary	Oct. 2	Nov. 16
90-162	Nov. 28	518	H. J. Res. 936			Nov. 28	Nov. 28
90-163	Nov. 29	518	H. R. 169			June 19	Nov. 20
90-164	Nov. 29	519	H. R. 168	344 Merchant Marine and Fisheries	791 Commerce	June 19	Nov. 20
90-165	Nov. 29	519	H. R. 1006	342 Merchant Marine and Fisheries	787 Commerce	June 19	Nov. 20
90-166	Nov. 29	519	S. 2428	347 Merchant Marine and Fisheries; 928 Armed Services	788 Commerce	Nov. 20	Nov. 13
90-167	Nov. 29	520	H. R. 3351	345 Merchant Marine and Fisheries	741 Armed Services; 789 Commerce	June 19	Nov. 20
90-168	Dec. 1	521	H. R. 2	13 Armed Services [Conference]	732 Armed Services	Feb. 20; Nov. 15	Nov. 8, 16
90-169	Dec. 1	526	H. J. Res. 859	925 Banking and Currency; 762 Interstate and Foreign Commerce	725 Labor and Public Welfare	Nov. 21	Nov. 22
90-170	Dec. 4	527	H. R. 6430	562 [Conference]		Sept. 20; Nov. 21	Nov. 6, 21
90-171	Dec. 4	531	H. R. 10442	954 Agriculture; 716 Agriculture	793 Agriculture and Forestry	Oct. 20, 23	Nov. 20
90-172	Dec. 4	532	S. 764	898 District of Columbia	340 District of Columbia	Nov. 20	June 13
90-173	Dec. 4	532	S. 770	899 District of Columbia	583 District of Columbia	Nov. 20, 20; Nov. 21	Oct. 10
90-174	Dec. 5	533	H. R. 6418	538 Interstate and Foreign Commerce [Conference]	724 Labor and Public Welfare	Nov. 21	Nov. 6, 21
90-175	Dec. 5	542	S. 1031	974 Foreign Affairs	223 Foreign Relations	Nov. 21	May 15
90-176	Dec. 6	542	H. R. 2529	807 District of Columbia; 115 District of Columbia	803 District of Columbia	Mar. 13	Nov. 27
90-177	Dec. 6	544	S. 706	918 Merchant Marine and Fisheries	472 Commerce	Nov. 20	Aug. 4
90-178	Dec. 8	544	H. R. 8582	378 District of Columbia	802 District of Columbia	June 26; Oct. 2; Nov. 20	Nov. 27
90-179	Dec. 8	545	H. R. 12910	710 Armed Services; 799 Appropriations	748 Armed Services	Oct. 24; Nov. 21	Nov. 16
90-180	Dec. 8	550	H. R. 13606	975 [Conference]; 948 Judiciary [Conference]	742 Appropriations		Nov. 13, 14, 21
90-181	Dec. 8	553	S. 2514 (H. R. 12010)	272 Interior and Insular Affairs	720 Public Works	Nov. 20	Nov. 6, 28
90-182	Dec. 8	559	H. R. 2154		816 Interior and Insular Affairs	June 5	Nov. 30
90-183	Dec. 10	559	S. 2211 (H. R. 13369)	923 Merchant Marine and Fisheries	717 Commerce	Nov. 20	Nov. 7, 29
90-184	Dec. 10	560	H. R. 4920	355 Interior and Insular Affairs	817 Interior and Insular Affairs	June 19	Nov. 30
90-185	Dec. 11	560	S. J. Res. 35	912 Interstate and Foreign Commerce	202 Interior and Insular Affairs	Nov. 20	May 4; Dec. 1
90-186	Dec. 12	566	S. 343	811 Public Works; 500 Judiciary	82 Public Works; 609 Judiciary	Dec. 4	Apr. 4
90-187	Dec. 12	567	H. R. 8629	987 [Conference]		Aug. 7; Nov. 29	Oct. 12; Nov. 28

Tracing Current Legislation

Even before a bill or resolution is introduced, activities which result in published materials may have taken place. Hearings on a problem of legislative concern may have been held prior to the introduction of a specific proposal to remedy the situation. In addition, presidential communications to the Congress appear prior to the measure's introduction "into the hopper." As noted, hearings are printed separately, and presidential messages may be found in the *Congressional Record, Weekly Compilation of Presidential Documents, Journals* of the House and Senate, and other places (see Chapter 7).

Useful bibliographic tools for determining the current status of legislation include the following.

CCH Congressional Index

This commercially produced looseleaf service is excellent because of its recency and comprehensive coverage. Legislation can be traced by subject, sponsor, bill number/date of introduction, and companion and identical bill numbers.

Moreover, CCH issues *Congressional Legislative Reporting Service*, which keeps subscribers in daily contact with action on public bills and resolutions whose subject matter is of interest to them. Full text copies of bills are also provided.

Congressional Record

The fortnightly index to the CR consists of an "Index to Proceedings" and a "History of Bills and Resolutions." These indexes afford access by subject, sponsor, and bill number.

Digest of Public General Bills

Although this does not have the recency of CCH's *Congressional Index*, its abstracting (digest) feature for measures is most valuable. Legislation in the cumulative issues of the *Digest* may be accessed by subject, sponsor, bill number, identical bill number or numbers, public law number, and keyword of title.

House Calendar

The Monday issue of the *Calendar* includes a subject index. Access to legislation using the *Calendar* is especially useful once a bill has been assigned to a committee. Access is by subject, bill number, public law number, and private law number.

CIS/Index

CIS/Index, which appears monthly, is valuable not so much for tracing current legislation as it is for its comprehensive coverage of congressional publications and its abstracting capabilities. Thus if one knows where the bill is in the legislative process, one can locate hearings, reports, and committee prints related to the legislation. Access is afforded by subject, author, popular name of bill or law, document and hearings titles, bill, report, and document numbers, and committee and subcommittee chairpersons.

Legislative Histories

Several useful sources for finding in one place citations to the appropriate publications that comprise the legislative history of a measure that has become law are noted, as follows.

Congressional Record—Daily Digest

The permanent, bound edition of the *Congressional Record* has an index volume which provides access by subject, sponsor, and bill number. The final issue of the *Daily Digest*, which is cumulated at the end of a session, contains a comprehensive status table for the session entitled "History of Bills Enacted into Public Law" (Figure 26). Preceding this table is a table arranged by Senate and House bill and resolution number, referencing the Public Law number. Following the status table is a subject index to the *Daily Digest*. Bill numbers are affixed to the subject references, which are further subdivided by action on the measures, including presidential communications. Accordingly, the subject approach is itself an account of the history of each bill and resolution.

Statutes at Large

As noted, the "Guide to Legislative History of Bills Enacted into Public Law" in the bound *Statutes* serves the same purpose as the *Daily Digest* table.

IHS—Legislative Histories on Microfiche

Typically, the legislative histories compiled by Information Handling Services include presidential communications if applicable; the bills and resolutions in all parliamentary stages, including amendments; committee hearings and prints; debates in the *Congressional Record*; and the law as enacted. Two indexes afford access to the microfiche texts. *Index I* cross-references each *History* under Public Law number, bill number, *Statute at Large* citation, and popular name. In addition, a section of *Index I* lists public laws by popular name, Congress, and year. *Index II*

Figure 26

CONGRESSIONAL RECORD: HISTORY OF BILLS ENACTED INTO PUBLIC LAW

CONGRESSIONAL RECORD—DAILY DIGEST

Title	Bill No.	Date introduced	Committees—Hearings House	Committees—Hearings Senate	Date reported House	Date reported Senate	Report No. House	Report No. Senate	Page of Congressional Record of passage House	Page of Congressional Record of passage Senate	Date of passage House	Date of passage Senate	Public Law Date approved	Public Law No.
Extending the time within which the President may transmit his budget message and economic report to the Congress.	H.J. Res. 1	Jan. 14			Feb. 3	Feb. 4			H 21	S 13	Jan. 14	Jan. 14	Jan. 24	94-1
Restoring to the Office of the Attorney General, effective February 4, 1975, annual salary level of $60,000, and other emoluments attached thereto.	S. 58	Jan. 15		POCS		Feb. 5		94-6	H 673	S 1590	Feb. 6	Feb. 5	Feb. 18	94-2
Providing a temporary increase in the debt limit from $495 billion to $531 billion, and extending the temporary debt limit through June 30, 1975.	H.R. 2634	Feb. 4		Fin		Feb. 17		94-12	H 595	S 2049	Feb. 5	Feb. 18	Feb. 19	94-3
To prohibit increases in the cost of coupons to food stamp recipients until December 30, 1975.	H.R. 1589 (S. 35)	Jan. 17	Agr	Agr	Jan. 31		94-2		H 506	S 1594	Feb. 4	Feb. 5	Feb. 20	94-4
Authorizing additional interim funding for maintenance and continued service of railroads operating under the Regional Railroad Reorganization Act.	S. 281 (H.R. 2051)	Jan. 21	IFC	Com	Feb. 10	Jan. 27	94-7	94-5	H 870	S 1197	Feb. 19	Jan. 29	Feb. 26	94-5
Making further urgent supplemental appropriations for fiscal year 1975 through June 30, 1975.	H.J. Res. 210	Feb. 18	App	App	Feb. 18	Feb. 25	94-14	94-21	H 953	S 2640	Feb. 20	Feb. 26	Feb. 28	94-6
To extend continuing appropriations for foreign assistance programs until March 25, 1975, and certain HEW programs until June 30, 1975.	H.J. Res. 219	Feb. 19	App	App	Feb. 20	Feb. 28	94-16	94-25	H 1053	S 2856	Feb. 25	Feb. 28	Mar. 14	94-7
Designating March 21, 1975, "Earth Day".	H.J. Res. 258	Feb. 27			Feb. 18	Feb. 25	94-14	94-21	H 1679	S 4299	Mar. 18	Mar. 18	Mar. 20	94-8
Extending from June 30, 1975, until December 31, 1975, certain authority contained in the Defense Production Act of 1950.	S.J. Res. 48	Mar. 6			Feb. 20	Feb. 28	94-16	94-25	H 1468	S 3395	Mar. 10	Mar. 6	Mar. 21	94-9
Authorizing approximately $562 million for certain maritime programs of the Department of Commerce for fiscal year 1975.	S. 332 (H.R. 3)	Jan. 23	MMF	Com	Feb. 10	Feb. 5	94-6	94-7	H 819	S 1821	Feb. 18	Feb. 12	Mar. 23	94-10
Making appropriations for foreign assistance programs for fiscal year 1975.	H.R. 4592	Feb. 10	App	App	Mar. 10	Mar. 17	94-53	94-39	H 1665	S 4350	Mar. 13	Mar. 19	Mar. 26	94-11
Tax Reduction Act of 1975.	H.R. 2166 / 2783 / 3260	Jan. 28 / Feb. 5 / Feb. 19	WM / BC&H / App	Fin	Feb. 25 / Mar. 14 / Feb. 20	Mar. 17 / Feb. 27	94-19 / 94-60 / 94-17	94-36 / 94-24	H 1198 / 1876 / 1069	S 4859 / 4705 / 4094	Mar. 27 / Mar. 18 / Feb. 25	Mar. 22 / Mar. 21 / Mar. 17	Mar. 29 / Apr. 8 / Apr. 8	94-12 / 94-13 / 94-14
Dealing with Presidential rescissions of budget authority as recommended in his messages embodied in House Documents 93-398, 94-39, and 94-50.	H.R. 4075	Mar. 3	App	App / Bud	Mar. 4	Mar. 12	94-26	94-35	H 1482	S 4073	Mar. 10	Mar. 17	Apr. 8	94-15
To defer the effective dates of certain provisions of the Commodity Futures Trading Commission Act of 1974.	H.J. Res. 335	Mar. 19	Agr	Agr	Apr. 7	Apr. 10	94-122	94-73	H 2507	S 5926	Apr. 8	Apr. 14	Apr. 16	94-16
Making additional appropriations for fiscal year 1975 for the Veterans' Administration for purpose of readjustment benefits.	H.J. Res. 375	Apr. 7	App	App	Apr. 10	Apr. 17	94-138	94-82	H 2746	S 6320	Apr. 15	Apr. 18	Apr. 24	94-17
Authorizing an additional $50.2 million for fiscal year 1975 for the Nuclear Regulatory Commission.	S. 994 (H.R. 4224)	Mar. 6	AE	AE	Mar. 20	Mar. 20	94-100	94-50	H 2560	S 4927	Apr. 10	Mar. 24	Apr. 25	94-18
To authorize the acceptance of additional land for inclusion in the home of Franklin D. Roosevelt National Historic Site, N.Y.	H.R. 2808	Feb. 5	IIA	IIA	Apr. 16	Apr. 29	94-149	94-98	H 2988	S 6921	Apr. 21	Apr. 29	Apr. 30	94-19
To continue through September 30, 1975, the special food service program for children.	S. 1310	Mar. 24	Agr	Agr		Mar. 24		94-57	H 2607	S 4979	Apr. 9	Mar. 26	May 2	94-20
Authorizing the President to proclaim the week beginning May 12, 1975, as "National Historic Preservation Week."	H.J. Res. 242	Feb. 25	POCS	Jud	Apr. 17	Apr. 30	94-153	94-100	H 2993	S 7249	Apr. 21	May 1	May 9	94-21

includes an alphabetical listing by popular name, with SuDocs class numbers and Serial Set number for reports cited in the legislative histories. The two hardcopy *Indexes* refer to the eye-legible microfiche card headers.

CCH—Congressional Index

Perhaps the most popular and widely used commercial source for tracing current legislation, *Congressional Index* is also useful for locating legislative histories of bills enacted into law. This looseleaf service cumulates current legislation with the usual subject, sponsor, and bill indexes. In the sections entitled "Status of House Bills" and "Status of Senate Bills," arrangement is by number, and a star preceding a bill or joint resolution number indicates that the measure has become law. Citations include the committee report numbers; public law numbers; and dates of chamber action, hearings, act sent to president, and approval.

House Calendar

The final edition of the *House Calendar* is a valuable source of legislative histories. The section entitled "Numerical Order of Bills and Resolutions Which Have Passed Either or Both Houses, and Bills Now Pending on the Calendars" is organized by House and Senate bills and resolutions. Committee report numbers, public law number, dates of passage by the chambers—all are given in this section.

Digest of Public General Bills and Resolutions

The final issue of the *Digest* for a Congress is yet another source for legislative histories of bills enacted into law. A section entitled "Public Laws" is arranged by PL number and contains digests of public laws with the important dates of consideration, passage, and enactment into law. In addition, committee report numbers are given as are roll call vote totals. For quick scanning, a "Cross Index of Public Law and Originating Legislation" may be used to reference bill number and brief title.

CIS/Annual

The most useful of all sources for citations to the significant publications that comprise the legislative history of bills signed by the President into law is the section on legislative histories in the *Abstracts* volume of each *CIS/Annual*. Much more information is provided in the *CIS/Annual* than in the other sources under discussion: depository Item number, hearings and committee prints, presidential communications. Following the abstract of the public law, references are to earlier *CIS/Annual* volumes where the abstracts of hearings and prints may be read. A useful feature is a separate section entitled "Revised Legislative Histories" for earlier laws supplementing the information already noted in the current annual volumes. Access to this information is through the *Index* volume by subjects and names, titles, bill, report and document numbers, committee and subcommittee chairpersons. The full text of legislative histories of public laws is available on CIS microfiche (Figure 27).

Figure 27

CIS/ANNUAL: SAMPLE LEGISLATIVE HISTORY

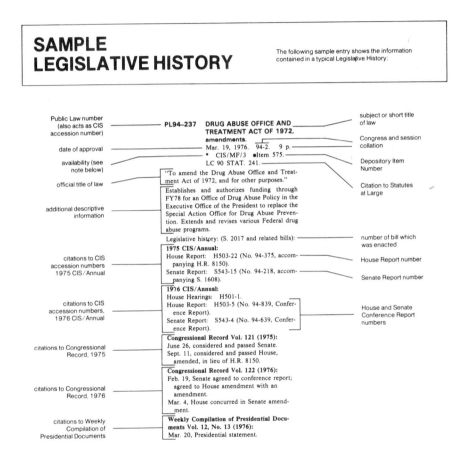

SAMPLE LEGISLATIVE HISTORY

The following sample entry shows the information contained in a typical Legislative History:

Public Law number (also acts as CIS accession number)	**PL94–237 DRUG ABUSE OFFICE AND TREATMENT ACT OF 1972, amendments.**
date of approval	Mar. 19, 1976. 94-2. 9 p.
availability (see note below)	• CIS/MF/3 •Item 575.
	LC 90 STAT. 241.
official title of law	"To amend the Drug Abuse Office and Treatment Act of 1972, and for other purposes."
additional descriptive information	Establishes and authorizes funding through FY78 for an Office of Drug Abuse Policy in the Executive Office of the President to replace the Special Action Office for Drug Abuse Prevention. Extends and revises various Federal drug abuse programs.
	Legislative history: (S. 2017 and related bills):
citations to CIS accession numbers 1975 CIS/Annual	**1975 CIS/Annual:** House Report: H503-22 (No. 94-375, accompanying H.R. 8150). Senate Report: S543-15 (No. 94-218, accompanying S. 1608).
citations to CIS accession numbers, 1976 CIS/Annual	**1976 CIS/Annual:** House Hearings: H501-1. House Report: H503-5 (No. 94-839, Conference Report). Senate Report: S543-4 (No. 94-639, Conference Report).
citations to Congressional Record, 1975	Congressional Record Vol. 121 (1975): June 26, considered and passed Senate. Sept. 11, considered and passed House, amended, in lieu of H.R. 8150.
citations to Congressional Record, 1976	Congressional Record Vol. 122 (1976): Feb. 19, Senate agreed to conference report; agreed to House amendment with an amendment. Mar. 4, House concurred in Senate amendment.
citations to Weekly Compilation of Presidential Documents	Weekly Compilation of Presidential Documents Vol. 12, No. 13 (1976): Mar. 20, Presidential statement.

Right-side labels:
- subject or short title of law
- Congress and session collation
- Depository Item Number
- Citation to Statutes at Large
- number of bill which was enacted
- House Report number
- Senate Report number
- House and Senate Conference Report numbers

NOTE—AVAILABILITY: All public laws are sold in "slip law" form by the Superintendent of Documents, Washington, D.C. 20402. The price varies from law to law, ranging usually between five cents and fifty cents per law. After the close of every Session, all the public laws passed during that Session and approved by the President are compiled in the Statutes at Large.

Veto Information

We noted that a retrospective compilation of presidential vetoes is found in the Senate General Publications series (see p. 165). Current veto information may be found in several places. A section titled "Bills Vetoed" in the *Daily Digest* of the CR (final issue) is arranged by bill number, with a notation if overriden. CCH's *Congressional Index* reports vetoes chronologically. Perhaps the best source is the final edition of the *House Calendar.* Sections include regular vetoes, acts which became laws without the President's approval, pocket vetoes after adjournment of Congress, pocket vetoes during recess, and acts which were vetoed but became law.

OTHER GUIDES TO LEGISLATION

Newspapers, magazines, newsletters, radio and television, commercial monographs—all carry information on the current and retrospective status of legislation. But these sources are usually selective. If, for example, the user needs only to know how one's Representative or Senator voted on a given measure, a local newspaper will usually provide the answer. However, there are a number of information sources that will furnish greater detail. A few selective sources of various aspects of the legislative process follow.

U.S.C.C.A.N.

U.S. Code Congressional and Administrative News (West Publishing Co.) is a useful secondary source for tracing legislation. Selective coverage of important legislation in U.S.C.C.A.N. includes a legislative history table of enacted laws arranged by public law number including, in parentheses, companion bills reported either in the Senate or the House. Another table, "Public Laws," references pages in U.S.C.C.A.N. where the text of the law is printed. Also printed are the texts of the appropriate House and Senate committee reports, including conference reports.

Washington Monitor, Inc. Publications

The Washington Monitor, a Washington, D.C., based publishing company, issues several useful publications. *The Congressional Monitor* is published daily when Congress is in session, and provides a schedule of all upcoming committee activity. *Congress in Print* is a weekly alert to just-released committee hearings, prints, and staff studies. Subscribers to *The Congressional Monitor* receive *Congress in Print* at no additional cost. The *Congressional Record Scanner* is an edited outline of the *Congressional Record* which enables users to locate quickly items of concern to them in an issue of the CR.

National Journal

National Journal is a weekly periodical published by the Government Research Corporation (Washington, D.C.) and devoted to subjects of public policy. Congressional activities are covered, as are newsworthy stories on the presidency, the executive and independent agencies, the media, and the private sector. Unfortunately, in 1976 the *Journal* discontinued its useful congressional voting charts because, in the words of the *Journal*'s editor, "similar information is available from other sources that libraries have access to." In its place, the magazine has expanded its "Washington Update" section and increased the number of analytical articles on public policy issues. A useful feature of *National Journal* is its cumulative index, which includes access by congressional committees and subcommittees. The other indexes include personal names, private organizations, government agencies, geographic areas, subject, and policy topics.

Congressional Quarterly, Inc. Publications

The quality of the many products issued by this Washington, D.C., based commercial publisher is universally acknowledged. Several sources dealing primarily or wholly with the activities of Congress are noteworthy:

CQ Weekly Report is a periodical that contains a wealth of information about congressional and political activity for the current week. "On the Floor" and "In Committee" sections follow important bills through the process; there is a status table of significant legislation, and votes of members are reported weekly. Quarterly indexes by names and subjects cumulate throughout the year.

CQ Almanac is published annually after each session of Congress. Well over 1,000 pages in length, it distills, reorganizes and cross-indexes the events of the year in Congress, politics and lobbying. Features typically include public laws, roll call charts, and highlights of congressional activity for the session.

Congress and the Nation 1945-1964 is a comprehensive summary and review of legislative, political and presidential developments covering that period. Supplementary volumes have covered the years 1965-1968, 1969-1972, and 1973-1976 (published in 1977).

Guides to Congress, Second Edition (1976) is an extensively revised version of *Guide to the Congress of the United States* (1971). It contains a vast wealth of information on the origins, history and procedures of Congress, with numerous reference tables and charts.

Members of Congress since 1789 (1977) includes basic biographical data on every person who has served in both chambers, including new members elected in 1976. The information is not as complete as that found in the *Biographical Directory of the American Congress.*

Congressional Roll Call is an annual volume which includes a chronology and analysis of all roll-call votes taken in the House and Senate during a session.

Origins and Development of Congress (1976) is a comprehensive history of the Congress from colonial America through the Watergate crisis. A companion volume, *Powers of Congress*, presents an analysis of the constitutional powers of Congress—their origins, evolution and current interpretation.

Inside Congress (1976) examines the behind-the-scene workings of Congress, the dance of legislation, committee power structures, etc.

Congressional Districts in the 1970s, Second Edition, gives complete demographic and political profiles of all 435 congressional districts including 1974 redistricting. Included are useful maps for each state and for large cities. There is a glossary of statistical terms.

Congressional Insight is a brief newsletter sent to subscribers weekly. It is a pithy compendium of key legislative activities, alerting the reader to significant trends and developments. Subscribers to *Insight* also receive, as a supplement, *News Futures*, a calendar of forthcoming events.

Moreover, Congressional Quarterly, Inc., now offers to subscribers complete congressional voting records covering the years 1961-1973 on microfiche. The microfiche edition includes over 2,000 pages of voting charts which were formerly scattered throughout many volumes.

The Congressional Quarterly Service is clearly a distinguished publisher of legislative and related activities. All libraries should be on the mailing list for the company's announcements.

The Almanac of American Politics

Published in revised editions for a Congress by E. P. Dutton & Co., the *Almanac* is over 1,000 pages in length and includes information on each state and congressional district, biographical data on members, committee assignments, ratings of performance by special interest groups such as the League of Women Voters, voting records on key legislation, and maps of each congressional district. It is a valuable compendium of information.

The multiplicity of sources published by government and the private sector permits depository and non-depository libraries alike the opportunity to render service in legislative matters. Large research libraries subscribe to virtually all the useful commercial tools. Most of the government publications are depository Items. Users and librarians with access to these materials and their several indexing and abstracting services tend to trace current and retrospective legislation with that source or those sources with which they are most at ease.

REFERENCES

1. As of May 1977 the House had 211 committees and subcommittees and the Senate 130 committees and subcommittees. See "Congress: Where the People Speak," *U.S. News & World Report* LXXXII: 49-51 (May 9, 1977).

2. *Legislative Branch Appropriations for 1978* (House), p. 101.

3. Ibid., p. 233.

4. *American Libraries* (May 1977), p. 232.

5. See Shirley Loo and Bruce E. Langdon, "Selective Dissemination of Information to Congress: The Congressional Research Service SDI Service," *LRTS* 19: 380-88 (Fall 1975), and Nancy E. Gwinn, "Capitol Hill's Hot Line," *Library Journal* 100: 640-43 (April 1, 1975).

6. *Daily Depository Shipping List 7838*, 3rd Shipment of June 20, 1975, p. 2.

7. An interesting analysis of CBO and the new budget system is found in "New Budget System Survives First Year Intact," *CQ Weekly Report* XXXIII:2863-69 (December 27, 1975).

8. See the author's "The Forlorn Passion of William Steiger," *The Serials Librarian* 1: 117-24 (Winter 1976-77).

9. *Legislative Branch Appropriations for 1978* (House), p. 466.

10. Craig H. Grau, "What Publications Are Most Frequently Quoted in the *Congressional Record*," *Journalism Quarterly* 53: 716-19 (Winter 1976).

11. *Congressional Record* (daily edition) 92/2:118/84, H4951.

12. 92-2: H. doc. 384, p. 26.

13. Rule XIII of the House provides that the *Union Calendar* be used for measures "raising revenue, general appropriations bills, and bills of a public character directly or indirectly appropriating money or property." Placed on the *House Calendar* are "all bills of a public character not raising revenue nor directly or indirectly appropriating money or property."

14. A useful discussion of private bills is found in *Guide to the Congress of the United States* (Washington: Congressional Quarterly, Inc., 1971), pp. 329-52.

15. A bill or resolution designated a *star print* means a printing that has been corrected. The "corrected print" is identified on the bill with a star and star prints are so indicated on the *Daily Depository Shipping List.* For a useful, although somewhat dated, discussion of some of the problems involved in the several printings of a bill, see John H. Thaxter, "Printing of Congressional Bills," *LRTS* 7: 237-43 (Summer 1963).

16. *Checklist of United States Public Documents, 1789-1909* (3d ed.; rev. and enlarged; Washington: Government Printing Office, 1911), p. 1507.

17. *Instructions to Depository Libraries* (rev. November 1977), p. 13.

18. *Inventory of Information Resources for the U.S. House of Representatives* (94-2: H. doc. 537), June 18, 1976, p. 45.

19. For example, *Briefing on Counterforce Attacks*, Hearing before the Sub-committee on Arms Control, International Law and Organization, Committee on Foreign Relations (Senate) was held September 11, 1974, but was "sanitized" and published January 10, 1975 (Y 4.F76/2: At 8; Item 1039).

20. *Daily Depository Shipping List 7720* (April 24, 1975) and 7842 (June 24, 1975) listed 18 Senate committees which had agreed to make their prints available on a continuing basis as depository distribution Items.

21. *Hinds' Precedents of the House of Representatives* (1907) and *Cannon's Precedents of the House of Representatives* (1936) are justly famous and simply known by their short titles, *Hinds' Precedents* and *Cannon's Precedents.*

22. Classes Y 5 and Y 6 are reserved in the SuDocs classification notation for Contested Elections and Impeachments, respectively.

23. Edward Kennedy's brief tribute to his brother, Robert, which was delivered not in the Congress but at St. Patrick's Cathedral on June 8, 1968, was issued in slip form and later incorporated into the bound set [13938].

24. Schmeckebier, pp. 109-116; 124-29; 150-66.

25. *Inventory of Information Resources . . .* , p. 46.

26. See statement by Supreme Court Justice Robert H. Jackson on the importance of committee reports, *Schwegmann Bros. v. Calvert Distillers Corp.* 341 U.S. 384 at 395-96 (1951).

27. *List of Classes*, March 1977 revised edition, p. 55.

28. See Mary Larsgaard, "Beginner's Guide to Indexes to the Nineteenth Century U.S. Serial Set," *Government Publications Review* 2: 303-311 (1975).

29. The value of the *CIS US Serial Set* for students of genealogy was observed in a perceptive article in the *Journal of Genealogy* (January 1977), pp. 15-21.

30. *How Our Laws Are Made: Bicentennial Edition* (94-2: H. doc. 509).

31. *How Our Laws Are Made*, above edition, shows examples of an engrossed bill and an Act print on pp. 58-59.

7

PUBLICATIONS OF THE PRESIDENCY

> The administration of government, in its largest sense, comprehends all
> the operations of the body politic, whether legislative, executive, or judiciary;
> but in its most usual, and perhaps its most precise signification, it is limited to
> executive details, and falls peculiarly within the province of the executive
> department.
>
> —*The Federalist*, LXXII (Hamilton)

INTRODUCTION

Article II of the Constitution states that "the executive power shall be vested in a President of the United States" who is charged "to take care that the laws be faithfully executed." The brevity of this constitutional injunction belies the complexity of the administrative task.

Inherent in any large administrative unit is a line and staff organization. When Jefferson was President, the entire federal government consisted of just over 2,000 persons—from the despised tax collectors to the marshalls of film and television immortality—while today there are at least that many units of federal administration. These agencies are organized in the familiar pyramid; each has its own hierarchical structure. Orders theoretically flow from the President, as the chief executive, to the department head, and down to the lesser units—bureaus, agencies, offices—where the work of government is carried out and where most of the publications of government are produced.

Of the over 2½ million civil servants, only a small percentage are presidential appointees. The control and direction of the vast administrative machinery in practice must be delegated by the President. However, the President has a staff whose job it is to advise and assist him in managing national affairs, and over this group the President has a large measure of control. Indeed, Presidents often choose their staff on the basis of loyalty first and competence second.

Presidential control abides in what has come to be known as the White House Office; this inner locus of power extends outward to what is called the Executive Office of the President, a complex of administrative units that reports directly to the President and whose officers are appointed by the President often without the advice and consent of the Senate. In his staff organization the President enjoys great flexibility. Moreover, Presidents have used their staff to execute responsibilities of greater moment than the corresponding duties of the Cabinet.

When we speak of publications of the presidency, we must abandon in part the principle of provenance. While the White House Office and the Executive Office of the President are issuing agencies for presidential documents, so are the Office of the Federal Register and the Department of State. Moreover, several kinds of presidential publications are sent from the White House to Congress and are ordered to be published as specific Congressional series. As we saw in Chapter 6, the relationship between executive and congressional authority is circular and not always discrete.

Owing to this pattern of multiple provenance in the issuance of publications related to presidential decision and action, there is much duplication of materials. The multiplicity is sometimes confusing, but, when sorted out, it is manageable if not uniform.

THE WHITE HOUSE OFFICE

Publications of the inner circle of presidential control and authority have been assigned the rubric "President of the United States" and bear a Pr notation in the SuDocs classification system. The number following the letters Pr indicates the chronology of persons who have held the office, thus, Nixon 37, Ford 38, Carter 39, etc.[1] Only a few Items are available in this category for subscription by depository libraries, but they are important publications.

Useful documents are often carried in the General Publications series (Pr 3-.2; Item 850). Of recent notoriety was *Submission of Recorded Presidential Conversations to the Committee on the Judiciary of the House of Representatives by President Richard Nixon*, 1974 (Pr 37.2:C76). Special Commissions and Committees [as appointed] (Pr 3-.8; Item 851-J) covers reports issued by ad hoc committees and commissions established by executive order. Materials issued under this classification are not to be confused with those in the Y 3 category (Commissions, Committees, and Boards), which subsumes publications of units established by act of Congress or under authority of an act of Congress.[2] Committees and Commissions of the President include the famous *Report of President's Commission on the Assassination of President John F. Kennedy* (Pr 36.8:K38/R29) in one volume, and the accompanying *Investigation of Assassination . . . , Hearings before President's Commission* (Pr 36.8:K38/H35) in 26 volumes.

Economic Report of the President (Pr 3-.9; Item 848) consists of the President's economic report to Congress and the Annual Report of the Council of Economic Advisors, an agency within the Executive Office of the President.[3] In 1947 and 1948 the Council's Report was issued separately. Now combined, the materials include the previous year's economic developments, with an analysis and indication of trends in major economic issues and recommendations for policy action. Appendixes relate to legislation, and statistical tables include figures on income, employment, and production.

In 1973 the *International Economic Report of the President* was issued for the first time, and for the years 1973-1977 the SuDocs notation for this publication was Pr 37.8:In8/3/R29/2/year (Item 851-J). These annual reports give information on prominent international economic policies from the standpoint of United States policy. Selected current international economic issues are discussed; included in the text are graphs and statistical tables.

Other series available to depository libraries in the Pr notation include *Federal Advisory Committees, Annual Report of the President* (Pr 3-.10; Item 848-C)[4] and *Federal Ocean Program, Annual Report of the President* (Pr 3-.11; Item 848-B). Unfortunately, the inconsistencies in assigning SuDocs class notation and Item numbers to some of these categories reflect an ineptitude too dismaying to be reviewed in these pages either in sorrow or in anger.

EXECUTIVE OFFICE OF THE PRESIDENT

The administrative structure of the Executive Office of the President is shaped by executive order or legislation. The several agencies within the Executive Office are under greater presidential control than is the civil service in the line organization. Under authority of the Reorganization Act of 1939 (53 Stat. 561; 5 U.S.C. 133-133r, 133t note), various agencies were transferred to the Office by the President's Reorganization Plans I and II, effective July 1, 1939. Executive Order 8248 (September 8, 1939) established the various divisions of the Office and defined their functions; subsequent legislation permitted creation of new units or a reordering of existing agencies.

In terms of national policy some of these agencies within the Executive Office of the President exercise enormous power and influence, while others have less impact on our lives. The letters assigned by SuDocs to this category are "PrEx," followed by the appropriate numbers for the subordinate units.[5]

Office of Management and Budget

A strong case can be made that this agency is the most important arm of executive power and intent in the presidency. Article II, Section 3 of the Constitution requires that the President "shall from time to time give to the Congress Information of the State of the Union, and recommend to their consideration such measures as he shall judge necessary and expedient." Furthermore, presidential initiative was expanded in the Budget and Accounting Act of 1921, which imposed on the President the duty to submit to Congress a plan of proposed expenditures for the executive agencies, including their financing. But a budget is not merely a mass of figures; it is a blueprint of public policy.

When the Congress specifically passed this duty to the Chief Executive, it acquiesced to presidential initiative in substantive policy measures. Unlike the statements in campaign rhetoric, the budget is an indication of exactly where the

President is willing to spend funds. Almost a year in advance of the fiscal year, the Office of Management and Budget (OMB) begins securing from the departments and agencies requests for review. When the budget is finally submitted, the Congress is, of course, not required to accept it. But it is an authoritative statement of executive intent.

For many years the agency was known as the Bureau of the Budget. When first created by the 1921 Act, it was located in the Treasury Department, although under the President's immediate direction. The 1939 Reorganization Act transferred it to the Executive Office. By Reorganization Plan 2 of 1970 the Bureau was redesignated (Executive Order 11541, July 1, 1970) and its mission was delegated to the director of the renamed Office of Management and Budget. The several functions of the Office demonstrate the power and scope of this unit, and the chief publications of the agency symbolize the importance of its duties.

Budget

The federal budget, probably this nation's most significant public document, is submitted by the President in late January. It represents a continuous process, involving a dialog among OMB, the Joint Economic Committee of the Congress, and the Congressional Budget Office (see Chapter 6). Data and analyses relating to the Fy 1978 budget were published in six documents.

The Budget of the United States Government (PrEx 2.8:year; Item 853) includes the budget message of the President, his budgetary philosophy and economic assumptions, and explanations of spending programs and estimated receipts.

The Budget of the United States Government, Appendix (PrEx 2.8:year/App.; Item 853) is a massive volume that runs over 1,000 pages. Detailed information for each agency includes the proposed text of appropriation language, budget schedules for each account, explanations of the work to be performed and the funds needed, proposed general provisions applicable to the appropriations of entire agencies or groups of agencies, and schedules of permanent positions.

Special Analyses, Budget of the United States Government (PrEx 2.8/5:year; Item 855-B) for FY 1978 contained seventeen special analyses designed to highlight specific program areas such as education, health, income security, environmental protection, etc.

The United States Budget in Brief (PrEx 2.8/2:year; Item 855-A) is an abridged statement of the budget, providing a more concise, less technical overview for the layman. Included are summary and historical tables with color charts.

Issues '78 (PrEx 2.2:Is 7/978; Item 854) was published for the first time with the 1977 budget bearing the title *Seventy Issues*. Intended for a general audience, it provides background information on major budget and program decisions reflected in the President's budget and on certain important issues confronting the nation.

The Budget of the United States Government, Supplement (PrEx 2.8:year/Sup.; Item 853) contains the President's recommendations on executive, legislative, and judicial salaries and is transmitted pursuant to section 225 of PL 90-206 (2 U.S.C. 351 *et. seq.*).

In addition to these six basic documents, there are two other FY 1978 publications of interest in the budget process. *Current Services Estimates for Fiscal Year 1978* (PrEx 2.2:Se 6; Item 854) as required by the Congressional Budget Act of 1974 (PL 93-344) consists of three parts. Part I discusses the current services concept. Part II discusses the current services totals and includes the underlying economic assumptions. Part III discusses the current services estimates by major function and includes information on programmatic assumptions as they affect each function. *Fiscal Year 1978 Budget Revisions* (PrEx 2.8/7:year; Item 853) transmits to the Congress in summary form the administration's revisions to the 1978 budget that was presented to the Congress January 17, 1977. This publication was also issued as 95-1: H. doc. 77.

OMB Statistical Services

The Statistical Policy Division of the Office of Management and Budget has been responsible for issuing several publications designed to coordinate the development of federal statistics. However, President Carter signed on October 7, 1977, Executive Order 12013, "Relating to the Transfer of Certain Statistical Policy Functions" which was published in the *Federal Register* for October 12, 1977. The effect of EO 12013 was to transfer certain statistical policy responsibilities from OMB to the Office of Federal Statistical Policy and Standards within the Department of Commerce. The core staff of the Statistical Policy Division of OMB was moved to the new entity. This reorganization affected the provenance of the monthly *Statistical Reporter* (C 1.69), which was formerly classed in PrEx 2.11; Item 855-C. The October 1977 issue of *Statistical Reporter* contains an article explaining the reorganization (pp. 1-7).

Other OMB issuances which, as time goes on, may be affected by the reorganization, include the following publications.

Federal Statistics: Coordination, Standards, and Guidelines (PrEx 2.6/2:St2; Item 854-A), first issued in 1976, is a handbook of basic documents designed to serve as a guide to federal statistical activities. Contained in one volume are the basic legislative authorities, circulars, regulations, standards, and guidelines affecting the development of federal statistics. *Social Indicators 1973* (PrEx 2.2:So 1/973; Item 854) is subtitled *Selected Statistics on Social Conditions and Trends in the United States.* Eight major social areas are examined in the 1973 edition: health, public safety, education, employment, income, housing, leisure and recreation, and population. In subsequent editions other areas may be added. *Federal Statistical Directory* (PrEx 2.10:976; Item 853-A) is designed to facilitate communication among the various federal offices working on statistical programs. It is a companion volume to the 1975 revised edition of *Statistical Services of the United States Government* (PrEx 2.2:St2/975; Item 854), which describes the federal statistical system and presents brief descriptions of the principal economic and social statistical series collected by government agencies. The *Standard Industrial Classification Manual 1972* (PrEx 2.6/2:In27/972; Item 854-A) and the *Enterprise Standard Industrial Classification Manual 1974* (PrEx 2.6/2:In27/2/974; Item 854-A) contain information on the classification by kind of activity of establishments and enterprises, respectively. The *Enterprise . . . Manual* provides a standard for promoting the comparability of statistics about the business enterprises of the nation, and allows statistics classified by this standard to be related to statistics of establishments classified by the Standard Industrial Classification. *Standard Metropolitan Statistical Areas*, 1975 revised edition (PrEx 2.2:M56/975; Item 854), contains the concept of a metropolitan area to meet the need for the presentation of general-purpose statistics for a recognized urban population nucleus of substantial size.

Rounding out these significant publications is an indispensable source of information, the *Catalog of Federal Domestic Assistance* (PrEx 2.20:year; Item 853-A-1). Issued in binder form to provide easy updating supplementation, the primary purpose of the *Catalog* is to assist state and local governments, public and private organizations, business, industry, labor, and individuals in identifying and obtaining federal assistance. Each program in the *Catalog* is described in terms of the specific type of assistance provided, the purpose for which it is available, who can apply, and how to apply. Included are grants, loan guarantees, scholarships, mortgage loans, insurance, technical assistance, counseling and training, statistical information, specialized technical and advisory services, and service activities of regulatory agencies. Access to this information is provided by five indexes. The *Catalog* is the single, authoritative compendium of this kind of information.

Central Intelligence Agency

In the summer of 1977 President Carter ordered all of the nation's intelligence-gathering agencies placed under the control of the Director of the Central Intelligence Agency (CIA). This reorganization was said to strengthen the role of the National Security Council (NSC), which is the basic decision-making body of what is usually called the United States "intelligence community," a congeries that includes the Departments of Defense, State, Treasury, the Federal Bureau of Investigation (FBI), the armed services, and other agencies.

The March 1977 *List of Classes* subsumed series issued by the CIA under the NSC rubric. They include Maps and Atlases (PrEx 3.10/4; Item 856-A-1) and CIA Publications (PrEx 3.10; Item 856-A-2). Under the former Item, a number of general reference maps have been published, cartographic endeavors for countries as disparate as Ecuador and Yemen. A useful publication in the CIA Publications Series is the *National Basic Intelligence Factbook* (PrEx 3.10:N21/year). Issued in semi-annual editions which supersede earlier ones, the *Factbook* is a compilation of basic data on worldwide political entities. Arrangement is alphabetical by countries, with much useful political, sociological, and economic data. Included are color folded maps of large geographical units like Canada, Africa, Oceania, etc.

Since January 1976, the Documents Expediting Project has made available on a subscription basis serial reports and monographs in the CIA's *Reference Aid* series. Titles include *Chinese Merchant Ship Production* (March 1976), *USSR Council of Ministers* (August, December 1976), *Economic Indicators* (weekly), and *Major Oil & Gas Fields of the Free World* (January 1976). In response to a query, an officer of the Agency provided an "explanation" of CIA's numbering system for these documents, which was published for the benefit of documents librarians in the March 1977 issue of DttP.[6] However, subscription to the Project's *Reference Aid* series by depository libraries was rendered unnecessary in December 1977, when the series became a depository Item (PrEx 3.11; Item 856-A-3).

Foreign Broadcast Information Service

Curiously, this agency within the Executive Office of the President is not mentioned in the 1976/77 edition of the *United States Government Manual.* Nevertheless, the unit is duly acknowledged in the *List of Classes* and is the issuing agency for the useful publication *Broadcasting Stations of the World* (PrEx 7.9:year/pts.; Item 856-B). Editions of this series are published in four parts. Part I, *Amplitude Modulation Broadcasting Stations*, is indexed alphabetically by country and city. Part II, *Amplitude Modulation Broadcasting Stations According to Frequency*, is indexed according to frequency in ascending order. Part III, *Frequency Modulation Broadcasting Stations*, consists of two sections, one indexed alphabetically by country and city, and the other indexed by frequency in ascending order. Part IV, *Television Stations*, has two sections indexed in the same manner as Part III (see Chapter 4).

OFFICE OF THE FEDERAL REGISTER

The Office of the Federal Register, a unit of the National Archives and Records Service, is the issuing agency for a number of important presidential documents, as follows.

Federal Register

Although the bulk of the *Federal Register* (FR) consists of the promulgated rules and regulations of the departments and agencies, including the so-called independent entities, there is a category entitled "Presidential Documents," which appears at the beginning of the *Register.* The most common kinds of presidential documents are executive orders and proclamations (Figures 28 and 29, pp. 216 and 217). Other presidential directives, which appear less frequently, go by names like Memoranda (Presidential Determinations), Letters, Directives, and Reorganization Plans. Classed in GS 4.107 (Item 573), the FR is issued daily (except Saturday, Sunday, and official Federal holidays). Access to presidential documents published in the FR is through a monthly, quarterly, and annual index.

Executive Orders

A presidential action legally expressed is rendered in print and given legitimacy in the form of an Executive Order or a Proclamation. The former has "never been defined by law or regulation," thus "in a general sense every act of the President authorizing or directing that an act be performed is an executive order."[7] But if a document is not specifically designed as an executive order, the decision as to whether or not it will be published as part of the public record is left to the discretion of the President and his advisers. Virtually all executive orders cite some authority upon which they are issued. Some rely exclusively upon the general, implicit powers of the President, some cite specific federal statutes, while a few of a transitory nature fail to cite any authority (for example, EO 10671).

Figure 28
EXECUTIVE ORDER: FEDERAL REGISTER

THE PRESIDENT

Executive Order 11969   February 2, 1977

Administration of the Emergency Natural Gas Act of 1977

By virtue of the authority vested in me by the Constitution and statutes of the United States of America, including Section 13 of the Emergency Natural Gas Act of 1977 (Public Law 95–2), and Section 301 of Title 3 of the United States Code, and as President of the United States of America, it is hereby ordered as follows:

SECTION 1. There is hereby delegated to the Chairman of the Federal Power Commission, hereafter the Chairman, all of the authority vested in the President by the Emergency Natural Gas Act of 1977, except for the authority to declare and terminate a natural gas emergency pursuant to Section 3 of said Act. Nothing in such delegation shall be construed as delegating such authority to the Federal Power Commission as a collective body, except insofar as the Chairman may further delegate his authority under Section 3 of this Order.

SEC. 2. The Chairman shall, to the extent he deems appropriate, consult with the Secretary of the Interior, the Administrator of the Federal Energy Administration, other members of the Federal Power Commission and the heads of other Executive agencies in exercising the authority delegated to him by this Order.

SEC. 3. All authority delegated to the Chairman by this Order may be further delegated, in whole or in part, by the Chairman to any other officer of the United States or to any Executive agency.

SEC. 4. The heads of all Executive agencies shall cooperate with and assist the Chairman in carrying out the authority delegated to him by this Order.

SEC. 5. All Executive agencies shall, to the extent permitted by law, provide the Chairman on request such administrative support and information as may be necessary to carry out the authority delegated to him by this Order.

Jimmy Carter

THE WHITE HOUSE,
February 2, 1977.

[FR Doc.77–3906 Filed 2–3–77;12:01 pm]

Figure 29

PROCLAMATION: FEDERAL REGISTER

THE PRESIDENT

Proclamation 4485   February 2. 1977

Declaring a Natural Gas Emergency

By the President of the United States of America

A Proclamation

Abnormal weather conditions have caused prevailing temperatures in the United States, particularly in the East and Midwest, to be well below normal for the past three months. Many interstate natural gas pipelines and local natural gas distribution companies do not have sufficient supplies of flowing or stored gas to meet current demand. The shortage of natural gas available to some interstate pipelines and local distribution companies has been so severe as to cause them to curtail or to be in imminent danger of curtailing natural gas supplies to residences, small commercial establishments and other high priority users, so as to endanger life or health, and risk damage to plant or other facilities.

Other interstate pipelines and distribution companies, however, have more than adequate supplies of natural gas to meet the needs of residences, small commercial establishments and other high priority users.

In light of the severe shortage of natural gas supplies available to some firms and the disparity of natural gas supplies in various regions of the United States, the exercise of extraordinary authority for emergency deliveries and transportation of natural gas pursuant to Section 4 of the Emergency Natural Gas Act of 1977 is necessary to assist in meeting the requirements of natural gas for residences, small commercial establishments, and other high priority users in the United States or regions thereof. No measures other than those authorized by Section 4 of the Emergency Natural Gas Act of 1977 are adequate to assist in meeting the requirements of natural gas for residences, small commercial establishments, and other high priority users in the United States or regions thereof.

NOW, THEREFORE, I, JIMMY CARTER, President of the United States of America, by virtue of the authority vested in me by the Constitution and statutes of the United States, including the Emergency Natural Gas Act of 1977, do hereby proclaim and declare that a natural gas emergency exists within the meaning of Section 3 of said Act.

IN WITNESS WHEREOF, I have hereunto set my hand this second day of ·February, in the year of our Lord nineteen hundred seventy-seven, and of the Independence of the United States of America the two hundred and first.

Jimmy Carter

[FR Doc.77-3907 Filed 2-3-77 ;12:02 pm]

There is no overall index or digest of executive orders. The Works Projects Administration (WPA) Historical Records Survey published in 1944 a two-volume index of EO's in the numbered series to EO 8030 (December 29, 1938) entitled *Presidential Executive Orders.* Volume 1 consists of a list and the second volume a subject index. But the work does not give the text or summaries of the orders.

Proclamations

In practice the distinction between calling a presidential action a "proclamation" or an "executive order" has never been clear. Generally, however, the occasion for this form is one of widespread interest, a decree addressed to the public at large. Some proclamations have legal effect (Proclamation No. 3884), while others do not have the force of law. In this latter category, we find the many hortatory designations of a ceremonial or celebratory nature: Thanksgiving, World Law Day, Fire Prevention Week, etc. Authority for proclamations is claimed by a President by virtue of his office, under existing legislation, or in response to a congressional joint resolution. Perhaps the most famous recent presidential directive issued as a proclamation was Ford's pardon of Richard Nixon (Proc. 4311, September 8, 1974; 3 CFR, 1971-75 Comp., p. 385; 39 FR 32601).

Other Presidential Documents

Rulings other than proclamations and executive orders include *Memoranda,* usually from the President to the heads of his departments; *Directives,* designating matters such as assignments for officials of agencies; *Letters,* such as instructions to chiefs of American diplomatic missions; and *Reorganization Plans,* by which a President under existing legislation has the right to make changes in the structure of agencies unless the Congress objects within a certain time period.

Code of Federal Regulations

"Title 3—The President" contains the full text of documents signed by the chief executive and issued annually. During the years 1971-1975, the title designation for the annual compilations was changed to Title 3A, an appendix to Title 3; during this period, Title 3 became the designation for a codification of certain regulatory presidential documents. With Title 3, 1976 Compilation, the editors of the *Code of Federal Regulations* (CFR) returned to the use of "Title 3—The President." The confusion thus generated may only be dissipated in time, with the publication of cumulative editions of Title 3.

Title 3 Compilations

Title 3 is one of the volumes of a series which began with Proclamation 2161 (March 19, 1936) and Executive Order 7316 (March 13, 1936). The series has been continued by means of annual compilations and periodic cumulations, as follows: 1936-1938, 1939-1942, 1943-1948, 1949-1953, 1954-1958, 1959-1963, 1964-1965, 1966-1970, 1971-1975. The contents of these compilations are by law prima facie evidence of the text of the original documents and are required to be judicially noticed (44 U.S.C. 1510).

Useful publications in this series are *Title 3, 1936-1965–Consolidated Indexes* and *Title 3, 1936-1965–Consolidated Tables.* The former consists of a consolidated subject index covering the period; the latter contains various tables to facilitate searching presidential documents covering the period.[8] Title 3 is classed in GS 4.108/2:year (Item 572). In addition to the text of the several presidential directives, Title 3 has tables which serve as finding aids and an index which affords a subject access.

Statutes at Large

As indicated in Chapter 6, the *United States Statutes at Large* is primarily a compilation of public and private session laws; however, it does include presidential materials. A list of reorganization plans, by number, topic and date and a list of proclamations, by number, title and date are included in the *Statutes.* Moreover, the text of proclamations and reorganization plans are published as well. Each volume of the *Statutes* has a subject index that refers the user to the materials.

Weekly Compilation of Presidential Documents

The *Weekly Compilation* (GS 4.114; Item 577-A) is called a "special edition" or supplement of the *Federal Register*; it did not begin publication until August 2, 1965. It is perhaps the single most useful collection of presidential activities in the public record.

Issued each Monday for the week ending the previous Saturday, the *Weekly Compilation* includes the text of proclamations and executive orders, addresses and remarks, appointments, letters, nominations submitted to the Senate, acts approved by the President, checklists of White House press releases, messages to Congress, and announcements of resignations and retirements. Excluded from the *Weekly Compilation* are lists of promotions of members of the uniformed services, nominations to the service academies, and nominations of Foreign Service officers. A useful feature of this periodical is a continuing cumulative index for each issue. Other index cumulations include a quarterly, plus semi-annual and annual subject indexes that are separately issued.

Public Papers of the Presidents

Annual volumes of the *Public Papers* (GS 4.113; Item 574-A) have been issued since 1957 in response to a recommendation of the National Historical Publications Commission. Until then, there had been no systematic publication of presidential papers. Many presidential documents could be found only in mimeographed White House releases or as reported in the press. The Commission thus recommended the establishment of an official series, which was incorporated in regulations issued pursuant to Section 6 of the Federal Register Act as amended. While contemporaneous compilations were mandated, provision was also made for a retrospective collection. Presidents covered in this series now include Hoover, Truman, Eisenhower, Kennedy, Johnson, Nixon, Ford, and Carter.[9]

It is advisable not to discard the *Weekly Compilation* upon receipt of the *Public Papers*, for the series is edited. Most of the public messages and statements, however, are included in the annual volumes. Materials are presented in chronological order with a subject index. White House releases not included in the main portion of the text, reports of presidential task forces, awards of Congressional Medals of Honor and of Presidential Unit Citations, presidential reports to Congress—these items are located in the several appendixes at the end of the volumes.[10]

DEPARTMENT OF STATE

The Constitution vests in the President command of two major instruments of foreign policy—the armed services and the diplomatic corps. Although Presidents can and do rely heavily on their staff for foreign policy implementation, the duly constituted line organization has the machinery in place for the administration of foreign relations.

The Department of State is the oldest executive body of the U.S. government. Its predecessors had limited functions and little real power until the creation, in 1781, of a separate Department of Foreign Affairs. In 1789, following the election of Washington, the Department was reconstituted, its name was changed to Department of State, and with Jefferson as the first Secretary of State its functions were expanded to make it the most important of the government offices within the executive establishment.

State Department publications are many and varied, but a few materials issued by state are directly and specifically presidential in nature. The President, of course, as chief executive, is responsible for the decisions and activities of the departments and their agencies, including State; but the treaty and agreement powers of the President, as they are made manifest by action, constitute a major category of President-related publications.

Department of State Bulletin

Since 1939 the *Department of State Bulletin* (S 1.3; Item 864) was issued weekly with semi-annual indexes. But beginning with the January 1978 issue, this official record of United States foreign policy became a monthly with an annual index. The change in frequency of issuance did not affect the substantive contents. They continue to include texts of all major foreign policy speeches, statements, and news conferences of the President, the Secretary of State, and senior Department officials.

The first notice of treaty or agreement information is often in the form of a mimeographed press release by State. Usually, but not always, the text of the press release is published in the *Bulletin.* Activities of the President in the field of foreign affairs is indexed under "Presidential Documents." In the last section of each *Bulletin* is found information on two important instruments by which foreign policy is recorded: notification of treaty action, and announcement of executive agreements reached.

Treaties and Agreements

Discussion of "treaties" and "executive agreements" is difficult; legal analysis of constitutional language regarding treaties and agreements have failed to distinguish precisely the procedures for implementing the provisions of such acts. In practice, "treaty" is used to refer to any international agreement designated by the executive branch to enter into force only after the Senate gives its "advice and consent" by two-thirds majority vote. "Executive agreement" is used to refer to those agreements, other than treaties, entered into without prior or subsequent legislative or treaty authority, but rather on the basis solely of constitutional authority interpreted as vested in the executive branch.

Between 1946 and 1972 the United States entered into some 6,045 international agreements which were published in the appropriate public documents. But other international transactions which may well constitute agreements are not reported to Congress and have not been published. The actual number of international agreements is almost certainly substantially larger than official documents indicate. Published treaties, however, during this period of time, have remained relatively steady, averaging about thirteen per year. The yearly volume of executive agreements jumped sharply in the early 1950s, but has remained relatively steady since then.

The Senate does not "ratify" treaties; this is done by the President with the advice and consent of two-thirds of the Senators present. If the Senate approves, a President proclaims the pact to be law (see Figure 30, p. 222). If the Senate disapproves, the treaty can be returned to the President, who may renegotiate it or abandon it. Conversely, a rejected pact can be held by the Senate Foreign Relations Committee until that body decides to recommend it once again for passage.

Other options open to the Senate include amending the treaty, which in effect would require that it be renegotiated. In practice, when an amendment seems likely, the State Department prefers that the Senate delay action until a protocol to the treaty can be worked out. Moreover, the Senate can attach "understandings," "reservations," or "interpretations" to a treaty even though it gives overall approval to the compact. These have no legal effect if they do not alter treaty terms; but if provisions of the treaty were changed, the other nation or nations could refuse to agree.[11]

Treaties in Force (TIF)

This annual volume (S 9.14; Item 900-A) is prepared by the Office of the Assistant Legal Adviser for Treaty Affairs and consists of a list of treaties and agreements to which the United States has become a party and which are in force as of the date of compilation. With each reference any later qualifying or modifying action is given. Text references are cited, so that the user can easily consult the appropriate act.

Figure 30
UNITED STATES TREATIES AND
OTHER INTERNATIONAL AGREEMENTS

UNITED KINGDOM OF GREAT BRITAIN AND NORTHERN IRELAND

Extradition

*Treaty, protocol of signature and exchange of notes signed at
London June 8, 1972;
Ratification advised by the Senate of the United States of America
June 21, 1976;
Ratified by the President of the United States of America Septem-
ber 10, 1976;
Ratifications exchanged at Washington October 21, 1976;
Proclaimed by the President of the United States of America
November 17, 1976;
Entered into force January 21, 1977.
With exchange of notes
Signed at Washington October 21, 1976.*

———

By the President of the United States of America

A PROCLAMATION

Considering that:

The Treaty on Extradition between the Government of the United States of America and the Government of the United Kingdom of Great Britain and Northern Ireland, a Protocol of Signature, and an exchange of notes were signed at London on June 8, 1972, the texts of which Treaty and related documents, are hereto annexed;

The Senate of the United States of America by its resolution of June 21, 1976, two-thirds of the Senators present concurring therein, gave its advice and consent to ratification of the Treaty and the related documents;

The Treaty and the related documents were ratified by the President of the United States of America on September 10, 1976, in pursuance of the advice and consent of the Senate, and were duly ratified on the part of the United Kingdom of Great Britain and Northern Ireland;

It is provided in Article XVI of the Treaty that the Treaty shall enter into force three months after the date of the exchange of instruments of ratification;

Treaties and Other International Acts Series (TIAS)

Pursuant to PL 89-497, approved July 8, 1966 (80 Stat. 271; 1 U.S.C. 113), this - numbered series, known by the acronym TIAS (S 9.10; Item 899), is competent evidence of the force and effect of the concluded treaty or other international act. Issued in unbound (slip) form, it includes the text of the acts. The "TIAS" citation is found in *Treaties in Force* and in the *Department of State Bulletin*, and is indexed in the *Monthly Catalog.*

United States Treaties and Other International Agreements (UST)

Just as public laws are bound together chronologically in the *Statutes at Large*, so the TIAS pamphlets are collected into *United States Treaties* (S 9.12; Item 899-A). The text of treaties and agreements that were proclaimed during a calendar year are arranged chronologically and accessed by a subject and country index. Before 1950, the full text of treaties was published in the *Statutes at Large.* Because the *Statutes* ceased publishing the text of treaties in 1949, volume 1 of *United States Treaties* began in 1950. Note that in our example (Figure 30, p. 222), the proclamation is preceded by a succinct chronology or "history."

Treaties and Other International Agreements of the United States of America, 1776-1949 (Bevans)

This long-awaited compilation (S 9.12/2; Item 899-A) by Charles I. Bevans is now the definitive edition of United States treaties and agreements up to the beginning of UST. It renders unnecessary the use of earlier compilations.[12]

Commercial Sources of Treaty Information

Wiktor, Christian L. *Unperfected Treaties of the United States of America, 1776-1976* (Dobbs Ferry, N.Y.: Oceana, 1976). Wiktor, who edited and annotated this series, has provided researchers with a valuable tool. Unperfected treaties are those which have not received Senate approval or have not been ratified by the President. A few unperfected treaties have appeared in congressional documents series, but published sources have been highly selective. The texts are reproduced from largely inaccessible sources, including original manuscripts in the National Archives. The series is projected to run five or six volumes.

Kavass, Igor I., and M. A. Michael (comps). *United States Treaties and Other International Agreements Cumulative Index 1776-1949* (Buffalo, N.Y.: Hein, 1975). A useful index which provides in four volumes access to the treaties and agreements by TIAS number, date, country or intergovernmental organization, and subject.

Its companion four-volume edition, compiled by Kavass and A. Sprudzs, entitled *UST Cumulative Index 1950-1970* (Hein, 1973), provides similar access to treaties and agreements to that for the earlier period.

International Law Digests

Compiled under the direction of Arthur W. Rovine, *Digest of U.S. Practice in International Law* (S 7.12/3:year; Item 864-A) is the latest in a distinguished series which began with Cadwalader and continued through a number of compilers.[13] Rovine's predecessor, Marjorie M. Whiteman, compiled a 15-volume set called *Digest of International Law* (S 7.12/2; Item 864-A). The Rovine series began with the year 1973, and concerns significant developments in the field of international law, particularly as they relate to U.S. practice. With its analyses and extensive documentation, the series may be considered a voluminous treatise.

CONGRESSIONAL SERIES

A final major category that includes a substantial number of publications associated with presidential activities is the Congress itself. As our discussion of the Serial Set in Chapter 6 demonstrated, a peculiarity of Congress as an issuing agency is that many so-called congressional publications do not originate in that body. For example, some of the materials reviewed in this chapter are assigned as House or Senate *documents* but are sent to depository libraries in their "departmental edition": *Economic Report of the President, Budget*, etc. Presidents by law are required to submit numerous reports to the Congress, many of which are ordered to be printed in the "congressional edition." Moreover, publications which originate in the Congress include presidential materials.

Congressional Record

The index entry for actions of the chief executive is "President of the United States" and there is also a subject approach. The kinds of presidential materials printed in the *Record* include proclamations, executive orders, addresses, messages (including vetoes), statements, and the like. Because a member can request that virtually anything be printed in the *Record*, it is reasonable to assume that at one time or another any presidential document may appear in its pages.

House and Senate Journals

Presidential materials in the *Journals* include addresses (for example, the State of the Union address), communications to the Congress (for instance, urging that certain legislation be passed), messages (*documents*) from the President transmitting legislation, and veto messages (published in the *Journal* of the chamber where the bill originated). The quadrennial inaugural address of a President is customarily printed in the Senate *Journal*. The index entry in the House *Journal* for presidential materials is "President"; in the *Journal* of the Senate, "President of the United States."

Serial Set

Presidential messages, reorganization plans, addresses, etc., are among the materials sent by a President to Congress and published in the House or Senate *documents* series (see Chapter 6).

United States Code

Although one would be inclined to search for executive orders and proclamations in 3 CFR, the full text of some of these presidential documents are found in the *United States Code* with the authorizing statutory section. Reorganization Plans are published in 5 U.S.C. Appendix following the specific Reorganization Act by which they were authorized.

Tables IV, V, and VI of the *Code* and its *Supplements* consist of finding aids to presidential materials. Table IV lists executive orders implementing general and permanent law. Table V lists proclamations that are referred to in the *Code*. Table VI lists those Reorganization Plans published in the *Code*.

Senate Executive Documents and Reports

As was noted in Chapter 6, Executive Documents and Reports are a Senate series only, are now depository Items, but are not part of the Serial Set. Senate Executive Documents seem to be confined to the text of treaties and other international agreements, along with messages and reports from the President and Secretary of State, transmitted to the Senate Foreign Relations Committee. Senate Executive Reports are issued by various committees of the Senate, but an executive report from the Foreign Relations Committee deals with treaty and other international agreement information.

Both executive reports and documents constitute a significant part of the legislative history of treaties. Examples of executive reports include *Tax Convention with U.S.S.R.*, December 11, 1975 (Exec. Rpt. 94-19; Y 1.94/1: rp. 19) and *Nomination of Paul C. Warnke*, February 25, 1977 (Exec. Rpt. 95-6; Y 1.95/1: rp. 6). In the former publication, the Foreign Relations Committee recommended to the full Senate that it consent to ratification of the income tax convention with the Soviet Union. In the latter report, the Committee recommended to the Senate that Warnke be confirmed as Director of the Arms Control and Disarmament Agency with the rank of Ambassador.

The executive report and document series are classified until released in limited quantity. Both series are indexed in the *Monthly Catalog* (thus available on Readex) and abstracted in *CIS/Index* (thus available in the CIS microform edition). For both executive documents and reports, *CIS/Index* provides maximum bibliographic information (Figures 31 and 32, p. 226).

Figure 31

SENATE EXECUTIVE DOCUMENT: ABSTRACT

S385–10   FIFTH INTERNATIONAL TIN
AGREEMENT, Message from
the President.
June 23, 1976.   94-2.
vii+47 p.   † CIS/MF/3
Exec. Doc. J, 94-2.
Y1.94/2:J.
MC 76-5641.

Request for Senate advice and consent to ratification of the Fifth International Tin Agreement
signed Mar. 11, 1976. Agreement attempts to
stablize world tin prices within agreed limits
through establishment of an International Tin
Council and development of a buffer stock of tin.

Figure 32

SENATE EXECUTIVE REPORT: ABSTRACT

S384–14   FIFTH INTERNATIONAL TIN
AGREEMENT.
Sept. 8, 1976.   94-2.
18 p. il.   † CIS/MF/3
Exec. Rpt. 94-37.
Y1.94/2:rp37.

Recommends Senate advice and consent to
ratification of the Fifth International Tin Agreement formulated at Geneva, Switzerland, June
1975.
   Includes tables on U.S. tin imports and international tin prices and production throughout.

COMMERCIAL SOURCES OF PRESIDENTIAL ACTIONS

Some of the commercial reporting services discussed in Chapter 6 may be
used for researching presidential materials. Although the primary value of a
particular source may concern agency or congressional activity, its utility as a
source of presidential documentation should not be overlooked.

CCH Congressional Index

Commerce Clearing House's *Congressional Index* contains a division entitled
"Reorganization Plans-Treaties-Nominations." Action on these measures is reported
in this division, preceded by a special index in which reorganization plans and
treaties are entered by topic, and nominations of the President by appointee and
agency or branch of the military service to which appointed.

CQ Weekly Report, etc.

The several sterling publications of Congressional Quarterly, Inc., often include the full text of important presidential press conferences, major statements, messages, and speeches.

U.S.C.C.A.N.

Tables 7 and 8 of *United States Code Congressional and Administrative News* list, by number, date, and subject, presidential proclamations and executive orders, respectively. References are to the pages in U.S.C.C.A.N. that contain the text of these materials. Moreover, this West Publishing Company service publishes on a selective basis U.S. treaties upon ratification.

CIS/Annual

The *CIS/Annual*, among its other virtues, is a comprehensive source of legislative histories. Citations, if applicable, to the *Weekly Compilation of Presidential Documents* are included in the legislative histories, so that the user may check the presidential statement which may have urged or initiated the measure.

Federal Index

Volume 1, number 1 of the *Federal Index*, a monthly publication of Predicasts, Inc. (Cleveland, Ohio), appeared in October 1976. The publication, which cumulates quarterly with a hardbound annual, covers material in the *Congressional Record, Federal Register, Weekly Compilation of Presidential Documents* and other governmental and commercial sources. Citations provide access to the FR and CFR, *United States Code*, public laws, congressional laws, resolutions, and reports.

SUMMARY

The foregoing has been an attempt to categorize the various publications that are generated by the presidency and that issue from the several units responsible for the "provenance" of these materials. Although the duplication of publications that carry the public record of presidential activity may be considered egregiously wasteful, such duplication does provide one clear advantage to libraries and other institutions that require these documents. By the very duplication, information centers small and large, non-depository and depository, indigent or affluent, may participate in the acquisition of at least some of these publications.

It is within the budget of a small library, for example, to subscribe to the *Weekly Compilation of Presidential Documents* or to the *Department of State Bulletin.* Moreover, most of the publications cited are depository Items. A selective policy for the several types of libraries should not be difficult to implement. Our tabular summary affords a convenient finding aid for the more important presidential initiatives and their location in government publications (Table 4).

Table 4

OFFICIAL PUBLIC DOCUMENTS CONTAINING
MAJOR PRESIDENTIAL ACTIVITIES

Type of Activity	Location
Addresses and Remarks	Dept. State Bulletin; Cong. Record; Journals; Serial Set; Weekly Comp./Public Papers
Executive Orders	Cong. Record; Fed. Register/CFR; Weekly Comp./Public Papers
Letters	Dept. State Bulletin; Cong. Record; Fed. Register/CFR; Weekly Comp./Public Papers
Messages	Dept. State Bulletin; Cong. Record; Journals; Senate Executive Documents; Serial Set; Weekly Comp./Public Papers
Press Releases	Weekly Comp./Public Papers
Proclamations	Dept. State Bulletin; Cong. Record; Fed. Register/CFR; Statutes at Large; Weekly Comp./Public Papers
Reorganization Plans	Cong. Record; Fed. Register/CFR; Serial Set; Statutes at Large; Public Papers; U.S.C.
Treaties and Agreements	Dept. State Bulletin/Treaties in Force (list); TIAS; U.S. Treaties & Other Int. Agreements (text); Bevans (text)

REFERENCES

1. According to a Department of State ruling, Grover Cleveland is counted twice, as the 22nd and the 24th President, because his two terms were not consecutive.

2. When the controversial *Report of the Commission on Obscenity and Pornography* was published, it was given a Y 3.Ob 7:1/970 notation. In this case, although the President appointed the members of the Commission, it was created by PL 90-100, and the report was made to the President from the Commission.

3. The General Publications series of the Council has its own notation: PrEx 6.2 (Item 857-E-1).

4. Problems in the documentation of advisory bodies are discussed in Chapter 11.

5. A good example of a publication issued in the General Publications series of the Executive Office is *The National Energy Plan* (PrEx 1.2:En2/2; Item 850), the text of President Carter's proposed energy program for the development and conservation of the nation's energy resources.

6. *Documents to the People* 5: 41 (March 1977).

7. Schmeckebier, p. 341. The haphazard manner of issuing executive orders and proclamations prior to 1936 is treated in the excellent committee print *Summary of Executive Orders in Times of War and National Emergency*, August 1974.

8. A two-volume set entitled *Proclamations and Executive Orders: Herbert Hoover, March 4, 1929 to March 4, 1933* (GS 4.113/2:H76/vols.; Item 574-A) was published by the Federal Register Office in 1974. It was issued as a companion volume to the Public Papers of the Presidents series for the Hoover administration. Because the period predated the FR and the CFR, it represents the first official printed compilation of the documents.

9. *The Complete Presidential Press Conferences of Franklin Delano Roosevelt* (New York: Da Capo Press, Inc.) in twelve volumes covering the years 1933-1945 was announced in the May 1973 issue of *College and University Libraries*.

10. An informative article on this topic is "The Scope, Accessibility, and History of Presidential Papers," written by Arnold Hirshon (*Government Publications Review* 1: 363-90, 1974).

11. See *International Agreements: An Analysis of Executive Regulations and Practices*, a committee print prepared for the use of the Senate Foreign Relations Committee by LC's Congressional Research Service, March 1977 (Y 4.F76/2:In8/47; Item 1039).

12. Bevans replaces the various series compiled by Malloy, Redmond, Trenwith, and Miller covering the same years.

13. Following Cadwalader, which consisted of a single volume, Wharton's series appeared in three volumes, Moore's in eight volumes, Hackworth's in eight volumes, and Whiteman's.

8

DEPARTMENT AND AGENCY PUBLICATIONS

Though we cannot acquiesce in the political heresy of the poet who says:
 "For forms of government let fools contest—
 That which is best administered is best,"—
yet we may safely pronounce, that the true test of a good government is its
aptitude and tendency to produce a good administration.

—The Federalist, LXVIII (Hamilton)

INTRODUCTION

In Chapter 7 we discussed some of the exemplary publications that reflect
presidential activities. But the President, as administrative head of the executive
branch of government, must delegate to the twelve departments and their numerous
subordinate agencies his mandate under the Constitution to insure "that the laws be
faithfully executed." To accomplish this task, a president must rely upon his
Cabinet, and that group of officers must rely upon the much maligned
"bureaucracy" to carry out the policies of the administration.

The Cabinet is an oddity. Although it has existed since George Washington's
administration, it is not mentioned by name in the Constitution. The only reference
to this body is in the 25th Amendment, which states that a Vice President "and a
majority of either the principal officers of the executive department or of such
other body as Congress may be law provide" may declare a President unable to
discharge the powers and duties of his office. Thus the Cabinet is a creation of
custom and tradition. A Cabinet officer is approved by the Senate and serves at the
President's pleasure.

There is a saying that whereas administrations come and go, the bureaucracy
endures forever. While this is an implied comment upon the limitations of
presidential power over the departments and agencies that the chief executive

titularly heads, it also misleadingly suggests a static quality. In fact, the bureaucracy endures while suffering many sea changes. Reorganization of existing agencies is an on-going process. New agencies and, indeed, departments themselves are created, enjoy their place in the federal sun, and die—sometimes with a bang, often with barely a whimper. The most common pattern of change consists of internal modifications at the subordinate bureau level, but the President has the authority to submit to the Congress formal plans for restructuring the executive branch.

As we have noted elsewhere in this text, government reorganization affects the issuance of public documents, sometimes in drastic and dramatic ways. Mergers and dissolutions that occur signify a change in the lines of issuing authority for publications. Sporadic bursts of economy may signal a publication's demise. A change in purpose carries with it a concommitant change in the content, periodicity, or even design of a document. And of course the classification notation of the Superintendent of Documents, based as it is on the principle of provenance, is affected by reorganization.

Authority

The basic document for presidential reorganization is the Reorganization Act of 1977 (PL 95-17; 91 Stat. 29; 5 U.S.C. 901), April 6, 1977. Under this legislation, a President may submit to Congress a reorganization plan that provides for the transfer of the whole or part of an agency to another agency's jurisdiction and control, the abolition of all or part of the functions of an agency, the consolidation or coordination of functions within an agency, and the abolition of an entire agency should it no longer have functions under the new plan.

Under PL 95-17 there are limitations on a President's power to reorganize. For example, a reorganization plan may not create a new entity at the departmental level or abolish a department or independent agency. Thus the Department of Energy (see Chapter 4) was not brought into being by a presidential reorganization plan. Moreover, reorganization plans cannot authorize an agency to exercise a function not expressly authorized by law at the time the plan is transmitted to Congress.

Reorganization plans are published in several places, among them the *Federal Register*, Title 3 of the CFR, *Statutes at Large*, and 5 U.S.C. App. (see Chapter 7).

Historical Background

President Hoover was the first chief executive to be given reorganization authority. The Executive Reorganization Act of 1932 gave the President permanent reorganization authority; but less than a year later, in a rider to an appropriation act, the reorganization authority was limited to two years' duration. Various acts since then have always carried a statutory limitation; and, indeed, the authority has not been continuous during this time. The 1977 version is effective for three years. Generally, Congress over the years since 1932 has restricted a President's authority to submit reorganization plans and increased its own control over the plans.[1]

An edited compilation of significant documents pertaining to the reorganization of the executive branch is entitled *Federal Reorganization: The*

Executive Branch (New York: Bowker, 1977). Part I deals with the consolidation of executive departments and agencies; Part II covers regulatory reform; Part III deals with Sunset legislation and Zero-based budgets. The 800-page volume includes a bibliography and appendixes containing a list of acronyms; congressional and Library of Congress reports and proposals; an index of included documents; and a subject and name index. The compilation was edited by Tyrus G. Fain in collaboration with Katharine C. Plant and Ross Milloy.

It would be an exercise in futility *even to list* all of the series issued by the hundreds of subordinate units within the twelve departments. For example, the March 1977 *List of Classes* indicates that there were, at the time the *List* was revised, 27 series available to depository libraries issued by the Office of Education, and 40 issued by the National Center for Education Statistics. These numbers, of course, account for only a small percentage of the production of documents on education issued or sponsored by the government. And while the field of education is large, it is not significant compared to the size and publishing proclivities of other agencies and departments of the federal establishment.

Yet, to pursue the point, every one of the series issued on various aspects of the educational enterprise is of some importance to a group of users or an individual consumer of this product. In that sense, every document that can be bibliographically verified (and many that cannot!) is of potential reference or research value. Conversely, any omission, deliberate or inadvertent, would be rightly if not righteously challenged. While it is true that important publications—those no librarian can long remain ignorant of—like the *United States Government Manual* and the *Statistical Abstract of the United States* seem to endure, there are too many documents whose apparent permanence was illusory. In 1970 the renowned *Bibliography of Agriculture* began to be published commercially. In 1974, the *Monthly Weather Review*, which had been published by the government for over 100 years, became a publication of the American Meterological Society.

Government reorganization, economies, changes in public policy, commercial encroachment on government publishing, the vagaries of things for which accountability is difficult to fix—all these factors and more render a discussion of "important" series and their exemplary titles fraught with danger. Accordingly, the titles mentioned in the pages that follow are, at best, hedged with caution. Users' needs cannot be circumscribed by one person's experience with documents; and this writer begs the reader's indulgence.

BASIC ADMINISTRATIVE SOURCES OF INFORMATION

Some basic guides to general issuances have been explored in Chapter 5 and elsewhere as appropriate. Before discussing a few representative series issued by the departments and their subordinate entities, it may be useful to acknowledge those sources which cut across and delineate all government units within the executive branch.

Federal Register

Presidential documents that appear in the *Federal Register* and in Title 3 of the *Code of Federal Regulations* were the proper concern of our discussions in Chapter 7. But the vast bulk of materials found in the FR are the pronouncements of the several agencies of the executive branch and the so-called independent agencies.

The Federal Register Act of 1935 (as codified in 44 U.S.C. 1501 *et. seq.*) provides that, in addition to presidential documents, the kinds of materials that are to be printed include "documents or classes of documents that . . . have general applicability and legal effect" and those "that may be required so to be published by Act of Congress." Moreover, notices of hearings or miscellaneous agency announcements, including those of proposed rules, are to be published and the public given timely notice to respond.[2] As a result of these categories, the documents published in the FR are grouped under the following headings:

1) *Presidential documents* (Chapter 7).

2) *Rules and regulations*; these normally take up the largest portion of any given issue of the FR. They have general, permanent applicability and legal effect. When published, they are codified as they are to appear in the CFR. Temporary rules having a time-expiration date or those of limited applicability are also published in the FR, but do not carry over into the CFR.

3) *Proposed rules*; these are the text of changes or amendments to already existing regulations, or new rules that an agency is considering. Their publication permits interested parties to comment on the proposals through hearings or by submitting written statements to the agency.

4) *Notices*; information other than rules or proposed rules is found in this section, but no codified material is printed here. Notices include but are not limited to a) changes in agency organization too small to be submitted as a reorganization plan; b) notices of opinions which are advisory and non-binding; c) timely notice of meetings of commissions, boards, and other bodies at which proposed rule changes will be discussed; and d) miscellaneous announcements, including grants.

Other useful reference features in the FR include *reminders* of rules going into effect that day, a list of dates for meetings, etc.; a *list of public laws* (but not the text) that have been recently signed; and various *finding aids*, which will be discussed later in this section. Moreover, the FR has published what are called "special issues." Useful titles in this series include *Protecting Your Right to Privacy—Digest of Systems of Records, Agency Rules, Research Aids* (GS 4.107/a:P 939; Item 573) and *Privacy Act Issues, 1976 Compilation, Volume 1—Systems of Records, Agency Rules* (GS 4.107/a:P 939/2/976; Item 573), the latter to be issued in five volumes.

The index to the FR is issued monthly, with quarterly and annual cumulations; it consists of subject entries and agency names arranged alphabetically and thereunder by rules, proposed rules, and notices.

Code of Federal Regulations

It is a useful analogy to compare the *Code of Federal Regulations* (CFR) to the *United States Code.* Just as the *Statutes at Large* are codified in the U.S.C., so are the daily issues of the FR codified in the CFR. The one represents statutory law, the other administrative law. The authority for publishing the CFR is found in 44 U.S.C. 1510.

The ferocious specificity of administrative rulings is evident when one notes that the volumes of the *United States Code* occupy only about one-third of the shelving space required for the volumes of the *Code of Federal Regulations.* Moreover, the CFR is divided into 50 titles, many of which parallel the titles of the U.S.C. Each volume of the CFR, unless no amendments were promulgated in the FR,[3] is revised at least once every CY and reissued on a quarterly schedule as follows:

Titles 1-16	as of January 1
Titles 17-27	April 1
Titles 28-41	July 1
Titles 42-50	October 1

As we noted in Chapter 7, Title 3 is set aside for presidential documents and its annual volumes cumulate. A list of current and superseded CFR volumes, and a list of CFR titles, subtitles, chapters, subchapters and parts are included in the subject index volume to the CFR; that volume is revised annually. In addition, individual CFR volumes include a Table of CFR Titles and Chapters, an Alphabetical List of CFR Subtitles and Chapters, and a List of CFR Sections Affected. This trio comprises the "finding aids" component of the CFR.

In the past, annual publications of the CFR included a *General Index* volume and a *Finding Aids* volume, both unnumbered. However, the two were combined in one unnumbered volume entitled *CFR Index and Finding Aids,* revised as of July 1, 1977. The *CFR Index* is to the entire *Code of Federal Regulations,* organized primarily by agencies with some broad subject headings included. Also included in this volume are several tables that formerly appeared in the *Finding Aids* volume. One table, entitled "Parallel Table of Statutory Authorities and Rules," is used to get from legislation to regulation; it contains sections of the U.S.C. cited by agencies as rulemaking authority. Another table, entitled "Presidential Documents Included or Cited in Currently Effective Rules," lists places in the CFR which carry a reference to a presidential ukase. This table was last revised as of January 1, 1976, in the separate *Finding Aids* volume of that date. The editors of the CFR feel that updating this table annually "would impose a considerable burden" on the staff and have no evidence of its usefulness. Figure 33 shows a typical example of a parallel table in this now combined index and finding aids volume.

Search Strategy Using the FR/CFR

The bibliographic apparatus which relates the FR to the CFR is relatively simple to understand.

Figure 33
PARALLEL TABLES: CFR INDEX AND FINDING AIDS VOLUME

5 U.S. C. 552   Finding Aids   **Table I—Authorities   5 U. S. C. 555**

United States Code	Code of Federal Regulations	United States Code	Code of Federal Regulations
5 U. S. C. 552 _____	15 CFR Part 911	5 U. S. C. 552 _____	40 CFR Parts 1–2
	Part 950		41 CFR Part 23-3
	16 CFR Part 14		Part 60–40
	17 CFR Part 140		Part 105–60
	Part 200		43 CFR Part 2
	18 CFR Part 3		45 CFR Part 5
	19 CFR Part 103		Part 1100
	21 CFR Part 2		Parts 1700–1701
	22 CFR Parts 5–6		46 CFR Part 2
	Part 212		Part 14
	Parts 302–303		Parts 50–59
	Parts 503–504		Part 63
	Parts 602–603		Part 162
	Part 1002		Part 175
	24 CFR Part 15		Part 380
	26 CFR Part 601		Parts 502–503
	27 CFR Part 71		47 CFR Parts 0–1
	28 CFR Part 16		49 CFR Part 73
	29 CFR Part 2		Parts 1000–1001
	Part 14		Part 1004
	Parts 70–71	553 _____	10 CFR Parts 1–2
	Part 570		Part 19
	Parts 1401–1404	553 _____	12 CFR Part 19
	Parts 1610–1801		14 CFR Part 221
	Part 1913		Part 250
	31 CFR Part 1		Part 302
	Part 256		Part 384
	Part 270		Part 387
	Part 323		Part 399
	32 CFR Part 64		15 CFR Part 4
	Part 66		Part 60
	Part 75		Part 903
	Part 100		Part 950
	Part 138		29 CFR Part 570
	Parts 168–169a		33 CFR Parts 1–2
	Part 213		36 CFR Parts 5–7
	Part 245		Part 25
	Part 275		41 CFR Part 60–2
	Parts 286–287		Part 60–60
	Parts 290–293		43 CFR Part 14
	Part 295		46 CFR Part 206
	Part 518		Part 251
	Part 735		Part 502
	Parts 806–806a		Part 522
	Part 813a		Part 530
	Part 1285		47 CFR Part 1
	Part 1480		49 CFR Part 1047
	Part 1701		Part 1065
	Part 1705		Part 1090
	Part 1813		Part 1123
	Part 1900		Part 1124
	33 CFR Part 1		Part 1131
	Part 3		Part 1203
	Parts 85–91		Part 1307
	Part 96	553v _____	49 CFR Part 1104
	Part 136	554 _____	10 CFR Part 2
	35 CFR Part 9		14 CFR Part 302
	36 CFR Part 200		18 CFR Part 13
	37 CFR Part 1		21 CFR Part 310
	39 CFR Part 111		Part 312
	Part 262		Part 314
	Part 601		Part 330
	Part 3002		47 CFR Part 1

    1)   To locate the title and the part one is concerned with, consult the *CFR Index and Finding Aids* volume.

    2)   Because the *CFR Index* is revised only once a year, bring it up to date by consulting a separate pamphlet, *LSA—List of CFR Sections Affected.* The *LSA—List* is designed to lead CFR users to amendatory actions published in the FR. It is arranged by titles of the CFR referencing pages in the FR. There is no longer a single annual issue of the *LSA—List.* Four publications must be saved: the December issue is the annual for Titles 1-16; the March issue is the annual for Titles 17-27; the June issue is the annual for Titles 28-41; the September issue is the annual for Titles 42-50.

    3)   To complete the updating to the most current (today's) issue of the FR, consult:

    a) "Cumulative List of Parts Affected during [Month]," located in the front of each issue of the FR. Titles of the CFR will reference pages in the FR for that month where amendatory matter may be found.

    b) "List of CFR Parts Affected in This Issue," also found in the front of that same day's issue of the FR. It is a list of the parts of each title of the CFR affected by documents published in the current issue.

Finding Aid Guide

A "Federal Register Finding Aid Guide" (34 FR 18785-94) provides a useful index to materials published not only in the FR and CFR but also in the *United States Government Manual, Weekly Compilation of Presidential Documents, Public Papers of the Presidents*, and *Statutes at Large.*

The Guide consists of an "Alphabetical List of Finding Aids" followed by four tables covering agency materials, presidential materials, statutory materials, and special information lists. The alphabetical list references the finding aid item.

In addition to this Guide, there is the unnumbered *CFR Index and Finding Aids,* noted above, and a Finding Aids section in all the CFR volumes. The latter contains a table of CFR Titles with breakdowns into chapters and parts; an alphabetical list of agencies with corresponding CFR subtitles and chapters; and a list of CFR sections affected, divided by year, since the Title was established.

Users Guide

Of value is a publication titled *The Federal Register: What It Is and How to Use It* (GS 4.6/2:F31; Item 569-B), published by the Office of the Federal Register in 1977. Contents of the 70-page document include the organization of the FR/CFR; a discussion of the several finding aids; the Federal Register Act; informal rulemaking procedures of the Administrative Procedures Act; and a finding aids summary.

Readability

The style of writing in the FR/CFR has come in for a great deal of criticism. Indeed, it is fashionable to make fun of the tortuous, obfuscating prose. But it is no laughing matter, because the regulatory activities of government extend into every facet of the nation's individual and collective activities. Witness these two examples:

An ingredient which is both a spice and a coloring, or both a flavoring and a coloring, shall be designated as spice and coloring, or flavoring and coloring, as the case may be, unless such ingredient is designated by its specific name.[4]

Order. (a) During the period Jan. 28, 1977, through Feb. 24, 1977, no handler shall handle any navel oranges grown in District 1 or District 3 which are of a size smaller than 2.20 inches in diameter, which shall be the largest measurement at a right angle to a straight line running from the stem to the blossom end of the fruit: provided, that not to exceed 5 percent, by count, of the navel oranges contained in any type of container may measure smaller than 2.20 inches in diameter . . .[5]

The Director of the Office of the Federal Register engages in an on-going struggle to try to make the FR/CFR at least a bit more readable. "Highlights" on the cover of each FR are selective but cover major items of general interest contained in a particular issue. The "Reminders" section noted above is an innovative feature. Before every ruling, a "preamble" must be written; it is supposed to contain the purpose of the rule, proposed rule history, results of public participation, and the like; and it is supposed to be written in language laypersons can understand. "Dial-a-Reg" permits one to telephone (202/523-5022) the day before, where a recorded voice gives selections from highlights of documents to be published in the next day's FR. The Office of the Federal Register is engaged in a project to automate the preparation and printing of the FR, CFR, and their finding aids. In March 1977 the Office announced the development of a thesaurus of subject headings to be used in indexing the FR, CFR, and related publications and invited comments.[6] A *Document Drafting Handbook* assists federal agencies in improving the quality of their regulatory programs and the writing of the documents that result from those programs.[7] And periodic workshops open to the public are conducted by members of the staff of the Office of the Federal Register.

But all of these excellent efforts will be of little help if the writers of the regulations do not communicate better with the public. The creation of the FR and CFR was an act of noble intent. It eliminated caprice and bibliographic chaos; it did away with "hip pocket" administrative law. How ironic, then, that having created the bibliographic machinery for this purpose, one cannot understand the regulations promulgated.

Microform Editions of the FR and CFR

In addition to the GPO micropublishing program, which used the CFR in a pilot project (Chapter 1), the following editions of the FR and CFR are available in a microformat.[8]

Federal Register

1) U.S. National Archives & Records Service, Publications Sales Branch (Washington, D.C.) on microfilm, 1936 to the present.
2) University Microfilms (Ann Arbor, Michigan) on microfilm, 1934-1974 and thereafter in film or microfiche.
3) Information Handling Services (Englewood, Colorado) on microfiche, 1936 to the present.
4) Princeton Microfilm Corporation (Princeton, New Jersey) on microfilm, 1955 to the present.
5) Brookhaven Press (Washington, D.C.) on microfilm, 1936 to the present.
6) Readex Microprint Corporation (New York, N.Y.) on microcard, 1956 to the present.

Code of Federal Regulations

1) Trans-Media Publishing Co. (Dobbs Ferry, N.Y.) on microfilm, 1939-1971, 1972-1976.
2) Readex Microprint Corporation (New York, N.Y.) on microcard, 1956 to the present.
3) Information Handling Services (Englewood, Colorado) on microfiche, 1938 to the present.

Looseleaf Services

The size and complexity of administrative regulations are rendered more manageable by the commercial publication of looseleaf services. Prominent commercial publishers include Commerce Clearing House, Prentice-Hall, the Bureau of National Affairs, and Pike & Fischer. Although the approach is by subject or topic (e.g., taxation, labor relations, securities, etc.), the services cover the administrative promulgations of the agency involved in the activity. A typical service includes all relevant materials on a given topic: texts of statutes, court decision, and administrative rulings. Editorial comments, indexes, rapid supplementation, tie the "package" together and save the researcher valuable time.

CSI Federal Register Report

Capitol Services, Inc. (CSI), a commercial firm based in Washington, D.C., which issues a daily abstract of *Congressional Record* proceedings (see Chapter 6), publishes the *Federal Register Report* and *Federal Register Abstracts, Master Edition*. The former is a customized daily service providing abstracts from the *Federal Register* in topic areas selected by the client. A subject checklist covers topics from agribusiness to veterans' pensions. The latter consists of a summary description of each entry in the FR, organized by subjects, with a useful "subject finder" guide included.

Before the FR and CFR

For the individual or business affected by government regulations, the current search strategy described above is the significant procedure. For the scholar or historian of administrative rulings, the task prior to 1936 is not so easy. Some agencies publish their own decisions and have been issuing compilations of rulings for many years. These compilations have usually been printed at the GPO. For example, *Treasury Decisions* go back to 1899, and the *Decisions of the Federal Trade Commission* exist from 1915 to date. Many of these compilations are available as depository Items, but it would be a mistake to use them instead of the FR and CFR because they lack adequate updating.

GPO and CFR

Commencing with the 1978 edition of the various titles of the CFR, the Library Division (SLL) of the SuDoc announced in a letter dated October 25, 1977, that it would begin distributing depository copies of the CFR in microfiche to those librarians indicating interest. Moreover, the Library Division stated that Item 572 is to be cancelled and replaced by Item 572-B for hardcopy, and Item 572-C for the microfiche copy. This selection will remain in effect for the complete 1978 edition of the CFR. The directive does not affect single copies of the CFR or sales copies, which will be available in hardcopy only through the sales program.

Summary

Libraries that enjoy heavy client use of the CFR should select the depository Item that calls for hardcopy. Except for Title 3, which cumulates, the CFR is kept current by replacement volumes. Consequently, continual discarding does not add a cumulative burden to a library's shelf space. Moreover, it is the writer's opinion that the current year's FR be subscribed to by depository libraries in paper copy. For earlier issues of the FR, a microformat is desirable.

The larger, crucial issue for the user is the ability to comprehend these important directives. From the womb to the tomb, government is involved in our individual and corporate destiny. If these rules cannot be read or understood save by those who wrote them, the body politic cannot effectively engage in a dialectic with its government.

United States Government Manual

The *United States Government Manual* is the official handbook of the federal government. It describes briefly the purposes and programs of most government agencies, and gives the names of chief personnel. The *Manual* is sold by SuDocs and is a depository Item (GS 4.109; Item 577).

Some new feature is introduced and another dropped in virtually every edition of the *Manual*. The basic information which does not vary includes descriptions of the programs and activities of the legislative, judicial, and executive branches, including the independent agencies; boards, committees and commissions; "quasi-official" agencies like the American National Red Cross; selected multilateral international organizations; and selected bilateral organizations. Appendixes include executive agencies and functions of the federal government abolished, transferred, or terminated subsequent to March 4, 1933; commonly used abbreviations and acronyms; the texts of the Freedom of Information Act as amended and the Privacy Act of 1974; and standard federal regions, councils and executive boards, along with a map of the standard federal regions. The *Manual* is indexed by name, subject, and agency.

New features of recent *Manuals* include a summary paragraph immediately following the personnel listing of most departments and agencies, which briefly epitomizes the agency's role and programs (1976/77); and a reference to the FR and CFR in which the most recent statement of organization has been published by the agency (1977/78). Continuing features include an introductory guide to government information, and a list of recent changes which occurred too late to be included in the text of the *Manual*.[9]

The *Supplement to the 1977/78 Manual* (GS 4.109:977-78/supp.; Item 577) contains changes in personnel and organization which occurred since May 1, 1977, the revision date for that edition of the *Manual*. Included in this *Supplement* are the structure and functions of the new Department of Energy and a list of those federal agencies affected by the creation of DOE.

Praeger Series

The Praeger Library of U.S. Government Departments and Agencies is a multi-volume series issued by Praeger Publishers (New York). Each title in the series deals with a government department or agency. Titles include Robert E. Kling, *The Government Printing Office* (1970), Stacy V. Jones, *The Patent Office* (1971), and Charles A. Goodrum, *The Library of Congress* (1974). The authors are all knowledgeable about the agencies they cover, several of them having been employees of the entity. More than seventy titles are planned for the series, and 43 of them are listed in Vladimir M. Palic's *Government Organization Manuals, A Bibliography* (Washington: U.S. Library of Congress, 1975), pp. 79-80.

Wall Chart

A large chart entitled *Organization of Federal Executive Departments and Agencies* is issued annually (data as of January 1, [year]) as a committee print of the Senate Committee on Governmental Affairs (formerly the Committee on Government Operations). It is sold by SuDocs and in 1977 was available to depository libraries (Y4. G 74/9: Ex 3; Item 1037-A). It provides a remarkably detailed breakdown of the federal establishment, including the independent agencies and selected commissions, with precise data on the number of federal employees by administrative unit. It is supplemented by a committee print issued in pamphlet form.[10]

Federal Yellow Book

The *Federal Yellow Book*, like its counterpart for Capitol Hill entitled the *Congressional Yellow Book* (Chapter 6), is a looseleaf locator directory published by The Washington Monitor, Inc. Purporting to be more up to date than the government agencies' own telephone directories, the *Federal Yellow Book* covers the White House, Executive Office of the President, and the federal departments and agencies. It lists approximately 25,000 federal employees by organization, with their names, titles, addresses, room and phone numbers. The directory is kept current by replacement pages issued irregularly several times a year, which constitutes at least two complete versions in every 12-month period. A year's subscription to the *Federal Yellow Book* in 1977 was $95.00.

Weekly Regulatory Monitor

Another publication of The Washington Monitor, Inc., is the *Weekly Regulatory Monitor*, a service which extracts from the *Federal Register* activities of regulatory agencies of some consequence, "translates" it into readable English if necessary, and packages it in a more convenient form than the basic official document. A regular feature of this periodical is entitled "This Week's Regularly Scheduled Meetings," which enables the user to review quickly agenda items of general regulatory interest scheduled by the several agencies. Subscription in 1977 to this weekly was $250.00.

SELECTED CATEGORIES OF DEPARTMENTAL PUBLICATIONS

Annual Reports

According to Schmeckebier, the annual reports "constitute the oldest series of government publications and are the sources where one is usually able to find full information regarding the operations of the several departments and agencies of the government."[11] Most of the annual reports of departments, and many of the reports of the subordinate units within a department, are available to depository libraries in their "departmental edition," while also issued in their "congressional edition" for those libraries designated to receive them as part of the Serial Set. Thus the annual report of the Secretary of Commerce is C 1.1 (Item 126) and that of the Economic Development Administration within the Commerce Department is C 46.1 (Item 130-F).

Bibliographies and Lists

Virtually all departments and agencies issue lists of their publications, either irregularly or on a periodic schedule. Many of these lists are also, like annual reports, available to depository libraries. Thus, for example, the Forest Service of the Department of Agriculture issues a miscellaneous series (A 13.11/2; Item 85-A), while the *Bureau of the Census Catalog* is issued quarterly with monthly supplements (C 3.163; Item 138). The various lists issued by agencies provide a useful complement to general tools like the MoCat. Moreover, in some instances agency and bureau lists, catalogs or bibliographies which are annotated may be better reference sources than the comprehensive indexes.

A useful compilation of catalogs, checklists, pricelists, indexes, accessions lists, and bibliographies issued by the federal agencies is found in Vladimir M. Palic, *Government Publications: A Guide to Bibliographic Tools* (4th ed.; Washington: Library of Congress, 1975), pp. 11-80.

Periodicals

Serials which have distinctive titles and appear more than once a year at regular intervals constitute an important vehicle for the dissemination of government information. Many periodicals (but by no means all) are recorded in the MoCat and other indexing sources. *Price List 36*, as we noted in Chapter 2, carries periodicals, including subscription services, available for sale from SuDocs.

As one might expect, the subject matter of federal government periodicals is as broad and varied as the interests of government. There is scarcely an agency of any size within the federal establishment that does not publish at least one periodical, and a number of periodicals are available to depository institutions. They range from magazines that the layperson can understand (*American Education, Airman*) to highly technical and specialized periodicals (*Journal of Research of the National Bureau of Standards*).

Some indication of the quantity of periodical publishing by the federal government may be gleaned from the following story: In 1972 Senator J. William Fulbright ordered the Department of Defense to submit a sample copy of all the periodicals it produced. An astonishing 1,402 titles surfaced, at an annual cost to the taxpayer of about $13 million. The list was published in the *Congressional Record* [daily edition] May 18, 1972, pp. S8102-8113. Moreover, DoD officials could *not affirm* that the number they found represented the total number of periodicals (including numerous internal newsletters and the like) issued by the Department and its several agencies.

American Statistics Index, which attempts to be comprehensive, covers approximately 800 federal government periodicals on statistical matters alone! A large number of these issuances are neither depository Items nor available for sale by the SuDocs.[12]

Index to U.S. Government Periodicals—Subtitled *A Computer-Generated Guide to Selected Titles by Author and Subject*, the *Index to U.S. Government Periodicals* covers over 150 titles from more than 100 government agencies. The publisher is Infordata International, Inc., a Chicago-based commercial firm.

Articles are not abstracted. The *Index* is issued quarterly with an annual cumulation. Annual volumes are being prepared for earlier years. The first quarterly issue covered the period January-March 1974. The *Index* clearly fills a gap, for although coverage is selective, it is the only indexing source that is devoted solely to the indexing of federal government periodicals. Microfiche of the text of all periodicals indexed is available in *Current U.S. Government Periodicals on Microfiche* (Glen Rock, N.J.: Microfilming Corporation of America).

An excellent study by Harleston and Stoffle in *Government Publications Review* 2: 323-43 (1975) describes the indexing and abstracting activities of 54 indexing services.[13] The "Appendix" to this article lists 704 federal government periodicals indexed or abstracted by at least one service. This extremely useful list is arranged as follows:

Class No.	Title	Where Indexed
C55.310	Commercial fisheries review	Biological Abstracts, Environmental Index

The study shows that *American Statistics Index* and the *Index to U.S. Government Periodicals* are the two services that index the most federal periodicals. Many of these 704 titles are indexed only by *American Statistics Index*. Conversely, the popular and well-known *Monthly Labor Review* (L 2.6; Item 770) is indexed by seventeen services. The list can be used by a small, non-depository library or a special library as a guide to periodical selection.

Another useful compilation is Philip A. Yannarella and Rao Aluri, *U.S. Government Scientific and Technical Periodicals* (Metuchen, N.J.: Scarecrow Press, 1976), an annotated list of 266 periodicals published either directly by a government agency or by grantees, contractors, and federally supported information analysis centers. Also included are some periodicals issued by so-called "quasi-official" agencies like the National Academy of Sciences, National Academy of Engineering, and the National Research Council.

The book is divided into two parts. Part 1, the entry section lists each periodical, with bibliographic information and the annotation. Part 2 consists of about 80 bibliographies and lists issued by federal agencies. The book is indexed by subject/title, agency, depository Item number, and SuDocs class number.

As useful as these several tools are, there is no comprehensive service for federal periodicals. Given the sheer amount and scatter-shot distribution pattern of periodicals, it is highly doubtful that they can be brought under exhaustive or reliable bibliographic control.

Handbooks and Yearbooks

The federal government issues a number of handbooks and yearbooks, many of which are of notable educational interest or reference value. Three of the more popular ones here noted will provide a brief sampling of these types of series.

Yearbooks of Agriculture

Perhaps the best known of federal government yearbooks, the Yearbooks of Agriculture are issued annually (A 1.10; Item 17), and each volume is devoted to one broad subject of interest to the general reader. Several yearbooks are kept in print and announced from time to time in *Selected U.S. Government Publications.* Until 1936 the yearbook consisted in part of the annual report of the Secretary of Agriculture.[14] The monographic concept began with the 1936-1937 two-volume *Better Plants and Animals* and continues to the present. Yearbooks are extremely popular sales publications of the SuDocs. Recent titles include *Landscape for Living* (1972), *Handbook for the Home* (1973), *Shopper's Guide* (1974), *The Face of Rural America* (1976), and *Gardening for Food and Fun* (1977).

Area Handbooks

Highly regarded are the "Area Handbook" series issued within the Department of the Army Pamphlet series (D 101.22; Item 327-J). A list of countries covered in SB (*Subject Bibliography*)-166 (February 1977) numbered over 100, and new Area Handbooks continue to be published. Countries span the world and alphabet, from Afghanistan to Zambia.

Each handbook discusses a foreign country's three basic institutions: social (history, geography, ethnic groups, religions); political (system of government, foreign relations); and economic (trade, agriculture, economic structure). All handbooks have bibliographies that enable readers to pursue further research.

Conservation Yearbooks

Issued by the Department of the Interior, the Conservation Yearbooks, a numbered series (I 1.95; Item 601-A), began in 1965 and continue to the present. These handsome, attractively illustrated monographs, like the Yearbooks of Agriculture, have different titles each year. Titles have included *Quest for Quality* (1965), *The Population Challenge* (1966), *The Third Wave* (1967), and *America 200: The Legacy of Our Lands* (1976).

"How to" Pamphlets, Manuals, and Brochures

In a myriad of publications, government agencies provide the public with information on how to do things. Indeed, the function of the "government as teacher" accounts for a publishing industry in itself. Titles representative of this large category of documents follow:

The Back-Yard Mechanic (D 301.72/A: M 46/v.1) is composed of articles from *Driver*, the magazine for military drivers issued by the U.S. Air Force. The instructions take one step-by-step, with illustrations, through the fine points of changing the oil, installing disc brake pads, and other routine maintenance procedures. The purpose of this 57-page compilation is to save the user money and give him a sense of "personal accomplishment."[15]

The "energy crisis" has generated a gaggle of publications such as *Tips for Energy Savers* and *Gasoline: More Miles Per Gallon.* The famous *Infant Care* and *Young Children and Accidents in the Home* instruct the reader in appropriate child-rearing practices. A number of pamphlets on nutrition are designed to help us eat better, look better, and stay healthy.

And no sample would be complete without mention of the publications of the Home and Garden Bulletin series (A 1.77; Item 11), Department of Agriculture: *Growing Flowering Perennials, Roses for the Home*, etc.

Many of these kinds of educational or self-help documents are listed in the *Consumer Information Catalog* and are available from the Consumer Information Center, Pueblo, Colorado. In addition, consulting the appropriate SB (*Subject Bibliography*) series will provide current ordering information.

SUMMARY

Whether published to instruct, regulate, provide statistics, list, direct, guide, or even to amuse, the publications of the executive branch are limited in quantity and variety only by budgetary realities and the imagination of the human mind. And whether the title is of profound significance (*Federal Register*) or of such a nature that the information could be found elsewhere (*How to Make Jellies, Jams, and Preserves at Home*), all purport to serve a legitimate function mandated by the purpose and mission of the agency.

Let us look at it another way. As of July 1977 the total number of federal civilian employees (excluding employees of the Central Intelligence Agency) was 2,901,973, and their annual salaries and wages exceeded $46 billion.[16] Since publishing is a means of establishing and validating the existence of government, perhaps the wonder is that the number of publications is so small.

REFERENCES

1. 95-1: H. rp. 105, pp. 494-95.

2. 44 U.S.C. 1505, 1508.

3. See "Special Notice" in *Daily Depository Shipping List 9877* (June 15, 1977).

4. Title 21, Chapter 1, Subchapter A, Part 1, Section 1.10, Paragraph (c), CFR. This is a regulation for the enforcement of the Federal Food, Drug and Cosmetic Act and the Fair Packaging and Labeling Act on the designation of ingredients.

5. Cited by Richard L. Madden, *New York Times* (city edition), February 19, 1977, p. 12.

6. "Notices," 42 FR 12986 (March 7, 1977).

7. U.S. Office of the Federal Register. *Document Drafting Handbook* (Washington: Government Printing Office, 1975).

8. Henry P. Tseng, *Complete Guide to Legal Materials in Microform* (Arlington, Va.: University Publications of America, 1976) and *1976 Supplement* (1977), *passim.*

9. Paul Axel-Lute has been supplying additions and corrections to the *Manual* and publishing them in various issues of *Documents to the People*, a very useful service.

10. *Supplement to [Year] Organization of Federal Executive Departments and Agencies: Agencies and Functions of the Federal Government Established, Continued, Abolished, Transferred, or Changed in Name by Legislative or Executive Action during Calendar Year [19— —].*

11. Laurence F. Schmeckebier and Roy B. Eastin, *Government Publications and Their Use* (2d rev. ed.; Washington: Brookings, 1969), p. 379.

12. *Periodicals and Sources: A List of Federal Statistical Publications and Their Issuing Sources* (Washington: Congressional Information Service, 1976).

13. Rebekah Harleston and Carla J. Stoffle, "Government Periodicals: Seven Years Later," *Government Publications Review* 2: 323-43 (1975).

14. The annual report of the Secretary is now a non-GPO Item available to depository libraries (A 1.1; Item 6).

15. *Selected U.S. Government Publications* (October 1977), p. 7.

16. "An Inside Look at Our Runaway Bureaucracy." *U.S. News & World Report* LXXXIII: 22-23 (October 3, 1977).

9

PUBLICATIONS OF THE JUDICIARY

The result of these observations to an intelligent mind must be clearly this, that if it be possible at any rate to construct a federal government capable of regulating the common concerns and preserving the general tranquility, it must be founded, as to the objects committed to its care, upon the reverse of the principle contended for by the opponents of the proposed Constitution. It must carry its agency to the persons of the citizens. It must stand in need of no intermediate legislations; but must itself be empowered to employ the arm of the ordinary magistrate to execute its own resolutions. The majesty of the national authority must be manifested through the medium of the courts of justice.

—The Federalist, XVI (Hamilton)

Regarding the due administration of Justice as the strongest cement of good government, I have considered the first organization of the Judicial Department as essential to the happiness of our Citizens, and to the stability of our political system. Under this impression it has been an invariable object of anxious solicitude with me to select the fittest Characters to expound the laws and dispense justice.

—George Washington, *Letter to John Rutledge*,
September 29, 1789

INTRODUCTION

The judicial branch of the federal establishment forms a pyramid. At the bottom of the pyramid stand the United States District Courts. On the next level stand the United States Courts of Appeals. At the pyramid's apex stands the Supreme Court, the highest tribunal in the land. Because our government is a dual one—federal and state—the powers of the United States courts are limited in that they can exercise only that authority granted by the Constitution. They are also limited in judicial function in that they cannot exercise authority belonging to the legislative or executive branches of the government.

State judicial systems have general, unlimited power to decide almost every type of case, subject only to the limitations of state law. They are comprised of a state supreme court, or state court of appeals, and a group of lower bodies, such as municipal, police, and justice-of-the-peace courts. These are the tribunals with which citizens most often have contact. The great bulk of legal business concerning divorce, the probate of estates, and all other matters except those assigned to the United States courts, is handled by state courts.[1]

The independence of the judicial branch is assured by the Constitution, even though federal judges are appointed by the President with the advice and consent of the Senate. Under the Constitution federal courts can be called upon to perform only judicial work, the application and interpretation of the law in the decision of real differences: that is, in the language of the Constitution, the decision of "Cases" and "Controversies." The courts cannot be called upon to make laws, which is the function of the legislative branch, nor to enforce and execute laws, the function of the executive. Federal judges hold their positions "during good behavior" and can be removed from office against their will only by impeachment. Independence is further insured by compensation that "shall not be diminished" during a judge's tenure in office; neither the President nor the Congress can reduce the salary of a federal magistrate.

Provision for a federal judiciary was stated with utmost simplicity in Article III, Section 1 of the Constitution: "The judicial Power of the United States shall be vested in one supreme Court, and in such inferior Courts as the Congress may from time to time ordain and establish." In accordance with this constitutional provision and by authority of the Judiciary Act of September 24, 1789, a Supreme Court, three circuit courts, and thirteen district courts were created. According to the 1976/77 edition of the *United States Government Manual* there are today eleven courts of appeals, eighty-nine district courts (plus the one in the District of Columbia), and territorial courts in Puerto Rico, Guam, the Virgin Islands, and the Canal Zone. The "Cases" and "Controversies" that can be decided in these courts are set forth in Article III, Section 2 of the Constitution.

Although independence and the concommitant ideal of integrity theoretically characterize the base of the federal judiciary, selection is largely a political process. Tradition has awarded to Senators of the President's party the prerogative of naming persons for federal judgeships within their states. If the Senators are not of the President's party, the White House looks to its party organization within that state for suggested nominees.

Judicial appointment is a powerful patronage lever for an incumbent President. Two sections of the Constitution govern appointment. Article II, Section 2 empowers a President to nominate, with the advice and consent of the Senate, "judges of the Supreme Court, and all other officers of the United States"; and Article II, Section 3 provides that a President "shall commission all the Officers of the United States." From these constitutional provisions evolved the stages in the selection process: nomination, appointment, commission.

Nomination involves considering many factors, not the least of them being political compatibility; but advice is also proffered by national, state, and local bar associations. Appointment is often a highly political act, involving as it does the consent of the Senate. Commission is a technicality in which the President gives the appointee the authority to carry out the duties of his office. In the selection of men and women to serve as judges and justices, ideological considerations loom significant if not paramount.[2]

A few important decisions of the district courts may be appealed directly to the Supreme Court, but the appellate process generally rises hierarchically from district court to court of appeals and then to the final tier of the tri-level pyramid, if the Supreme Court has jurisdiction. The courts of appeals review decisions of the district courts within their circuit and also some of the actions of the independent regulatory agencies. One Supreme Court justice is assigned to each circuit, but his duties as circuit justice are nominal.

Lower court judges are required to follow the precedents established by the Supreme Court, but the system is not a monolithic unit in which, like the military chain of command, orders flow from the top. District and circuit judges have wide latitude in determining the lineaments of Supreme Court decisions. Those at the lower levels often take a different point of view toward legal disputes than do the members of the high court. And, since few of the thousands of cases reach the Supreme Court, the magistrates of the lower federal courts are important policy-makers. The federal judiciary, like the executive and legislative branches, reflects in its judgments the shifting and variegated interests of the body politic.

REFERENCE AND RESEARCH AIDS

The scope of legal reference and bibliography is vast and at first seemingly complex. But the bibliographic apparatus of the law is one of the easiest to master, in large part because it adheres to a logic not evident in other areas of government publications. The account that follows is intended merely to introduce the reader to some of the salient materials supportive of federal case law. The nature of publications in this field is such that a host of commercial materials surrounds and amplifies a relatively small number of official government documents.

Basic Sources

For the beginner, Morris L. Cohen's *Legal Research in a Nutshell* (St. Paul, Minnesota: West Publishing Co., 1978), now in its third edition, affords a concise though limited introduction to legal bibliography. As the author notes in his "Preface," the narrative "for best effect should be followed by some form of bibliographic exposure in a library setting."

Comprehensive introductory works include Morris L. Cohen (ed.) *How to Find the Law* (7th ed.; St. Paul, Minnesota: West Publishing Co., 1976), and J. Myron Jacobstein and Roy M. Mersky *Fundamentals of Legal Research* (Mineola, N.Y.: The Foundation Press, 1977). The latter, now in its fifth edition, is the successor to *Pollack's Fundamentals of Legal Research* (1973). Still of value although becoming dated is Miles O. Price and Harry Bitner *Effective Legal Research* (Boston: Little, Brown, 1969).

Bernard D. Reams, Jr. (ed.), *Reader in Law Librarianship* (Englewood, Colorado: Information Handling Services, 1976) is a collection of 42 articles that deal with various aspects of law librarianship, including legal research, the environment of law libraries, law librarianship, and new directions for law libraries.

Bibliographic guides include the annual *Bibliographic Guide to Law* (Boston: G. K. Hall), a compilation of sources in United States and international law cataloged by the Library of Congress; S. W. Beal, *Legal Reference Collections for Non-Law Libraries: A Survey of Holdings in the Academic Community* (Ann Arbor, Mich.: Pierian, 1973); and *Law Books Recommended for Libraries* (Rothman Reprints, Inc.), a list prepared by the Association of American Law Schools (AALS). The latter is being made available in full text by Rothman on microfiche.

In the Legal Almanac series (Dobbs Ferry, N.Y.: Oceana), number 44 is Roy M. Mersky's *Law Books for Non-Law Librarians and Laymen—A Bibliography* (1969) and number 74, David Lloyd's *Finding the Law: A Guide to Legal Research* (1974).

Encyclopedias

Two general legal encyclopedias dominate the field and provide topical coverage of the law in narrative form; they are *American Jurisprudence Second* (Am. Jur.2d) and *Corpus Juris Secundum* (C.J.S.). The former is published by Lawyers Co-operative Publishing Company, the latter is issued by West Publishing Company. As will become evident, these two publishers are responsible for producing most of the tools of legal bibliography.

Both encyclopedias are multi-volume works arranged alphabetically by topic with a general index to supplement the index in each volume. Both have scope notes and definitions and are supplemented annually by pocket parts. Each cites decisions found in its own sister publications. Neither encyclopedia has a table of cases.

Legal scholars warn that encyclopedias are often slow to reflect subtle changes in the law and lack the careful analysis and fine distinctions of a good treatise. Nevertheless, they are useful as a starting point in a legal search and, although not binding on courts, are often cited in judicial opinions.

Dictionaries

Legal dictionaries vary in size and purpose. Standard one-volume dictionaries include *Black's Law Dictionary* (West Publishing Co., 1968) and Ballentine, *Law Dictionary, with Pronunciations* (Lawyers Co-op, 1969). Each gives court citations with its definitions. A massive multi-volume *Words and Phrases* (West, 1940-) covers definitions used in reported cases from earliest times to the present. This work is kept current by annual pocket supplements. Legal dictionaries usually define maxims and, of course, the dictionary function of legal encyclopedias must not be overlooked.

Directories

The superior entry in this form is the annual, five-volume *Martindale-Hubbell Law Directory* (Summit, N.J.: Martindale-Hubbell, Inc.). Subdivided by states, it lists the names of attorneys and firms alphabetically by city and town. *Martindale-Hubbell* contains a section on federal law that includes digests of United States copyright, patent, tax, and trademark law. The directory also includes a list of key personnel, jurisdiction, terms and calendars of federal, District of Columbia, Canal Zone, and state courts.

Indexes to Legal Periodicals

The Wilson Company's *Index to Legal Periodicals* is arranged by subject and author. Coverage includes the major legal periodicals published in the United States, Canada, Great Britain, Australia, and New Zealand. The index also contains a table of cases arranged alphabetically by name of plaintiff; case notes of insufficient length to be indexed as articles are cited at the end of each subject under the subheading "Cases." The Book Review Section lists reviews under the name of the author of the book, or under the title if the author is unknown. Published monthly except September, *Index to Legal Periodicals* cumulates annually and triennially.

The *Jones-Chipman Index to Legal Periodicals*, the forerunner of the current *Index to Legal Periodicals*, provides coverage of English language periodicals for the years 1886-1937. Arranged by subject and author, it was issued in six volumes.

Current Index to Legal Periodicals is issued jointly by the University of Washington (Seattle) Law Library and the Washington Law Review on a weekly basis. Articles indexed are arranged in a broad subject format—e.g., Bankruptcy, Civil Rights, Contracts, etc. The service is mimeographed and purports to supplement material found in *Index to Legal Periodicals*. Subscribers to *Current Index* were advised to discard issues prior to the January 11, 1974, number because material covered in earlier issues was now indexed in the February 1974 issue of *Index to Legal Periodicals*.

Index to Periodical Articles Related to Law, a quarterly, lists articles of legal interest that are of research significance. Edited by Jacobstein and Mersky (Dobbs Ferry, N.Y.: Glanville), it has a subject arrangement with a separate index for authors and periodicals.

L. W. Morse (comp.), *Checklist of Anglo-American Legal Periodicals 1962-1974*, is a guide to issues and pagination of all English language periodicals worldwide. This was issued in looseleaf form, and permitted libraries an opportunity to check their holdings. Only a limited quantity of complete sets covering the years 1962-1974 are available from Glanville, an affiliate of Oceana Publications.

Eugene M. Wypyski, *Legal Periodicals in English* (Dobbs Ferry, N.Y.: Glanville, 1975-) is the successor service to the *Morse Checklist*. Broader and more detailed than the former, it offers information in depth about all legal periodicals published in English worldwide. Cumulative indexes will appear with each new volume, with periodic supplementation. A projected five to six volumes in looseleaf binders, volume 1 became available in 1976 and additional volumes are issued quarterly until completion.

A special citator service of Shepard's, called *Shepard's Law Review Citations*, covers over 100 law reviews and legal periodicals. Updated by cumulative supplements three times a year, the service permits the user to determine if any law review article written since 1947 has been referred to in any other law review article or federal or state court decision since 1957.

Looseleaf Services

We noted in Chapter 6 the value of a looseleaf service like CCH's *Congressional Index.* There are numerous looseleaf services prepared for the legal community. They provide fast updating. The "package" format permits the user to find in one source all relevant documentation. They are indexed thoroughly. They cover all jurisdictions. They combine full text materials with editorial comment, historical notes, and annotations.

Typically, looseleaf reporters are devoted to a topic. The major publishers of these services are Commerce Clearing House, Inc., Prentice-Hall, Inc., and the Bureau of National Affairs, Inc. Topics include tax law, securities, corporations, labor law, trade, and the like. Indexing of looseleaf services is usually by subject, case name, and finding lists of administrative and statutory provisions. Moreover, citator tables are a feature of the tax services.

Citators

Because the law is a dynamic process, the lawyer must know what cases or acts are valid and may properly be cited as authority. Case citators provide a record for tracing the judicial history of a case, establishing whether it is still effective law, and finding later cases that have cited the principal case. In addition, the citator process permits one to develop research leads to periodical articles, opinions of the Attorney General, law review comments, and annotated reports comments on cases.

The most complete and well-known citator system is Shepard's *Citations.* Indeed, the word "Shepardizing" is used in legal parlance to describe the operations in determining the applicability of statutes and cases as authority. Shepard's *Citations* cover all federal statutes and cases, labor law, administrative decisions, District of Columbia reports and statutes, regional and state law.

Supreme Court coverage is found in Shepard's *United States Citations* (Colorado Springs, Colorado: Shepard's Citations, Inc.). The work is divided into two parts, the *Case Edition* and the *Statute Edition.*

Case Edition

Citations shown are found for opinions reported in 1) *United States Reports* (Ju 6.8; Item 741), the official GPO edition; 2) West Publishing Company's *The Supreme Court Reporter*; and 3) *United States Supreme Court Reports, Lawyers' Edition*, published by Lawyers Co-operative Publishing Company. Both official and unofficial reports are citable in courts. To save space, Shepardizing information is given under the official *United States Reports*, with parenthetical reference to the case in the *Supreme Court Reporter* and *Lawyers' Edition.*

Statute Edition

Shepardizing legislation is complicated because, as noted in Chapter 6, session laws published chronologically in the *Statutes at Large* and statutes in force published in topical order in the *United States Code* are both official sources, although usually only one of these forms is the authoritative text. Moreover, the U.S. Constitution is amended, codes are amended and repealed and at intervals revised, and there are jurisdictional problems of statutory coverage in our federal system. Accordingly, the process involves tracing subsequent action on a given law and subsequent judicial action construing the legislation.

The Statute Edition of *United States Citations* includes citations to the Constitution, the *United States Code*, official edition (Y 1.2/5; Item 991), the *United States Code Annotated* (West Publishing Co.), *United States Code Service* (Lawyers Co-operative Publishing Co.), *U.S. Statutes at Large* (GS 4.111; Item 576), *U.S. Treaties and Other International Agreements* (S 9.12; Item 899-A), and various rules of court.

The concept of Shepardizing is the essence of simplicity, and librarians who have any familiarity with *Science Citation Index* or *Social Science Citation Index* will not find Shepardizing to be difficult. However, since the very thought of learning the citator system strikes fear among the neophyte, the following sources for preparation are recommended:

> *How to Use Shepard's Citations* (Colorado Springs, Colorado: Shepard's Citations, Inc., 1975).
>
> Cohen, M. L., *How to Find the Law* (7th ed.; 1976), pp. 160-83.
>
> Price and Bitner, *Effective Legal Research* (1969), pp. 239-65.

Digests

Digests, simply defined, are indexes to judicial decisions. Cohen's definition of these finding aids is clear and succinct:

> A digest to judicial decisions superimposes a subject classification upon chronologically published cases. The classification consists of an alphabetically arranged scheme of legal topics and subtopics which can be approached through a detailed index. Brief abstracts of the points of law in decided cases are classified by subject and set out in the digests under appropriate topical headings. They are then located and retrieved by the researcher through the index to the digest.[3]

West Publishing Company's *American Digest System* is the most comprehensive of case digests for this country. It consists of the *Century Edition* and *Decennial Digests*, and purports to cover "all standard law reports from appellate courts rendering written decisions from 1658 to date. It also digests selective opinions from certain courts of first instance, such as the federal district courts and some lower state courts."[4]

The pattern of publishing the *American Digest System* is as follows:

Name	Years Covered
Century Digest	1658-1896
First Decennial	1897-1906
Second Decennial	1906-1916
Third Decennial	1916-1926
Fourth Decennial	1926-1936
Fifth Decennial	1936-1946
Sixth Decennial	1946-1956
Seventh Decennial	1956-1966
Eighth Decennial	1966-1976
General Digest, 5th Series	1976 to date

The *General Digest* covers cases decided since the end of the most recent decennial. If the publishers continue to follow this scheme, *General Digest, 5th Series* will continue until the issuing of the *Ninth Decennial Digest* in 1986, when a new *General Digest* will begin.

Digests are abstracts of points of law decided in a court case. They reference (using West's key number system) the units of the *National Reporter System*, bringing together all cases on a similar point of law. A *Descriptive-Word Index* includes all topics of the digest classification, key-number section lines and editorial reference lines in the *Decennial Digests*, and "catch" words and phrases descriptive of the facts and points of law of the abstracts contained in that digest. There is a separate *Descriptive-Word Index* to each of the *Decennial Digests* and to the *General Digest*. For our purposes, there are specialized digests for federal case law.

Federal Digests (West)

The *Federal Digest* is the permanent index to federal case law from the eighteenth century to 1938. *Modern Federal Practice Digest* includes cases reported in the various West reporters from 1939-1961. *Federal Practice Digest 2nd*, which began in 1976, covers cases from 1962 to date. Individual volumes are updated by cumulative pocket supplements, and pamphlet supplements are issued three times a year. The *Descriptive-Word Index* of *Modern Federal Practice Digest* also covers the *Federal Digest*.

United States Supreme Court Digest contains abstracts of all cases decided by the U.S. Supreme Court, thus duplicating the digests in *Federal Digest* and *Modern Federal Practice Digest*. Volume 1 comprises the *Descriptive-Word Index*, and volume 14 has a table of cases.

Digest of United States Supreme Court Reports, Lawyers' Edition

This digest, published by Lawyers Co-operative Publishing Company, does not employ West's key number classification scheme, but is useful in other respects. Volume 16 is the *Word Index*; volumes 15 and 15A include table of cases; volumes 17 and 18 cover federal court rules. Volume 17 also contains the text of the United States Constitution, referencing topics in the *Digest* covering the subject matter. There are several valuable finding aid tables, including in volume 14, lists of citations to the *Revised Statutes, Statutes at Large*, and *U.S. Code*.

Annotations

American Law Reports (A.L.R.) comprise a selective number of appellate court decisions. This series, published by Lawyers Co-operative Publishing Company (and its affiliate, the Bancroft-Whitney Company), is characterized by decisions of widespread interest followed by what the publishers call *annotations*. These *annotations* are usually expository encyclopedic essays of varying length (from one page to three hundred pages). The editorial staff presents a discussion and explication of a point of law based on all relevant cases on the subject. In effect, *annotations* are monographs that analyze and restructure the entire body of law on point.

The *American Law Reports* are published in four series, as follows:

Series	Cited As	Years Covered
First	A.L.R.	1919-1948
Second	A.L.R.2d	1948-1965
Third	A.L.R.3d	1965 to date
Federal	A.L.R.Fed.	1969 to date

A.L.R.Fed. includes only decisions from the federal courts. Leading decisions of the federal courts are published, followed by an annotation as described above.

The A.L.R. series are supplemented as follows:

Series	Supplementation
First	A.L.R. Blue Book of Supplemental Decisions
Second	A.L.R.2d Later Case Service
Third	pocket supplement
Federal	pocket supplement

Any A.L.R. *annotation* may subsequently be *supplemented* or *superseded*. A *supplemental annotation* is one in which the cases in point since the original *annotation* was written are gathered, and a new *annotation* is written. However, one should read the new *annotation* in connection with the earlier one. A *superseded annotation* is one that is completely rewritten, so that the earlier one is no longer required to be read. The easiest way to determine if an *annotation* has been *supplemented* or *superseded* is to use the "Historical Table," which is found in the back of the *Quick Index* to A.L.R.3d.

Each of the four sets has a one-volume index called *Quick Index*. These are arranged alphabetically to the *annotations* in the A.L.R. volumes and are subdivided by topics and facts; the *annotations* are listed by their titles.[5]

Other

The bibliographic structure of American law also encompasses federal practice and procedure, treatises, restatements, model codes, uniform laws, citations, and form books. For these and other topics the reader is advised to consult one of the basic texts noted at the beginning of this chapter.

FEDERAL COURT REPORTS

The magisterial bibliographic apparatus created and maintained by commercial publishers like West and Lawyers Co-operative is necessary in large measure because of the doctrine of *stare decisis*, which holds that precedents should be followed. That is, principles of law established by judicial decision must be accepted as authoritative in cases similar to those from which such principles were derived. From this construct, it follows that an attorney must have access to the latest cases in order to advise his client correctly. Commercial publishing of case law is geared to prompt reporting, not only of the opinions and decisions of courts but of the indexes and other finding aids. The process is crucial to effective legal deliberation.[6]

Decisions relied upon as precedent are usually those of appellate courts. Consequently, availability of published decisions and opinions increases in ascending order of the federal court hierarchy. Whereas only selected decisions of district courts are readily available to those with a need to know, almost all written and *per curiam* (literally "by the court") decisions of the appellate courts, special courts, and the Supreme Court are reported either officially or unofficially. Nevertheless, total bibliographic control does not exist; Price and Bitner state that "not all decisions of any federal court, even of the Supreme Court, are reported."[7]

District and Appellate Courts

During most of the nineteenth century, decisions of United States district courts and U.S. circuit courts of appeals were published in a number of separate series cited by the names of their official reporters. This "nominative" reporting, which caused bibliographic confusion, was rectified by the publication of a thirty-volume series known as *Federal Cases* (West Publishing Co.); the series was arranged by title and arbitrary case number, with a table translating the nominative report series to *Federal Cases* notation. The new series incorporated selected lower court decisions of importance from 1789 to 1879.

For the years 1880 to the present three units of West's National Reporter System are consulted for the reports of the lower federal courts.

Federal Reporter (West)

The *Federal Reporter* consists of two series. The first series (F.) covers three hundred volumes; the second series (F2d.) began anew with volume 1. From 1880 to 1932 the *Federal Reporter* covered cases reported in district courts, courts of appeals, U.S. Court of Customs and Patent Appeals, Court of Appeals of the District of Columbia, and Court of Claims. From 1932 to the present the *Federal Reporter* has primarily covered the courts of appeals and cases adjudged in the U.S. Court of Customs and Patent Appeals. From 1942 to 1961 cases reported from the U.S. Emergency Court of Appeals were published. And from 1960 to date cases of the Court of Claims have been included.

Federal Supplement (West)

Federal Supplement (F.Supp.) was created in 1932 to cover selectively the U.S. district courts. From 1932 to 1960 it included the Court of Claims. And from 1949 to date coverage has included the U.S. Customs Court.

Federal Rules Decisions (West)

Federal Rules Decisions (F.R.D.) began in 1940 with coverage of cases relating to the various federal procedural rules. It began with cases concerning the federal rules of civil procedure and in 1946 included the rules of criminal procedure as well.

It is important to remember that these three units publish on a *selective basis* the decisions of the several courts, a departure from West's policy of comprehensive coverage.

"Special" Courts

In addition to the Supreme Court, the courts of appeals, and the district courts, the Congress has created from time to time special courts to deal with particular types of cases. Appeals from the decisions of these courts may ultimately be reviewed in the Supreme Court. The official district and appellate court reports have been discontinued, but the GPO still publishes reports from some of the special courts. What follows are reports available to depository libraries. Keep in mind that these are not annotated, and are selectively reported by West (except for the Tax Court).

Court of Claims

Cases Decided in the Court of Claims of the United States (Ju 3.9; Item 730) have, in addition to the decisions of the court, abstracts of the decisions of the Supreme Court in Court of Claims cases.

Court of Customs and Patent Appeals

Beginning with volume 17, reports have been issued in two separate volumes, one called *Customs Cases Adjudged*, and the other titled *Patent Cases Adjudged* (Ju 7.5; Item 733).

Customs Court

United States Customs Court Reports (Ju 9.5; Item 736) are issued on a semi-annual basis and are available for sale through SuDocs.[8]

Tax Court

The United States Tax Court is a court of record under Article I of the Constitution. *Reports of the Tax Court* (Ju 11.7; Item 742) are issued semi-annually in bound volumes and are sold by SuDocs. But tax law is best researched through looseleaf services provided by commercial firms such as CCH and Prentice-Hall. The former issues a number of tax reporters. *Tax Court Reports* present full-text decisions along with all the editorial and index-digest aids the looseleaf services typically provide. *Tax Court Memorandum Decisions* and the weekly *Standard Federal Tax Reports* are two other examples of CCH's in-depth coverage of this topic. Prentice-Hall's *Federal Tax Library* is a useful multi-volume looseleaf service.

Court of Military Appeals

The United States Court of Military Appeals is the final tribunal to review court-martial convictions of all the services. It is exclusively an appellate criminal court. In addition, the Court is required by law to work jointly with the Judge Advocates General of the armed services and the General Counsel of the Transportation Department and to report annually to the Congress on the progress of the military justice system under the Uniform Code of Military Justice and to recommend improvements wherever necessary. Publications of the Court are under the provenance of the Department of Defense: *Report of the Court of Military Appeals* (D 1.19; Item 311-A) and *Digests and Digested Opinions of the Court of Military Appeals, Annotated* (D 1.19/3; Item 311-B).

THE SUPREME COURT

Background

Article III, Section 2 of the Constitution, sets forth the areas of original and appellate jurisdiction of the Supreme Court. While the Congress has no authority to change or amend the original jurisdiction of this Court, appellate jurisdiction has been conferred by various statutes under the authority given Congress by the Constitution. Furthermore, Congress has from time to time conferred upon the Supreme Court power to prescribe rules of procedure to be followed by the lower courts of the United States. Pursuant to these statutes are rules governing civil and criminal cases in the district courts, bankruptcy proceedings, admiralty and copyright cases, appellate proceedings, and minor criminal offense proceedings before United States magistrates.

After the appointment of John Jay as the first Chief Justice, the Supreme Court opened its first session in New York on February 2, 1790. The judges wore gowns of black and scarlet, but honored Jefferson's appeal to "discard the monstrous wig which makes the English judges look like rats peeping through bunches of oakum."[9] Today the Supreme Court comprises the Chief Justice and "such number of Associate Justices as may be fixed by Congress." Under that authority and by virtue of the act of June 25, 1948 (62 Stat. 869), the number of associate justices is eight. Nominated by the President and appointed by and with the advice and consent of the Senate, justices serve life terms.

Curiously, there are no specific qualifications for the office of Supreme Court justice. However, the Senate's role in the process of advisement and consent is designed to insure that only the highly qualified attain the position. Indeed, from 1789 to 1973, twenty-seven Supreme Court nominations failed to receive Senate confirmation. Although most justices have retired in advanced age and several have died in office, some have resigned to accept other positions or have quit for other reasons. Abe Fortas was the first justice to resign, in 1969, under charges of extra-judicial misconduct. Samuel Chase was the only Supreme Court justice to be impeached. In 1804 the House of Representatives charged him with "harsh and partisan conduct on the bench and with unfairness to litigants"; however, he was acquitted by the Senate.[10]

Popular civics hold that the Supreme Court is an ultimate court of appeals for all, a bulwark of freedom to which every citizen can press his claim under federal law or the Constitution. That concept has long since ceased to be a physical possibility. In addition to the jurisdictional limitations prescribed by the Constitution, the high court over the years has been further restricted in its range of judicial authority by the Congress. Yet the number of cases has grown. In 1945 the docket showed 1,448 cases; in 1971 the Court heard 4,533 cases, an increase which some justices found alarming. A committee appointed by the Chief Justice in 1972 to review the workload recommended the creation of a National Court of Appeals, whose chief function would involve the preliminary winnowing of cases for Supreme Court review. The suggestion aroused considerable opposition from judges, lawyers, and a few justices themselves, on the grounds that the rights of litigants to appeal to the Court would be severely abridged.[11]

With its power of judicial review—the authority of the Court to strike down acts it deems unconstitutional—the decisions of this tribunal are both legally and politically of momentous consequence. Lawyers are accustomed to say that the truth is in the Supreme Court record; that is, it is not unusual for the passage of time to show that some dissenting justice saw the case more clearly than did the majority. Justice Jackson's epigram voices precisely the Court's power and influence in the structure of the federal establishment: "We are not final because we are infallible, but we are infallible because we are final."[1][2]

Sources of Information

The following editions contain the full-text decisions of the Supreme Court, with appropriate finding aids and other access tools.

United States Reports (Official Edition)

The unannotated edition of Supreme Court reports is issued in three stages; in order of recency they are as follows:

1) *Slip opinions* (Ju 6.8/b; Item 740-A) are printed individually when rendered by the high court. They are not headnoted or indexed. Typically the only information given is the docket number, names of parties to the dispute, date of opinion, and name of justice who wrote the opinion.

2) *Preliminary prints* (Ju 6.8/a; Item 740-B) are also known as advance parts. Issued in paperbound form, the text is enhanced by a summary of the case and headnotes supplied by the official Reporter of Decisions. The pagination of the preliminary prints is the same as that which will appear in the bound volumes, thus making early citations possible.

3) *United States Reports* (Ju 6.8; Item 741), cited as *U.S.*, has as its full title *United States Reports, Cases Adjudged in [the] Supreme Court at [the] October Term [date]*. The bound volumes contain tables of cases reported and cited, a table of statutes cited, and a subject or topical index. Like the material included in the preliminary prints, the *United States Reports* contain decisions *per curiam* and miscellaneous orders.

United States Supreme Court Reports, Lawyers' Edition

In this "unofficial" annotated edition published by Lawyers Co-operative Publishing Company, case summaries precede the headnotes. Headnotes are classified to the *U.S. Supreme Court Digest, Lawyers' Edition.* There are *Total Client-Service Library* references to Am.Jur.2d, U.S.C.S., etc., and *annotation* references. The official syllabus by the Reporter of Decisions is included, followed by the opinion of the court.

In the *Lawyers' Edition, 2d Series,* a *Later Case Service* is used to keep the annotations that appear in this set current. Advance parts appear every two weeks. As of 1977, the advance parts include a "Current Awareness Commentary" at the beginning of the issue. It consists of a discussion on a selective basis of recent cases accepted for review but which will not be argued until the court's next term; and a section discussing major issues decided by the court in opinions handed down too late to be included in the advance part at hand, but which will appear in the following one. Advance parts have cumulative tables of cases and statutes, and a cumulative index. Figure 34 shows the first page of a Supreme Court report as it appears in an advance part of the *Lawyers' Edition*.[13]

Figure 34

ADVANCE PART: UNITED STATES SUPREME COURT REPORTS, LAWYERS' EDITION

UNITED STATES, Petitioner,

v

GABRIEL FRANCIS ANTELOPE et al.

— US —, 51 L Ed 2d 701, 97 S Ct —

[No. 75–661]

Argued January 18, 1977. Decided April 19, 1977.

SUMMARY

Certain Indians, who were enrolled members of the Coeur d'Alene Tribe, were convicted in the United States District Court for the District of Idaho of first-degree murder under the felony murder provisions of the federal enclave murder statute (18 USCS § 1111), as made applicable to Indians by the Major Crimes Act (18 USCS § 1153), which provides that any Indian who commits any of certain specified offenses within Indian country (including murder) shall be subject to the same laws and penalties as other persons committing any such offenses within the exclusive jurisdiction of the United States. On appeal, the defendants argued that their convictions were unlawful as products of invidious racial discrimination, because if a non-Indian had committed the crime—the killing of a non-Indian during a burglary and robbery within the boundaries of the Indian reservation—the case would have been prosecuted under the law of the state where the reservation was located (Idaho), and under such law, proof of premeditation and deliberation would have been required, whereas no such elements were required under the applicable federal law. The United States Court of Appeals for the Ninth Circuit reversed the convictions, holding that the disparity between state and federal law violated equal protection requirements implicit in the due process clause of the Fifth Amendment (523 F2d 400).

On certiorari, the United States Supreme Court reversed and remanded. In an opinion by Burger, Ch. J., expressing the unanimous view of the court, it was held that equal protection requirements were not violated, notwithstanding the disparity between state and federal law, since (1) the federal statutes were not based upon impermissible racial classifications, the defendants not being subjected to federal criminal jurisdiction because they were of the Indian race but because they were enrolled members of the

701

Supreme Court Reporter (West)

This is a special unit of West's *National Reporter System*, and as such shares all the typical features of the key number classification scheme. The full text of the decisions is accompanied by edited headnotes referencing topic and key number. Summaries of arguments of counsel are not included. The advance parts contain a number of cumulative tables: cases reported, statutes construed, Supreme Court rules, etc. There is also a cumulative "Words and Phrases" and a cumulative Key Number Digest. Figure 35 shows the first page of a Supreme Court report as it appears in an advance part of the West edition.

Figure 35

ADVANCE PART: SUPREME COURT REPORTER

UNITED STATES v. ANTELOPE   **1395**
Cite as 97 S.Ct. 1395 (1977)

UNITED STATES, Petitioner,

v.

Gabriel Francis ANTELOPE et al.

No. 75–661.

Argued Jan. 18, 1977.

Decided April 19, 1977.

Two enrolled Coeur d'Alene Indians were convicted in the United States District Court for the District of Idaho for first-degree murder under the felony-murder provisions of the federal enclave murder statute, made applicable to the Indians by the Major Crimes Act, and were also convicted of burglary and robbery, while third Indian was convicted of second-degree murder, and they appealed. The United States Court of Appeals for the Ninth Circuit, 523 F.2d 400, reversed the murder convictions, and certiorari was granted. The Supreme Court, Mr. Chief Justice Burger, held that federal legislation with respect to Indian tribes, though relating to Indians as such, is not based on impermissible racial classifications; and that prosecution of defendants under federal felony-murder statute for murder of a non-Indian within Indian country, subject to the same body of laws as any other individual charged with first-degree murder committed in a federal enclave, did not deny them due process or equal protection despite fact that a non-Indian charged with the same crime would have been tried under Idaho law which lacks a felony-murder provision, so that the prosecution would have been required to prove premeditation and deliberation.

Judgment of Court of Appeals reversed and cause remanded.

1. Indians ⊜32, 38(2)

Except for the offenses enumerated in the Major Crimes Act, all crimes committed by enrolled Indians against other Indians within Indian country are subject to the jurisdiction of tribal courts, but a non-Indi-

an charged with committing crimes against other non-Indians in Indian country is subject to prosecution under state law. 18 U.S.C.A. §§ 1152, 1153.

2. Indians ⊜2

Federal legislation with respect to Indian tribes, though relating to Indians as such, is not based on impermissible racial classification but is instead rooted in the unique status of Indians as "a separate people" with their own political institutions, and amounts to governance of once-sovereign communities, rather than legislation of a "racial" group consisting of Indians. U.S. C.A.Const. art. 1, § 8.

3. Indians ⊜38(2)

Members of Indian tribes whose official status has been terminated by congressional enactment are no longer subject, by virtue of their status, to federal criminal jurisdiction under the Major Crimes Act, and crimes by enrolled tribal members occurring elsewhere than within the confines of Indian country are not subject to exclusive federal jurisdiction. 18 U.S.C.A. § 1153.

4. Constitutional Law ⊜250.2(1), 257

Enrolled members of the Coeur d'Alene Indian Tribe who were prosecuted under the Major Crimes Act for felony-murder of a non-Indian within the boundaries of Indian reservation and who were subject to the same body of laws as any other individual charged with first-degree murder committed within a federal enclave were not denied due process or equal protection on ground that, if they had not been Indians, they would have been prosecuted under Idaho law which, unlike federal law, lacked felony-murder provision so that the prosecution would have been required to prove premeditation and deliberation. U.S.C.A. Const. Amend. 5; 18 U.S.C.A. §§ 1111, 1153, 3242; I.C. § 18-4003.

5. Indians ⊜36

Congress has undoubted constitutional power to prescribe a criminal code applicable in Indian country.

United States Supreme Court Bulletin (CCH)

A useful Commerce Clearing House looseleaf service, the *Bulletin* consists of facsimile reprints of the opinions, a statement of official court actions for the preceding week, court rules, a table of cases on the docket, highlights of recently docketed cases, and the usual detailed indexing.

United States Law Week (BNA)

Another useful looseleaf service published by the Bureau of National Affairs and issued weekly, *United States Law Week* (U.S.L.Week) consists of two sections, a Supreme Court section and a General Law section. Subject, case, and docket number indexes cumulate during the term. Other useful features enhance the text of the opinions.

For current awareness, the CCH and BNA services are most useful; older decisions may most profitably be accessed through the West and Lawyers Co-operative volumes.

Decisions of the United States Supreme Court

If the researcher does not need comprehensive coverage of the full text of Supreme Court opinions, a useful source is published annually by Lawyers Co-operative Publishing Company. Titled *Decisions of the United States Supreme Court, [year] Term*, it is designed to serve as a quick reference guide to the work of the court.

Features include a list of the personnel of the Court accompanied by biographical sketches of each Justice; a "Survey of the Term"—a succinct narrative statement highlighting the term; "Summaries of Decisions"—a *selective* summary of important decisions, reprinted from the summaries in the *Lawyers' Edition*; a glossary of common legal terms in layman's language; a table of cases; and a detailed, alphabetical word index.

Method of Citing

Because of the publishing of official and so-called "unofficial" reports, the proper procedure is to cite the official publication. If the unofficial versions are also cited, the official citation must be cited first. Thus in a typical Supreme Court opinion, one finds a reference to a case as follows:

Allied Stores of Ohio, Inc. v Bowers, 358 US 523, 3 L ed 2d 480, 79 S Ct 437 (1959).

The pattern is that of volume, reporter, page, and finally year. US refers to *United States Reports* (official), L Ed 2d is *Lawyers' Edition, 2d Series*, and S Ct is West's *Supreme Court Reporter*.

The first ninety volumes of the *U.S. Reports* are cited by the names of their reporters. Thus, a citation to an early report would be phrased as follows:

Ward v Maryland, 79 US (12 Wall) 418, 20 L Ed 449 (1871)

Because the first ninety volumes, from Dallas through Wallace, were later numbered consecutively, we can use a conversion table to determine that Wallace's reports (*Wall*), in 23 volumes, were numbered volumes 68-90 (1863-1874), and the *Lawyers' Edition* (first series) may be used.[14]

Ancillary Sources of Information

Advice and Consent on Supreme Court Nominations (1976) is a committee print issued by the Subcommittee on Separation of Powers of the Senate Judiciary Committee. It is essentially a record of the proceedings of a symposium on the subject of the Senate's role in the advice and consent procedure, with distinguished lawyers and scholars presenting their opinions on the matter.

The Supreme Court of the United States: Hearings and Reports on Successful and Unsuccessful Nominations of Supreme Court Justices by the Senate Judiciary Committee, 1916-1972 (Buffalo, N.Y.: Hein, 1975) is a twelve-volume set compiled by Mersky and Jacobstein which brings together all existing Senate documents relevant to hearings on the nominations of Supreme Court Justices. The set includes hearings which have never been made public before; these hearings were located in the National Archives and reproduced for publication with the permission of the Senate Judiciary Committee.

ADMINISTRATION OF THE FEDERAL JUDICIARY

Two agencies of the judicial branch help administer the business of the federal courts and seek to improve judicial administration.

Administrative Office of the United States Courts

The director of this unit is the chief administrative officer of the United States courts (except the Supreme Court). The director and deputy director are appointed by the Supreme Court. Their duties are set forth in succinct form in the current issue of the *United States Government Manual.*

Publications issued to depository libraries from this provenance begin with the *Annual Report of the Director of the Administrative Office of the United States Courts* (Ju 10.1; Item 728), wherein the business of all federal courts except the Court of Military Appeals and the Tax Court is discussed in detail; the text is complemented by statistical data on various aspects of the courts and their workloads.

Other publications include the *Report of the Proceedings of the Regular Annual Meeting of the Judicial Conference of the United States* (Ju 10.10; Item 729); *Juror Utilization in United States District Courts* (Ju 10.13; Item 717-Y), an annual; and a fiscal year *Management Statistics for United States Courts* (Ju 10.14; Item 717-X). Interesting periodicals include *The Third Branch* (Ju 10.3/2; Item 728-B), a monthly with the subtitle "A Bulletin of the Federal Courts"; and the excellent *Federal Probation* (Ju 10.8; Item 717-T).

Federal Judicial Center

The Center was created by an act of Congress approved December 20, 1967 (81 Stat. 664; 28 U.S.C. 620). Its purpose is to further the development and adoption of improved judicial administration in the federal courts. Its activities are supervised by a Board composed of the Chief Justice of the United States and judges from the lower federal courts. The director of the Administrative Office of the United States Courts is a permanent member of the Board.

Publications include an *Annual Report* (Ju 13.1; Item 742-A-1) and a General Publications series (Ju 13.2; Item 743-C-1).

LEGAL INFORMATION RETRIEVAL SYSTEMS

A growing number of articles on legal computer systems in law journals attest to the importance of the computer in this field.[15] An early proponent of the impact of the computer on the legal field noted that, because of its capabilities,

> the lawyer will be freed to do his distinctively legal tasks. Thus freed from the insuperable burden of plodding from library to library, refreshing his recollection upon index systems of various books, pulling them out and ploughing through them, and then making laborious notes in longhand, the lawyer can devote his time and mind to the social, political, and economic aspects of law and justice. No longer will the true value of his wisdom be lost to society. No longer will courts hand down unintentionally conflicting decisions. No longer need lawyers give erroneous advice to clients and cause loss to them. No longer will legislators unwittingly confuse the law.[16]

The over three decades since that was written have not seen the ushering in of the Millennium, but there are a number of legal retrieval systems which show great promise. A sampling of the significant systems follows.

WESTLAW

The data base of WESTLAW (West Publishing Company) in 1975 consisted of headnotes classified to West's own key number/topic arrangement. In 1978 West began to include the full text of the opinion. The scope of WESTLAW comprises the reported opinions in West's *National Reporter System*: all federal courts from 1961 to the present, all state appellate courts from 1967 to date.

For federal case law, the files include those contained in West's *Supreme Court Reporter, Federal Reporter, Federal Supplement*, and *Federal Rules Decisions.* Only one file can be searched at a time. Search strategies are varied and flexible. The files may be accessed by descriptive words, topic/key number, name or citation of case, court rule, or natural language. Information retrieved and displayed is ranked by the computer on the basis of the frequency of occurrence of different search terms in each document. When a citation that the searcher finds relevant is displayed, he or she may 1) use the appropriate volume of the *National Reporter System* in hardcopy to read the case; 2) summon the full text on the terminal; or 3) request a print-out of the case.

WESTLAW does not include statutes, constitutions, or administrative regulations. West's editorial opinion on this deliberate omission is that "since retrieval of case material is the primary need of most lawyers, the base of only case material . . . is justified."[17]

Hardware for the components of the WESTLAW system includes a central computer located at West headquarters in St. Paul, Minnesota, a video display terminal for office or library linked to the central computer, and a printer which allows one to obtain copies of any document displayed on the screen.

LEXIS

LEXIS is a full-text data bank available commercially by Mead Data Central, Inc. (New York). It is composed of "libraries"; each "library" is divided into files which are searched separately after the jurisdictional interest is determined.

Libraries are being added to the LEXIS data base regularly, and include a General Federal Library, Federal Tax Library, Federal Securities Library, Federal Trade Regulation Library, and several state libraries. The General Federal Library includes *U.S. Reports*, federal appellate court and district court cases, and the *United States Code*. The Federal Tax Library includes *U.S. Reports*, the *Internal Revenue Code* (Title 26 of the *U.S. Code*), and various files of Tax Court memoranda and decisions. Thus LEXIS does include more than case law. Retrieval strategies employ KWIC (key-word-in-context), and the general features of command language using Boolean connectors.[18]

The documents in the LEXIS files are not pre-indexed. The searcher interacts on a one-to-one basis with the terminal. As Dee and Kessler make clear, "It is essential to realize in searching through LEXIS that one's success will be in proportion to his ability to predict the terminology used in the kind of document he hopes to summon. As we all know, statutory language is expressed differently from that in court decisions; and historic court decisions use terminology no longer employed today. A searcher must be flexible in his choice of words and phrases, and the more versatility he possesses the more profitable his research is likely to be."[19]

FLITE

Federal Legal Information through Electronics (FLITE) was developed by the Judge Advocate General, U.S. Air Force. A full-text system, its availability is not limited to the federal government; FLITE is available to state and local governments.

Some of the data bases in this system include *Decisions of the Comptroller General of the United States, Board of Contract Appeals, U.S. Reports*, and *Court of Claims Reports*. FLITE is constantly adding data bases to its system. Among these bases are *Federal Reporter, 2d Series, Federal Supplement*, U.S.C.A., U.S.C.C.A.N., *Statutes at Large*, and the CFR.[20]

JURIS

JURIS is a system in the Department of Justice. Development of the system began in early 1970, but until 1974 the only file in the data base that was productive was the *U.S. Code*. In mid-1974 JURIS contracted with Mead Data for access to the LEXIS system. However, in August 1975 the LEXIS contract expired, and its base lost to JURIS. To make up for this loss of federal case law, JURIS borrowed the case law data base from FLITE. In addition, JURIS has continually under review the possibility of picking up other data bases or information services.

A full-text system, JURIS holds two basic types of data files: 1) federal statutory and case law; and 2) the "work product" of the Justice Department: briefs, memoranda, policy directives, procedural manuals, and other materials generated by the attorneys in Justice in their day-to-day work routines.

"Libraries" in the JURIS data bank include files such as *U.S. Court of Claims Decisions, U.S. Code*, current Executive Orders, and selected titles from the CFR. JURIS is not available commercially.[21]

Other Systems

Acronyms abound in computerized information systems for the law. ASPEN (Aspen Systems Corporation) has a legal data base consisting of the full text of the *U.S. Code* and all state statutes. AUTO-CITE, developed by Lawyers Co-operative Publishing Company, is a computer-assisted case verification system. BIBNET, developed by Information Dynamics Corporation, has a specialized legal data service within its larger program; it combines the law catalogs of the Library of Congress and the Harvard Law School library for on-line searching. And there are many small computerized services that go by names like DATUM, LIS, GYPSY, for regional users.[22]

LEGAL MATERIALS IN MICROFORM

The revolution in micropublishing has encompassed sources of the law as well as government publications generally. Fortunately, a master guide to the literature of the law in microform has been published, a notable achievement. What follows is a sampling of legal information in various microformats, designed to give some flavor of the scope of the enterprise.

Basic Guide

One bibliographic source dominates this field. Henry P. Tseng, *Complete Guide to Legal Materials in Microform* (Arlington, Virginia: University Publications of America, 1976) lists all law and law-related microforms known to Mr. Tseng "whether domestic or international, English or foreign languages (such as Chinese, French, Indonesian, Japanese, Russian, and Spanish), and believed to be in print or in the process of completion as of November 2, 1975."[23] As of this writing, Tseng has issued a *1976 Supplement* to his *Complete Guide*, covering November 1975-November 1976 and published by University Publications of America in 1977.

The scope and arrangement of the parent volume and the *1976 Supplement* are virtually identical. Entries are alphabetically interfiled by personal or government author and title. Journals, periodicals, and series are entered by title. Archival materials, government documents, and manuscripts are entered as listed by publishing organization, with added cross references under title or editor. The basic volume of this comprehensive work has over 15,000 entries.

All bibliographic and ordering information is based upon that given in the micropublishers' catalogs or other brochures. Appendixes include a selected glossary of microform terms, a directory of publishers in alphabetical order (with address, phone number, and acronym or abbreviation), and a directory of publishers by alphabetical designations.

The *1976 Supplement* should be used with the basic volume. So volatile is the micropublishing world that some publishers that appeared in the parent volume have discontinued micropublishing, while others have merged, been acquired, ceased to exist, or changed names since 1975. These changes are reflected in Appendix II of the *1976 Supplement.*

Selected Series in Microform

The following represent some of the important issuances in the area of case law.

National Reporter System

West's ultrafiche editions of the *National Reporter System* now include the entire regional reporters first series, as follows:

Reporter	Volumes
Atlantic Reporter, 1st Series	1-200
North Eastern Reporter, 1st Series	1-200
South Eastern Reporter, 1st Series	1-200
Southern Reporter, 1st Series	1-200
North Western Reporter, 1st Series	1-300
Pacific Reporter, 1st Series	1-300
South Western Reporter, 1st Series	1-300
New York Supplement, 1st Series	1-300

Moreover, West has made its *Federal Reporter, 1st Series* (Volumes 1-300) and its *Federal Reporter, 2d Series* (Volumes 1-150) available on ultrafiche. Readers and reader-printer-copiers are available for sale from the company.

CCH Ultrafiche Tax Library

Available from Commerce Clearing House are ultrafiche editions of retrospective and current CCH reporters, as follows.

Retrospective

Series	Years Covered
U.S. Tax Cases	1913-1976
Tax Court Memorandum Decisions	1943-1975
Board of Tax Appeals Reports	1924-1942
Tax Court Reports	1943-1975
Cumulative Bulletins	1919-1975-2

These issues on ultrafiche were reproduced from prior bound volumes published by CCH. *Reports of the Board of Tax Appeals* is a completed set. After 1942, the series became known as *Tax Court Reports*.[24] *Cumulative Bulletins* are reproduced from the official bi-weekly *Internal Revenue Bulletin* (T 22.23; Item 957), which in its semi-annual cumulations, is called *Cumulative Bulletin* (T 22.25; Item 960).

Current

With the exception of the completed *Board of Tax Appeals Reports*, the four series above are currently offered in ultrafiche volumes. CCH also makes available for sale a Vantage I (HMV) Reader compatible with ultrafiche.

United States Reports

The Supreme Court reports, official edition, are available from the following micropublishers: University Microfilms (Ann Arbor), a Xerox Company affiliate, v. 1-414 (1754-1973); William S. Hein & Co., Inc. (Buffalo, N.Y.), v. 1-410, with reader; Lawyers Microfilm, Inc. (Rogers, Ark.), v. 411 1970) to date; and Information Handling Services (Englewood, Colo.), v. 127 to date (1887-).

U.S. Supreme Court Records and Briefs

Two commercial micropublishing companies have editions of the Supreme Court records and briefs.

1) Information Handling Services offers retrospective series of argued cases in the following formats: a) on 35mm microfilm from 1832-1896, full opinion, *per curiam* and *certiorari denied* cases are available; b) on microfiche *per curiam* cases

from 1950-1975; c) on microfiche full opinion cases from 1897-1975; and d) on microfilm *certiorari denied* cases from 1950-1975.

2) Law Reprints, Inc. (New York, N.Y.) offers a *current* edition of all argued cases (1976-1977 term). In addition, Law Reprints offers on microfiche "non-argued cases" filmed from the printed records and briefs of cases disposed of but not argued. A comparative review by Margaret A. Leary of the current services of the "argued cases" series of IHS and Law Reprints provides a useful guide to the strengths and weaknesses of both products.[25]

CONCLUSION

When viewed bibliographically, it is said "that the law is a seamless web. . . . [T]he various sources of law are inter-related and rarely meaningful or usable in isolation. To understand a statute, one needs the decisions which have interpreted it; to understand a court's decision, one needs the statute which it has applied; to understand an administrative regulation, one must see the statute by which it was authorized; even to read a legal periodical article or a treatise, one needs access to all of the primary sources it cites and discusses."[26] Statutory and administrative law have been treated in earlier chapters of this text. The foregoing discussion of the sources of case law should enable the reader to relate its bibliographic structure to that of legislative activities and promulgated regulations.

REFERENCES

1. A concise account of the basic functions, organization, jurisdiction, and procedure of the courts is found in a House Judiciary committee print, *United States Courts: Their Jurisdiction and Work* (Y 4.J89/1:C83/6/year). Revised periodically, this useful brochure gives an illustration of the distinction among cases that may be tried in state or federal courts.

2. *The Supreme Court: Justice and the Law* (Washington: Congressional Quarterly, Inc., 1973), pp. 6-7, 65-68.

3. M. L. Cohen, *Legal Research in a Nutshell*, pp. 40-41.

4. Price and Bitner, *Effective Legal Research* (1969), p. 188.

5. The A.L.R. series are the most prominent feature of Lawyers Co-operative Publishing Company's *Total Client-Service Library*, which also includes *United States Supreme Court Reports, Lawyers' Edition, United States Code Service, American Jurisprudence 2d, American Jurisprudence Legal Forms, American Jurisprudence Pleading and Practice Forms, American Jurisprudence Proof of Facts,* and *American Jurisprudence Trials.*

6. A useful discussion of *stare decisis*, the *ratio decidendi* of a case, and other characteristics of the law, is found in Cohen, *How to Find the Law*, pp. 2-11.

7. Price and Bitner, p. 128. *Per curiam* refers to an unsigned opinion of the court, or an opinion written by the whole court.

8. A weekly *Customs Bulletin* (T 1.11/3; Item 950-D), issued by the Treasury Department, contains regulations, rulings, decisions, and notices concerning customs and related matters; and decisions of the Court of Customs and Patent Appeals and of the Customs Court.

9. Samuel Eliot Morison, *The Oxford History of the American People* (New York: Oxford University Press, 1965), pp. 321-22.

10. Congressional Quarterly, Inc., *Guide to the Congress of the United States* (Washington, 1971), p. 270.

11. In 1973 a joint congressional commission, appointed ad hoc to study the structure of the lower courts system, recommended the creation of two new circuits for the Courts of Appeals in order to lessen the workload.

12. *Brown v. Allen*, 344 U.S. 433 (1953).

13. Advance parts in the *Lawyers' Edition* do *not* have annotations. The subject index to the annotations in the bound volumes is a separate publication titled *Supreme Court Reports Index to Annotations*; it also provides subject access to *A.L.R.Fed.*

14. The authoritative guide for legal citations is *A Uniform System of Citation* 12th edition (1976), published by the Harvard Law Review Association.

15. Sources of law-computer literature are summarized in Peter Nycum, "Law and Computers: Overview Update 1975," *Law Library Journal* 68: 251-53 *et passim* (August 1975).

16. "Does the Law Need a Technological Revolution?" *Rocky Mountain Law Review* 18: 391 (1946).

17. Mathew F. Dee and R. M. Kessler, "The Impact of Computerized Methods on Legal Research Courses: A Survey of LEXIS Experience and Some Probable Effects of WESTLAW," *Law Library Journal* 69: 180 (May 1976).

18. Summoning code sections and cases on LEXIS is without benefit of annotations, which are copyrighted materials of the commercial publishers like West.

19. Dee and Kessler, p. 165.

20. Nycum, pp. 245-46.

21. James E. Hambleton, "JURIS: Legal Information in the Department of Justice," *Law Library Journal* 69: 199-202 (May 1976).

22. A useful summary of other systems is provided by Oscar M. Trelles, "Automation in Law Libraries: The State of the Art," *Law Library Journal* 68: 209-233 (August 1975).

23. Tseng, *Complete Guide* (1976), p. xvii.

24. It should be noted that *U.S. Board of Tax Appeals Reports, 1924-1942* are also available in microfilm from Brookhaven Press (Washington) and Princeton Microfilm Corporation (Princeton, N.J.).

25. Reviewed in *Microform Review* 4: 224 (July 1975).

26. Cohen, *How to Find the Law*, p. xvi.

10

DOCUMENTS OF INDEPENDENT AND REGULATORY AGENCIES

The rise of administrative bodies probably has been the most significant legal trend of the last century and perhaps more values today are affected by their decisions than by those of all the courts, review of administrative decisions apart. They also have begun to have important consequences on personal rights. . . . They have become a veritable fourth branch of the Government, which has deranged our three-branch legal theories much as the concept of a fourth dimension unsettles our three-dimensional thinking.

Courts have differed in assigning a place to these seemingly necessary bodies in our constitutional system. Administrative agencies have been called quasi-legislative, quasi-executive or quasi-judicial, as the occasion required, in order to validate their functions within the separation-of-powers scheme of the Constitution. The mere retreat to the qualifying "quasi" is implicit with confession that all recognized classifications have broken down, and "quasi" is a smooth cover which we draw over our confusion as we might use a counterpane to conceal a disordered bed.

—Supreme Court Justice Robert H. Jackson,
FTC v. Ruberoid, 343 U.S. 470 (1952)

Quis custodiet ipsos custodes?

—Juvenal

INTRODUCTION

The legislative, executive, and judicial powers are set forth in Articles I, II, and III of the Constitution. Advisory committees and commissions serve at various times the three duly constituted branches. But Justice Jackson, in the above quote, recognized the peculiar place of the independent and regulatory agencies outside the constitutional system. With their power to issue rules and adjudicate matters within their jurisdiction, they have indeed become "a veritable fourth branch of government."

Students of government find it convenient to divide the independent establishments into two categories: the regulatory bodies, and the other agencies that exist structurally outside the formal executive departments. The *United States Government Manual* makes no such distinction. In its 1977/78 edition, the *Manual* in its "Contents" pages following a list of the Departments, has a section called "Agencies." There ensues an alphabetical listing of 58 "independent agencies," some of which have more regulatory authority than others.

Political scientists Burns and Peltason attempted, in the absence of any satisfactory definition, to state what constitutes an independent agency:

Broadly speaking, all agencies that are not corporations and that do not fall under an executive department (such as Treasury or Interior) are called independent agencies. Many of these agencies, however, are no more independent of the President and Congress than are the executive departments themselves.[1]

But the 1977/78 *Manual* includes in its list of independent agencies the Federal Deposit Insurance Corporation (FDIC), Overseas Private Investment Corporation (OPIC), and the Pension Benefit Guaranty Corporation (PBGC). The imprecise terminology employed by the federal government may be the problem here; among the so-called independent agencies there are titles of entities in which the words conference, commission, board, administration, government, service, foundation, authority, company, and agency appear.

It is useful to identify those independent establishments that perform significant *regulatory* functions. While most independent agencies have regulatory activities, it is also true that many of the agencies within the executive branch departments have important regulatory activities. The autonomy of the so-called independent agencies is circumscribed by a President's appointive power, by Congress's power of the purse, and by the courts' power of judicial review. On the other hand, independent agencies plan and execute decisions relatively independent of a President's direction. They make administrative rulings independent of Congress, which defers to their putative expertise. And they are empowered to render certain decisions independent of the courts.

All this provides the scholar with a bumper theoretical crop to harvest. For our purposes, we ought to recognize that any agency which promulgates its regulations in the *Federal Register* and in the *Code of Federal Regulations* has, *ipso facto* and *ipso jure*, regulatory authority. Thus the FR and CFR are the basic documents in any bibliographic accounting of regulatory activities. The basic documents concerning the "independence" of an agency, as opposed to its status within the executive office of the President or within the structure of a department, are the statutes which created the entities.

It has been popular among scholars writing about regulatory bodies to isolate from among the over fifty independent establishments listed in the *Manual* seven agencies.[2] These became known as the "Big Seven," owing to their vast powers and their degree of independence:

Name	Year Established
Interstate Commerce Commission (ICC)	1887
Federal Trade Commission (FTC)	1915
Federal Power Commissions (FPC)	1920
Federal Communications Commission (FCC)	1934
Securities and Exchange Commission (SEC)	1934
National Labor Relations Board (NLRB)	1935
Civil Aeronautics Board (CAB)	1938

The Federal Power Commission was abolished in the legislation that created the Department of Energy (91 Stat. 565), but the six remaining bodies still possess enormous regulatory authority. In recent decades, however, other regulatory entities have been created, and these have been given large powers to affect by their rules and regulations "the food that people eat, the cars they drive, the fuel they use, the clothes they wear, the houses they live in, the investments they make, the water they drink and even the air they breathe."[3] Thus an updated list would certainly include, as exemplary, the following independent, regulatory bodies:

Name	Year Established
Equal Employment Opportunity Commission (EEOC)	1964
Occupational Safety and Health Review Commission (OSHRC)	1970
Postal Rate Commission (PRC)	1970
Environmental Protection Agency (EPA)	1970
Consumer Product Safety Commission	1972
Federal Election Commission	1974
Nuclear Regulatory Commission (NRC)	1975

There is another way to look at the influence of regulatory agencies, and that is to ignore the distinction between independent entities and departmental units. Thus, *U.S. News & World Report* divides the "fourth branch of government" into two categories: "the agencies that operate within a Cabinet Department and those that are completely [sic] independent." Accordingly, the editors of that magazine include, as "major federal regulators," the Food and Drug Administration

(FDA) within the Department of Health, Education and Welfare (HEW); and the Federal Aviation Administration (FAA) within the Department of Transportation (DOT).[4]

Moreover, entities like the Federal Reserve Board (Fed) and, obviously, the Internal Revenue Service (IRS) of the Treasury Department, are extraordinarily powerful units of government which exercise vast amounts of influence over our individual and corporate existence. Discriminating among these entities becomes a matter of academic puntilio, which can lead to sterile discourse. For our purposes, it is sufficient to characterize the independent and regulatory agencies as those listed as such in the *Manual*, while acknowledging that such a taxonomy may be simplistic.

SELECTED CATEGORIES OF PUBLICATIONS

Independent and regulatory bodies which have been long established contribute a number of series to the depository library system. For example, the first of the "Big Seven" regulatory establishments, the Interstate Commerce Commission (ICC), issues over thirty series available to depository institutions.

Publications of the ICC follow the regular form of classification for materials of the Commission as a whole, such as annual reports (IC 1.1), general publications (IC 1.2), rules of practice (IC 1.6), etc. But there is also a subject grouping, employed by SuDocs because the Commission had no subordinate agency and bureau breakdowns at the time class notations were assigned.[5] Subject designation takes the form of adding the first three or four letters of the subject word to the main agency designation of IC 1, as follows:

Symbol	Publications Relating to:
IC 1 acco.	Accounts
IC 1 act.	Acts to regulate commerce
IC 1 blo.	Block signals
IC 1 def.	Defense Transportation Administration
IC 1 elec.	Electric railways
IC 1 exp.	Express companies
IC 1 hou.	Hours of service
IC 1 loc.	Locomotive inspection
IC 1 mot.	Motor carriers
IC 1 pip.	Pipe line companies
IC 1 rat.	Rates
IC 1 saf.	Safety
IC 1 sle.	Sleeping car companies
IC 1 ste.	Steam roads
IC 1 val.	Valuation of property
IC 1 wat.	Water carriers

It is interesting to note that of all the above categories of ICC series, only five are in the March 1977 *List of Classes* as being available to depository libraries: Accounts, Acts to regulate commerce, Motor carriers, Steam roads, and Water carriers.

Other regulatory bodies such as the FTC, NLRB, CAB, etc., offer typical series discussed in Chapter 8: reports, periodicals, bibliographies and lists, handbooks and manuals. However, being regulatory bodies, compilations of rules and regulations are distinctive features of the publishing activities of these entities. Thus, for instance, the Federal Trade Commission offers to depository institutions series called Rules of Practice (FT 1.7; Item 538) and Regulations, Rules, Instructions (FT 1.8; Item 537). Similarly, series of Decisions and Orders, Laws, Related Court Decisions, etc., are prominent issuances of the publications of these agencies.

It is important to reiterate, as we noted in Chapter 8, that compilations of regulations, decisions, and laws are better researched through the appropriate tools that are current and that have supplementation. Rather than directing a patron to a compilation of the above, however current, research should be pursued through the FR/CFR, an annotated code, a commercial looseleaf service, or a combination of the three.

Table 5 shows a selected list of regulatory bodies and the location in the *Code of Federal Regulations* where current administrative edicts of the agency may be found:

Table 5
SELECTED REGULATORY AGENCIES AND CFR REFERENCES

Agency	CRF Title and Subtitle or Chapter Reference
Civil Aeronautics Board	14, II
Consumer Product Safety Commission	16, II
Environmental Protection Agency	40, I; 41, 15, 115
Federal Communications Commission	47, I
Federal Reserve System	12, II; 32A, XV
Federal Trade Commission	16, I
Interstate Commerce Commission	49, X
National Labor Relations Board	29, I
Nuclear Regulatory Commission	10, I
Occupational Safety and Health Review Commission	29, XX
Postal Rate Commission	39, III

NTIS

As we noted in Chapter 4, regulatory bodies that participate in the NTIS data base include the Environmental Protection Agency, Federal Communications Commission, Federal Trade Commission, and Nuclear Regulatory Commission. Other independent agencies that may or may not have regulatory authority but that also participate in the NTIS system include the United States Civil Service Commission, National Aeronautics and Space Administration, and National Science Foundation.

Example: The Environmental Protection Agency

As of January 1, 1977, the EPA had 11,428 employees.[6] It was established as an independent agency pursuant to Reorganization Plan No. 3 of 1970, effective December 2, 1970. Its purpose is "to protect and enhance our environment today and for future generations to the fullest extent possible under the laws enacted by Congress. The Agency's mission is to control and abate pollution in the areas of air, water, solid waste, pesticides, noise, and radiation. EPA's mandate is to mount an integrated, coordinated attack on environmental pollution in cooperation with State and local governments."[7]

EPA's research and development function is one of coordination and support involving state and local governments, private and public groups, individuals, and educational institutions. Its regulatory functions include enforcement of pollution control. Thus R&D publishing is managed through the NTIS system, while a number of agency publications are available through the depository program.[8] In the latter mechanism it issues an annual report (EP 1.1; Item 431-I-4); laws (EP 1.5; Item 431-I-2); rules and regulations (EP 1.6; Item 431-I-56); handbooks, manuals, and guides (EP 1.8; Item 431-K); a grants administration manual (EP 1.8/2; Item 431-I-10); bibliographies and lists of publications (EP 1.21; Item 431-I-9); and final environmental impact statements (EP 1.57/3; Item 431-I-55). Those whose philosophy of government leans toward less regulative activity frequently cite EPA's power and size in pejorative terms.

Example: OSHRC and OSHA

The Occupational Safety and Health Review Commission (OSHRC) is an independent adjudicatory agency established by the Occupational Safety and Health Act of 1970 (84 Stat. 1590; 29 U.S.C. 651). It adjudicates cases forwarded to it by the Labor Department when disagreements arise "over the results of safety and health inspections performed by the Department."[9] But the responsibility for inspection is the function of the Occupational Safety and Health Administration (OSHA), a subordinate agency within the Department of Labor. OSHA is not an independent establishment, but it develops and promulgates occupational safety and health standards. Moreover, it issues regulations and proposes penalties for noncompliance with health and safety standards. The working relationship between OSHA and OSHRC is a good example of the distinction between regulatory entities that are (relatively) "independent" and those within an executive Department that have powerful regulatory functions.[10]

While OSHRC participates minimally in the depository library system, OSHA issues a number of series available to depositories, and is one of the components of the Labor Department that registers reports with NTIS. OSHRC is classed in Y3.Oc 1, while OSHA is classed in L 35. The March 1977 *List of Classes* showed nineteen series from OSHA available to depository libraries.

Thus while OSHRC is the "independent" agency, OSHA's regulatory activities are far more significant to the business community. Indeed, OSHA has the dubious distinction of being the federal government's most criticized regulatory body. Complaints of enforcement of meaningless or trivial safety regulations amounting to harrassment find their way with frequency into the *Congressional Record.* Trivial information found in OSHA publications has come in for criticism too:

> Taxpayers are paying $466,700 to inform farmers that floors covered with manure tend to be slippery, 2nd District Rep. Tom Hagedorn charged today.

> Such advice is contained in one of a series of pamphlets promoting farm safety being published by the Department of Labor through the Occupational Safety and Health Administration (OSHA), Hagedorn said. He said the information contained in the pamphlets is of little educational value to farmers. . . .[11]

OSHA regulations published in the *Federal Register* suffer from that obscurantist bafflegab we noted in Chapter 8:

> The angle (a) between the loaded and unloaded rails and the horizontal is to be calculated from the trigonometric equation: Sine a = difference in defection 9, ladder width.

Concerning OSHA regulations, the Federation of American Scientists said: "Regulations are voluminous and complex, the language convoluted beyond recognition except by a scientist or lawyer. . . . Businessmen who have no legal or scientific training are unable to understand OSHA regulations. Unfortunately, few efforts are being made to translate the information into readable language. . . . Equally unnerving to the businesses is the sheer volume of the regulations—thousands of them apply to one small operation."[12]

Critics in Congress and in the business community contend that OSHA runs "a vast bureaucracy armed with constitutionally questionable powers which imposes an unacceptable burden on the employers and cost consumers and taxpayers untold billions—to achieve a statistically insignificant impact on the safety record of American industry."[13]

Many contend that the fault lies with the badly written and constitutionally dubious enabling legislation; federal district courts have held that sections of 84 Stat. 1590 violate the Fourth Amendment of the Constitution. The bureaucrats who have the unhappy task of administering the Act find themselves caught between business and labor and health groups. The former complain that OSHA is too severe in enforcing meaningless or silly regulations; the latter are upset that the health provisions of the Act are being slighted in OSHA's zeal to enforce the safety provisions. And of OSHA's 1,400 inspectors, whose mandate it is to protect the health and safety of 65 million workers in 5 million workplaces, 1,000 are safety specialists while only 400 are health specialists.[14]

The anatomy of a regulatory body like OSHA, and that of its "independent" sister EPA, epitomizes the ambivalence within and without government over the proper role of regulatory activities.

SUMMARY

We have observed that it is somewhat difficult to categorize and distinguish among independent entities and those within and without the departmental structure of the executive branch. Two final examples will suffice. The Commission on Civil Rights was created by the Civil Rights Act of 1957 (71 Stat. 634) and it exists independent of the President and the Cabinet. It has investigatory authority, can make findings of act, but has no enforcement powers. Although its findings and recommendations, which are submitted both to the President and to the Congress, may be highly persuasive depending upon the political climate, it cannot be called a true regulatory agency. The only series available to depository libraries as of the March 1977 *List of Classes* is its Reports and Publications (CR 1; Item 288-A).

On the other hand, the Consumer Product Safety Commission was established in 1972 (86 Stat. 1207) as an *independent regulatory* agency; it has authority, for example, to ban hazardous consumer products. Like a true regulatory agency, it possesses quasi-executive, quasi-legislative, and quasi-judicial power. And it too has a degree of independence from both the executive and the Congress, thus purporting to insure freedom from political pressures. Publications of the Commission are classed in Y3.C 76/3 and among the series it offers to depository libraries are its annual reports (Y3.C76/3:1; Item 1062-C-5), bibliographies and lists of publications (Y3.C 76/3:13; Item 1062-C-8), and a monthly serial entitled *Banned Products* (Y3.C76/3:9; Item 1064-B).

Administrative Conference of the United States

The task of developing improvements in the legal procedures by which federal agencies administer regulatory programs is the charge of a body called the Administrative Conference of the United States. Itself an independent entity, the unit was established by the Administrative Conference Act of 1964 (5 U.S.C. 571-76) to conduct studies of procedures that fix the rights and obligations of private persons and business interests through agency adjudication, rulemaking, and investigative proceedings. Its membership includes high-level agency officials, private lawyers, university faculty members and others qualified in law and government.

The Conference makes available to depository institutions an annual report (Y3. Ad 6:1; Item 1049-G), interim *Recommendations and Reports* (Y3.Ad 6.9; Item 1049-H) and a handbooks, manuals, and guides series (Y3.Ad 6:8; Item 1049-H-1).

Quis Custodiet?

The role of independent agencies is never wholly free from the political process. Independent bodies with regulatory powers are given theoretical autonomy, but it is almost impossible to remain independent of the Congress, the executive, the courts, and—most vexing of all—the influence of the institutions they regulate.

Moreover, some regulatory entities seem to have overlapping, if not competing, functions. The Federal Communications Commission's mandate includes radio and television broadcasting; telephone, telegraph, and cable television operation; two-way radio and radio operators; and satellite communication. Meanwhile, the Office of Telecommunications Policy in the Executive Office of the President is responsible for overall supervision of national communications matters.[15] Radio and television from time to time feel the political pressure of the not-so-independent Office of Telecommunications Policy, which in turn watches the FCC. Regulatory commissions like the FCC have always found it difficult to please simultaneously the executive and legislative branches and the regulated industry. Thus these "seemingly necessary bodies," in Justice Jackson's phrase, pose difficult constitutional problems. No satisfactory resolution of their role within the framework of the constitutional trinity seems philosophically possible. We are thus inescapably brought back to Juvenal's great, unanswered question, a question posed two thousand years ago: *Quis custodiet ipsos custodes?*

REFERENCES

1. J. M. Burns and J. W. Peltason, *Government By the People* (5th rev. ed.; Englewood Cliffs, N.J.: Prentice-Hall, 1963), p. 464.

2. Richard L. Worsnop, "Federal Regulatory Agencies: Fourth Branch of Government," *Editorial Research Reports*, February 5, 1969, pp. 87-89.

3. "Federal Regulators: Impact on Every American," *U.S. News & World Report* LXXXIII: 61 (May 9, 1977).

4. Ibid., pp. 61-62.

5. U.S. Public Documents Department. *An Explanation of the Superintendent of Documents Classification System* (1973), pp. 3-4, 9.

6. U.S. Senate. Committee on Governmental Affairs. *Organization of Federal Executive Departments and Agencies* (Committee Print; January 1, 1977).

7. *United States Government Manual, 1977/78*, p. 488.

8. The March 1977 *List of Classes* listed over 100 EPA series available to depository institutions.

9. *United States Government Manual, 1977/78*, p. 601.

10. From a *U.S. Department of Labor Office of Information News* release dated October 14, 1976: "From its inception OSHA has conducted 337,079 inspections resulting in the issuance of 245,138 citations alleging 1,270,212 violations, for which penalties of $34,634,729 were proposed."

11. *Congressional Record* (daily edition), June 8, 1976, p. E3173.

12. *Congressional Record* (daily edition), March 3, 1977, p. E1194.

13. Ibid., pp. E1194-95.

14. "Stressing Health Over Safety—A Switch in On-the-Job Rules," *U.S. News & World Report* LXXXIII: 65 (July 11, 1977).

15. *United States Government Manual, 1977/78,* pp. 100, 502.

11

REPORTS OF ADVISORY COMMITTEES AND COMMISSIONS

Upon the testimony of these facts [the Whiskey Insurrection] an associate justice of the Supreme Court of the United States notified to me that "in the counties of Washington and Allegheny, in Pennsylvania, laws of the United States were opposed, and the execution thereof obstructed, by combinations too powerful to be suppressed by the ordinary course of judicial proceedings or by the powers vested in the marshal of that district."

My proclamation of the 7th of August last was accordingly issued, and accompanied by the appointment of commissioners, who were charged to repair to the scene of insurrection. They were authorized to confer with any bodies of men or individuals. . . .

Although the report of the commissioners marks their firmness and abilities, and must unite all virtuous men, by showing that the means of conciliation have been exhuasted, all of those who had committed or abetted the tumults did not subscribe the mild form which was proposed as the atonement, and the indications of a peaceable temper were neither sufficiently general nor conclusive to recommend or warrant the further suspension of the march of the militia.

Thus the painful alternative could not be discarded. I ordered the militia to march, after once more admonishing the insurgents in my proclamation of the 25th of September last.

–George Washington, *Sixth Annual Address*,
November 19, 1794

INTRODUCTION

In the summer of 1794, farmers in western Pennsylvania resisted the efforts of the federal government to enforce an excise tax on distilled liquors by resorting to violence. They attacked federal revenue officers who tried to collect the tax and in some cases tarred and feathered them. The rebellion appeared to be organized; it became too powerful to be suppressed by the normal course of judicial proceedings or by the powers vested in the marshal of the territory. Indeed, Hamilton, who was Secretary of the Treasury, saw in the resistance a plot to destroy the federal government. The uprising came to be known as the Whiskey Insurrection.

Under authority granted by Congress, President Washington on August 7, 1794, issued a proclamation appointing commissioners who were authorized to confer with the rebels to assay a peaceful settlement. Although the report of the commissioners called for a relatively mild atonement, it was rejected by the rebels whereupon Washington called up the militia. Some 13,000 troops occupied the region; opposition melted away and the rebels surrendered without a battle. The historic incident was hailed by Federalists as the triumph of national authority over internal rebellion. Moreover, a significant precedent was established in that state governments supported the enforcement of federal law within the states. As a footnote to history, Washington's action is considered to have created the first advisory body to the federal government in our history.

That the commissioners failed in negotiating a compromise with the rebels did not negate the value of their appointment or the importance of their report to the President. It seemed necessary at the time, and continues to be of consequence today, that government receive advice from private citizens in the making of policy. Government probably came into being through the effort of committees, and after Washington's precedent, advisory bodies commonly were established to assist a President, the departments and agencies, and the Congress on matters of greater or lesser moment. Indeed, there appears to be an overwhelming tendency to appoint a committee or commission whenever a problem arises which at the time seems vexing or difficult of resolution. Ideally, the advisory body effects a significant contribution by the governed to the government; it provides a means by which the best brains and experience in business, labor, and the professions can be made available. Inevitably, as government has increased in size and responsibilities, the number of advisory groups has grown.

While the growth of advisory units has been substantial, their functions and management have been haphazard. Many statutes exist which either have established specific committees or have granted the President and the agencies broad authority to create advisory groups. The vast majority of committees and commissions come into being in the latter way. From time to time Congresses and administrations have engaged in housecleaning of committees which have become obsolete. But this process, known as "committee-killing" or "committee flushing," has been counterpoised by the penchant of government to create large numbers of new or reconstituted advisory bodies. The runaway nature of committee growth led President Kennedy, in 1962, to issue Executive Order 11007 (27 FR 1875; 3 CFR, 1959-1963 Comp., p. 573). Titled "Prescribing Regulations for the Formation and Use of Advisory Committees," it attempted to impose upon advisory bodies throughout the government uniform standards for their formation and activities.

Section 2(a) of EO 11007 defined the term "advisory committee" to mean "any committee, board, commission, council, conference, panel, task force, or other similar group, or any subcommittee or other subgroup thereof, that is formed by a department or agency of the Government in the interest of obtaining advice or recommendations, or for any other purpose, and that is not composed wholly of officers or employees of the Government. The term also includes any committee, board, commission, council, conference, panel, task force, or other similar group, or any subcommittee or other subgroup thereof, that is not formed by a department or agency, but only during any period when it is being utilized by a department or agency in the same manner as a Government-formed advisory committee." The EO further signified an "industry advisory committee" to be one composed predominately of "members or representatives of a single industry or group of related industries, or of any subdivision of a single industry made on a geographic, service or product basis."

While EO 11007 prescribed regulations for the formation and use of advisory committees in the executive branch, it did not provide for executive review of the formation, management and use of those bodies. Moreover, it did not suggest guidelines for funding the advisory units, was not inclusive enough, and contained only vague provisions for reporting and records access. In short, EO 11007 afforded minimum basic management control over an insufficient portion of the advisory committee mechanism.

In December 1970 the House Committee on Government Operations issued a report based upon a study of advisory bodies by its Special Studies Subcommittee. Entitled *The Role and Effectiveness of Federal Advisory Committees* (91-2: H. rp. 1731), the study reviewed the operations and effectiveness of committees advising the government, assessed the possibility of abuse and over-use of the committee device, and made recommendations for improving the machinery. Findings and recommendations resulted in EO 11671 (37 FR 11307; 3 CFR, 1971-1975 Comp., p. 710) of June 5, 1972, which superseded EO 11007 and established a centralized management system. Finally, Congress passed the Federal Advisory Committee Act (PL 92-463; 86 Stat. 770) which was signed into law on October 6, 1972. One day later, EO 11686 (37 FR 21421; 3 CFR, 1971-1975 Comp., p. 728) revoked EO 11671 (which had been intended as an interim Executive Order designed to create the administrative machinery in anticipation of passage of the new act) and directed that all executive agencies comply with the act's provisions.

PROVISIONS OF THE
FEDERAL ADVISORY COMMITTEE ACT

The Federal Advisory Committee Act (FACA) mandates a Committee Management Secretariat within the Office of Management and Budget to review each advisory body in order to determine if it is carrying out its purpose and if its responsibilities should be revised, merged, or abolished. Under the provisions of Section 6 of the act, the President is required to submit an annual report to the Congress. The report "shall contain the name of every advisory committee, the date of and authority for its creation, its termination date or the date it is to make a report, its functions, a reference to the reports it has submitted, a statement of whether it is an ad hoc or continuing body, the dates of its meetings, the names and occupations of its current members, and the total estimated annual cost to the United States to fund, service, supply, and maintain such committee." Moreover, the report is to include a list of committees abolished by the President, and in the case of advisory groups established by statute, a list of committees the President wishes to be terminated along with his reasons therefor. Section 11 of the act requires that agencies with advisory bodies make available to the public copies of transcripts of proceedings or meetings. Section 13 designates the Library of Congress as a depository for "at least eight copies of each report made by every advisory committee and, where appropriate, background papers prepared by consultants"; these documents "shall be available to public inspection and use."

A significant "sunshine" provision of the Federal Advisory Committee Act is found in Section 10: "Each advisory committee meeting shall be open to the public." Furthermore, with the exception of meetings where national security (that pernicious abstraction) mandates executive session, "timely notice of each such meeting shall be published in the *Federal Register*" to insure "that all interested persons are notified of such meeting prior thereto." What follows is paradigmatic of the imprecise process by which statutory law is translated into administrative fiat.

An OMB/Department of Justice Memorandum was written to provide guidance in the implementing machinery. Public participation in meetings of advisory bodies is subject to exceptions under Section 10(d) of the act, which cites 5 U.S.C. 552(b)—the nine categories of information that the Freedom of Information Act exempts from mandatory public disclosure. If portions of a meeting are to involve discussion of one or more of the categories, the appropriate portion is to be closed; in all cases the discretion of a President or agency head is the determining factor establishing openness or concealment. The act reads that "any such determination [of the necessity for secret sessions] shall be in writing and shall contain the reasons for such determination." The Memorandum further refines the wording of the act by stating that "the determination of the agency head or the Director shall be in writing and shall contain a brief statement of the reasons for closing the meeting (or portion)." The "timely notice" provisions were construed by the Memorandum to mean "at least 7 days before the date of the meeting" excepting emergency situations and on occasions "when 7-days notice is impracticable."

CONGRESSIONAL OVERSIGHT

While OMB is responsible for executive oversight concerning the operations of federal advisory bodies, the Subcommittee on Budgeting, Management and Expenditures of the Senate Committee on Governmental Affairs is the Congressional unit responsible for legislative review of the administration of the act. The late Senator Lee Metcalf, chairman of the subcommittee, noted deficiencies in the application of exemption (5) of the Freedom of Information Act and in the interpretation of the "timely notice" provision. Exemption (5) allows the withholding of "inter-agency or intra-agency memorandums or letters which would not be available by law to a party other than any agency in litigation with the agency." But, as the Senator pointed out, "an advisory committee is not an agency, and in most cases its members are not government officials. Generally, an intra- or inter-agency communication which the agency exempts from disclosure under (5) should lose its confidential privilege when introduced into an advisory committee meeting." As construed, an agency need only insert an "internal document" into the agenda to justify closing the meeting. Moreover, Metcalf noted that "there appears to be no requirement that any such written determination—with reasons—made by the Director or the agency head to close meetings under any exception be made public." This, he averred, was clearly in contravention of statutory intent.

Concerning notice in the *Federal Register*, Metcalf reported that "numerous notices have appeared . . . only one or two days before the meeting, without stating a time, place or purpose of the meeting." Because Metcalf's comments were made six months after the Federal Advisory Committee Act became effective, he was annoyed that such deficiencies in notification still obtained.[1]

If Metcalf found pockets of non-compliance with the intent of the act after six months of operation, a later, even more critical assessment was determined by Gerald D. Sturges, a congressional staff aid. Taking a week's sample of meetings of advisory bodies, Sturges found that 65 percent of the sessions were either closed or subject to restrictions. Other weekly samples showed a 74 percent closed or partially-closed pattern. "Timely notice," which had been extended to 15 days due to pressure from Metcalf's subcommittee, was found to be alarmingly disregarded. Sturges cited gross violations, among them a one-day notice of a meeting of the Wholesale Petroleum Advisory Group, a body created to advise the Federal Energy Administration. The agenda that day included no-lead gasoline problems and two-tier pricing and allocation discussions.[2]

EFFECT OF THE ACT

In the August 8, 1977, issue of *Newsweek* magazine, a squib titled "Brzezinski's Baby" aptly illustrated the difficulties involved in taming the widespread use and lack of accountability of advisory bodies, almost five years after passage of FACA:

> National-security adviser Zbigniew Brzezinski, angry that NASA failed to consult with him before agreeing to joint space-shuttle operations with the Russians, has ordered up a new interagency committee to coordinate talks with the Soviets. Brzezinski's brainchild—the Interagency Coordinating Committee of U.S.-Soviet Affairs—hopes to offer President Carter expert advice on Soviet matters and make sure that all upper-echelon Administration officials are aware of any impending deals with the Russians. But the committee got off to an inauspicious start: Carter learned of its existence from a newspaper story.[3]

Indeed, one has good reason to be concerned about the effective implementation of FACA. Senator Metcalf was again obliged to wax wroth in the pages of the *Congressional Record* in late 1975. Noting that in enacting FACA, the Congress declared that "new advisory committees should be established only when they are determined to be essential and their number should be kept to the minimum necessary," Metcalf proceeded to demonstrate that the number of advisory committees had actually risen, during the first seven months of 1975, from 1,242 to 1,307. Members of Congress "had introduced more than 750 bills establishing, authorizing or otherwise affecting advisory bodies." And the Senator had the list of bills read into the *Record.*[4]

FACA, 1972-1976

Initial compliance with Section 6 of the act was accomplished in two distinct forms. Detailed information was sent to the Senate Committee on Governmental Affairs by OMB. In turn that committee's Subcommittee on Budgeting, Management, and Expenditures issued a massive amount of data in five parts as a committee print. Titled *Federal Advisory Committees: First Annual Report of the President to the Congress, Including Data on Individual Committees* (Y 4.G74/6:Ad9/4/973/pts.), it was regrettably not issued to depository libraries. The other form of reporting consisted of a one-volume issuance titled *Federal Advisory Committees: First Annual Report of the President* (Pr 37.12:973; Item 848-C). In it are listed 1,439 advisory bodies which were in existence on December 31, 1972, arranged by department and agency without benefit of an index. Appendixes included the text of PL 92-463, EO 11686, a Draft OMB Circular, and a Draft OMB/Department of Justice Memorandum.

The pattern of this latter report has not essentially changed. *Federal Advisory Committees: Fifth Annual Report of the President* (Pr 38.10:976; Item 848-C) shows a slight decrease in the number of advisory bodies. Covering calendar year (CY) 1976, the *Fifth Annual Report* indicates that 180 new committees were established, while 287 committees were merged, abolished, or expired during CY 1976. By comparison, in CY 1972, a total of 211 new advisory committees were established while 187 were terminated. Looking at it another way, there were 1,439 advisory bodies extant as of December 31, 1972. As of December 31, 1976, there were 1,159 advisory committees in existence. In the four years of the FACA, the government was able to eliminate only 280 committees.[5]

Advisory committee management is currently governed by EO 11769 (39 FR 7125; 3 CFR, 1971-1975 Comp., p. 855) of February 21, 1974. A copy of this Executive Order is published as an appendix to the *Fifth Annual Report*, along with an OMB Circular and three OMB Transmittal Memoranda. Also included as Appendix material are GSA Federal Property Management Regulations prescribing records management procedures and forms. The main entry section is simply a list of current federal advisory committees, arranged alphabetically.

PROVENANCE

In the May 1973 revised *Explanation of the Superintendent of Documents Classification System* the following information is given under the heading, *Boards, Commissions, and Committees*:

Those agencies established by act of Congress or under authority of act of Congress, not specifically designated in the Executive Branch of the Government nor as completely independent agencies, are grouped under one of the agency symbols assigned to Congressional publications—namely, Y3. This place in the scheme is reserved for all such agencies.

When a President appoints an advisory committee or commission by executive order, the report that eventually issues from that body is properly to be classed in Pr (President of the United States). However, committees listed in the *First Annual Report* under the heading "Presidential Advisory Committees" have had their publications classed in either Y3 or Pr. The distinction appears to be a subtle one, because executive orders may be issued by a president in virtue of his office or pursuant to legislation. Consequently, one finds in this report Presidential advisory committees such as the Advisory Council on Historic Preservation (Y3.H62), Committee for the Preservation of the White House (Y3.W58/10), National Advisory Council on the Oceans and Atmosphere (Y3.Oc2), and Joint Commission on the Coinage (Y3.C66/1) issued under one class, whereas reports of committees to advise the President such as the Citizen's Advisory Commission on Environmental Quality (Pr 37.8:En 8) and the President's Council on Physical Fitness and Sports (Pr 37.8:P56/2) issued under the Office of the President. Moreover, the *First Annual Report*, in some instances, lists the very same committee as advising a Department or agency *and* serving as a "Presidential Advisory Committee."[6]

It is instructive to note that the 1976/77 edition of the *United States Government Manual* distinguishes between certain kinds of entities known by various names. In the section "Guide to Boards, Committees, and Commissions," there is an alphabetical list (with directory information) of "Federal boards, centers, commissions, councils, panels, study groups, task forces, etc., not listed elsewhere in the *Manual*, which were established by Congressional or Presidential action and whose functions are not strictly limited to the internal operations of a parent department or agency." The editors further note that "Federal Advisory Committees, as defined by the Federal Advisory Committee Act . . . have not been included here." Among those bodies which, according to the *Manual*, do not qualify as "Federal Advisory Committees," are the Federal Library Committee, Commission on Federal Paperwork, National Commission on Libraries and Information Science, and the California Debris Commission.[7]

ACCESSING ADVISORY COMMITTEE PUBLICATIONS

Sources of information on the publications of advisory bodies range from those which give somewhat detailed indexing and bibliographic information to those which are little more than verification and location devices. A selected account of these sources of information follows.

Monthly Catalog

Access through the *Monthly Catalog* is provided by personal or government author, title, and subject. A typical entry in the MoCat for an advisory committee publication is given below:

76-1020

Pr 37.8:En 8/T 68

United States. Citizens' Advisory Committee on Environmental
Quality.

From rails to trails. -- Washington : Citizens' Advisory
Committee on Environmental Quality : for sale by the Supt.
of Doc., U.S. Govt. Print. Off., 1975.

68 p. : ill. ; 23 cm.

Bibliography: p. 43-44.

Cover title.

Item 851-J

S/N 040-000-00330-4

pbk. : $1.50

1. Cycling paths. 2. Trails--United States. 3. Railroads
--United States--Abandonment. 4. Railroads--United States
--Right of way. I. Title.

HD2051975.U54 1975   75-601269

3850MZO.0973

OCLC 1258325

Tollefson & Chang

A Bibliography of Presidential Commissions, Committees, Councils, Panels, and Task Forces, 1961-1972 (Minneapolis: Government Publications Division, University of Minnesota Libraries, 1973) was compiled and edited by Alan M. Tollefson and Henry C. Chang. The *Bibliography* is selective in scope; 243 publications are arranged alphabetically by main entry. There is a "popular name" index as well as a title and subject/keyword index. Entries include SuDocs class number.

Gale Research Company

The Second Edition (1975) of the *Encyclopedia of Governmental Advisory Organizations* (Detroit: Gale Research Co.) covers 2,678 groups functioning in an advisory capacity to the President and to the several government agencies. Emphasis is on currently active advisory committees, but the *Encyclopedia* also includes some defunct bodies of historical interest.

Entries include the body's official name, acronym, popular name, address, phone number, name of executive secretary, date of establishment, type of organization, sponsoring agency, anticipated duration, program and activities, number of members, and the like. Publications and reports are given, with titles and frequency of issuance. The work is accessed through a subject/keyword index. This edition was edited by L. E. Sullivan and A. T. Kruzas.

The same editors are responsible for an updating service entitled *New Governmental Advisory Organizations.* A periodical supplement to the *Encyclopedia*, the arrangement is similar to the basic volume.

It is obvious that the *Encyclopedia* includes over 1,000 *more* entities acting in an advisory capacity than the official figures reveal. It would be useful for the compilers of the Federal Advisory Committee *Annual Reports* to compare their information with that gathered by Sullivan and Kruzas.

Popular Name Catalog

The Third Edition (1976) of *Popular Names of U.S. Government Reports: A Catalog* (LC 6.2:G 74/976; Item 818-F) was prepared in the Serial Division of LC. This edition represents a considerable improvement over earlier editions.

As with previous editions, the most attractive feature of the volume is the identification of the popular name of government reports. The news media will inevitably latch on to the name of the chairperson of an advisory committee. The more newsworthy the committee becomes, the more the popular name is used. Indexing tools such as the *Monthly Catalog* are not likely to include popular names of reports.

The *Popular Name Catalog* is still selective, but the Third Edition has a number of features which make it a vastly improved source for accessing those elusive documents. The reports are arranged alphabetically by popular name. Coverage includes not only "advisory" bodies as delineated by the *United States Government Manual* or FACA, but selected congressional committee reports, prints, or hearings known by the name of the chairperson or chief investigative officer. The entries include SuDocs class number and citation to the *Checklist of United States Public Documents, 1789-1909, Document Catalog*, or *Monthly Catalog* (date-entry number). An index has also been provided; each entry is indexed by the main subject of the report.

In addition, there is an added feature of great value. The compilers have included a section under the heading "Impeachment Inquiry." An attempt was made to include all reports, hearings, and miscellaneous documents printed by the GPO pertaining to the Watergate affair and related matters. Subdivisions include presidential documents; bills and resolutions; and hearings and reports. The whole (pp. 212-44) is perhaps the most complete listing in one place of official documents encompassing the impeachment inquiry.

Finally, the edition contains a section called "Unidentified Reports" for which minimal bibliographic information was available at the time of publication. The editors request the aid of documents librarians to identify reports so that they may be included in the next edition.

Despite the increased coverage of this edition, and the various ways of accessing reports of advisory bodies in the MoCat, there yet remains *no one source* that comprehensively and reliably indexes documents of this nature in *all* bibliographic ways.

CONCLUSION

Both the President and Congress often fail to make use of a committee's findings. In fact, creation of a committee can be used to delay, stall, or thwart solution or resolution of a problem. When a controversy erupts, the announcement of a committee to study the problem may be a ploy to mollify public concern or outrage. Incidents that create headlines often result in the creation of a presidential "blue-ribbon panel" to conduct an "in-depth" study. When the report is finally issued, a President is frequently obliged, for political or other reasons, to ignore, pigeonhole, or even denounce the findings.[8]

In early 1977 President Carter expressed concern about the number of advisory bodies and their usefulness. He ordered a government-wide, zero-base review of all committees. This directive was translated into specific instructions published in the *Federal Register*. Agencies were to report on each advisory body under their sponsorship. OMB provided a "review coversheet" for transmitting information on each body proposed to be terminated.[9]

But because previous administrations have ignored the recommendations of these groups, it might be thought that advisory bodies in general do not wield enough influence to worry about. Not so. The Sturges article quotes a professor of law at Georgetown University Law Center who is nationally known as an expert in the area of advisory committees: "I believe they are vastly underrated as policy-makers, mostly because those who do the rating—scholars, journalists and others—are only occasional observers of the advisory committee process."[10]

Indeed, the influence of advisory groups was underscored in the House Government Operations Committee report:

> Advisory groups are present throughout the legislative, executive, and judicial branches of Government and are created to advise either the officer or the agency in the performance of its responsibility, or as a communication aid in coordinating functions. There are, even, committees to advise advisory committees. Their functional use and growth have led to the description, "Government by Committee." The number, scope and use of the advisory committees appear to entitle committees to be termed the "fifth arm of the Federal establishment"—along with the constitutionally created legislative, executive, and judicial arms as the first three branches of government, and the regulatory boards, possessing administrative, judicial, and executive functions as the fourth arm.[11]

REFERENCES

1. *Congressional Record* (daily edition), July 16, 1973, pp. S 13566-69.

2. Sturges's comments were carried in a District of Columbia newspaper over 16 months after the act had been in existence. See "Advising Government from the Closet," *Washington Star-News* (May 26, 1974), pp. F 3-4.

3. *Newsweek* (August 8, 1977), p. 15.

4. *Congressional Record* (daily edition), September 15, 1975, pp. S 15917-24.

5. When the *Second Annual Report of the President* (Pr 37.12:974) was submitted in June, 1974, it showed that although 216 advisory committees were created during calendar year 1973, 390 had been terminated. The net decrease of 174 advisory bodies brought the total number in existence to 1,250. As an example of inadequate reporting, however, Senator Metcalf noted that the *Second Annual Report did not list* the advisory bodies abolished. Consequently, that information was printed in the *Congressional Record* (daily edition), June 20, 1974, pp. S 11145-49.

6. For example, one finds the President's Committee on Mental Retardation listed on page 1 under "Presidential Advisory Committees" and on page 41 as a committee to advise HEW. The summary tables on pages 4-6 of the one-volume annual report indicate that certain so-called presidential advisory committees are assigned to the appropriate federal agency for jurisdiction.

7. *United States Government Manual, 1976/77*, pp. 657-62.

8. The report of the Commission on Obscenity and Pornography (Lockhart Report) was scored by Spiro Agnew when he promised that "as long as Richard Nixon is President, Main Street is not going to turn into Smut Alley." The report of the President's Commission on Campus Unrest (Scranton Report) was ridiculed by Agnew as "pablum for permissiveness." And the report of the Commission on Marihuana and Drug Abuse (Shafer Report) was categorically rejected by the Nixon administration *before* it was made public.

9. 42 FR 13638-39 (March 11, 1977).

10. Sturges, "Advising Government from the Closet," p. F3.

11. 91-2: H. rp. 1731, p. 5.

APPENDIX A

SPECIAL PROBLEMS IN DOCUMENTS LIBRARIANSHIP

I–FEDERAL MAPPING AND CHARTING ACTIVITIES

INTRODUCTION

The task of providing an introduction to the mapping, charting, geodesy, surveying and related cartographic activities of the federal government is dismaying. Two comments will illustrate this discouraging feeling:

> The last major study of Federal surveying and mapping nearly 40 years ago found a disturbing proliferation and duplication of activity among many different agencies. Today these activities are found among an even greater number, suggesting that over the years the conventional budgetary process alone could not constrain the growth of surveying and mapping outside the core agencies, which apparently were not getting the job done. Now a new generation of problems–urban sprawl, pollution, energy crisis–are creating additional pressures which threaten even further lag in services and diffusion of effort.[1]

* * * *

It is difficult and often impossible to locate current special forms of printed material on a desired subject; maps are not an exception. E. B. Espenshade, in an article written in 1950, noted that the major problems were a lack of well-established bibliographic aids, the multitude of sources of maps, and the fugitive and documentary nature of maps. These are the same problems existing today–there is still no comprehensive index to U.S. government-published maps.[2]

Within the federal establishment there are agencies that sell maps and related cartographic materials but do not produce them, agencies that produce maps but do not issue or sell them, and agencies that both produce and sell their cartographic products. All the confusion that is engendered by the multiple bibliographic sales and acquisition patterns of federally funded research reports (see Chapter 4) is evident, perhaps even more dramatically, in the federal mapping enterprise. In the following pages an attempt will be made to indicate the nature and scope of the problem. The solution, according to experts who have studied the fragmented activities of the agencies, is massive reorganization of the federal mapping community resulting in a strong central mapping agency.[3]

CURRENT SOURCES OF INFORMATION
ABOUT FEDERAL MAPPING

The literature about mapping is rather extensive, and the best information is either problem-oriented or state-of-the-art surveys. Materials on federal cartography, for our purposes, may be divided into those issued as official government publications and those published in non-governmental sources.

Commercial Sources

The best current account of federal activities in this area is Jane Grant-Mackay Low, "The Acquisition of Maps and Charts Published by the United States Government," *University of Illinois Graduate School of Library Science Occasional Papers No. 125* (November 1976). Low, Science and Documents Reference Librarian at Trinity University in San Antonio, Texas, has rendered the documents community a great service with her excellent paper on federal maps and charts. The contents of the paper include current selection tools, map evaluation, federal agencies distributing maps, the map depository program, and a detailed account of federal departments and agencies which publish these materials. Her extensive list of references provides a worthy bibliography for further study. Her paper should be consulted by anyone involved in mapping work in libraries.

Laurence F. Schmeckebier and Roy B. Eastin, *Government Publications and Their Use* (2d rev. ed.; Washington: Brookings, 1969) devote Chapter 16 (pp. 406-440) of their book to federal mapping activities. Included in this useful discussion are state, county, topographic, geologic, agricultural, and weather maps.

Mary Larsgaard, *Map Librarianship: An Introduction* (Littleton, Colo.: Libraries Unlimited, Inc., 1978), in a section entitled "U.S. Government-Produced Maps" (pp. 42-47), provides a brief survey of the departments and agencies of the federal government that issue maps and includes a list of the types of maps and names of the issuing entities.

Donald A. Wise, "Cartographic Sources and Procurement Problems," *Special Libraries* 68: 198-205 (May/June 1977) discusses the several sources where cartographic materials may be acquired and the problems in developing a procurement policy. An appendix to the article contains a selected list of United States dealers in out-of-print maps and atlases.

Robert Sivers, "Federal Map and Chart Depositories," *Government Publications Review* 2: 9-15 (1975) discusses the depository program which the Defense Mapping Agency, National Ocean Survey, and U.S. Geological Survey maintain with libraries.

The May 1974 issue of *Illinois Libraries* is devoted to the topic of map collections. Although the articles cover maps and related materials in general, some contain useful information on federal government activities and sources.

Richard W. Stephenson (ed.), *Federal Government Map Collecting: A Brief History* (Washington: Special Libraries Association, Washington, D.C., Chapter, 1969) consists of papers presented at a meeting of the Geography and Map Group of the Washington, D.C., Chapter of SLA. Federal collections discussed include the Army Map Service, Congress's first map collection, early years in the Map Division of LC, and the National Archives as a repository of the official records of American cartography.[4]

Government Publications

Types of Maps Published by Government Agencies (I 19.2:M32/10/year; Item 621) is issued by the U.S. Geological Survey. The 1977 edition of this 15-page brochure contains a most useful list of the kinds of mapping and charting activities of selected agencies, arranged as shown in these examples:

Type	Publishing Agency	Available from
Congressional Districts	Bureau of the Census	Superintendent of Documents
Indian Reservations	Bureau of Indian Affairs	Superintendent of Documents
World Maps	Defense Mapping Agency	Defense Mapping Agency Topographic Center

Following the basic list, the several publishing and distributing agencies are given with their address. It is instructive to note that *Types of Maps* lists no fewer than 29 publishing and distributing agencies. The National Cartographic Information Center (NCIC) provides a central source of information for United States maps and charts, aerial photographs and space imagery, geodetic control, and digital and related cartographic data. NCIC is located in Reston, Virginia.

Report of the Federal Mapping Task Force on Mapping, Charting, Geodesy and Surveying, July 1973 (PrEx 2.2:F31/2/973; Item 854) was issued by the Office of Management and Budget and prepared by an interagency task force consisting of members of the Departments of Interior, Commerce, Agriculture, and Defense, and the OMB. The task force proposed a reorganization of mapping activities and discussed existing federal programs under the topics of Land Surveys; Land Mapping; Marine Mapping and Charting; Technical Services, including printing and distribution; and Map and Chart Pricing. The report constituted the first major study of federal activities in these areas since the 1930s.

GENERAL BIBLIOGRAPHIC SOURCES

In addition to the references cited in the articles and monographs above, which serve as official and unofficial sources, the following are examples of general sources of information on the publications of maps and other cartographic materials:

Library of Congress. Copyright Office. *Catalog of Copyright Entries: Third Series, Part 6, Maps and Atlases.* This is an important official document for identifying new maps, atlases, and globes. During FY 1975 for example, "338 atlases, 4 globes, and 1,804 maps were deposited in the Copyright Office and transferred to the cartographic collections of the Library of Congress."[5] Registrations for maps covering the period January-June 1976 totalled 847 and renewals 140. *Maps and Atlases* registered with the Copyright Office and listed in Part 6 of the *Catalog* are produced primarily by individuals, companies and corporations, associations, cities and counties.

Monthly Catalog of United States Government Publications. Presumably, publications available for sale by the Superintendent of Documents find their way into the *Monthly Catalog.* But *Types of Maps Published by Government Agencies* identifies SuDocs as but one of 29 distributing agencies for cartographic materials. Both Low and Wise indicate that the MoCat does not provide comprehensive coverage of cartographic publications.[6]

Moreover, a number of maps listed in the MoCat are distributed by other agencies through sale or deposit. Here is an example of a MoCat listing illustrating this pattern:

Monthly Catalog, July 1976

76-156

C 55.220:44

Graff, Werner.
   Synoptic maps of solar 9.1 cm microwave emission from June 1962 to August 1973/by Werner Graff and Ronald N. Bracewell ; Radio Astronomy Institute, Stanford University.   --Boulder, Colo: World Data Center A for Solar-Terrestrial Physics; Asheville, N.C.: distributed by the National Climatic Center, 1975.
      ii, 183 p.: ill.; 27 cm.--(World Data Center A for Solar-Terrestrial Physics report UAG ; 44)
      Chiefly tables.
      Bibliography: p. 181.
      Subscription price: $25.20 a yr., foreign $37.20. pbk. : $2.55
      1. Solar radiation--Charts, diagrams, etc. 2. Emissivity--Measurement, 3. Microwave measurements. I. Bracewell, Ronald N., jt. auth. II. National Climatic Center. III. IGY World Data Center A for Solar-Terrestrial Physics. IV. Title. V. Series.
   OCLC 2046945

Popular maps are advertised for sale through the Superintendent in *Selected U.S. Government Publications* and, in greater detail, in *Subject Bibliography 102, Maps (United States and Foreign)*. A related SB series is *Subject Bibliography 183, Surveying and Mapping*, which lists publications like *Engineering Field Tables, Elements of Surveying*, and various manuals of instructions with their supplements.

SB-102 took the place of the several *Price Lists* that included maps and charts. The August 1977 edition of SB-102 is typical of those cartographic issuances sold by SuDocs. Map-producing agencies whose publications are listed in SB-102 include Census, Central Intelligence Agency, Bureau of Indian Affairs, National Park Service, Department of Transportation, National Oceanic and Atmospheric Administration (NOAA), Fish and Wildlife Service, and the now-abolished Federal Power Commission. In quantity, it would appear that the Bureau of the Census is the agency that produces and issues the largest number of maps through the sales offices of the Superintendent of Documents.

All cartographic materials available for sale through the SuDocs are in the *Publications Reference File* (PRF), the microfiche in-print sales catalog issued by the Superintendent and described in Chapter 2. The PRF provides access by GPO stock number, SuDocs class number, and an alphabetical dictionary index of interfiled titles, agency series or report numbers, key words or phrases, and subjects.

Finally, library-oriented journals provide non-governmental sources of titles. Among these is the column by Alan Edward Schorr entitled "United States Government Publications Relating to Geography and Cartography" in the *SLA Geography and Map Division Bulletin*, in which issuing agency, title, year of publication, price if applicable, and SuDocs number are given. Low mentions other commercial sources in her section "Current Selection Tools" (pp. 3-5) of "The Acquisition of Maps and Charts Published by the United States Government."

FEDERAL CARTOGRAPHIC INFORMATION AGENCIES

The Superintendent of Documents, through its several sales catalogs and bibliographies, announces the availability of mapping and related materials. But, as Low noted, SuDocs "primarily distributes maps for federal agencies issuing a relatively small quantity of maps."[7] Moreover, certain federal agencies that do not produce maps nevertheless are important in the overall federal mapping enterprise:

National Cartographic Information Center. This entity, which is operated by the U.S. Geological Survey (USGS), "collects, processes, and disseminates information concerning maps, aerial photography geodetic positions, and elevations."[8] Accordingly, answers to questions involving the sale and distribution of maps produced by other federal agencies may be found at NCIC. Moreover, the Center publishes various brochures which have useful information. Many of these informational materials are free and often are received by depository libraries in the Geological Survey's General Publications series (I 19.2; Item 621). Although NCIC acts as a central clearinghouse for cartographic information, one cannot order needed materials from the Center.[9]

Cartographic Archives Division. This agency within the National Archives and Records Service (NARS), "houses more than 1,600,000 maps and approximately 2,250,000 aerial photographs." The Division issues various informational documents describing the kinds of materials which are available to the general public for research on location.[10]

Geography and Map Division. This unit of the Library of Congress houses over 3 million maps and over 35,000 atlases, and provides reference service by correspondence and telephone. The LC Photoduplication Service (see Chapter 4) sells reproductions of these materials which are not subject to copyright or other restrictions.[11] For depository libraries the General Publications series of the Division is available (LC 5.2; Item 811-A).

SELECTED MAP PRODUCING AGENCIES

In her excellent account, Low discusses thoroughly a number of important map-producing and issuing agencies within the federal establishment. Included are the Geological Survey (Interior Department); several components of the Commerce Department, including the National Ocean Survey and the Bureau of the Census; the Defense Mapping Agency (DoD); the Army Corps of Engineers (Department of the Army); components of the Department of Agriculture like the Forest Service and Soil Conservation Service; the Departments of State, Transportation, and Housing and Urban Development; the CIA; and independent agencies like the Tennessee Valley Authority (TVA) and Civil Aeronautics Board (CAB). The reader is referred to this account, which contains a wealth of information, and to the specialized lists and catalogs of the agencies themselves.

Of the many entities publishing cartographic materials, "the majority of maps and charts . . . are distributed through three main agencies: the Defense Mapping Agency, the National Ocean Survey, and the U.S. Geological Survey." Moreover, "these agencies publish and/or distribute maps for other agencies, yet not all the maps available are listed in the publications lists of these three agencies."[12] This lack of bibliographic consistency further confounds an already difficult situation.

Geological Survey

Perhaps the best known of this agency's activities is the production of topographic maps. Regional mapping units of NCIC sell or distribute USGS topographic maps or map reproducibles. Moreover, there are some 1,500 map dealers throughout the United States that sell topographic maps. Formerly the names of dealers and their addresses were located on the back of each state's topographic map index. Current publishing plans are to list map dealers in a catalog of published maps by states, one catalog for each state to accompany the topographic index. A basic source of information on topographic maps and other USGS products and services is *A Guide to Obtaining Information from the USGS, 1978* (I 19.4/2:977; Item 620-A). Issued as Geological Survey Circular 777, the *Guide* includes valuable information on purchasing, specialized subjects, map reference libraries, and other USGS products and services.

Topographic maps are produced with the cooperation of other agencies like Defense Mapping, National Ocean Survey (NOS), the TVA, Forest Service, and Mississippi River Commission. In addition, state or local agencies on occasion participate in mapping projects.[13] But the USGS does not issue topographic series only; indeed, the "thematic mapping of the USGS includes geologic maps at large and small scales, mineral resource maps, hydrologic maps and geophysical maps."[14]

Over twenty depository series are available from USGS through the regular depository system. It should be noted that series like the Professional Papers (I 19.16; Item 624) and Bulletins (I 19.3; Item 620) include individual publications that contain maps in the pocket of the document. Also, important documents like *The National Atlas of the United States* (I 19.2:N 21a; Item 621) are sometimes made available to depository institutions.

Guide to U.S. Government Maps (John L. Andriot, Documents Index, McLean, Virginia), covering *Geologic and Hydrologic Maps* published by the USGS through December 1974, is an annotated list which references the individual maps themselves. The entries and annotations were taken from the cumulative volumes of *Publications of the Geological Survey*, 1879-1961 and 1962-1970; the annual supplements for 1971-1973; and the monthly lists of *New Publications of the Geological Survey* for 1962 through 1974.

National Ocean Survey

According to the 1977-1978 edition of the *United States Government Manual*, the National Ocean Survey (NOS) emerged in its current hierarchial place after some interesting reorganization maneuvers. Its initial name, the Coast Survey, was established in 1807 for the purpose of preparing navigational charts of U.S. coastal waters. The Coast Survey was redesignated as the Coast and Geodetic Survey by act of June 20, 1878. In consolidating the functions of the Survey and of the Weather Bureau, the Environmental Science Services Administration (ESSA) was created by Reorganization Plan 2 of 1965. But ESSA itself was absorbed into the National Oceanic and Atmospheric Administration (NOAA),[15] and the functions of the Coast and Geodetic Survey were structured into a new entity, the National Ocean Survey.

NOS "is the primary publisher of nautical charting for U.S. marine waters including its dependencies and Puerto Rico, the Great Lakes and certain other navigable waterways."[16] The agency's "principal products . . . are nautical and aeronautical charts, which are basic tools needed to maintain the nation's sea and air transportation system."[17] As "Chartmaker to the Nation," NOS and NOAA issue approximately 43 million copies of navigational charts each year; a free catalog of this activity can be obtained from the National Ocean Survey, Distribution Division (C44), Riverdale, Maryland 20840.[18] Also, nautical charts are available for purchase from the Survey itself and from its more than 1,400 authorized sales agents throughout the United States.

NOS issues several series for depository libraries, including Tide Tables, Coast Pilots, and Tidal Current Tables. But the regular depository program does not provide the majority of charts issued by NOS. Indeed, like the USGS, collection-building of NOS cartographic activities must be accomplished through purchase[19] or participation in the Survey's specialized chart depository arrangements.

It should be noted that the National Weather Service, Environmental Data Service, and NOAA itself as an issuing agency all publish numerous mapping and charting materials. But the most prolific of the sub-units within NOAA is the National Ocean Survey.

Defense Mapping Agency

The Defense Mapping Agency (DMA) was established in 1972 to unify all Department of Defense (DoD) mapping operations and to separate the intelligence functions of DoD from its mapping activities. DMA absorbed most of the staff and functions of the former Mapping and Charting Division, Defense Intelligence Agency, including the Secretary, U.S. Board on Geographic Names.

DMA field activities provide topographic, aerospace and nautical products; the agency's components "make DMA one of the largest mapping organizations in the world." Moreover, though DMA produces some mapping of the United States, its primary activity "is the compilation and publication of small, medium and large scale topographic mapping, thematic mapping, nautical and aeronautical charting for world areas exclusive of the United States, its territorial waters, its dependencies and Puerto Rico."[20]

According to Low, "of the 90 million maps and charts annually distributed, the majority is used by the federal government, civilian and military agencies. Relatively few of the agency's products are available to the public."[21] Of those that are, however, ordering information is given in the 1977-1978 edition of the *United States Government Manual*, pages 232-33. Also, the DMA Topographic Center has a map depository program, although, as Sivers points out, membership can only be obtained when an established member withdraws; there is an "approved waiting list."[22]

Concerning the regular depository library program, DMA issues three series: a weekly *Notice to Mariners* (D 5.315; Item 379-A); *Summary of Chart Corrections* (D 5.315/2; Item 379-A); and numbered Hydrographic Center Publications. Of the latter, there is the well-known *Sailing Directions* (D 5.317; Item 378-E). Both *Notice to Mariners* and *Sailing Directions* were formerly issued by the U.S. Naval Oceanographic Center.

Bureau of the Census

The statistical activities of this famous agency and its resultant published data tend to obscure the Bureau's cartographic endeavors. Indeed, geography plays a crucial role in taking censuses, and the geographic work for a census includes preparing appropriate maps. In this activity, a number of tools and products that are helpful to the data user as well as to the Census Bureau have been developed: new types of maps, computerized geographic coding, mapping, and graphic display systems.

Census Maps

Census maps are necessary for virtually all uses of small-area census data. They are needed to locate specific census geographic or statistical areas and to analyze their spatial relationships. Outline maps are used to show boundaries, and display maps serve to portray data.

Outline maps are produced by the Bureau for counties, urbanized areas of Standard Metropolitan Statistical Areas (SMSA) and Enumeration Districts (ED), tracts, county subdivisions, places, central business districts, and major retail centers. Display maps show geographic distributions of various social and economic data and large SMSAs. Both types of maps are available either from the Superintendent of Documents; Bureau of the Census Library (Washington, D.C. 20233) on microfiche; Subscriber Services (Publications), Bureau of the Census; or Customer Services Branch, Data User Services Division, Bureau of the Census. There are also a number of private summary tape processing centers that are able to provide computer tape copies to their customers.

GBF/DIME Files

GBF/DIME files (geographic base file/dual independent map encoding) were developed for nearly 200 SMSAs following the 1970 census to assign geographic codes to the census records. They are computerized versions of the Metropolitan Map Series plus block-by-block address ranges, ZIP codes, and X-Y coordinate values at intersections. The Bureau has developed a number of computer programs for creating, editing, and maintaining GBF/DIME files and for user applications. These are used to perform tasks, such as geographic coding of local records, computer mapping, and the like. A list of these programs is available on request from the Data User Services Division in Washington.

Other geographic reference products are discussed in *Factfinder for the Nation* (C3.252:8; Item 131-F) issued September 1977, along with a list of sources which provide additional explanations and descriptions of census geography and its various aspects.

Unlike the other agencies discussed above, the Census Bureau participates actively in the regular depository program. Numerous series are available to depository institutions. For example, most of the reports on population statistics are accompanied by maps and charts. In addition, much useful census information is actually published in graphic form. The GE-50 (C 3.62/4) and GE-70 (C 3.62/8) map series, which utilize color coding as well as lines and dots, show the distribution of people by a variety of characteristics. The GE-80 (C 3.62/7) series, *Urban Atlas: Tract Data for SMSAs,* provide through the use of computer-mapping techniques, selected 1970 census tract statistics. All three GE series are available under Item 146-K. The *Congressional District Atlas* depicts boundaries of the 435 congressional districts. This extremely useful reference source shows each county that is divided between two or more congressional districts, and each small complexly divided area where congressional district boundaries follow streets, corporate limits, streams, and other difficult-to-locate line features. County and place listings accompany the maps. Like the GE series above, the *Atlas* is available to depository libraries (C 3.62/5; Item 140-B).

Township Atlas of the United States: Named Townships (John L. Andriot Associates, Box 195, McLean, Virginia 22101), in two volumes, consist of state and county maps reproduced from various Census Bureau maps and publications issued in connection with the 1970 Census of Population; Public Land Survey townships are included.

CARTOGRAPHIC DEPOSITORY PROGRAMS

The basic depository library system of the federal government has been discussed at length in Chapter 3 and elsewhere as noted. But there are a number of specialized programs in which certain libraries become depositories for specific kinds of materials. Some of the specialized types of materials include or have included Housing and Urban Development planning reports, patents, census materials, and maps. Census Depository Libraries, for example, were chosen on the basis of population (in the case of a municipal institution) or enrollment (in the case of a college or university library). But this program is being phased out and census materials are currently available through the regular depository system.

Unfortunately, these specialized depository programs do not publish information about their arrangements with the specificity of the normal depository system of the GPO. As Hamilton notes, "documentation on special depository systems is not abundant. Information on depository status requirements is not generally published. Formal agreements to accept and maintain the depository designation are not used by the agencies contacted. Only one agency conducts periodic canvasses of its depositories to determine whether changes are in order. None of the agencies could provide specific information on the retention practices, organization, use patterns, or service policies for their materials on deposit in various libraries."[23] That is, we have nothing like the listing of depositories in the September MoCat, the April joint committee print, published *Instructions to Depository Libraries*, etc.[24]

Selective depository systems exist to satisfy one or more of the following purposes:

1. to supplement the Government Depository Library system,
2. to insure that unusual storage and handling requirements will be met,
3. to insure that special collections are available at research centers where heavy use is anticipated, or
4. to insure that collections are in relatively convenient locations for public use.[25]

Before we discuss some of the specialized depository programs for mapping agencies, it is important to note that the GPO depository program is not excluded from mapping activities. For example, some (not an exhaustive list) agencies supplying maps, charts, atlases, and other materials to any depository that wishes to subscribe include:

Issuing Agency	Series	Item No.
Central Intelligency Agency	CIA Maps and Atlases	856-A-1
Bureau of Indian Affairs	Maps	627-C
National Park Service	Maps	651-A
National Oceanic and Atmospheric Administration	NOAA Atlases	250-E-9
Bureau of Land Management	Maps and Map folders	629-B

Geological Survey

The Survey designates selected public, college, and professional society libraries as "map reference libraries" for deposit of its topographic, geologic and hydrologic maps. The designated institution must have adequate facilities for proper storage, preferably in map file cabinets, and a member of the library staff must be responsible for maintaining the collection. Maps provided must be made available for reference use to the public and must not be sold.

Topographic quadrangle maps are deposited for one state, a group of states, or all states; but other topographic maps, such as state base maps, national parks, and the U.S. 1:250,000-scale series are sent by full series, without geographic selectivity.

Geologic and hydrologic maps, however, are all sent by full series instead of selectively by state. These categories are distributed as a rule only to colleges that offer a degree in geology. New and revised maps are supplied monthly to map reference libraries, but USGS does not include reprinted maps. As in the regular depository program, materials are not issued retroactive to the library's designation as a depository. USGS will, however, supply maps of a local area to form the nucleus of a map reference library collection and, on request, will replace maps that become worn by frequent use.

The responsible librarian signs a "map reference library agreement" declaring his or her staff and facilities "fully capable of compliance with all requirements necessary for designation as a Map Reference Library for U.S. Geological Survey maps." The original of the agreement is returned to the U.S. Geological Survey, 329 National Center, Reston, Virginia 22092, and a copy is retained in the institution's files as a record of the official date of designation as a map reference library.[26]

A list of USGS map depository libraries is published at the bottom of the index maps of each state. The USGS does attempt to keep in touch with its depository libraries by means of an "annual canvass to identify what changes, if any, are necessary in distributing maps to its depositories." However, these "canvasses are sometimes delayed, especially when adequate staff is not available to handle them."[27]

National Ocean Survey

According to Sivers, "full or partial NOS depositories are available to libraries in the United States which can provide evidence of adequate storage capacity, and agree to give public access to revised charts as furnished." A list of *some* depository libraries can be found in the map library directory, and these are signified by "USC&GS" [United States Coast and Geodetic Survey], the initials of a predecessor agency.[28]

Defense Mapping Agency

Depository materials consist primarily of medium and small scale topographic maps, aeronautical and nautical charts. Membership in DMA's program is limited. During the 1960s the agency, then known as the Army Map Service (AMS), stopped accepting additional depository members. Membership is by invitation from DMA, but "only when an established member withdraws from the program, and the DMA gives permission for transfer of the depository to a library on an approved waiting list."[29] Materials are deposited on "an indefinite loan basis subject to recall by the Defense Mapping Agency. Depository maps and charts should be clearly marked as such and should be processed into an active file where they may be readily retrieved." Units within DMA producing maps for depository distribution include its Topographic Center, Hydrographic Center, and Aerospace Center. Inquiries concerning this program should be sent to the DMA Topographic Center (DMATC) in Washington, D.C.[30]

As is the case with all depository library programs within the federal government, terms of membership and other criteria change from time to time. Accordingly, it is necessary to obtain from the appropriate agency the most current information available when contemplating membership.[31]

SUMMARY

The Federal Mapping Task Force found numerous problems in the production and distribution of cartographic activities within the federal establishment. Most work is accomplished in-house at many facilities throughout the country. Agencies creating computer-assisted automated systems have made no concerted effort to develop compatible techniques. The Joint Committee on Printing has made little effort to remedy duplication or waste in the printing operations of the mapping agencies or their commercial contract printers. Millions of maps and charts are distributed by different agencies; customers do not know where to turn for correct ordering information.[32]

To remedy this lack of coordination, the Task Force recommended a centralized cartographic agency to provide:

Single-agency liaison with GPO and JCP to handle all Federal map and chart printing, whether or not the products were compiled by the central agency.

More consistency in printing standards and specifications.

Better use of all in-house plants through creation of services of common concern.

Single-source information service for all users to acquire map and chart products.

Consolidated implementation of modern, efficient merchandising techniques.[33]

The Task Force recommended giving a new, central agency full responsibility and authority for managing the printing and distribution of federal map and chart products, including authority to contract map and chart printing directly with private industry. It has been noted that consolidation of DoD mapping into the

Defense Mapping Agency has improved that entity's capabilities. Perhaps a single agency for all cartographic products would accomplish what the Task Force believes. If that is the case, then the present bibliographic confusion could be allayed.

REFERENCES

1. U.S. Office of Management and Budget. *Report of the Federal Mapping Task Force on Mapping, Charting, Geodesy and Surveying* (PrEx 2.2:F31/2; Item 854), July 1973, p. i.

2. Jane Grant-Mackay Low, "The Acquisition of Maps and Charts Published by the United States Government," *University of Illinois Graduate School of Library Science Occasional Papers No. 125* (November 1976), p. 3.

3. *Report of the Federal Mapping Task Force . . .* , p. iii.

4. The Stephenson compilation is cited in the section on "Maps, Geography, and Cartography" (pp. 66-67) in *Draft Syllabus of Resources for Teaching Government Publications* (ED 125 668), 1976, prepared by the Education Task Force of GODORT.

5. Donald A. Wise, "Cartographic Sources and Procurement Problems," *Special Libraries* 68: 198 (May/June 1977).

6. Low, pp. 4, 29; Wise, pp. 198-99.

7. Low, p. 9.

8. *United States Government Manual, 1977/78*, p. 314.

9. Low, p. 8.

10. Ibid., pp. 9-10.

11. Ibid., p. 9.

12. Ibid., p. 29.

13. Ibid., p. 12.

14. Robert Sivers, "Federal Map and Chart Depositories," *Government Publications Review* 2: 13-14 (1975).

15. Reorganization Plan No. 4, 1970.

16. Sivers, p. 12.

17. Low, p. 14.

18. *Business Service Checklist* (July 8, 1977), p. 1.

19. Each chart catalog, available from the central office in Riverdale, Maryland, contains a list of authorized dealers from which NOS charts may be purchased.

20. Sivers, p. 11.

21. Low, p. 21.

22. Sivers, p. 11.

23. Beth A. Hamilton, "Selected Special Depository Libraries in H.E.W. Region V," *Illinois Libraries* 56: 285 (April 1974).

24. Patents seem to be an exception; a list of Patent Copy Depository Libraries is published in Volume II of the annual *Index of Patents* (C 21.5/2; Item 255).

25. Hamilton, p. 285.

26. USGS map reference library agreement, 1977.

27. Hamilton, p. 288.

28. Sivers, p. 13.

29. Ibid., p. 11.

30. Defense Mapping Agency. Map and Chart Depository Program. *Terms of Membership* (1974).

31. Low, p. 28.

32. *Report of the Federal Mapping Task Force....*, pp. 147-52.

33. Ibid., pp. 152-53.

II–CENSUS BUREAU INFORMATION

INTRODUCTION

The statistical system of the federal government is a decentralized one. Students of numerical facts like to distinguish among agencies involved in statistics: "the analytic and research agencies, the administrative and regulatory agencies, and the general purpose statistical ones." The latter have as their primary function the collection of statistics and include the "Bureau of the Census, the Bureau of Labor Statistics, the Statistical Reporting Service of the Department of Agriculture, the National Center for Educational Statistics, and the National Center for Health Statistics."[1]

Of all the vast statistical generating and gathering machinery, that of the Census Bureau is best known and, owing to its complexity, is apt to consume a good deal of the reference time allotted to the documents librarian. Census publications are the core of any collection of statistical data. The information that is obtained from the publications which the Bureau issues is used in a variety of fields. Businessmen, school administrators, neighborhood citizens' groups, housing authorities, indeed virtually all types of persons and occupations, find census information significant to their activities. Data, moreover, are used by governments to set public policy and plan for the future.

The first decennial census was taken in 1790 and was repeated each succeeding decade. In 1902, the Bureau of the Census was established as a permanent office (32 Stat. 51). By laws codified as Title 13, *U.S. Code*, and in virtue of Article I, Section 2 of the Constitution, the Bureau is enjoined to take a census of the population every ten years. On January 1, 1972, the Social and Economic Statistics Administration (SESA) was established, thus creating an intermediate management layer in order to integrate the Bureau of the Census and the Bureau of Economic Analysis. SESA was terminated by Department of Commerce Organization Order 10-2, effective August 4, 1975 (40 FR 42765, September 16, 1975). The decision to terminate SESA was based "principally on the failure of President Nixon's Departmental Reorganization Program to be enacted." Thus Census and the Bureau of Economic Analysis (BEA) were restored as primary operating units reporting directly to the Assistant Secretary for Economic Affairs, Commerce Department.[2] Unfortunately, during SESA's short life as an agency, the Superintendent of Documents managed to classify a number of Bureau publications in "C 56." Presently, publications of the Census Bureau are found in both the "C 3." and "C 56." notations.[3]

Census Bureau Activities

As a general purpose statistical agency, the Bureau's primary function is to collect, process, compile, and disseminate statistical data for the use of other government agencies and the general public. Census publishes more statistics than other federal agencies do, covers a wider range of subjects, and serves a greater variety of needs. The Census laws guarantee the confidentiality of replies to Census inquiries; indeed, Census Bureau employees take an oath to protect that confidentiality. Accordingly, tabulations that reveal confidential data for individual respondents or establishments are not published.

The first census, taken in 1790, counted the number of free and slave persons in each state; the national total was nearly 4 million inhabitants. Today the Bureau is responsible for taking all censuses authorized by federal law, including:

Census	Periodicity	Recent Census
Population	10 year	1970
Housing	10 year	1970
Agriculture	5 year	1974 *1978, 1982,*
Business	5 year	1977 *,1982, 1987*
Construction Industries	5 year	1977
Governments	5 year	1977
Manufactures	5 year	1977
Mineral Industries	5 year	1977
Transportation	5 year	1977

(handwritten annotation under Agriculture: RETAIL; under Business: WHOLESALE, SELECTED SERVICES)

In addition the Bureau is responsible for tabulating and publishing the official statistics on the foreign trade of the United States, and issues periodic reports in this field.

Reports between Censuses

Because many persons, organizations, and government units need information provided more frequently than on a decennial or quinquennial schedule, and more promptly than data from a full-scale census can be tabulated, the Bureau gathers and reports statistics on many census subjects in the form of current reports. These include population, manufacturing activity and commodity production, retail and wholesale trade, state and local government finances, and housing characteristics and vacancies. These reports are issued at different intervals: annually, quarterly, monthly, even weekly. Moreover, many local governments seek more frequent population figures than are afforded by the decennial censuses. Occasionally a local government requests the Census Bureau to conduct a "special census" of its area. Some 1,600 of these counts, made at the expense of local governments, were taken between 1960 and 1970.

International Assistance

Many foreign nations avail themselves of services provided by the Bureau in order to strengthen their statistical programs. Training is conducted for foreign statisticians and specialists interested in studying American census-taking procedures and related statistical techniques that can be usefully applied in other countries. American statistical knowledge is also transmitted through advisory services of United States officials. At any given time, there may be over 40 census and statistical advisors or technicians serving in these roles overseas.

Services for Other Federal Agencies

Because of its resources, the Census Bureau performs services for other agencies, such as data collection, sample design, machine tabulation, or consultation on methods and procedures. Three examples will suffice. Census collects and compiles household interview data for the national health survey program of the Public Health Service. Monthly employment and unemployment figures are collected by Census for the Bureau of Labor Statistics (BLS). And the Bureau maintains an international assistance program under arrangements with the Agency for International Development (AID).

Personal Data Search

The Bureau maintains a staff of employees at Pittsburg, Kansas, whose function is to search the various federal censuses of population and provide at a nominal cost personal data from these records to individuals who lack other documents of birth or citizenship. Extracts from these records are often accepted as evidence of age and place of birth, for obtaining employment, social security benefits, old-age assistance, passports, naturalization papers, delayed birth certificates, and the like. Confidential information may be furnished only if desired for a proper purpose upon the written request of the person seeking the information or his or her legal representative.[4] Inquiries should be addressed to Personal Census Service Branch, Walnut and Pine Streets, Pittsburg, Kansas 66762.

RELEASING CENSUS DATA

According to Judith Rowe, census material exists in several physical forms: in a conventional printed document, a microform copy of that printed report, a machine-readable data file, or in microfilm consisting of some of the computer summary tape data. For agencies like Census, where the data are so massive, computers are being used more frequently for the storage, manipulation, and printing of information. "This means that not only do all the data found in printed government documents usually exist in machine-readable form but also that for every piece of information eventually printed, a much larger body of data is stored in machine-readable form."[5]

Printed Reports

Information in printed form has long been, and probably still remains, the most common means of releasing census data. If the information required is not in great detail, the printed reports will be the most convenient and readily available source.

Census data contained in printed reports are arranged in tables. For example, population and housing characteristics for specified geographic areas are reported, such as the number of rented housing units in a block, the number of families below specified income levels in a census tract, or the number of persons who have had vocational training in a city or county.

Reports are released in a number of different series. Many series consist of one report for each state plus a United States summary; other series contain one report for each SMSA or urbanized area. Some reports are issued by topic rather than by area. Series related to the 1970 census include PC (1)-A, *Number of Inhabitants*; PC (1)-B, *General Population Characteristics*; PC (1)-C, *General Social and Economic Characteristics*; and HC (1)-A, *General Housing Characteristics*. Other series for the 1970 census include HC (3), *Block Statistics*; and PHC (1), *Census Tract Reports. Block Statistics* consist of one report for each urbanized area (UA), while *Census Tract Reports* consist of one report for each SMSA.[6]

Virtually all printed reports are available through the regular depository library system. In addition many printed reports are available for sale through SuDocs; Subscriber Services Section (Publications), Bureau of the Census, Washington, D.C. 20233; or the many U.S. Department of Commerce District Offices, the names and addresses of which are usually published on the back cover of every issue of the *Bureau of the Census Catalog.*

Microfiche

Microfiche copy of any printed report can be obtained from the Bureau of the Census Library, Washington, D.C. 20233. In addition, census data on microfiche can be obtained through NTIS, as the reports are listed in GRA&I (see Chapter 4). Other publishers of census materials in microform, known to the Census Bureau Library staff as of October 1975, are listed in Paul T. Zeisset,

"Micropublishing at the Bureau of the Census," *Illinois Libraries* 58: 209-211 (March 1976). These include a mixture of government and private concerns as follows:

> Publications Sales Branch (NEPS)
> National Archives (GSA)
> Washington, D.C. 20408
> First eleven censuses, 1790-1890 on 35mm positive microfilm.

> Research Publications, Inc.
> 12 Lunar Drive
> New Haven, Conn. 06525
> Decennial Census Publications, 1790-1970 on 35mm positive microfilm.

> Population Division
> Bureau of the Census
> Washington, D.C. 20233
> 1960 Censuses of Population and Housing, on microfilm.

> Readex Microprint Corporation
> 101 Fifth Avenue
> New York, N.Y. 10003
> Census publications listed in the MoCat, 1958 to date, in microprint edition.

> Congressional Information Service (CIS)
> 7101 Wisconsin Avenue
> Washington, D.C. 20014
> Census publications indexed/abstracted in *American Statistics Index* (ASI), on microfiche.

> Greenwood Press
> 51 Riverside Avenue
> Westport, Conn. 06880
> Census publications 1820-1945 and 1946-1967 exclusive of decennial census publications, on microfiche.

Data Maps

The spatial distribution of the population and its characteristics are visualized in two types of wall-size maps using colors to represent values: National maps showing data by county (GE-50 and GE-70 series) and SMSA maps showing data by census tract (*Urban Atlases*, GE-80, for 65 SMSAs). Order forms for census maps can be obtained from the Bureau's Subscriber Services Section. The cartographic endeavors of the agency were discussed in more detail in Appendix A (I) on federal mapping activities.

Summary Tapes

The raw materials for statistical tables are the individual replies to the census questionnaires. There is virtually an unlimited number of combinations or cross-tabulations of census data that may be prepared. For example, in reporting for a particular county, a count of females could be given, or a count of males by single years of age, or a count of males and females by single years of age by race, and so on. Summaries may appear in printed tables, as we noted, or on punched cards, magnetic tape, or in the memory of a computer. In a printed table, the summary count is expressed in the familiar Arabic numerals, but in the data storage of a computer it is expressed in coded patterns which require transformation through use of processing equipment to make the summary count readily intelligible to the user.

Computer summary tapes are the medium most frequently used to deliver census data in a computer-readable format. They are the magnetic tape recordings of strings of numbers in the form of magnetized dots or bits in the metallic oxide which coats one side of the tape. The numbers represent a series of accumulations or tallies of responses on a set of questionnaires. Each number is a total for a particular characteristic at the level at which the summarization was made—usually a geographic unit such as tract, county, state, etc.

By themselves, summary tapes are useless. Only when they are accompanied by a description of the numbers recorded and their location can the tapes be used. At the Census Bureau, the description is called "technical documentation," and it is an essential part of the summary tape package. With this documentation, programmers can instruct computers to read the tapes, perform operations on the numbers, and print out the desired information as eye-readable numbers. For many users, the printed reports will be sufficient. But if frequent and extensive use is planned, summary data on computer tapes may be the best approach because of the speed, relative convenience of computer processing, and greater detail. Tapes contain many cross-classifications of variables and more geographic areas than printed reports; therefore, some users may find this additional information essential to meet their data requirements. That is, the summary tapes have the same kind of data as found in printed reports—there is just more of it.

The Bureau maintains data files of two basic types: those containing the basic records of individual respondents, and those containing statistical totals— summarizations for small areas or for detailed subject classifications. The individual records are "untabulated" and are seldom published. Because of the Bureau's legal requirements and historical standards of confidentiality, this information—known as microdata—can be released "only after it has been divested of names and other identifying information."[7]

There are six major series of summary tapes, called "counts." The files in each count cover geographic units like blocks, minor civil divisions (MCDs), tracts, congressional districts, 3- and 5-digit ZIP areas, and SMSAs. *Data Access Descriptions* (DAD) series issued in printed form by the Bureau describe each count in detail.

The user will need maps to accompany the summary tapes. It is patently of no value to know that 103 people live in block no. 205 if one doesn't know where block no. 205 is. Printed report users do not have this problem, because the appropriate maps are included with each report. But persons using summary tapes must either buy maps separately from the Bureau or obtain those printed reports which include the necessary maps.

Summary tape users will also need computer programs to display data from the tapes and a listing of geographic areas with their code numbers to interpret the code on the tapes. For this purpose, the Bureau has prepared a Master Enumeration District List (MEDList). MEDList is a hierarchical code list relating each state, county, MCD, and place segment by name to all relevant geographic codes. Components down to the basic enumeration districts or block groups are listed within each unit. Census tracts, enumeration districts or block groups, and blocks are defined by maps prepared by the Geography Division of the Bureau and are available from the Data User Services Division of the Bureau.[8]

Unpublished census data are available in microform. Zeisset notes that selected unpublished data from the 1960 census are available on 35mm microfilm. 1970 census files available on computer output microfilm include the above-mentioned MEDList, MCD/CCD statistics, and household income special tabulations. Information on these materials is available from Data User Service Division.[9]

Summary Tape Processing Centers

If the user needs data found only on the tapes but does not wish to do the necessary processing, there are a number of Summary Tape Processing Centers that provide census data products and services. As Rowe points out, one might be better off utilizing the services of these Centers: they "are more user-oriented, are more likely to produce adequate documentation, and are likely to have cleaned up errors and inconsistencies in the data or at least to have flagged them." Moreover, obtaining data from one of these organizations may be no more expensive than buying the products from the Census Bureau. And even if the charges are higher, the services provided may be worth the additional expense.[10]

The Centers are not franchised, established, or supported by the Bureau. They tend to develop through local initiative and respond to needs recognized by their organizers. But they are recognized when they file a statement with Census indicating their intention to service the needs of census data users and specifying their planned activities. They are representative of various segments of the private and public sector. Examples of Centers and their locations follow:

> Data Use and Access Laboratories (DUALabs)
> Arlington, Virginia
>
> New York State Department of Commerce
> Albany, New York
>
> Princeton-Rutgers Census Data Project
> Princeton University Computer Center
> Princeton, New Jersey
>
> UNITEL Census Program
> Massachusetts Institute of Technology
> Cambridge, Massachusetts

Market Opinion Research
Detroit, Michigan

Each Processing Center creates its own computer software package and establishes its own cost structure for services. Information on these Centers is found in the following places: U.S. Bureau of the Census. *Summary Tape Processing Centers: Location, Activities, Tapes* (1972); U.S. Bureau of the Census. *Summary Tape Processing Centers: Address List* (1975); *Data User News* (monthly Census Bureau publication wherein new Centers are announced); and Clearinghouse and Laboratory for Census Data. *Census Processing Center Catalog* (Arlington, Virginia, 1974). The Bureau of the Census welcomes these Centers. It considers the public listings of the Centers as a useful means of calling attention to their programs, thereby encouraging the pooling of resources and avoiding duplication of effort and extra expense to census data users.

SELECTED SOURCES OF INFORMATION

As the statistical activities of the Census Bureau are abundant, so are the published materials it issues. What follows are some of the sources of information about the Bureau's products and services and other supportive aids.[11]

Resource Guides

Reference Manual on Population and Housing Statistics from the Census Bureau (C 3.6/2:P 81; Item 146-A). This publication, dated March 1977, presents a comprehensive introduction to demographic data from the Bureau, with emphasis on population and housing information. Its purpose is to provide an up-to-date starting point for the new or prospective user, and a useful reference for the experienced user. Fifty reference charts and illustrations are included, along with numerous cross-references to other publications where more detailed information can be obtained.

Guide to Programs and Publications: Subjects and Areas, 1973 (C56.208:P94; Item 146-A) is an annotated listing of the programs and reports issued by the Bureau during the 1960s and early 1970s. It includes the subjects, areas, frequency, and scope of the agency's programs and publications in agriculture, the economic censuses and surveys, geographic reports and maps, governments, population, housing, and studies of foreign countries.

1970 Census Users' Guide (C 3.6/2:C33/2/yr./pts.; Item 146-A) is organized in two parts. Part I describes census concepts and procedures and has a Census Users' Dictionary. Part II includes the technical documentation for the first through fourth count summary tapes. Census data products are listed and described in detail in the *Guide*, as are general applications of the use of census data.

In-Print Information

For Census Bureau publications sold by the Bureau or by SuDocs, there are several in-print sources: *Publications Reference File*; *Selected U.S. Government Publications*; the current *Bureau of the Census Catalog*; and *Subject Bibliography* (SB) series numbers 146 (Census of Manufactures), 149 (Census of Transportation), 152 (Census of Business), 156 (Census of Governments), 157 (Census of Construction), 181 (Census of Population), 242 (Census of Housing), and 277 (Census of Agriculture).

Indexes

Among the standard indexes where Census Bureau materials may be accessed are *American Statistics Index*, the *Monthly Catalog*, and GRA&I. Special indexes, in addition, are devoted entirely to Bureau publications. These include the *Index to Selected 1970 Census Reports* (C 3.223: In 2; Item 154) and the *Index to 1970 Census Summary Tapes* (C 3.223:Su 6/970; Item 154). The former is an exhaustive index to data tables in various report series, with a cross reference guide to census terminology and computer-generated index entries listed alphabetically by subject. The latter is a comprehensive index to data tables in the summary tapes, first through sixth counts.

Periodicals and Series

Data User News (C 56.217; Item 148-C) is a monthly newsletter which provides information on plans for future censuses and the use of products and services of the Bureau. Moreover, as noted, this publication lists new Summary Tape Processing Centers registered with the Census Bureau. *Data User News* was formerly called *Small-Area Data Notes*.

Factfinder for the Nation (C 3.252; Item 131-F) is a series of topical brochures issued irregularly. Each brochure describes the range of census materials available on a given subject and suggests some of their uses. Subjects in the series have included agricultural statistics, reference sources, geographic tools, and the history and organization of the Census Bureau.

Data Access Descriptions (C 3.240/7; Item 142-D) are also issued on an irregular basis. They serve as introductions to means of access to Census Bureau data. Numbered consecutively by date of issue, they have included subjects like current survey statistics and data on selected racial groups.

The Basic Catalog

The indispensable tool for Census Bureau users is the *Bureau of the Census Catalog* (C 3.163/3; Item 138). Divided into two parts, Part I lists and describes reports from censuses and surveys; Part II describes the data files and selected tabulations currently available, and provides information on how these materials may be obtained. Additional features include highlights of new publications;

selected publications of other federal agencies based on Census Bureau data; selected reports on congressional hearings relating to the work of the Bureau; and occasional consolidated listings of reports of formal census programs, procedural histories, methodological studies, and special publications series. The *Catalog* is issued quarterly with monthly supplements. There is an annual cumulation. The *Catalog* is available for sale from the Superintendent of Documents.

The Bureau of the Census Catalog of Publications, 1790-1972 (C56.222/2-2:790-972; Item 138) is a massive volume which provides a comprehensive historical bibliography of sources for Census Bureau statistics covering these years. The *Catalog* is presented in two sections. The first section is a reprint of the *Catalog of United States Census Publications, 1790-1945*, prepared by Henry J. Dubester, Chief, Census Library Project, Library of Congress. It is a compilation of all materials issued by the Bureau and its predecessor organizations starting with the first decennial report of 1790. The second section, *Bureau of the Census Catalog of Publications, 1946-1972* updates and complements its historical predecessor. Information in this section is a compilation of data published in the annual issues of the *Bureau of the Census Catalogs* from 1946 to 1972.

Statistical Compendia

The following sources are also indispensable tools for libraries. They serve a dual function: the sources present data from the Census Bureau and from a wide variety of other entities, including some non-governmental sources; and through citations, source notes, and other bibliographic references, they direct the user to more extensive and detailed data.

Statistical Abstract of the United States (C 3.134; Item 150) is considered the authoritative source of facts on the social, economic and political aspects of the United States. Like the annual issues of the *United States Government Manual*, each yearly edition of the *Statistical Abstract* adds, drops, or refines a feature. Basic data on population, health, social welfare, the labor force, income, education, housing, government, and dozens of other topics are presented. There are close to 1,500 tables, a guide to sources, metropolitan area concepts and components, and, in the 1976 edition, a new section on statistical reliability and methodology. Information from private companies, states, and individual regions is given.

One outstanding feature of this renowned reference work is its *source notes*. Following every table, these source notes refer the user to the issuing entity where more comprehensive data can be found. If the source note indicates "unpublished data," one may write the appropriate agency for further information.

Pocket Data Book, USA (C3.143/3; Item 150-A) is called a "supplement" to the *Statistical Abstract* and consists of condensed data taken from the parent volume. Designed for quick and easy reference, it contains graphic and tabular presentations of summary statistics on a wide variety of subjects.

The following reference works are also considered "supplements" to the *Statistical Abstract*:

Historical Statistics of the United States, Colonial Times to 1970 (C 3.134/2:H 62/789-970; Item 151) is the "Bicentennial Edition" of this well-known work. This edition is a two-part compendium which updates and expands the predecessor volume *Historical Statistics of the United States, Colonial*

Times to 1957. It contains over 12,500 time series, primarily annual, covering United States social, economic, political, and geographic development during periods from 1610 to 1970. As in the annual *Statistical Abstract,* source notes serves as a guide to original documents which may be consulted for further study and additional information. Over 300 of the 1,298 pages cover definitions of terms, development and reliability of the data, and references to other sources. There are a table of contents, introduction, time period index, and alphabetical subject index included in each part.

Congressional District Data Book (C3.134/2:C 76; Item 151) presents over 250 statistical items for every congressional district on population and housing characteristics from the 1970 census and elections data for 1968, 1970, and 1972. It also includes congressional district maps for each state. The *Data Book* for the 93d Congress is also valid for the 95th Congress.

County and City Data Book (C 3.134/2: C83/2; Item 151) presents a variety of statistical information for counties, SMSAs, cities, urbanized areas, and unincorporated places. The 1972 edition contains economic and social data from the 1970 census of population and housing and from other censuses. Covered in this edition are the 50 states, 243 metropolitan areas, 840 cities, 245 urbanized areas, and 76 unincorporated places. The *County and City Data Book* is over 1,000 pages.[12]

CENSUSES OF POPULATION AND HOUSING

Among the resources recommended for all depository libraries as basic and available for immediate use are the Census of Population and the Census of Housing for the state in which the depository library is located.[13] An examination of the components of these two censuses will illustrate the publishing activities of the Census Bureau, for they seem to be the most sought-after materials.

Population

The Census of Population is the oldest of the censuses taken by the Bureau. It has been taken every ten years since 1790. At first, the census included little more than a count of inhabitants, which is required according to the Constitution to determine the apportionment of representatives to the Congress among the states. Very soon, however, the census was recognized as a convenient vehicle for obtaining various types of social and economic information, and inquiries were expanded. In the 1970 census, three types of questionnaires were used throughout the country. Five population questions were asked of every household (relationship to head of household; color or race; age; sex; marital status). A number of additional questions were asked on a 5- and 15-percent sample basis; and certain items common to both these questionnaires resulted in a 20 percent sample.

A vast amount of detailed information was generated thereby. The data are valuable in showing the characteristics of the population of states, counties, cities, and towns, and in analyzing specific subjects such as marital status or education. Between decennial censuses, information is needed on changes in employment, school enrollment, income, family status, and other economic and social characteristics. To get this information, the Bureau undertakes monthly, quarterly, and annual sample surveys. It also assists various jurisdictions (cities, towns, villages, counties, townships, and school districts) that need up-to-date census figures by conducting special censuses at the expense of the communities. The results of special censuses of certain of these areas are published in the P-28 series, *Special Censuses.*[14]

Population Census Reports

Taking the 1970 Census as an example, population census reports fall into three categories: preliminary, advance, and final. *Preliminary reports* consist of three series; data were based on preliminary population counts compiled in the census field offices. "Counts" designate major elements of the Bureau's tabulation program by the order in which they were produced and the results made available. The figures in all the preliminary reports were superseded by those in the advance and final reports. The series is available to depository institutions (C 3.223/2; Item 159-A-1 through 159-A-54). *Advance reports* in two series presented selected data prior to their publication in the final reports. Each series consisted of a report for each state and the District of Columbia, as well as a U.S. summary report. Advance reports series are available to depository libraries in C3.223/4 (Items 159-A-1 through 159-A-54).

The *final reports* came in two volumes. Volume I included characteristics of the population; number of inhabitants, general population characteristics; general social and economic characteristics; detailed characteristics. Volume II consisted of data on particular subjects such as national origin and race, fertility, migration, occupation, income, etc. Volume I was issued in 58 numbered parts, one for the United States, each of the 50 states, the District of Columbia, Puerto Rico, Guam, Virgin Islands, American Samoa, Canal Zone, and Trust Territory of the Pacific Islands. For each of the 58 areas, the data were first issued in four separate paperbound chapters, designated as A, B, C, and D. The four chapters were then assembled and issued in a hardcover edition, designated as Part A. For the outlying areas other than Puerto Rico, all the data on characteristics of the population were included in Chapter B. For depository institutions, subscribing to Items 159 and 159-A-1 through 159-A-54 will insure receipt of these data, according to the June 30, 1977, revised *List of Classes.*

Of great value to census users is a series called *Current Population Reports* (C3.186; Item 142-C). These consist of continuing and up-to-date statistics on population counts, characteristics, and other special studies on the American people. Data are issued in seven separate series: population characteristics (P-20); special studies (P-23); population estimates and projections (P-25); federal-state cooperative program for population estimates (P-26); farm population (P-27); special censuses, noted above (P-28); and consumer income (P-60).

Another useful series on population data is entitled *Supplementary Reports* (C3.223/12; Item 154). For the 1970 census this series presented miscellaneous types of population data: special compilations which could not be accommodated in the regular final reports, and selected tables from large reports to permit distribution of the particular figures in an inexpensive format.

Housing

The first census of housing was taken in 1940, although counts of "dwelling houses" were obtained in earlier censuses of population. Beginning in 1940, a census of housing has been taken every ten years in conjunction with the census of population. In the 1970 census, a number of questions were asked of every household, additional housing questions were asked on a 5- and 15-percent sample basis, and certain items common to both questionnaires resulted in a 20-percent sample. Although the Bureau gets most of its information on the number and characteristics of the nation's housing from the decennial census, current information on housing is collected monthly and there are quarterly and annual publications between the decennial censuses.[15]

Housing Census Reports

For the 1970 census, housing data followed the issuing pattern of population statistics: preliminary, advance, and final series. *Preliminary reports* consisted of a report for each state presenting housing unit counts for each place of 10,000 inhabitants or more, as compiled in the census field offices. And these figures, too, were superseded by those in the advance and final reports. *Advance reports* consisted of a report for each state and the District of Columbia, as well as a U.S. summary report. *Final reports* were issued in seven volumes. Volume I, *Housing Characteristics for States, Cities, and Counties*, consisted of separate reports for the United States, each of the 50 states, and the other components noted above for population final reports. The other volumes contained information on subjects like metropolitan housing characteristics, block statistics, plumbing facilities, estimates of dilapidated housing, and the like. *Supplementary reports* presented miscellaneous types of housing data. These series are classed in C3.224/numbers and are available to depository libraries under Items 155 and 156-A-1 through 156-A-54.

A useful publication is titled *Annual Housing Survey* (C3.215/year; Item 141-A), a sample survey of housing units in the United States. The series consists of six parts issued jointly by the Department of Housing and Urban Development and the Census Bureau and is composed of two samples: a national sample of housing units to be visited every year, and a metropolitan sample in 60 SMSAs. This is a typical example of the Census Bureau as a data-gathering agency for other governmental units: HUD sponsors the *Annual Housing Survey* while Census conducts it.

Joint Population-Housing Reports

Series PHC (1), *Census Tract Reports* (C3.223/11; Item 159) for the 1970 census included one report for each SMSA and showed data for most of the population and housing subjects included in the 1970 Census. Some tables in this series are based on the 100 percent tabulation, others on the sample tabulation.

Series PHC (2), *General Demographic Trends for Metropolitan Areas, 1960-1970* (C 3.223/13; Items 159-A-1 through 159-A-54), consisted of one report for each state and the District of Columbia, as well as a national summary report. Statistics were presented for the state and for SMSAs and their central cities and constituent counties. Comparative 1960 and 1970 data are shown on population counts by age and race, and on such housing subjects as value, contract rent, and plumbing facilities.

Series PHC (3), *Employment Profiles of Selected Low-Income Areas* (C3.223 /17; Items 159-A-1 through 159-A-54), consisted of 75 reports, each presenting statistics on the social and economic characteristics of the residents of a particular low-income area, as well as a United States summary.

Computer Summary Tape Program

The major portion of the results of the 1970 Census was produced in six tabulation counts which yielded the statistics presented in the printed reports discussed above. But these counts were also designed to provide data in much greater subject and geographic detail than feasible or desirable to publish in printed reports. The additional data tabulated are available—subject to suppression of certain detail where necessary to protect confidentiality—on magnetic computer tape, and in some cases on printouts and microfilm. This information is available from the Bureau at the cost of preparing the copy or from Summary Tape Processing Centers.

The first three counts relate to the subject items collected on a 100 percent basis in the census. The second three counts relate to the subject items collected on a sample basis, but also include the 100 percent items for purposes of cross-classification. The counts consist of "cells" of population and housing data. This term refers to each figure or statistic in the tabulation for a specific geographic area. For example, in the Third Count there are six cells for a cross-classification of race by sex: three categories of race by two categories of sex.

The *First Count* contains approximately 400 cells of data for each of about 250,000 enumeration districts. File A contains the data for enumeration districts, one to eight reels of tape per state. File B contains summations by place, county, etc., one or two reels per state.

The *Second Count* contains approximately 3,500 cells of data for each of about 35,000 tracts and 35,000 census county subdivisions. File A contains the data for tracts, one to ten reels per state. File B contains the data for county subdivisions and the summations by place, county, etc., one to nine reels per state.

The *Third Count* consists of about 250 cells of data for each of about 1,500,000 blocks. The file contains one to twenty-three reels per state.

The *Fourth Count* contains approximately 13,000 cells of data for each of about 35,000 tracts and 35,000 census county subdivisions, and also about 30,000 cells of data for each county. File A contains the data for tracts, File B for county subdivisions, and File C the summations by place, county, etc. The population data appear in File A on one to fifteen reels of tape per state, in File B on one to seven reels, and in File C on one to six reels. The housing data appear in File A on one to twenty-three reels of tape per state, in File B on one to twelve reels, and in File C on one to six reels.

The *Fifth Count* consists of about 900 cells of data for 5-digit ZIP code areas in SMSAs and 3-digit ZIP code areas outside SMSAs. Available only on tape, one reel contains all data for all 3-digit ZIP code areas inside and outside SMSAs. Twelve reels contain all the data for the SMSA 5-digit ZIP code areas.

The *Sixth Count* consists of about 260,000 cells of data for each state, SMSA, and the larger cities and counties. The population data appear on one to fourteen reels per state and the housing data on one to fourteen reels per state.[16]

In addition to the tapes available for these six counts, other summary tapes are available from the tabulations made to prepare the Population Series and Housing Series subject reports. As Jones points out, "for extensive socio-economic analysis of small areas, the Count Four Population and Housing files are basic. Count Four is one of the largest numeric data bases in the world." Moreover, the several Summary Tape Processing Centers "should have a basic expertise in the use of census data, the appropriate computer equipment (hardware) and software." The software permits this vast quantity of data to be retrieved from the city block level through state and national areas and also provides the technique for managing the arithmetic computations. "Thus, a basic procedure has been developed to retrieve, manipulate, and print out census data in a package customized to meet the needs of the user."[17]

CONCLUSION

Even as data from the 1970 Census were being processed and published, plans for future censuses were being laid by the assiduous employees of the Census Bureau. Census "dress rehearsals," for example, were conducted by the Bureau in 1978. These were actual censuses in which plans and techniques for collecting, processing, and tabulating the 1980 nationwide census were used. Major processing centers were developed to handle the approximately 86 million census forms expected to be returned in the 1980 census. The processing operations include microfilming of the specially designed forms and conversions of the microfilm images into electronic data fields for direct transmission to the Bureau's computers in Suitland, Maryland, just outside Washington, D.C. Delivery of the data to the President is targeted for January 1, 1981.[18]

As more sophisticated uses of census data are employed, the demand for Summary Tape information will surely increase. Similarly, Bureau officials expect the demand for microform to increase; and future Census Bureau *Catalogs* will give more prominent treatment to microfiche. The Bureau conducts workshops for librarians throughout the country, and representatives are aggressively pushing the agency's microfiche services. Printed reports, of course, will continue to satisfy the research or informational needs of many users; but increased use of microform and Summary Tapes seems inevitable.

REFERENCES

1. J. E. Morton, "A Student's Guide to American Federal Government Statistics," *Journal of Economic Literature* 10: 372 (June 1972).

2. U.S. Department of Commerce. Office of the Secretary. *News Release* (G 75-126), July 17, 1975.

3. BEA publications are found in C56 and C59 notations.

4. Bureau of the Census. *Guide to Programs and Publications: Subjects and Areas 1973* (Washington: Government Printing Office, 1973), p. 3.

5. Judith Rowe, "The Use and Misuse of Government Produced Statistical Data Files," *RQ* 14: 201 (Spring 1975).

6. A summary of major 1970 census reports is found in *The 1970 Census and You* (C 3.2:C33/27/977), revised September 1977, pp. 10-11.

7. Rowe, p. 202.

8. A useful account of computerized census services is Ray Jones, "U.S. Census and Census Tapes," *Documents to the People* 3: 36-38 (March 1975).

9. Paul T. Zeisset, "Micropublishing at the Bureau of the Census," *Illinois Libraries* 58: 210-11 (March 1976).

10. Rowe, p. 203.

11. The reader is referred to the useful analysis of various sources in *Documents to the People* 4: 20-25 (November 1976).

12. The apparent discrepancy of C56 and C3 SuDocs notations is due to the vicissitudes of government reorganization. It is SuDoc's policy to return to the C3 classification all new issuances of Census publications which were reclassified into C56 during the years 1972-1975.

13. "Proposed Standards and Guidelines (Revised)," *Public Documents Highlights, Special Supplement*, August 1977 (GP 3.27:23), pp. 3, 6.

14. *Guide to Programs and Publications: Subjects and Areas 1973*, p. 117.

15. Ibid., p. 75.

16. Bureau of the Census. *Publication and Computer Summary Tape Program* (C 3.223:P96/4/970-3; Item 154), June 1973, p. 5.

17. Ray Jones, "U.S. Census and Census Tapes," *Documents to the People* 3: 36 (March 1975).

18. *United States Department of Commerce News*, October 6, 1977.

III–COMPUTER-BASED BIBLIOGRAPHIC SERVICES

INTRODUCTION

Computer-based bibliographic services are a dramatic and swiftly growing development in the world of information and are effecting major changes in the way libraries operate. Data bases for searching federal government materials have been discussed in various places throughout this text where appropriate, but this summary will attempt to note the scope and coverage of the field as it existed in 1977. For the present, the state-of-the-art is one of intense competition among the purveyors of these systems, and the results are often chaotic. Nevertheless, the field is of such importance that it cannot be overlooked.

According to Martha E. Williams, writing in the 1974 *Annual Review of Information Science*, a "data base is an organized set of machine-readable records containing bibliographic or document-related data."[1] Bibliographic data bases contain information identifying the document. A typical data base entry of this kind contains a citation plus an abstract of the material. In some cases the data base consists only of index entries and the accession numbers of the cited documents. Text data bases contain the text of the document or a usable condensation of it.

The benefits of data bases to the user have been discussed with great frequency approaching shrillness. A computer-aided search takes only a fraction of the time of a manual search and, in terms of the cost of a researcher's time, can be less expensive (see Chapter 9). Moreover, machine-readable data bases are usually more comprehensive, more deeply indexed, and more readily updated than printed bibliographic tools. An interactive, machine-aided search can be expanded, narrowed or redirected instantly on the basis of results achieved. And a skilled searcher can "combine terms, concepts and strategies in ways that are extremely difficult or even impossible during a manual search."[2]

The current role of libraries providing data bases is not unlike their role in providing other kinds of information. On-line terminals are used by the patron for the citation, and if the library can provide the printed text, the user's need is satisfied. As Christian points out, "very few libraries acquire, maintain, and process the taped data bases themselves—that would require a vast investment and heavy on-going expenses." It is interesting to note that data base services increase the demand for more conventional library services: interlibrary loans, photocopying, supplemental manual research, and the like. By and large, individual libraries prefer "to function as local 'windows' into the data bases made available by other organizations."[3]

THE DATA BASE INDUSTRY

Generally, the organizations involved with machine-readable bibliographic data bases are of three kinds: *publishers, distributors*, and *users*. The publishers actually produce the bibliographic files and make them available on magnetic computer tape. Distributors, also called brokers or vendors, subscribe to the taped data bases of several different publishers "and process (search) them, either off-line or on-line, as a service to institutions or corporations who do not themselves have the facilities or desire to do so. Also in this category are the companies that provide the communications facilities over which the on-line data bases are remotely searched, and over which the search results may be transmitted back to the data base user." Users, of course, are organizations like libraries and their clientele; that is, those who have need for the information that resides in the data bases.

But this tripartite structure is not that discrete. In practice, "the lines of distinction become very blurred, and the competitive situation is confused, if not chaotic. Some of the firms providing communications services to data base processors offer data base services of their own. Some data base publishers market their wares both to academic and special libraries (users) and to commercial vendors who themselves market to academic and special libraries. Conversely, some libraries and non-profit information centers simultaneously buy data base services from commercial vendors and compete with the same vendors for user customers."

To add to this bewildering picture, the federal government "sells, buys, and distributes data bases and data base services, both to and from—and often in competition with—elements of the private sector, both commercial and non-profit.... The pricing picture, complicated as it is by a variety of missions, objectives, sponsorship, subsidies and expectations, is equally confused, and subject to frequent changes." Nevertheless, it is useful to consider the three components as consisting of publishers, distributors, and users.[4]

SELECTED DATA BASES FOR
FEDERAL GOVERNMENT INFORMATION

Typical of the publishers of data bases are NTIS and CIS, the former a government agency, the latter a commercial organization. Commercial vendors of machine-readable bibliographic data bases in on-line formats include System Development Corporation (SDC), Lockheed Information Systems (LIS), and Bibliographic Retrieval Services (BRS). In February 1977 a representative of SDC explained to the author that the thirty data bases it had then would be expanded to one-hundred in the next five years, adding one data base approximately every thirty days. Each data file in these systems has a different vocabulary structure, some controlled, others uncontrolled. Computer-connect time costs vary from one data base to the next. These costs depend on the number of citations in the data base, the number of correlations to be made to complete the search, and the like. Vendors must pay royalties to some of the publishers of the data bases, and that in turn dictates the fees charged by the vendors.

In the January 1977 issue of *Online*, the *CIS/Index* data base was reviewed and the data base specifications for this publisher provide a useful example of critical analysis of these systems. Specifications include the subject matter in the file, the types of source documents, their language, the size of the data base, transmission speeds, availability of a thesaurus online or in print, availability of offline prints, microforms of the original documents, frequency of updating, restrictions on use, price per connect hour, etc. The picture thus presented enables libraries or other users to determine whether to subscribe to this service.[5]

While some data bases are devoted to a specific subject or discipline (e.g., Agriculture, Oceanography, Patents), others cover a broad range of disciplines; the most obvious example of the latter is *Government Reports Announcements & Index*, which was discussed in Chapter 4. The following data bases represent a selection of machine-readable citations that the user can access in searching for information produced by the federal government. It is important to note that many of these data bases contain information from private sources as well as government-generated or sponsored data.[6]

AGRICOLA

AGRICOLA is a cataloging and indexing (CAIN) data base providing worldwide coverage of agriculture from the National Agricultural Library. The vendors are BRS, LIS, and SDC. Coverage began in January 1970, and there is a monthly updating frequency.

Air Pollution Abstracts

The *Air Pollution Abstracts* data base contains air quality and air pollution prevention and control information from the Environmental Protection Agency. LIS is the vendor. The file dates from January 1966 and is updated monthly.

American Statistics Index (ASI)

ASI, as we noted in Chapter 5, covers comprehensively the statistical production of the federal government. SDC is the vendor. The coverage is from January 1973 although data go back some ten years prior to 1973 for certain statistical series. Updating is monthly, and the publisher is Congressional Information Service, Inc.

APIPAT

APIPAT is one of several data bases covering United States patents; in this file are petroleum patents on a restricted availability basis. *APIPAT*'s file began in January 1964. The publisher is the American Petroleum Institute, the vendor is SDC, and the updating frequency is monthly.[7]

CLAIMS/GEM

CLAIMS/GEM, from IFI/Plenum Data Company, contains information on general, electrical and mechanical United States patents. The file began in January 1975, LIS is the broker, and the updating is quarterly.

Congressional Information Service

Publications of the U.S. Congress (see Chapters 5 and 6): hearings, prints, reports and documents produced by CIS, Inc. The distributor is SDC. *CIS/Index* serves as the thesaurus. Coverage is from January 1970 and updating is monthly.

CRECORD

CRECORD (*Congressional Record*) data base provides over 300 capsulations of congressional proceedings indexed and cross-referenced in 275 legislative areas. Prepared by Capitol Service, Inc., the vendor is SDC. The base begins in January 1976 and is updated weekly.

Current Research Information Systems

This data base covers current research in agriculture and related areas from the U.S. Department of Agriculture Cooperative State Research Service. The vendor is LIS. Coverage is from July 1974. Updating frequency is monthly.

Defense Market Measures System

The coverage is U.S. Department of Defense contract awards. Information in the data base includes receiving contractor, awarding agency, and dollar amount of contract. Prepared by Frost and Sullivan, Inc., the vendor is LIS. The entry date is January 1975 and updating is quarterly.

Energy Information Abstracts

The *ENERGYLINE* data base covers energy economics, U.S. policy and planning, environmental impact, etc. The publisher is Environment Information

Center, Inc. The broker is SDC. Entry date is January 1971 and updating is bimonthly.

ERIC

As discussed in Chapter 4, this data base includes CIJE and RIE citations. Prepared by the Educational Resources Information Center, the vendors are BRS, LIS, and SDC. The entry date is January 1966 and updating is monthly. ERIC's parent agency is the National Institute of Education.

Federal Index

Federal Index covers federal publications such as the *Congressional Record, Federal Register, Commerce Business Daily,* and the *Weekly Compilation of Presidential Documents.* Available from Predicasts, Inc., the distributor is LIS. From its entry in October 1976, the data base is updated monthly.

Medlars

Medlars is a data base that provides worldwide coverage of biomedical journal literature from the National Library of Medicine. The broker is BRS; the entry date is January 1966, and updating is monthly.

MGA

Meteorological and Geoastrophysical Abstracts (MGA) contains current citations in English for important literature in these disciplines from both United States and foreign sources. Availability is through the American Meteorological Society and the Environmental Sciences Information Center, NOAA. The vendor is LIS. Coverage begins in January 1972 and is updated monthly.

NTIS

Broad coverage in *Government Reports Announcements & Index* (see Chapter 4) characterizes this large data base. Vendors include BRS, LIS, and SDC. BRS has coverage from January 1970 and updates monthly. SDC has coverage from January 1970 and updates biweekly. LIS has coverage from January 1964 and updates biweekly also.

Oceanic Abstracts

The federal agency NOAA participates in this data base in cooperation with Data Courier, Inc. Worldwide coverage of oceanography and marine-related literature is cited. The vendor is LIS, coverage extends from January 1976, and the file is updated monthly.

Smithsonian Science Information Exchange

SSIE covers on-going and recently completed research in the life, physical and social sciences. Research in progress is included from over 1,300 funding organizations, including the federal government. The vendor is SDC. The entry date is FY 1974 and updating is monthly.

* * *

It will be noted from this sample that LIS, called the Lockheed/DIALOG system, and SDC, using a retrieval system called ORBIT III, provide the largest number of data bases in their respective systems. Note, too, that there is duplication. AGRICOLA, ERIC, and NTIS have as vendors all three systems, including BRS. Data bases commercially on-line exclusively through the SDC Search Service include APIPAT, ASI, *CIS/Index*, CRECORD, and ENERGYLINE. Lockheed is the sole vendor for Current Research Information Systems, Defense Market Measures System, *Federal Index*, MGA, *Oceanic Abstracts*, and *Patent Concordance*. Bibliographic Retrieval Services, in addition to being the vendor for *Medlars*, shares with LIS and SDC data bases like Biological Abstracts, Chemical Abstracts, and INFORM, which covers business, finance, and related fields. By far the smallest of the three vendors, BRS—using a system called STAIRS—came into being in 1976 and has shown little inclination to expand in a manner characteristic of LIS and SDC.

COMMUNICATIONS VENDORS

LIS, SDC and BRS serve their customers by communications links with names like TELENET and TYMNET. Tymshare, Inc., "a commercial service company that serves principal cities throughout the U.S. and, via trans-Atlantic cable to a subnet headquartered in Paris, most of Europe and Scandinavia," has improved data communications greatly. For example, TYMNET, which has been operating since 1970, is the prototype of three or four "value added networks" in operation. Users have only to dial a local number or the number of the nearest input node "in order to contact any computer or data base available on the entire network. Moreover, once connected to the system, a user can switch instantly from one service or data base to another at will—a kind of electronic browsing." And TYMNET charges are less by far than direct distance dialing. Tymshare's distributed, nationwide network, permits brokers like SDC and LIS to market machine-readable data bases more effectively.[8]

CONCLUSION

Studies of legal information retrieval systems like WESTLAW and LEXIS (Chapter 9) seem to indicate that machine searching is cost effective. And Christian notes that in a number of studies made of the comparative costs of manual versus computer searching, "the results tend to strongly favor the electronic approach. In fact, one team estimates that manual searching costs 50% more than machine searching."[9] However, the cost of providing computer-aided bibliographic services to libraries is great. And this cost factor has raised the sensitive question of "user fees" for this type of service. "Those in favor of user fees argue that electronic services are similar to the photocopier services offered for a fee in many libraries; that the expensive equipment, purchased services and specially-trained staff involved, burden the library's scarce resources to cater to a small, identifiable segment of its total clientele; and that it's unfair to other library patrons and to commercial competitors for the library to expand its subsidies to provide these services at high cost to itself and no cost to the few users. A further argument is that each computer search is a service custom-tailored to a single individual's information needs—unlike the purchase of a book, which can be used by many patrons."

With respect to the issue of user fees for computerized searches, the argument, as Christian notes, is largely academic: "The economic realities are such that libraries that cannot or will not recover at least some of the costs of providing these expensive services will not long be able to provide them at all."[10]

As electronic bibliographic or full text services evolve, one can be sure that the vast literature generated by or for the federal government will be found in ever greater quantity in machine-readable form. The result, almost unforeseeable in its consequences, will surely be profound for the library community.

REFERENCES

1. Quoted in Roger W. Christian, *The Electronic Library: Bibliographic Data Bases 1975-76* (White Plains, N.Y.: Knowledge Industry Publications, 1975), p. 8.

2. Christian, pp. 2-3.

3. Ibid., pp. 3-4.

4. Ibid., pp. 25-26.

5. Lynn Allen Green, "Data Base Review: CIS Index," *Online* 1: 47-50 (January 1977). The magazine covers online information systems.

6. This information is taken from the *Bulletin of the American Society for Information Science* 3: 18-23 (June 1977).

7. Other data bases with U.S. patent information include WPI, prepared by Derwent Publications, Ltd.; and RINGDOC, also prepared by Derwent. Both are distributed by SDC. *Patent Concordance* correlates patents issued by different countries for the same basic invention; the vendor is LIS.

8. Christian, pp. 38-41. SDC, for example, uses both TELENET and TYMNET depending upon geographical location.

9. Ibid., p. 52.

10. Ibid., pp. 71-72.

IV—FEDERAL AUDIOVISUAL INFORMATION

INTRODUCTION

One can search in vain for any reference to audiovisual information in the Subject Index of the 1977/78 edition of the *United States Government Manual.* Indeed, the National Audiovisual Center, National Archives and Records Service, General Services Administration—which serves as the central information source on federal audiovisual materials—is not listed in the Agency Index of the *Government Manual.* Yet there are many units of the federal government that employ audiovisual personnel. The sixth edition (1977) of the *Directory of U.S. Government Audiovisual Personnel* (GS 4.24:977; Item 567-B) indicates that audiovisual personnel staff divisions and departments within the Congress, GPO, Library of Congress, CIA, the major departments, some twenty-six independent agencies, and eight Boards, Committees, and Commissions.

Bibliographic control of federal audiovisual activities, like that of federal mapping and charting, is (to be charitable) not a well-developed apparatus. The situation was somewhat improved when, in 1968, the National Audiovisual Center was authorized by Bureau of the Budget *Bulletin No. 69-7*, and was established by General Services Administration *Bulletin FPMR B-21*, December 9, 1969. In the brief summary that follows, an attempt will be made to indicate some of the basic sources of audiovisual materials produced by or for government agencies, and their sales, loans, and rental services.

GENERAL GUIDES TO AUDIOVISUAL INFORMATION

Official documents that serve as guides include *Subject Bibliography* (SB) 073, *Motion Pictures, Films, and Audiovisual Information.* The May 1977 edition of SB 073 lists a mere fourteen titles, including the *Catalog of Copyright Entries, Cumulative Series, Motion Pictures and Filmstrips.* Typical titles for sale through SuDocs are *Color Filmstrips and Slide Sets of the United States Department of Agriculture* (A 1.38:1107/3; Item 13-A), *Employment Outlook for*

Motion Picture Projectionists (L2.3:1875-11; Item 768-A-1), and *Veterans Administration Film Catalog* (VA 1.20/4:6). A related *Subject Bibliography* is SB 057, *Posters, Charts, Picture Sets, and Decals.* The May 1977 edition of this SB includes an *America the Beautiful* series, 52 natural-color photographs of lakes, farmlands, pastures, cattle, etc., issued by USDA's Soil Conservation Service; *The American Soldier*, armed forces posters; and a number of Bicentennial posters commemorating historical themes.

Although the PRF, MoCat, and *Selected U.S. Government Publications* provide some access to catalogs and directories that list certain audiovisual information, they do not occupy a prominent bibliographic position in this large area. And, when we turn to commercial sources, the information is not any better. The well-known *Audiovisual Market Place*, published annually by the R. R. Bowker Company, lists a few federal agencies that produce, distribute or loan "audiovisual software." Among the agencies listed in the 1977 *Audiovisual Market Place* were the Departments of Agriculture, Commerce, and HUD; ERDA; the U.S. Navy Office of Information; NARS; the Geological Survey; and the National Audiovisual Center itself. Bowker notes that Commerce and Agriculture did not even respond to a questionnaire sent by the company. However, Bowker ascertained that these departments do indeed produce audiovisual products.[1]

For these government entities listed, AVMP 1977 gives basic directory information and a listing of products and other services. A typical listing for USGS appears in this form:

```
UNITED STATES GEOLOGICAL
  SURVEY
National Center, Reston, VA 22092
Tel (Switchboard): 703-860-7000
Information Officer:  Frank H.
  Forrester.  Tel: 703-760-7444

Distributes:  16mm films. Subject
  Areas: earth science, mapping,
  water resources. Grade Levels:
  senior high, college, adult.
```

NATIONAL AUDIOVISUAL CENTER

As noted, the National AudioVisual[2] Center (NAC) was established in 1969 to provide government agencies and the general public with a central information, loan, sales, and rental service for audiovisual materials produced by or for executive agencies. The materials are either instructional or promotional. The Center maintains a reference service to help the public learn what federal AV materials are distributed through the Center, other federal agencies, or nongovernmental services. In this respect, the function of the Center is analogous to the clearinghouse function of the National Cartographic Information Center for mapping and charting.

NAC Publications

A Reference List of Audiovisual Materials Produced by the United States Government, 1978 (GS 4.2: Au 2/978; Item 569)

This basic *Reference List* provides over 6,000 titles selected from over 10,000 programs produced by 175 federal agencies. Major subject concentrations in the Center's collection include medicine, dentistry, education, science, social studies, safety, and the environmental sciences. The *Reference List* has a subject section that lists titles under a broad range of subject headings. The title section consists of entries containing all pertinent bibliographic information. Under each title, arranged alphabetically, data on producing organization, availability, NAC control number for ordering, sponsoring organization, and description of the material are given. Rental and purchase policies and a price list are additional features of this basic catalog.

The 1978 edition of the *Reference List* marked the first time that this important tool was made available to depository libraries. Predecessors of the *Reference List* included *A Catalog of United States Government Produced Audiovisual Materials, 1974-75* and *U.S. Government Films: A Catalog of Motion Pictures and Filmstrips for Sale by the National Audiovisual Center* (1969).

NAC Supplemental Information

Several brochures and catalogs appear, usually at irregular intervals, which serve as listings available for sale and/or rental. One series, *National Audio Visual Center: Select List*, a monthly, was made available to depository libraries in September 1977.[3] The *Select Lists* cover topics or agency-produced materials. For example, *National Park Service Films: U.S. History-Earth Sciences-Recreational Areas*, and *Career Education*. This series is available to depository institutions under Item 569-C-1 (GS 4.17/5). A typical annotated entry from a *Select List* appears in this form:

```
Coke Making in the Beehive Oven
18 Min, 16mm, color, 1975
#010066/EA                                    $115

Photographed at Bretz, West Virginia, this
film documents an early American industrial
process of making blast furnace coke using
techniques and equipment from the 19th
century.
```

Another series, *Selected U.S. Government Audiovisuals*, is issued by subject. The individual pamphlets, which can run thirty or more pages, contain annotated entries and the appropriate ordering information. Some titles issued during 1977 in this series include *Special Education, Career Education, Engineering, Dentistry*, and *Safety*. In prefatory material preceding the entries, NAC notes that it has over

9,000 titles in its computer data file. Materials for use fall under the categories of educational, informational, technical, and professional training. These individual brochures serve to advise users of new AV materials until the publication of a new comprehensive catalog. Producer/Sponsor Codes are listed on the back cover of the booklets. NAC indicates that, as of late 1977, it distributes programs produced or sponsored by more than 150 offices or agencies of the federal government. As expected, a large number of sponsored organizations are educational institutions and instructional materials centers.

Price Change List

In August 1976 the prices of the 16mm motion pictures in *A Catalog of United States Government Produced Audiovisual Materials, 1974-75* were increased, representing the first general price rise since 1971. Because the NAC, like NTIS, operates a self-supporting program, it was obliged to raise prices. The vehicle for this announcement was *Price Change List*, a document issued by the Center which applied only to the 16mm motion pictures in the *Catalog*. The *List* itemized, in alphabetical order, the pictures by title and included title number, rental rates where applicable, and the new purchase prices. When the *Reference List of Audiovisual Materials Produced by the United States Government* was issued in 1978, the increased prices were reflected.

AV Personnel Directory

A *Directory of U.S. Government Audiovisual Personnel* (GS 4.24:year; Item 567-B) lists federal government agencies and their audiovisual personnel, defined as those involved in radio, television, motion pictures, still photography, sound recordings, and exhibits. The "Introduction" to the sixth edition (1977) of the *Directory* notes that "it is not an exhaustive listing of all persons involved in Federal audiovisual activities, but it is an effort to list each agency's key audiovisual personnel." The organization of the *Directory* follows the format of the *United States Government Manual*. Personnel are listed by name, title, phone number, and mailing address. The *Directory* is accessed by a name and organization index.

Basic Language Courses

Depository libraries that subscribe to Item 872-A receive a series of manuals for language study, which range from commonly known European tongues to exotic species such as Urdu. This series, called Basic Language Courses, Foreign Service Institute (S 1.114/2), is complemented by language tapes designed to accompany many of the texts. Because the language tapes, irrationally, are not available as depository Items, one must make inquiries by writing the National Audiovisual Center, attention: Reference Section, General Services Administration, Washington, D.C. 20409. A catalog of the language tapes was released by NAC, but librarians must write the Center to secure a copy.

How to Order from NAC

For the individual titles in the *Selected U.S. Government Audiovisuals* series there are order forms for the materials distributed by the National Audiovisual Center. The following procedures were in effect in late 1977:[4]

Purchase: Materials listed for sale are offered at the net prices indicated in the entries. Minimal information on the order forms or by letter must include title number, title, quantity, unit price, and total price. All prices are subject to change without notice. Orders will be shipped as quickly as possible. If there is a delay, the subscriber will be notified. Purchased materials cannot be returned for replacement or credit without the Center's prior approval. Replacement footage for damaged portions of previously purchased motion pictures involves a fee set at a specific price per foot and a minimum charge per section. For customers interested in purchasing materials in formats other than 16mm, the NAC will provide price quotations for converting 16mm to any desired format.

Rental: For 16mm films, some of the more popular titles are available for rental. There are rental periods and rates. The user should schedule rentals as far in advance as possible and list alternate dates. The NAC assumes the cost of mailing the rental print. Moreover, most rental films can be purchased on a "rental-applied-to-purchase" basis. The most recent rental fee may be applied to the purchase price within 90 days of the rental invoice date. Order forms for rentals require the user to indicate title number, title, rental 3-day fee price, first-choice date, second-choice date, and first available date.

Preview Prints: Free preview of 16mm motion pictures will be provided "to qualified customers when prints are available." If the Center does not have a preview print of the requested title, it will attempt to refer the customer to other sources. NAC requests that the user does not ask for previews unless he or she is authorized to buy and has the funds for purchase. The preview service is not available for rentals or for materials other than 16mm motion pictures.

Restrictions: Titles marked with restrictions such as "professionally interested groups only" have been so designated by the producing agency or sponsored organization, and prints will be rented or sold only as indicated. Where known, the type of TV clearance is indicated. In addition, the government does not always have full rights to the films it produces. Rental or sale does not constitute authorization for reproduction, showing for profit, resale, or use of the materials in any manner other than in their original form, or as otherwise may be stated in the description.

User Guides: The NAC provides accompanying materials such as study guides or teacher manuals, if the producing agency has made them available.

Other: NAC accepts Mastercharge and BankAmericard/VISA. For direct payments, checks should be made payable to National Archives Trust Fund (NAC). All orders should be addressed to:

National Audiovisual Center
National Archives and Records Service
General Services Administration
Order Section DA
Washington, D.C. 20409

DEPOSITORY DISTRIBUTION OF AV INFORMATION

The existence of a central clearinghouse like the NAC is virtually indispensable in attempting to keep up with the amount of audiovisual materials available for purchase or rental. But if one is willing to take the trouble, there are a number of agencies that publish lists and catalogs of their audiovisual products. Many, but not all, of these bibliographic sources are available to depository libraries. A sample of these catalogs and guides follow:

Item No.	Agency	Title
83-A	Forest Service	Forest Service Films Available on Loan . . .
425	Air Force Department	Air Force Audiovisual Directory
475-F	Food and Drug Administration	Catalogue of FDA Publications and Audiovisual Materials for Consumers
499-F-2	National Institute for Occupational Safety and Health	NIOSH Films and Filmstrips on Occupational Safety and Health
507-B-10	National Institute of Mental Health	Selected Mental Health Audiovisuals
603	Interior Department	Film Catalog
717	Justice Department	Criminal Justice Audiovisual Materials Directory

NATIONAL MEDICAL AUDIOVISUAL CENTER

The National Medical Audiovisual Center (NMAC), a component of the National Library of Medicine, acquires and distributes evaluated medical and dental instructional materials. The Center issues a *National Medical Audiovisual Center Catalog* (HE 20.3608/4; Item 497-A) which lists 16mm motion pictures and videocassettes available on short-term loan for use in professional education programs in the health sciences. The 1977 edition of the *Catalog* is in two sections: a subject section and a name/title section.

In the subject section, films and videotapes are listed under terms selected from the National Library of Medicine's *Medical Subject Headings* (MeSH), the controlled vocabulary used by NLM in the preparation of *Index Medicus* as well. The full bibliographic citation appears in the name/title section, in which titles are arranged alphabetically by first significant word. This section also contains the names of persons appearing in the film or identified by the producer as "credits."

Materials listed in the Center's *Catalog* are available for health sciences professional educational use only. Selected titles are listed in *NMAC News*, single-page brochures issued by the Center. Audiovisual materials are produced either by the Center or by medical schools and related institutions supported by funds from NLM and NMAC.

Although loans of films and videotapes are made without charge to qualified requesters, many of the audiovisuals listed in the *Catalog* may be purchased from the NAC. Requests for loans, however, must be sent to the Materials Utilization Branch, NMAC (Annex), Station K, Atlanta, Georgia 30324.

CONCLUSION

Although the NAC plays an important role in making accessible information on the audiovisual activities of federal entities, it is highly unlikely that its catalogs and lists plus those of specific agencies constitute a total bibliographic picture. There is, for example, no master list to federally produced or sponsored audiovisuals. Nor is there any list, to the author's knowledge, of materials produced but not available to the general public. The number of training films alone produced by DoD and its components seems limitless, as anyone who has served in the armed forces will attest.

However, for general-purpose informational and educational viewing, products distributed through NAC may be quite satisfactory to the needs of schools in their educational materials programs.

REFERENCES

1. "Preface" to *Audiovisual Market Place: A Multimedia Guide* (New York: Bowker, 1977), p. vii.

2. Some publications of the Center use the capital "V" in the agency's name, others do not.

3. *Daily Depository Shipping List No. 10,178* (September 23, 1977), p. 3.

4. Information and explanations taken from *Selected U.S. Government Audiovisuals* series, unnumbered pages after entries, and *A Reference List of Audiovisual Materials Produced by the United States Government, 1978.*

V—MICROFORM SUMMARY

INTRODUCTION

A number of microform materials produced or distributed by government agencies and commercial sources have been mentioned in this text in the appropriate chapters and appendixes. No attempt has been made to cover all titles and series available in a microformat. The growth of the micropublishing industry renders exhaustive treatment of this area impossible in an introductory text. A full-length treatise on microformatted federal government information is needed.

The following comments are intended merely to summarize the micropublishing scene as it relates to public documents and legal materials, and to add some sources not discussed in the earlier pages.

The Micrographics Industry

There seems little doubt that government information will increasingly be found in micropublished format. Economic circumstances relevant both to the producer and the purchaser justify this statement. Micropublishing reduces the costs of conventional paper publishing dramatically. Microform material is less than one-tenth the cost of paper; printing speeds are several orders of magnitude faster than paper printing; and microform distribution costs are a fraction of the paper equivalent. In other words, paper has become a luxury that fewer and fewer consumers of information can afford.

With limited budgets and rising costs of title acquisition, libraries must closely examine the relative importance of each title that is acquired. Moreover, storage has become a primary consumer argument for materials in microform—it takes up very little space. These arguments have been voiced for years by the producers, but they are inescapable facts.

Categories

Gary suggests that the term "micropublishing" is perhaps a misnomer "as few companies under this umbrella term truly publish anything." Instead, he attempts to define the categories of companies engaged in the microform enterprise.

Micropublishing Organization

This is an organization that produces its own current output (reports, journals, etc.) in microform instead of hardcopy or as an optional alternative to paper. "At present only a small minority of publishers fall under this category."

Microprinting Organization

This is a firm that takes another organization's data base (typically back issues), converts it to microform, and either sells it directly or returns it to the owner for sale. "At present, this represents the largest segment of the industry. Most societal journals and magazines available in microform are produced in this manner."

Microrepublishing Organization

This is a firm that takes data from various sources, and either edits, categorizes, or indexes the data in such a fashion as to produce a proprietary special interest package for sale. Gary points out that this "is the newest and most rapidly growing segment of the industry."

Trends

Gary's survey of government agencies and commercial firms revealed the following immediate if not long-term trends for which there was a general consensus.

Film Formats

There seems to be no chance for a single microform to evolve in the near future.

Paper Copy/Microform

It can be expected that more journal publishers, either directly or by subcontracting, will initiate simultaneous paper and microform publishing. "This will be accomplished in microfiche format at current NMA [National Micrographics

Association] standards (98 image, 24x, 4x6). There will be no significant cost reduction attached to the purchase of the fiche itself as the cost to produce the film for a limited market . . . will be as high as the paper copy."

Microprinting

The major trend within this portion of the industry will be the increase "of titles (of back issues) that will become available in the near term. 35mm roll film will become almost extinct," except perhaps for newspaper microfilming.

Microrepublishing

Most of the materials issued by the several microrepublishers are already being produced on microfiche. "It is anticipated that as new special interest topics are defined [environment, energy, social legislation, etc.], more and more data bases will become available in microform." The creation of numerous specialized information packages will continue to thrive.[1]

GUIDES TO MICROFORMS

MIMC Microforms Annual

Microforms International Marketing Corporation (MIMC), a subsidiary of Pergamon Press, Inc., issues an *Annual* covering micropublications produced and/or currently distributed by MIMC. Pergamon's policy since 1970 has been to make available microforms as an option to all its journals and as an alternative to the firm's out-of-print books. The 1977/78 edition of *MIMC Microforms Annual* contains sections on *Index Medicus* and *Cumulated Index Medicus*; NTIS Library Reference Files; the National Nuclear Energy Series (including the Manhattan Project) of the now defunct Atomic Energy Commission; and United States government serials publications in microform.

Index Medicus and *Cumulated Index Medicus* are published with the permission of the National Library of Medicine and are available from MIMC on microfiche or microfilm. *Cumulated Index Medicus* backfiles prior to 1975 on microfiche are being prepared.

The *NTIS Library Reference Files 1943-1972* cover over one million federal government R&D reports by over 225 federal agencies. The files consist of report/accession number, 1943-1971; cumulative subject indexes, 1943-1971; and cumulative personal author, corporate author, and contract number indexes, 1964-1971; Libraries may order either 16mm reels or cartridges, or 35mm reels in positive or negative microfilm.

Microfiche editions of government periodicals include titles such as *Air Pollution Abstracts, Business Conditions Digest, American Education, Problems of Communism, Survey of Current Business*, and *Foreign Trade Reports*. Many of the journals are also available on microfilm.

Microform Review, Inc.

Microform Review, Inc. (Westport, Connecticut) issues comprehensive guides to materials in microform. Coverage is worldwide. Their series follow.

Guide to Microforms in Print

Edited by John J. Walsh, the 1977 edition of this annual listing of microform titles includes books, journals, newspapers, archival material, and government publications. The contents include introductory information in English, French, German, and Spanish; a directory of publishers; and the main entry section. Listings in the *Guide* are entered in alphabetical sequence according to an author-title arrangement, including corporate (government) author. Included in the single alphabetical sequence are journal and newspaper entries. A government entry appears in the *Guide* in this way:

> U.S. Congress. REGISTER OF DEBATES. 1824-1837. $100.00/HDI/1. With hardbound index. $119.00/ HDI/1

The Directory of Publishers by Codes (acronyms) shows that this series is available from the United States Historical Documents Institute (see Chapter 5).

Subject Guide to Microforms in Print

Also edited by John J. Walsh, this *Subject Guide* is the companion volume to the *Guide to Microforms in Print.* Titles are listed under subject divisions derived from LC subject headings. Within each subject division, micropublications are listed in alphabetical sequence. The same titles, of course, are listed in an author-title sequence in the *Guide to Microforms in Print.* Government documents like debates, official gazettes, legislative proceedings, etc., are grouped in the subject scheme together regardless of country.

Micropublishers' Trade List Annual

This work, called the MTLA, is simply a microfiche collection of the catalogs of micropublishers worldwide. Over 12,000 pages from hundreds of catalogs and brochures are included in the 1977 edition of MTLA. The catalogs are issued as diazo positive transparencies. To find a micropublisher's catalog, use the printed index which lists publishers alphabetically. Reference is to the corresponding fiche number which is found on the lower-right-hand corner of the microfiche title stripe. The fiche headers provide the names of the first and last micropublishers appearing on each fiche.

Complete Guide to Legal Materials in Microform

Henry P. Tseng's *Complete Guide to Legal Materials in Microform* and *1976 Supplement* were discussed in Chapter 9. It is important to note here that the title of Tseng's excellent work is misleading. The author includes not only the basic micropublishers of legal materials but also a large number of distributors and producers of federal government publications. In the *1976 Supplement*, for example, Tseng lists 97 "law and law-related microform publishers," including those mentioned in this text. If, as planned, Tseng continues updating his *Guide* with annual supplementation, it will become a standard source for government documents librarians.

OTHER SOURCES OF MICROFORM INFORMATION

The principal journal for librarians in the field is *Microform Review*, published six times a year by Microform Review, Inc., the publishers of the in-print *Guides* mentioned above. Each year *Microform Review* (MR) devotes one issue to the "unique problems of handling government documents and microforms."[2] The September 1977 issue of MR was their annual government documents issue, and it contained excellent articles on problems of government publications in a microformat. The reviews in MR are models of specificity. Following the narrative, there is a standard "Microform Evaluation" section which serves as a valuable guide to the potential customer. Segments of this evaluation include the type of microformat, quantity, film type, reduction ratio, film polarity, safety base, resolution test chart, external finding aids, internal finding aids, sequence, project editor(s), selected parts available, replacement policy, time payments available, whether registered in the *National Register of Microform Masters*, and any additional remarks. In addition to commenting on microform products and services generally, MR claims to be "the only publication that reviews micropublished government documents collections."[3]

Bibliographic Aids in the Periodical Literature

The admirable *Illinois Libraries* devoted their March 1976 issue to "Documents in Microform." In addition to the useful articles, which consist of papers presented at the sixth annual documents workshop sponsored by the Illinois State Library and the Illinois Library Association in Chicago in 1974, there were two bibliographic contributions to the issue.[4] Geneva Finn, "Bibliography on Government Publications in Microform," contains a selected list of references on micrographics, including some on government micropublishing; and a selected list of reports from DttP. The bibliography is annotated. Janet Lyons, "Documents in Microform: A Selective Bibliography," consists primarily of reviews of documents in microform and reviews of some materials "that can be considered supplementary to a government publications collection and some sets that partially contain document material." The author has updated her bibliography in the September 1977 issue of *Microform Review.*[5]

CONCLUSION

The conclusion of this account roughly coincides with the advent in earnest of the GPO microform distribution program. We noted in Chapters 1 and 3 that, once permission was granted by the JCP to provide depository libraries with publications in a microformat, little time was lost in doing so. *Government Printing Office Instruction 565.1* was dated September 30, 1977; it set forth procedures for implementing the program. History of a sort was made with *Daily Depository Shipping List 10,301* (November 3, 1977), when depository institutions that subscribed to Item 546-D received a shipment of 355 titles in the *GAO Reports to Congress* series on microfiche. In comments following the 23-page listing of titles, J. D. Livsey reminded librarians that "in the weeks ahead there will be approximately 24 microfiche titles on each *Shipping List.*" This, he wrote, "is material called 'non-Depository non-GPO' because copies were not available in sufficient quantity for distribution to Depository Libraries."[6]

The other major part of the Depository Library Microform Project is the conversion of "GPO depository" titles to microfiche. At the October 1977 meeting of the Depository Library Council to the Public Printer, Livsey presented a list of specific titles and categories of documents for conversion to microfiche to the Council Committee on Micrographics and asked for their recommendations. While the "non-GPO" phase of the program has been generally well received by librarians, the "GPO depository" titles to be made available in microform *only* is a subject of grave concern. So it should be, for there is great difficulty in selections that have no alternate options.

The decision is fraught with danger. The JCP gave GPO the authority to convert existing depository series into microfiche if such conversion will provide substantial economic savings. Thus the convenience of the library's public and the realities of publishing economics meet at the cutting edge of the microform.[7] Would you or I, as a user, prefer to peruse the contents of the *Congressional Record* or *Federal Register* in microform or in printed copy? How about bills, resolutions, documents or reports, those crucial publications of the Congress of the United States?

One of the great occupational hazards that afflict librarians is the temptation to perceive reality through their own eyes rather than through the eyes of users. If this temptation can be overcome, decisions on the wise and prudent selection of microform collections, whether distributed by the GPO or by a commercial firm, can be made that will satisfy user needs without sacrificing internal management policies. Knowing my colleagues in this profession, I am confident that wisdom will prevail.

REFERENCES

1. Philip J. Gary, *Development of a Model Library Microform Center* (Washington: U.S. Environmental Protection Agency, Library Systems Branch, August 1976), pp. 1-10. The author of this study submitted to the EPA is head of Micrographic Systems Consulting Services, Marina del Rey, California.

2. *Microform Review* 6: 257 (September 1977).

3. Publisher's message to GODORT members. MR states that more than 100 government documents collections worth over $1 million have been reviewed in MR from 1972 to 1977.

4. *Illinois Libraries* 58: 227-29; 229-32.

5. *Microform Review* 6: 299-301.

6. *Daily Depository Shipping List 10,301* (November 3, 1977), p. 23.

7. See the "Report of the Council Committee on Micrographics," which was attached to the Secretary's Summary of Meeting of the Council, October 16-18, 1977 (mimeographed).

APPENDIX B

ABBREVIATIONS, ACRONYMS, CITATIONS, AND POPULAR NAMES USED IN THIS TEXT

ABBREVIATIONS, ACRONYMS, CITATIONS, AND POPULAR NAMES USED IN THIS TEXT

AACR	Anglo-American Cataloging Rules
AALS	Association of American Law Schools
AEC	Atomic Energy Commission
AID	Agency for International Development
A.L.R.	American Law Reports
A.L.R.Fed.	American Law Reports Federal
Am.Jur.2d	American Jurisprudence, Second Series
AMS	Army Map Service
API	American Petroleum Institute
AV	Audiovisual
AVMP	Audiovisual Market Place
BEA	Bureau of Economic Analysis
Bevans	Treaties and Other International Agreements of the United States of America, 1776-1949
BLS	Bureau of Labor Statistics
BNA	Bureau of National Affairs
BRS	Bibliographic Retrieval Services
CAB	Civil Aeronautics Board
CBO	Congressional Budget Office
CCD	Census County Division
CCH	Commerce Clearing House
CETA	Comprehensive Employment and Training Act
CFR	Code of Federal Regulations
CIA	Central Intelligence Agency
CIH	Committee on Information Hang-Ups
CIJE	Current Index to Journals in Education
CIS	Congressional Information Service
C.J.S.	Corpus Juris Secundum
CONSER	Conversion of Serials
COSATI	Committee on Scientific and Technical Information

CP	Carrollton Press
CPI	Consumer Price Index
CQ	Congressional Quarterly
CR	Congressional Record
CRS	Congressional Research Service
CY	Calendar Year
DAD	Data Access Description
DDC	Defense Documentation Center
DMA	Defense Mapping Agency
DMATC	Defense Mapping Agency Topographic Center
DOC	Documents Office Classification
DocEx	Documents Expediting Project
DoD	Department of Defense
DOE	Department of Energy
DOT	Department of Transportation
DttP	Documents to the People
ED	Enumeration District
EDRS	ERIC Document Reproduction Service
EEOC	Equal Employment Opportunity Commission
Ei	Engineering Index
EO	Executive Order
EPA	Environmental Protection Agency
ERA	Energy Research Abstracts
ERDA	Energy Research and Development Administration
ERIC	Educational Resources Information Center
ESSA	Environmental Science Services Administration
Exec. Doc.	Senate Executive Document
Exec. Rpt.	Senate Executive Report
F.	Federal Reporter
FAA	Federal Aviation Administration
FACA	Federal Advisory Committee Act
FBIS	Foreign Broadcast Information Service
FCC	Federal Communications Commission
FDA	Food and Drug Administration
FDIC	Federal Deposit Insurance Corporation
FEA	Federal Energy Administration
Fed	Federal Reserve Board
FLECC	Federal Libraries' Experiment in Cooperative Cataloging
FLITE	Federal Legal Information through Electronics
FPC	Federal Power Commission
FR	Federal Register
F.R.D.	Federal Rules Decisions
F.Supp.	Federal Supplement
FTC	Federal Trade Commission
FY	Fiscal Year
GAO	General Accounting Office
GBF/DIME	Geographic Base File/Dual Independent Map Encoding
GODORT	Government Documents Round Table
GPO	Government Printing Office

GRA&I	Government Reports Announcements & Index
H.Con.Res.	House Concurrent Resolution
H.doc.	House Document
HEW	Department of Health, Education, and Welfare
Hickcox	United States Government Publications: A Monthly Catalogue, 1885-1894
H.J.Res.	House Joint Resolution
H.R.	House of Representatives Bill
H.Res.	House Resolution
H.rp.	House Report
HUD	Department of Housing and Urban Development
IAEA	International Atomic Energy Agency
ICC	Interstate Commerce Commission
IHS	Information Handling Services
INIS	International Nuclear Information System
IR	ERIC Clearinghouse on Information Resources
IRS	Internal Revenue Service
JCP	Joint Committee on Printing
JPRS	Joint Publications Research Service
KWIC	Key Word in Context
LC	Library of Congress
L.Ed.	United States Supreme Court Reports, Lawyers' Edition
LIS	Lockheed Information Systems
LRTS	Library Resources & Technical Services
MARC	Machine-Readable Cataloging
MCD	Minor Civil Division
MEDList	Master Enumeration District List
MeSH	Medical Subject Headings
MGA	Meteorological and Geoastrophysical Abstracts
MIMC	Microforms International Marketing Corporation
MoCat	Monthly Catalog of United States Government Publications
MR	Microform Review
MTLA	Micropublishers' Trade List Annual
NAC	National Audiovisual Center
NARS	National Archives and Records Service
NASA	National Aeronautics and Space Administration
NCIC	National Cartographic Information Center
NIE	National Institute of Education
NIOSH	National Institute for Occupational Safety and Health
NLM	National Library of Medicine
NLRB	National Labor Relations Board
NMA	National Micrographics Association
NMAC	National Medical Audiovisual Center
NOAA	National Oceanic and Atmospheric Administration
NOS	National Ocean Survey
NRC	Nuclear Regulatory Commission
NSA	Nuclear Science Abstracts
NSC	National Security Council
NTIS	National Technical Information Service

OCLC	Ohio College Library Center
OMB	Office of Management and Budget
OPIC	Overseas Private Investment Corporation
OSHA	Occupational Safety and Health Administration
OSHRC	Occupational Safety and Health Review Commission
PBGC	Pension Benefit Guaranty Corporation
PDH	Public Documents Highlights
PL	Price List
PL	Public Law
PRC	Postal Rate Commission
PRF	Publications Reference File
Proc.	Proclamation
R&D	Research and Development
RIE	Resources in Education
Rovine	Digest of U.S. Practice in International Law
RSR	Reference Services Review
RTOPs	NASA Research and Technology Operating Plans
S.	Senate Bill
SB	Subject Bibliographies
S.Con.Res.	Senate Concurrent Resolution
S.Ct.	Supreme Court Reporter
SDC	System Development Corporation
SDI	Selective Dissemination of Information
S.doc.	Senate Document
SEC	Securities and Exchange Commission
SESA	Social and Economic Statistics Administration
SIC	Standard Industrial Classification
S.J.Res.	Senate Joint Resolution
SLA	Special Libraries Association
SMSA	Standard Metropolitan Statistical Area
SOIS	Sales Order and Information System
SOS	Standing Order Service
S.Res.	Senate Resolution
SRIM	Selected Research in Microfiche
S.rp.	Senate Report
SSIE	Smithsonian Science Information Exchange
STAR	Scientific and Technical Aerospace Reports
Stat.	Statutes at Large
SuDocs	Superintendent of Documents
TAB	Technical Abstract Bulletin
TIAS	Treaties and Other International Acts Series
TIF	Treaties in Force
TVA	Tennessee Valley Authority
UA	Urbanized Area
UMI	University Microfilms International
U.S.	United States Reports
U.S.C.	United States Code
U.S.C.A.	United States Code Annotated
U.S.C.C.A.N.	United States Code Congressional and Administrative News

U.S.C.S.	United States Code Service
USGS	United States Geological Survey
USHDI	United States Historical Documents Institute
U.S.L.Week	United States Law Week
UST	United States Treaties and Other International Agreements
WGA	Weekly Government Abstracts
Whiteman	Digest of International Law
WPA	Works Projects Administration
WPI	World Patents Index

PERSONAL AUTHOR INDEX

SELECTED TITLE/SERIES INDEX

SUBJECT INDEX